POLITICAL CHANGE IN JAPAN: ELECTORAL BEHAVIOR, PARTY REALIGNMENT, AND THE KOIZUMI REFORMS

**Edited by
Steven R. Reed, Kenneth Mori McElwain,
and Kay Shimizu**

SHORENSTEIN
APARC
STANFORD

THE WALTER H. SHORENSTEIN
ASIA-PACIFIC RESEARCH CENTER

THE WALTER H. SHORENSTEIN ASIA-PACIFIC RESEARCH CENTER (Shorenstein APARC) is a unique Stanford University institution focused on the interdisciplinary study of contemporary Asia. Shorenstein APARC's mission is to produce and publish outstanding interdisciplinary, Asia-Pacific–focused research; to educate students, scholars, and corporate and governmental affiliates; to promote constructive interaction to influence U.S. policy toward the Asia-Pacific; and to guide Asian nations on key issues of societal transition, development, U.S.-Asia relations, and regional cooperation.

The Walter H. Shorenstein Asia-Pacific Research Center
Freeman Spogli Institute for International Studies
Stanford University
Encina Hall
Stanford, CA 94305-6055
tel. 650-723-9741
fax 650-723-6530
http://APARC.stanford.edu

Political Change in Japan: Electoral Behavior, Party Realignment, and the Koizumi Reforms may be ordered from:
The Brookings Institution
c/o DFS, P.O. Box 50370, Baltimore, MD, USA
tel. 1-800-537-5487 or 410-516-6956
fax 410-516-6998
http://www.brookings.edu/press

First printing, 2009.
13-digit ISBN 978-1-931368-14-8

POLITICAL CHANGE IN JAPAN: ELECTORAL BEHAVIOR, PARTY REALIGNMENT, AND THE KOIZUMI REFORMS

SHORENSTEIN
APARC
STANFORD

THE WALTER H. SHORENSTEIN
ASIA-PACIFIC RESEARCH CENTER

CONTENTS

Preface   VII

INTRODUCTION   3
1. An Overview of Postwar Japanese Politics   5
   Steven R. Reed and Kay Shimizu

ELECTORAL POLITICS   27
2. Avoiding a Two-Party System: The Liberal Democratic Party versus   29
   Duverger's Law
   Steven R. Reed and Kay Shimizu
3. Has the Electoral-System Reform Made Japanese Elections Party-   47
   Centered?
   Ko Maeda
4. Pork-Barrel Politics and Partisan Realignment in Japan   67
   Jun Saito
5. Declining Electoral Competitiveness in Japan: Postreform Trends and   87
   Theoretical Pessimism
   Robert J. Weiner

KOIZUMI   107
6. How Koizumi Won   109
   Chao-Chi Lin
7. How Long Are Koizumi's Coattails? Party-Leader Visits in the 2005   133
   Election
   Kenneth Mori McElwain
8. Two Steps Forward, One Step Back: Japanese Postal Privatization as   157
   a Window on Political and Policymaking Change
   Patricia L. Maclachlan

BEYOND ELECTORAL POLITICS   181
9. The Slow Government Response to Japan's Bank Crisis: A New
   Interpretation
   Ethan Scheiner and Michio Muramatsu
10. Stealing Elections: A Comparison of Election-Night Corruption in   199
    Japan, Canada, and the United States
    Ray Christensen and Kyle Colvin

WOMEN IN POLITICS   219
11. The Puzzle of the Japanese Gender Gap in Liberal Democratic Party   221
    Support
    Barry C. Burden

12. Women Running for National Office in Japan: Are Koizumi's Female   239
   "Children" a Short-Term Anomaly or a Lasting Phenomenon?
   Alisa Gaunder
13. Surrogate Representation: Building Sustainable Linkage Structures in   261
   Contemporary Japanese Politics
   Sherry L. Martin

CONCLUSION   279
14. Japanese Politics in the Koizumi Era: Temporary Anomaly or a   281
   Paradigm Shift?
   Kenneth Mori McElwain and Steven R. Reed

Index   293
About the Contributors   317

PREFACE

People study the politics of particular countries for various reasons. Often, the motivation is personal: you study the country you were born in or you live in, since it affects you directly. International salience may matter: American elections, economic performance, and foreign policy are interesting because the United States is the dominant nation in the global arena today. Japanologists, however, typically cite a different and more controversial justification: Japan is somehow *different* from comparable advanced industrialized democracies. The postwar performance of the Japanese state seemed to validate the limelight; the economy grew at an unprecedented rate while minimizing wealth disparities and social unrest.

The stated reasons for Japanese exceptionalism vary—from cultural characteristics and unique historical trajectories to distinct institutional frameworks. Some of these purportedly sui generis logics are more questionable than others. However, two facets of Japanese politics are genuinely puzzling. First, the Liberal Democratic Party (LDP) held a continuous majority in the Japanese parliament (the Diet) for thirty-eight years (1955–1993). In 1994, after only a nine-month interruption, the LDP resumed its rule through a coalition government. Such long tenure in the legislative and executive functions of government is unseen in other stable democracies. Second, one-party dominance has given the Japanese bureaucracy a legislative autonomy that is uncommon in most democratic states. Japanese laws are largely drafted by bureaucrats, not legislators, and the elite ministries have broad jurisdiction over economic and social issues that give them significant say over how the country is run. Indeed, a common argument is that bureaucratic insulation explained Japan's rapid economic growth: long-serving civil service elites simply made better managers than reelection-maximizing, short-sighted politicians.

Because Japan does not fit into classical typologies of cross-country analysis—it is not part of Europe or the British Commonwealth or North America—comparable cases tend to vary with the issue under question. Scholars who examine government longevity, for example, tend to examine the LDP in Japan with reference to the Social Democrats in Sweden, Labor in Israel, or the Christian Democrats in Italy. Those interested in public administration from a Weberian perspective, however, contrast Japan with France (strong bureaucrats) or the United States (weak bureaucrats). Indeed, Japan is fascinating to scholars of comparative politics because its component parts share similarities with a diverse range of cases, but its whole is distinct from the state structures of most democracies.

Since the 1990s, however, the myth of Japanese exceptionalism—at least in the positive sense of the term—has dissipated, and the Japan that was studied as an exemplary model in the past is now viewed as inflexible and outmoded. The economy's "lost decade" punctured theories that Japan presents an alternative, state-centric model of democracy, and the bureaucratic scandals of that period dispelled the pristine aura of the civil service. Even the keystone of Japanese politics, the LDP, crumbled in 1993, when the party lost its parliamentary majority for the first time since its formation. Although the LDP swiftly returned to power, it has done so in a diminished capacity, relying on coalition arrangements with various conservative and centrist parties. In some ways, Japan is increasingly seen as an example of what *not* to be—an eccentric democracy, not an exemplar.

When Ichiro Ozawa, a major figure within the LDP, left his party in 1993, he argued that for Japan to be economically competitive, politically accountable, and internationally relevant, it needed to become a so-called normal nation. His motivation came from failings in Japanese foreign policy, particularly the inability of the Japanese government to take decisive action in the first Gulf War, but his prescriptions for transformation were straightforwardly domestic and institutional. Ozawa became an ardent supporter of electoral reform, with the goal of encouraging the multiple opposition parties to coalesce into a single viable alternative to the LDP. A two-party system would result in coherent ideological competition, stronger government leadership built on a clear electoral mandate, and more frequent alternations in power. In other words, the goal was to make Japan more like other democracies, or at least like Ozawa's conception of Britain and the United States.

Perhaps no leader epitomized these expectations for political transformation as much as Junichiro Koizumi. Koizumi was the first LDP president elected in a primary in over two decades, and he entered—and more importantly, left—the political limelight as one of the most popular prime ministers in postwar history. During his tenure, LDP factionalism weakened, the cabinet seized greater control over policymaking from the bureaucracy, major policy reforms became the focus of electoral competition, and public interest in politics exploded. There has scarcely been a time when so much *appeared* to be changing, justifying many observers' excitement in unfolding events.

There is a precedent for pessimism, however. To repeat the oft-quoted adage: the definition of insanity is doing the same thing over and over again and expecting different results. With a bit of creative license, we can apply this malady to Japan researchers—including ourselves. The demise of LDP politics—sometimes labeled the "1955 system"—was predicted for over thirty years: in the mid-1970s, when internecine warfare over Tanaka's pork-barrel politics and corruption divided the LDP; in the late 1970s through the mid-1980s, when a splinter faction left the LDP and formed the New Liberal Club; and in the early 1990s, when the LDP's stranglehold over government was finally loosened. Each time, analysts predicted a fundamental shift in the nature of Japanese politics: parties would prioritize ideological platforms over clientelist appeals, factional power-balancing would give way to meritocratic cabinet appointments and pluralism in policy input, and governments would alternate between political parties. And in each case, we saw changes in the process and output of policymaking around the margins, but signs of structural transformation were elusive.

The overriding question of this book is thus whether recent events and apparent transformations in Japanese politics will stick. Koizumi *seemed* to embody strong latent desires for political reform, and we have seen important changes (or at least we *think* we have seen changes) in policymaking processes and outcomes. But will these changes persist, or will traditional structures regain their place of prominence? Already we have seen the fall of Shinzo Abe, who many thought was cut from the same cloth as Koizumi. The next prime minister, Yasuo Fukuda, was less of a firebrand and more of a competent manager—exactly the type of leader that factions have historically preferred. These recent events do not indicate a reversion to the past, but hopes for change have not always been rewarded. Our apologies for mixing metaphors, but even a broken clock is right twice a day.

Each author in this volume has tackled an important issue in contemporary Japan, with an eye toward evaluating deep-rooted as opposed to surface-level changes. We have explored what tangible effects Koizumi has had on Japanese politics, and whether his tenure was merely a brief pause in long-running conservatism or the harbinger of new politics. While we hesitate to arrive at definitive conclusions, we believe there is sufficient data to identify concrete changes, or at least to separate cases of "slow change" from "no change." As with the best studies of Japan in the past, we analyze Japan in the context of empirical and theoretical findings from other countries. This is particularly relevant to understanding transitional processes, since many arguments for and against institutional or policy reforms were made with reference to similar experiences abroad. To take one example, the expectation that switching to an electoral system combining single-member districts (SMDs) and proportional representation (PR) would result in two-party competition was based on how SMDs have shaped politics in the United States and Great Britain. As such, we can best understand the successes and failures of Japanese reforms by looking outside the country and teasing apart the factors that are unique to Japan from larger global trends.

This book touches on a number of themes, some of which have a venerable academic tradition and others that have been understudied with respect to Japan. The introductory first chapter provides an overview of electoral and party politics in postwar Japan. It focuses on the emergence and evolution of LDP politics, including factionalism, leadership, and electoral trends, and provides a context for the analytical content found in later chapters.

The first section of the book looks at electoral politics in both the pre- and post-1993 period. In chapter 2, Steven R. Reed and Kay Shimizu examine the prospects of two-party competition and government alternation under the new electoral system. They argue that the increasing volatility of public opinion, coupled with the growing irrelevance of other minor parties, suggest the possibility of opposition victories and government turnover in the future. In chapter 3, Ko Maeda demonstrates that the party label has played a greater role in recent elections, in contrast to the candidate-heavy nature of earlier competition. Using data from the 1990s, he finds that there is growing correspondence in vote swings in the SMD tier (typically the more candidate-centered choice) and the PR tier (typically the more party-centered choice). In chapter 4, Jun Saito looks at bipartisanship from the perspective of legislators. He finds that party-switching, which was rampant in the first few years after electoral reform, was motivated by a combination of ideological and particularistic interests. As legislators' demand for pork-barrel projects to their districts decline, however, we can expect more stable partisanship in the future. In chapter 5, Robert J. Weiner adds an important word of caution to our expectations that two-party politics means greater political accountability. He finds that bipartisanism at the national level masks relatively uncompetitive contests within individual districts, suggesting that incumbents in "safe" districts may become less attuned to the demands of minority groups within their jurisdictions.

The second section of the book examines the emergence and success of Junichiro Koizumi, the most prominent Japanese prime minister in recent memory. In chapter 6, Chao-Chi Lin studies the factors that led to Koizumi's surprising ascension to the role of LDP party leader. She argues that the LDP's decision to switch to local primaries for leader selection allowed Koizumi, who had strong support from voters, to win a surprising victory over the establishment candidate, Ryutaro Hashimoto. In chapter 7, Kenneth Mori McElwain analyzes the electoral impact of Koizumi's popularity. Utilizing statistical analyses of the 2005 House of Representatives elections, he finds that Koizumi generated important coattail effects by making personal appearances and swinging crucial votes in close district races, facilitating the LDP's historic victory. In chapter 8, Patricia L. Maclachlan studies Koizumi's impact on policymaking through the lens of postal-privatization reform. She argues that Koizumi succeeded in pushing through a bill with little bureaucratic or legislative backing by establishing and staffing policymaking councils within the cabinet agency instead of locating decision-making in individual ministries or within the LDP.

The third section, titled "Beyond Electoral Politics," focuses on the legislative and administrative aspects of Japanese government. In chapter 9, Ethan Scheiner and Michio Muramatsu compare the relationship between LDP politicians and government bureaucrats before and after the LDP's ouster in 1993. They argue that the bureaucrats' willingness to cooperate with the opposition parties in 1993–1994 generated LDP mistrust, and the new, competitive relationship between these two pillars of government led to bungled policy responses to the nonperforming loans crisis of the 1990s. In chapter 10, Ray Christensen and Kyle Colvin study a relatively unexplored aspect of elections: last-minute ballot stuffing, or "election-night corruption." Despite widely acknowledged corruption problems in other aspects of governance, they find that Japanese elections are relatively clean, due in part to the delegation of election management to a nonpoliticized administrative agency.

The book's final section examines an issue important to the future of Japanese politics: the involvement of women in the political process. In chapter 11, Barry C. Burden analyzes the gender gap in postwar voting trends and finds that unlike in other advanced industrialized democracies, Japanese men and women respond to political stimuli in similar ways. An important exception is the role of political leaders: Japanese women are more likely to link support for the LDP to support for the prime minister, raising the stakes for finding popular leaders to ensure electoral victory. In chapter 12, Alisa Gaunder looks at the factors that constrain or enable the electoral success of female candidates. She notes the emergence of nonprofit and civil-society organizations that provide funding and training to potential candidates, but argues that the biggest reductions in the parliamentary gender gap occur only with the backing of strong political leaders such as Koizumi. In chapter 13, Sherry L. Martin looks at voters' perceptions of legitimacy and satisfaction with respect to the political process. While most voters who support a particular party are happy with the legislative process, even if their party is not in government, she finds that nonpartisan voters are much less likely to express satisfaction, a problem that is pronounced for the disproportionately large number of women in the nonpartisan pool.

Finally, we bring these issues full circle in chapter 14, in which we evaluate the arguments and evidence of these chapters from the perspective of three principal questions that will affect Japanese politics in the long run: the importance of political leaders, the potential for government alternation, and pluralism in the policymaking process.

This project's conception was a conference at Stanford University, organized by two of the editors, Kenneth Mori McElwain and Kay Shimizu, and by Robert J. Weiner, who is now at the Naval Postgraduate School. We were all affiliated with Stanford at the time, and we were united by our interest in Japanese politics. The two-day "2007 Stanford Conference on Electoral and Legislative Politics in Japan," as it came to be called, was (we think) a huge success, with fifteen papers and twenty participants from around the country. It could not have materialized without the long-suffering, wonderfully kind, and extremely efficient staff members of the Walter H. Shorenstein Asia-Pacific Research Center (Shorenstein APARC) at Stanford University. Dan Okimoto, Gi-Wook Shin, Dan Sneider, and Bob Carroll helped us work out the conference's purpose and budget, while Neeley Main, Denise Matsumoto, Debbie Warren, Huma Shaikh, and Vivian Beebe efficiently managed the conference logistics. Shorenstein APARC was the primary funder of this conference, but we also received invaluable contributions from Stanford's Center for East Asian Studies (CEAS) and the Freeman Spogli Institute for International Studies.

From the beginning, we hoped to make this conference a stepping stone for a book project, focusing on recent events and their significance to the future of Japan. To this end, Steven R. Reed kindly came on board as the senior editor, since the rest of us lacked the temperament to crack the editorial whip when deadlines approached. As it turned out, the authors did a wonderful job of policing themselves. The participants utilized original data sets, personal interviews, new statistical techniques, and their deep knowledge of relevant cases to write chapters that not only add to our understanding of Japan, but also open new avenues for research in the future. We collectively received fantastic feedback from discussants at the 2007 Stanford conference, who helped all the authors with theoretical, empirical, and methodological suggestions. This volume would be much poorer without the advice of Frances Rosenbluth, Mike Thies, Len Schoppa, Laurie Freeman, Ben Nyblade, Shigeo Hirano, and Meg McKean. Barbara Milligan and Fayre Makeig did a great job copyediting and proofing all the chapters. Victoria Tomkinson, Shorenstein APARC's wonderfully patient editor, helped us all the way from picking a book cover to fixing up and organizing the chapters, thereby making this book much more than the sum of its parts.

Finally, Kenneth Mori McElwain would like to thank Shorenstein APARC and the Division of International, Comparative and Area Studies (ICA) at Stanford University for the support he received while working on this book, along with other projects. Dan Okimoto has been a wonderful inspiration and great sounding board for various paper and conference ideas. Kenneth also thanks his mother, Setsuko, and his partner, Tomoka, for their helpful advice in making this manuscript relevant to a broader audience.

Kay Shimizu would like to thank Dan Okimoto for getting her hooked on the study of Japanese politics and for continually encouraging her to dig deep, beyond the surface story. Kay would also like to thank her family and friends, especially her IUP family in Beijing for their support and understanding this year.

Steven R. Reed would like to thank Kay and Kenneth for their energy and Victoria for her help and patience.

Steven R. Reed
Kenneth Mori McElwain
Kay Shimizu
June 2009

INTRODUCTION

An Overview of Postwar Japanese Politics

Steven R. Reed and Kay Shimizu

This chapter provides basic background on postwar Japanese politics as well as more specific information on the recent events addressed in this volume. We begin with a short history of the dominant Liberal Democratic Party (LDP) and then turn to the alternatives offered to voters. We describe the events that led to the LDP's 1993 loss of power and the 1994 enactment of political reform. We then look at how politics has evolved since reform, focusing on the dramatic events of the Koizumi era and its aftermath.

The Liberal Democratic Party (LDP)

The LDP was founded in 1955 and remained at the helm of Japanese politics until losing its majority in 1993. The party returned to power less than a year later—this time in coalition—and has served as the senior coalition partner in every government since. It was and continues to be the party in power.

From Fragmentation to Factionalization

The LDP was created from a merger of two conservative parties—the Liberals and the Democrats—as an antisocialist alliance based largely on the voting support of farmers and the financial support of big business. Its first several years were chaotic; the party's survival was often at risk. Factions then emerged inside the party (originally divided between ex-Liberals and ex-Democrats—a line that later blurred). It was the presence and stable coexistence of internal factions that prevented the rupture of the LDP into separate parties.

A key event was the 1956 election of the party leader, who, as such, would also become prime minister. The leading candidate was Nobusuke Kishi (grandfather of the recent prime minister Shinzo Abe). The other two candidates in the race agreed to direct their supporters to vote for whoever finished second in the first round of voting. Unexpectedly, enough faction members followed the instructions of their leaders to defeat Kishi. Although Kishi still became prime minister, it was only when the candidate who defeated him fell ill and was forced to resign. Thereafter, prime ministerial hopefuls began organizing their own factions; in fact, being a faction leader became a necessary prerequisite. Between 1956 and 1976 (with the rise of Kakuei Tanaka, discussed later in this chapter), factions were primarily vehicles for electing party leaders.

Japanese politics was in turmoil from the end of World War II in 1945 through 1960, and political parties, as a rule, were more concerned with winning elections than with policy. Civil servants from the bureaucracy took this opportunity to step into the policymaking vacuum. Japan's postwar bureaucracy, an outgrowth of the prewar tradition of an imperial bureaucracy, was further strengthened by the U.S. occupation's decision to purge the prewar Diet but leave the old bureaucracy largely intact. The postwar era thus began with a group of experienced bureaucrats, accustomed to exercising power in the name of the emperor, facing an inexperienced group of politicians. Because of these factors, the LDP was both disunited on policy priorities and unable to exercise much policy leadership even after it had gained a stable majority. In addition, Prime Minister Shigeru Yoshida's decision to recruit twenty-five bureaucrats to run for his Liberal Party in the 1949 elections, and the return of purged bureaucrats to public life following the end of the occupation in 1952, created an influx of ex-bureaucrats into both of the conservative parties that merged to form the LDP (Reed 1988). Ex-bureaucrats assumed leadership roles in the LDP, contributing to a bureaucratic style of decision-making in the party.

From Ideology to Pragmatism

1960 was a tumultuous year in Japanese politics. In that year, Prime Minister Kishi attempted to force an amended version of the U.S.-Japan Security Treaty (known in Japan as Ampo) through the Diet (Packard 1966). The opposition, led by the Japan Socialist Party (JSP), opposed this move with every means at its disposal, using both legislative maneuvers and extraparliamentary demonstrations. The bill was nevertheless passed and the treaty revised, but Prime Minister Kishi's public support plummeted and he was forced to resign.[1] Thereafter, the LDP dropped all talk of rearmament and constitutional revision.[1] Instead, Hayato Ikeda, the new prime minister, campaigned on his "income-doubling plan," a promise to double the income of all Japanese voters within ten years. This was actually more of a forecast than a policy, but it was excellent electoral politics, especially when Japanese economic growth doubled incomes even faster than had been promised.

In the following years, the LDP continued to be identified with the conservative position on Ampo, but it was now the progressive peace pole that attracted voters. Since peace was the Socialist Party's best issue, it continued to return to this theme, but the LDP refused to fight back, focusing instead on the growing economy. Periodically, an LDP politician would make noise about constitutional revision and rearmament, but the party would treat it as a *shitsugen* ("misstatement"), making the topic a political taboo. But the events of 1960 left their mark on Japanese politics. Though the division over foreign policy weakened over time, it has yet to be erased (Flanagan 1984). Now, principled opposition to constitutional revision is represented by the Socialist and Communist parties but draws little popular support. Nor is there popular support for conservative proposals to revise the constitution, particularly those proposals that involve changing the "peace clause." Thus, arguments over the constitution that drew both sides into the streets in 1960 are still of concern to some political elites but move very few votes.

Consensus-Based Policymaking

The consolidation of LDP one-party dominance required the maintenance of party unity. From its founding, the LDP was plagued by the threat that members might defect to start a new party (and the procedures and precedents for starting a new party were naturally well understood by all founding members). Ikeda's successor, Eisaku Sato, solved this problem by developing a consensus-based policymaking system that not only took into account all party opinions but also balanced the allocation of posts within the party and the government. Internal party politics was thus designed to keep all members happy—at least happy enough not to defect. But this system had a number of side effects. Avoiding divisive policy initiatives further increased the dominance of bureaucrats in policymaking, and frequent cabinet reshuffles—necessary to give as many people as possible the chance to become a cabinet minister—became unavoidable. Such reshuffles are more similar to those of Italy's recent administrations than is usually recognized.

Unfortunately, solutions to interparty conflict did not necessarily lead to electoral victory, and the LDP was losing votes at each election in the 1960s, despite the favorable circumstances of rapid economic growth. Sato's consensus-based politics was a good way to avoid fracture and to maintain a dominant position in the short run, but the party needed to provide more dynamic leadership to win continued voter support. LDP governments enacted only the lowest-common-denominator policies that could gain a consensus from all concerned, excluding only the Communists and the left wing of the Socialists. It is hard to campaign on such an insipid platform. After 1963 the LDP maintained its majority only because the opposition proved incapable of coordinating their nominations, thereby splitting the anti-LDP vote and allowing the LDP to win a majority of the Diet seats without a majority of the votes. In 1972, fearing that the end was near, the party turned to an "outsider," Kakuei Tanaka, to lead it out of its predicament.

A Clientelist Electoral Machine

Kakuei Tanaka became the leader of the LDP in 1972—in circumstances that resembled those faced by Junichiro Koizumi in 2000. But while Koizumi was a policy maverick within the party, Tanaka was an outsider in a different sense: he had not even graduated from college, when most of his predecessors had been elite bureaucrats. Like Koizumi, he was also a reformer of sorts. The electoral reform bill passed in 1994 was very similar to the one Tanaka had proposed in 1973 (which failed to pass). Tanaka introduced new ideas and strategies to stem the party's slide in the polls, but the party that Tanaka created in the 1970s was one that badly needed reform by the 1990s.

Tanaka's solution to the LDP's electoral woes was his best-selling book *Remodeling the Japanese Archipelago*,[2] which essentially detailed a massive construction project designed to bring industrialization to every corner of Japan. When Tanaka tried to implement his ideas, however, it produced both inflation and a drop in public support.[3] Tanaka's plans also coincided with serious environmental pollution problems. He was promising a factory for every corner of Japan just when antipollution citizens' movements across the country were protesting the factories built during the period of rapid postwar growth. Some localities remained anxious to attract development, but others proved willing to forgo their chance at industrialization if it meant accepting polluted air and water. The slogan "remodeling the archipelago" had to be abandoned. Fiscal conservative Takeo Fukuda (who later served as prime minister and who is the father of the recent prime minister Yasuo Fukuda) was installed as minister of finance, and inflation was brought under control. Though inflation lost votes, fiscal rectitude did not win votes, so the party was subsequently left with little choice but to depend upon clientelist and pork-barrel politics to win elections (Scheiner 2006). Herbert Kitschelt best describes the essence of a clientelist system and, in so doing, the LDP's electoral strategy since Tanaka: "First, resource-rich but vote-poor constituencies provide politicians with money in exchange for material favors. . . . Second, vote-rich but resource-poor constituencies receive selective material incentives before and after elections for surrendering their vote" (2000:849).

Building the Clientelist System

The LDP, like Italy's Christian Democrats, used the land reforms of the early postwar period as a way of building clientelist networks in rural areas, taking credit for public projects in a manner common to democratic parties worldwide. *Noukyou*, the farm cooperatives, were the first solid organizational support base for the party. By the 1970s, however, the LDP needed something more to maintain support. Tanaka's contribution was to systematize and extend the clientelist system. New clienteles were added even if their interests were in direct conflict with those already included under the LDP umbrella. For example, the abortion debate in Japan featured an antiabortion religious group, Seicho-No-Ie, versus pro-abortion doctors—and both supported the LDP (Norgen 2001). Policymaking in the Tanaka LDP was a matter of compromise and negotiation; any group willing to negotiate was welcome. In the 1974 House of Councillors elections, for example, individual candidates were supported by specific interest groups such as the Toyota sales distribution network, Hitachi home electronics, the cosmetics industry, Seicho-No-Ie (which was divided into eastern and western branches, each supporting a different candidate), tobacco companies, pharmacists, the Self-Defense Forces, the Association of the War Bereaved, nurses, dentists, midwives, chefs, and an opera association.[4] Most of these groups were not directly involved in politics prior to being mobilized by the LDP, but the LDP gradually extended its reach into groups that had supported the opposition, including some labor unions. A large proportion of the candidates elected by these newly mobilized groups joined the Tanaka faction.

The LDP's response to election losses was to invite yet another interest group into the inner circle. Thus, interest groups were left with the choice of expressing their policy preferences by voting for an opposition party and being excluded from power or voting for an LDP candidate and gaining a seat at the bargaining table. Groups that opposed a given LDP policy found that the most effective way of exerting influence was to vote for an LDP candidate who also opposed this policy. The result of this continued incorporation of interest groups, however, was a party incapable of taking a coherent policy stance.

The party did not—indeed, could not—enforce party discipline in election campaigns. Nonetheless, when the internal party negotiations were complete, LDP members of the Diet were expected to vote for the resulting compromise.

Thus, under Tanaka, the LDP came closer to fitting the model of a "mass clientelism party," a term originally coined to describe Italy's Christian Democratic Party (Belloni, Caciagli, and Mattina 1979). Both parties used public policy to create mass support bases, which they otherwise lacked. One particularly clear example of this process was the LDP's *tochi kairyo jigyo* ("land- improvement associations"). The system was simple: any group of farmers who successfully applied for a public project to improve its land could receive subsidies (George Mulgan 2000:80–82). Unsurprisingly, candidates for public office proved to be particularly active entrepreneurs in forming these associations, which not only received large sums of public money but also served as campaign organizations for the candidate in question. These associations were often involved in political corruption scandals.

Factions in Tanaka's LDP

The Tanaka faction evolved into a political organization quite different from the factions founded in 1956. First, and by design, the Tanaka faction was much more involved in elections. It became less a parliamentary vehicle for electing the party leader and more a political machine for electing faction members (Johnson 1986). The faction operated like a *gundan* ("military unit") in exercising discipline over its members—including not only elected politicians but also their political secretaries and potential future candidates—and like a *sogo byoin* ("general hospital") when processing requests from a wide range of constituents and interest groups. Other factions were forced to adapt and became more like political machines themselves, changing the nature of LDP factions more generally.

The Tanaka era also—albeit not by design—decoupled faction leadership from party-leader elections. Tanaka was arrested in the Lockheed scandal of 1976 and convicted in 1983, thus becoming one of several world leaders caught in a scandal that originated in a U.S. congressional investigation into American companies paying bribes to foreign officials. Although many people, including Tanaka himself, thought that he would return to lead the party after the Lockheed storm had blown over, it soon became clear that this was not to be. Previously, a faction leader who was no longer a viable candidate for party leader would be replaced or the faction would lose members to those that were led by potential prime ministers. The Tanaka faction, however, had become something different, allowing Tanaka to hold onto the reins of political influence. He was thus able to prevent the large number of ambitious young politicians in his faction from running for party leader. The fact that the largest faction had no candidate for party leader also allowed Tanaka to play the role of "kingmaker," as the Tanaka faction plus any one of the other major factions had enough votes to elect a party leader. For several years Japan experienced a bizarre political situation in which the most powerful politician in all of Japan (with respect to leadership selection if not necessarily public policy) was on trial for corruption and, while technically not even a member of the LDP, was actually the leader of the largest faction within the LDP.

In the end, the Tanaka strategy suffered from two major problems. First, the escalation of mass clientelism produced periodic corruption scandals. Japan is ranked second to Italy in most international comparisons of corruption levels in industrialized democracies (see, for example, Gerring and Thacker 2004). Major scandals affected elections in 1947, 1955, and 1967, but corruption increased and diversified dramatically following the 1972 ascension of Tanaka (Johnson 1986; MacDougall 1988). The 1974 House of Councillors elections set new records for both campaign money spent and election laws broken. The style of exchange also shifted subtly away from interest groups buying off politicians, toward politicians extorting money from interest groups (Reed 1996). Tanaka is also credited with spreading money politics to the bureaucracy. Bureaucratic corruption is understudied, but bureaucrats too were arrested in each of the major postwar scandals, and it is clear that the bureaucracy became significantly more corrupt under the Tanaka regime and thereafter. The rise of *zoku giin*—politicians who have intimate ties to specific industries and lobby on their behalf (Inoguchi and Iwai 1987)—is directly linked to bureaucratic corruption. The relationship between politicians and bureaucrats has changed since Tanaka, but we know little about the new relationship.

The second problem with Tanaka's clientelist solution to the LDP's electoral woes was that its effectiveness declined over time. Not only did the LDP continue to lose votes to scandals, but it also lost votes due to the increasing number of voters who ignored the recommendations of their organizations. The decline of the "organizational vote" has been widely discussed in Japan and is analogous to the weakening of linkages and increased availability of voters seen in Europe (Mair, Muller, and Plasser 2004).

Alternatives to the LDP

Given the weaknesses of the LDP and the continued decline of its popularity, why have Japanese voters not simply voted the party out of office? The answer lies mainly in the nature of the alternatives. Until the 1993 election, whenever voters were angered by an LDP scandal, they were faced with a narrow and uninspiring set of alternatives. In 1993 three new nonsocialist parties, two of which were formed by defectors from the LDP, forced the LDP into opposition for the first time in its history.

From the founding of the LDP after the 1955 election until the 1993 election, the largest opposition party was the JSP. The JSP fought against rearmament and constitutional revision in the 1940s and 1950s, winning votes primarily based on its pro-peace stance, with its other left-leaning positions notably less attractive to voters (Curtis 1988, chapter 4). This stance was electorally productive as long as the conservatives continued to stand for rearmament and constitutional revision. Except for the disaster of 1949, when the JSP was severely punished for its role in an ineffective and scandal-ridden coalition government, the socialist vote grew continuously—due to the pro-peace stance—from 1946 through the 1960 elections. In 1960, however, the LDP changed its strategy, newly emphasizing its economic policies instead of its support for rearmament. The JSP's anti-rearmament stance—which had appealed to voters and worked so well for the JSP from 1952 through 1960—proved ineffective thereafter, but the party never adjusted to this new reality despite voters' hunger for fresh ideas. There was a reform movement inside the JSP, led by Saburo Eda, but it was repeatedly stymied by the left wing, and in 1978 Eda finally gave up on his attempts to reform the JSP, defecting to form the Social Democratic League (SDL, Shaminren). But Eda died soon afterward and the SDL never developed into a significant force in Japanese politics.

Both the LDP and the JSP vote thus declined in the 1960s and 1970s, and the newly available votes were picked up by several smaller parties in a process the Japanese called *tatoka* (literally, "multipartization"). New parties emerged in succession to take advantage of otherwise unoccupied niches in the Japanese electorate. Precisely because they occupied niches, however, they could not expand much beyond their respective constituencies and had no prospects of ever winning a majority in the Diet. The possibility of forming an opposition coalition to defeat the LDP seemed more feasible, and efforts were made in that direction but without success (Christensen 2000). Each party had a greater need to protect its own niche than to defeat the LDP.

The Democratic Socialist Party (DSP) was formed from a split of the JSP in 1960. Komei, a religious party, entered national politics in 1967. Neither of these parties, however, attracted broad support. The Japan Communist Party (JCP) ran in every postwar election—indeed, in every electoral district beginning in 1960—but also experienced little success until 1972 (Berton 1992). In 1972 the party's primary appeal was its opposition of Tanaka's plan to remodel the archipelago. In the 1960s and 1970s the JSP allied itself with the JCP, winning several major gubernatorial elections (Maeda 1995). But neither the DSP nor Komei would accept JCP cooperation. Forced to choose between a leftist alliance with the JCP and a centrist alliance with the DSP and Komei, the JSP finally chose the latter and the JCP was forced back into its corner. By 1993 no party considered the JCP an acceptable coalition partner. Therefore, any vote for the JCP was simply a "wasted" protest vote.

In the absence of opposition-party coordination, an alternative strategy was to attract LDP politicians into a new party. This simultaneously gained seats and weakened the LDP. As Curtis accurately forecast at the time, "For the foreseeable future at least, the end of LDP rule, if it is to occur at all, is most likely to result from a split in the LDP itself" (Curtis 1988:240). The first successful defection from the LDP occurred during the Lockheed scandal election of 1976. Five members of the Lower House of the Diet defected from the LDP to form the New Liberal Club (NLC) (Pharr 1982). But the NLC fielded candidates in only 25 districts (out of 124), the minimum requirement for legal recognition as a political party. Thus, although the electorate responded enthusiastically, the NLC failed to attract mainstream support because only a very small proportion of the electorate was given the opportunity to respond at all (Reed 1997). Nevertheless, the "NLC boom" of 1976 provided the future reformers of 1993 with many valuable lessons. The most optimistic lesson learned was that the electorate was ready for a change and a new reformist party could expect a substantial boom in its first election. The most difficult lesson was that a party could be "new" only once. The NLC faded in its second election and eventually returned to the LDP fold after the 1986 election.

The 1993 Election

Between the 1990 and 1993 elections, a series of scandals rocked the LDP. These scandals were similar to those of the past except that they broke almost immediately after the Recruit scandal of 1989, leaving the LDP no respite. After every major scandal up to this point, the LDP had studied the possibility of electoral reform, but, in the past, talk of reform faded in concert with public interest in the most recent scandal. This time, reform plans were already on the table when the next scandal started (Reed 1999), and when the LDP government failed to enact change under two successive cabinets in the midst of two successive scandals, LDP reformers decided to exit and start their own parties (Kato 1998; Reed and Scheiner 2003; Saito, chapter 4, this volume).

The July 18, 1993, election was precipitated by the decision of 39 members of the LDP to vote in favor of a motion of no confidence against their own government. Eighteen more abstained. The LDP's inability to enact political reform had frustrated the public and fractured the LDP, and a total of 46 LDP defectors formed 2 new parties. First, on June 21, 1993,

Masayoshi Takemura led a group of reformers out of the LDP to found the New Party Harbinger (Shinto Sakigake) (Otake 1997). Two days later, on June 23, 1993, the LDP faction led by Tsutomu Hata and Ichiro Ozawa defected en masse to form the Japan Renewal Party (Shinsei). These two new parties fell into step with a third new party, the Japan New Party (JNP, Nihon Shinto), which had been founded before the 1992 House of Councillors elections by Morihiro Hosokawa, the governor of rural Kumamoto prefecture. The key word in each of the party names was *shin* ("new").

Not only did all three new parties gain votes in 1993, but the newer the party's image, the better it fared at the polls. The average change in votes received by the defecting candidates gives us a simple estimate of how many votes a given party label was worth. The JNP label was, on average, worth forty-two thousand additional votes per candidate, while the other two new party labels were worth over thirty thousand additional votes each. The message was clear: the Japanese electorate wanted change. Yet voters did not abandon the LDP. The LDP label cost a candidate only about five thousand votes on the average. If all the defectors had run under the LDP label and had lost five thousand votes each, the LDP would still have finished with 29 percent of the electorate and 43 percent of the vote, likely maintaining its majority in the Diet. The defections were a necessary condition of unseating the LDP; the LDP was defeated by the interaction between the seats directly lost by LDP defections and the favorable response of the electorate to the new-party boom.

The 1993 election thus ended the 1955 party system. The LDP was out of power for the first time in its history, and more important, the election had produced three new alternatives to the LDP. The mold had been broken, but what would replace it? After the 1993 general election, Japanese politics entered a phase of remarkable fluidity. Many new parties were founded and many more proposed, but the LDP remained basically intact as the largest party in the system.

Forming a Non-LDP Government

After the 1993 elections, independents who had won joined various parties and a few more defections occurred, but the non-LDP, non-Communist forces had a majority of 260 seats to the LDP's 233. The non-LDP forces were divided into a total of 8 parties. In a normal process of coalition formation, one would have expected the LDP to be able to find a coalition partner. The non-LDP parties were united on nothing except the necessity of political reform, and the LDP was now expressing a commitment to political reform and could thus play the role of center party, necessary for any policy-based coalition. In the end, however, the non-LDP parties were able to form a coalition and establish a government led by the JNP's Hosokawa; the logic of coalition formation was overpowered by that of preparing for the next election and the emotional appeal of grasping a historical opportunity. The exclusion of the LDP was hardly inevitable, and was accomplished in large part due to the skilled and tireless advocacy of Ozawa

(Curtis 1999:111–14). Table 1.1 shows the Lower and Upper House election results (each party's vote and seat shares) since 1990.

The eight-party, anti-LDP, non-JCP coalition's only accomplishment was to enact political reform for changing the electoral system. The new electoral system, still current, combines the mixed-member systems now popular around the world with single-member districts (SMDs) and proportional representation (PR) (on mixed-member systems, see Shugart and Wattenberg 2001; on the Japanese version, see Maeda, chapter 3, and Reed and Shimizu, chapter 2, this volume). Once political reform was enacted, however, the coalition lost all coherence. The various parties agreed on nothing else and began concentrating on reorganizing themselves into larger parties that might challenge the LDP. Ozawa led the most successful movement, but his efforts forced those not included, the JSP and Sakigake, out of the coalition. Those two parties, as a result, joined an LDP-led coalition, and the LDP thus returned to power with the help of its traditional rival, the JSP. The key to forming this coalition of "strange bedfellows" (Kabashima and Reed 2001) was the LDP's historic concession to the Socialists of the prime ministership, a position the LDP had not ceded since its creation in 1955.

Japanese Politics Since Reform

The 1993 electoral-system reform has changed Japanese politics in a multitude of ways, many of which will be documented in the chapters that follow. Both the LDP and its alternatives have changed. Under the leadership of Junichiro Koizumi from 2001 to 2006, the LDP seemed poised to reinvent itself, but Koizumi's successors have since guided the party back to its conservative roots. The opposition now faces the task of organizing new parties and merging them into a single relevant challenger to the LDP. Though there has yet to be a post-1993 loss of LDP power, evolution toward a two-party system is clearly visible at each successive election. The opposition is slowly but surely consolidating into a single challenger, and an alternation in power appears to be on the horizon.

The Return of the LDP

In the 1996 election, the LDP was challenged by two new parties, the New Frontier Party (NFP, Shinshinto), the result of Ozawa's organizational efforts, and the Democratic Party of Japan (DPJ, Minshuto). The DPJ was formed immediately preceding the election, primarily from Sakigake and moderate elements of the JSP. The LDP won a qualified victory due to the opposition's failure to coordinate, picking up 239 of the 500 seats (a gain of 16 from before) with a little less than 39 percent of the vote, and coming in first primarily because of its advantage in the SMDs. The NFP came in second, winning 156 seats with 28 percent of the vote, while the DPJ finished a rather dismal third, winning 51 seats with almost 11 percent of the vote. Soon after the election, however, the NFP disintegrated into its constituent parts.

Table 1.1 General Election Results, 1990–2005 (%)

	1990		1993		1996		2000		2003		2005	
	Votes	Seats	Votes	Seats	Votes	Seats	Votes	Seats	Votes	Seats	Votes	Seats
LDP	46.1	53.7	36.6	43.6	35.7	47.8	34.7	48.5	39.4	49.4	43.0	61.7
JSP/SDP	24.4	26.6	15.4	13.7	4.3	3.0	6.6	4.0	4.0	1.3	3.5	1.5
NFP					28.0	31.2						
DPJ					13.3	10.4	26.4	26.5	37.0	36.9	33.7	23.5
Komei (CGP)	8.0	8.8	8.1	10.0			7.4	6.5	8.1	7.1	7.3	6.5
JCP	8.0	3.1	7.7	2.9	12.8		11.7	4.2	7.9	1.9	7.3	1.9
DSP	4.8	2.7	3.5	2.9								
Shinsei (Renewal)			10.1	10.8								
Sakigake (Harbinger)			2.6	2.5	1.2	0.4						
JNP			8.0	6.8								
Liberal							7.2	4.6				
Conservative							1.2	1.5	0.7	0.8		
Kokumin (PNP)											1.2	0.8
Others	8.7	5.1	7.8	6.7	4.7	2.0	4.8	4.4	2.8	2.7	4.0	4.2

Source: Calculated from data provided by Kenneth Mori McElwain.
Note: Grey shading = government parties. Only parties competing in at least *two* elections *or* that won at least 1 percent of votes and/or seats are included.

15

One of the parties that subsequently reemerged from the NFP was Komei, Japan's only religious party. This party would play a major role in the events that followed. In 1967 Komei (the "clean government party"), a local party based on the Soka Gakkai Buddhist sect, entered the national arena (White 1970). Komei mobilized many new voters who had otherwise tended not to vote at all. Though only about half their votes come from members of the Soka Gakkai (Watanuki 1991:77), the party has proved remarkably effective, turning out not only to support Komei candidates but also to support candidates from other parties. But Komei has generally not been able to attract many voters from other parties, even in exchange for the disciplined support of Komei voters in other elections (Christensen 2000:95). The Soka Gakkai's intolerance toward other sects, its use of aggressive recruitment techniques, and the mixing of religion with politics give Komei one of the most negative images of any party in Japan, second only to that of the Communists.

After the 1996 election, the LDP needed new allies because the big losers of the election were its former allies, the JSP and Sakigake. At the time, the only party that could give the LDP a majority in both houses of the Diet was Komei; when Komei initially refused, the LDP coalesced with the Liberals, the fragment of the NFP led by Ozawa. The LDP, however, persisted in pursuing Komei, and the result was a three-party coalition in which the Liberals became an unnecessary appendage. Ozawa proposed that the LDP and Liberals dissolve to form a new party. It was also widely reported but never confirmed that he asked to be allowed to rejoin the LDP, as the NLC and many from the NFP had done previously. In the end, neither plan proved feasible, so Ozawa led the Liberals out of the coalition in preparation for the next election. About half the party, however, remained behind, calling themselves the Conservative Party, and most of them eventually found their way back into the LDP.

Table 1.2 shows the party composition of the Japanese government since Prime Minister Miyazawa's administration in 1991.

In the 2000 election, the LDP-Komei coalition faced a fragmented opposition led by the DPJ. The LDP gained in the SMDs, largely because the DPJ could not find good candidates to run in rural districts, and the coalition held its ground. Consequently, although the DPJ more than doubled its votes and seats, it failed to offer the LDP as strong a challenge as the NFP had in 1996. In 2003, however, the DPJ continued to grow and actually defeated the LDP in the PR voting. Nonetheless, just when it looked as if it would take only one more push to unseat the LDP-Komei coalition, the LDP nominated Koizumi as its leader (Lin, chapter 6, this volume).

Table 1.2 Government Composition, 1991–2007

Dates	Prime minister	Parties in the coalition
Nov. 5, 1991–Aug. 9, 1993	Miyazawa (LDP)	LDP
Aug. 9, 1993–Apr. 28, 1994	Hosokawa (JNP)	JNP, JSP, Shinsei, Sakigake, Komie, DSP, SDF, DRP
Apr. 28, 2004–Jun. 30, 1994	Hata (Shinsei)	Shinsei, JNP, Komei, DSP, Liberal, DRP
Jun. 30, 1994–Jan. 11, 1996	Muruyama (JSP)	JSP, LDP, Sakigake
Jan. 11, 1996–Nov. 7, 1996	Hashimoto 1 (LDP)	LDP, SDP (formerly JSP), Sakigake
Nov. 7, 1996–Jul. 30, 1998	Hashimoto 2 (LDP)	LDP (minority)
Jul. 30, 1998–Jan. 14, 1999	Obuchi 1 (LDP)	LDP (minority)
Jan. 14, 1999–Oct. 5, 1999	Obuchi 2 (LDP)	LDR, Liberal
Oct. 5, 1999–Apr. 5, 2000	Obuchi 3 (LDP)	LDP, Komei, Liberal*
Apr. 5, 2000–Apr. 6, 2001	Mori (LDP)	LDP, Komei, Conservative**
Apr. 6, 2001–Sept. 26, 2006	Koizumi (LDP)	LDP, Komei
Sept. 26, 2006–Sept. 26, 2007	Abe (LDP)	LDP, Komei
Sept. 26, 2007–	Fukuda (LDP)	LDP, Komei

Source: Calculated from data provided by Kenneth Mori McElwain.
Note: * Apr. 1, 2000—Liberal Party splits into the Liberal and New Conservative Parties. The Liberals leave the Obuchi cabinet, but the Conservatives remain.
** Nov. 21, 2003—Conservative Party merges with the LDP.

Junichiro Koizumi and the "New LDP"

Junichiro Koizumi was first elected in 1972, after failing in his first attempt to succeed his father. His father had served in the prewar Diet and won his first postwar election in 1952, after the U.S. occupation ended. Koizumi soon developed a reputation as a maverick, periodically getting himself reprimanded for "antiparty" activities or statements. He also developed an image of a somewhat eccentric reformer. He was a member of the reformist YKK group (Taku Yamazaki, Koichi Kato, and Koizumi), but when Kato and Yamazaki led their factions in an abortive attempt to vote for a motion of no confidence in their own government (Saito, chapter 4, this volume), Koizumi declined to participate. He was also somewhat inexplicably committed to postal reform, an issue that drew neither popular support nor much interest from other members of the Diet. A further eccentricity was his decision to run in every party leadership election despite embarrassing showings in his first two runs. Koizumi's career might well have ended in obscurity but for the convergence of circumstances that led to victory in his third leadership bid in 2001.

Once he became prime minister, Koizumi's quirkiness proved remarkably popular, spanning the generations. He certainly did not look, act, or talk like any previous LDP leader or prime minister and was therefore able to symbolize change. The LDP found itself actually making money on sales of Koizumi posters, Koizumi dolls—and anything with Koizumi's image on it. In the 2001 House of Councillors elections, Koizumi promised to "change the LDP in order to change Japan"; if the LDP refused to reform, he would "bust it up" (*buchikowasu*). A Koizumi cabinet could and would do things that no previous LDP cabinet could do. Compared to the fledgling DPJ, Koizumi promised change without risk. In 2001 he led the LDP to its first clear electoral victory since 1986.

After the 2001 election, however, progress toward reform was bogged down in the LDP's consensus-based policymaking process. Although Koizumi earned popular support by going to North Korea and bringing back several abductees, there was little evidence to indicate that the LDP had changed. Running as a "normal" LDP prime minister, and acting just like his predecessors and nothing like the eccentric reformer of 2001, Koizumi suffered what had come to be "normal" LDP defeats in the 2003 general election and the 2004 House of Councillors elections. Koizumi's postal-reform bill also suffered defeat in the Diet at the hands of his own party. At this point, however, Koizumi took extraordinary steps that snatched victory from the jaws of defeat. Despite his cabinet and party's low poll ratings (45 percent support for the cabinet and 33 percent for the party, according to the *Yomiuri Shimbun* poll published August 11, 2005) and internal disarray, he dissolved the Diet on August 8, 2005, and called for new elections. He then not only refused to nominate those incumbents who had voted against postal reform (the "postal rebels") but also nominated challengers (dubbed "assassins") to run against them. Koizumi was keeping his promise to pass reform and bust up the LDP if the party did not cooperate. His popularity soared and the LDP won an overwhelming victory, electing 83 new members, who were immediately labeled "Koizumi's children." Running against the LDP, his own party, proved as popular in 2005 as it had in 2001. Postal reform was passed and Koizumi kept one more promise: to retire after two terms.

In these two "miracle" elections (2001 and 2005), Koizumi drew DPJ supporters back into the LDP fold. He produced an image of a "new LDP" analogous to Tony Blair's New Labour in Great Britain. He also kept his promise to change the LDP, at least temporarily, ignoring many of the LDP's traditional practices that went back to the Hayato Ikeda and Eisaku Sato administrations. Most notably, he largely ignored factions in his cabinet appointments. The 2005 election was the first time that the LDP had run on a clear policy platform and enforced agreement of all party nominees. When he retired, it was possible to imagine the LDP reinventing itself and winning elections on issues and leadership instead of pork-barrel clientelism. Instead, Koizumi's successors returned to LDP traditions.

Koizumi's chosen successor was Shinzo Abe. As the prime minister, Abe soon squandered all the popularity that Koizumi had built up. Abe allowed the winning (but not the losing) postal rebels to return to the LDP, with no objection from Koizumi, a measure unpopular with the public. Moreover, Abe's primary policy goal was to revise the constitution, which proved uninteresting to the public and divisive within the party. The Abe cabinet also soon proved incompetent and prone to scandal. In 2007 Abe fell ill and resigned the day after giving his Crown speech (a statement of his administration's policy objectives, adopted from the British tradition) and before the Diet session had even begun. The LDP scrambled to select a new leader, choosing party stalwart Yasuo Fukuda, who led the party until September 2008. Fukuda proved to be a competent manager in the LDP tradition, which has lost votes in every election since 1993.

The opposition also remained active during the Koizumi administration. As mentioned earlier, after 2003 it seemed as if just one more push would unseat the LDP, but Koizumi pulled off his second "miracle" and led the LDP to a historic victory in the 2005 election. It was not until 2007, when the DPJ turned to Ozawa to lead the party, that the LDP lost in the House of Councillors elections, producing the first divided government in postwar Japanese political history. The LDP had been in a House of Councillors in which it was not the majority party, but not in one led by an opposition party.

An Evolution toward Two-Party Dynamics

The fundamental dynamic of a two-party system is alternation in power. This has yet to occur in Japan (Reed and Shimizu, chapter 2, this volume). Although the opposition has made substantial gains and did defeat the LDP in the 2007 House of Councillors elections, the LDP remains in power. But several other dynamics typical of two-party systems have already begun to emerge.

First, policy issues and the images of party leaders have begun to play an increasing role in election campaigns (Maeda, chapter 3, this volume). In 2003 the DPJ produced a party manifesto to which every single nominee signed his or her name—a first in Japanese political history. In 2005 the election was fought over postal reform, the clearest case of a single issue dominating an election since the 1960 Ampo election. The 2007 election, when the DPJ took control of the House of Councillors, saw the emergence of more open debate in the Diet. Following this loss, the LDP reacted as it always did to defeat: with an offer to bargain with the winners. But the DPJ, after some waffling by Ozawa, refused, arguing that debates should take place in the Diet and not behind closed doors. Since this decision, debate has indeed moved into the Diet and onto Japanese TV screens. Two debates, one concerning the role of the Self-Defense Forces in the War on Terror and the other over what to do about the bureaucracy's misplacement of fifty million public pension records, have drawn public attention and dominated the media. In these debates the two parties appear divided by an unbridgeable gulf, producing good drama and wide public debate. Despite this open debate, however, compromises are being made and bills passed at a respectable pace. The pension problem itself is an example of a two-party dynamic: more information is being made available to the public. Since winning control of the House of Councillors, the DPJ is better able to obtain information from the bureaucracy. The party's discovery and publicization of the pension problem occurred just as one would envision it in a two-party system.

Meanwhile, important changes are occurring in the role of women in politics and in the relationship between politicians and bureaucrats. Japan has long been one of the most male-dominated industrialized democracies, but there are signs that this trend may be fading. The entry of women into Japanese politics, both as candidates and as a key voting bloc, has the potential to change the nature of Japanese democracy. In addition, Japan has long seen bureaucrats dominate politics. The relationship between politicians and bureaucrats has been well chronicled and hotly debated, but the recent spate of bureaucratic corruption and incompetence suggests that the relationship is changing in fundamental ways. The LDP is no longer able to simply delegate policymaking to the bureaucracy, because of both increased electoral competition and bureaucratic failures.

A Note on Women and Politics

With the temporary exception of the very first postwar election in 1946, women have historically played a very small role in Japanese politics (Burden, chapter 11, and Martin, chapter 13, this volume). The initial glimmer of change occurred in 1989 and 1990 when Takako Doi, the first female leader of any major Japanese political party, led the JSP to its first victories since the 1950s (Gaunder, chapter 12, this volume). For a period, the SDP, led by Doi, seemed to be reinventing itself as a women's party, and since the 1990s, women have been considered good candidates, symbolizing a commitment to change. When Koizumi decided to send "assassins" to defeat the postal rebels, he often chose women, with three of those women becoming prominent symbols of his cabinet and administration. Moreover, the women chosen were strong and ambitious, guaranteeing that they would not be quiet tokens content to stay in the background. "Compared to the period from 1955 to 1993, women are now [since reform] more than *twenty* times as likely to be in the cabinet" (Pekkanen 2008:7). Young Japanese women today see the promise of a prominent role in politics. We should expect gains in gender equality not only to continue but possibly to accelerate.

Another glimmer of change can be found in the several elections in which powerful LDP politicians were the subjects of sex scandals and were roundly defeated. Until recently such sex scandals were not given much press coverage and had little if any effect on election results. Since 1996, however, sex scandals have had the most devastating electoral repercussions of any type. Here we recount the three most prominent examples.

Taku Yamazaki, first elected in 1972, was a coleader of the YKK group mentioned earlier. He now leads his own faction and has ambitions to become party leader some day. In the 2003 election, however, he found himself running from behind because of a sex scandal widely publicized in the weekly magazines that represent Japan's popular press. Although he managed to increase his vote by one thousand, the DPJ was able to increase its vote by twenty thousand and defeat the LDP stalwart. Yamazaki was extremely lucky that his Democratic opponent had lied about his educational qualifications and was forced to resign. Yamazaki won the by-election and returned to the Diet, but his loss showed the power of sex scandals to move votes.

In the same election and in a neighboring district, Seiichi Ota made a statement that lost him the election. First elected in 1980, Ota had a solid base in his district and was seen as a politician with great potential. When asked about a gang-rape incident that was making the news, however, he responded that he was pleased that Japanese youth (presumably referring to males only) still had lots of energy (*genki ga aru*). He apologized profusely thereafter but lost ten thousand votes, while his opponent gained over twenty thousand votes from previously dormant voters. Although Ota returned to the Diet in the 2005 election, at least partly on the basis of the Koizumi miracle, his future remains in some doubt as of this writing.

Naka Funada, a third-generation conservative politician who won his district overwhelmingly in 1996 lost in 2000 largely because he had divorced his wife and married a younger woman (a member of the House of Councillors). He campaigned with his new wife and lost thirty-five thousand votes while his opponents gained forty thousand. In the 2003 election, after wisely moving his new wife to the background during the campaign, he regained thirty thousand votes and his seat.

These three cases await statistical confirmation, but they do indicate that issues involving women are gaining in importance and that women as voters—and candidates—are having a greater impact on Japanese politics.

A Note on the Japanese Bureaucracy

One of the most widely shared perceptions of the Japanese government is that it boasts an efficient and clean bureaucracy (Johnson 1982). As noted in the previous section, however, this image has been exaggerated. Bureaucrats and ex-bureaucrat politicians have been deeply involved in all the major postwar scandals. There have also been many purely bureaucratic scandals that have not been widely covered in the press or studied by academics. Bureaucrats appear "clean" only when compared to the Tanaka-led LDP, and bureaucratic corruption appears to have increased under Tanaka's tenure. Moreover, political reform has not noticeably diminished corruption; bureaucratic corruption appears in the press intermittently, although seldom resulting in sustained calls for investigation. Most recently, when Koizumi appointed LDP maverick Makiko Tanaka (Kakuei Tanaka's daughter) as the minister of foreign affairs, she uncovered serious systematic corruption; this discovery was one reason she was fired from that post. In 2007 allegations directed at the vice-minister of defense, Takemasa Moriya, received wide and continuing coverage. Those allegations were lodged by another female, Defense Minister Yuriko Koike, who was also soon removed from office.

One long-recognized source of bureaucratic corruption is the practice of *amakudari* (literally, "descent from heaven"). In this practice, retiring bureaucrats are given lucrative jobs, with correspondingly lucrative retirement benefits, by their ex-clients. Attitudes toward *amakudari* divide the parties as consistently as any issue. Criticism of *amakudari,* and of bureaucratic influence more generally, has been one of the DPJ's most popular issues, while the LDP has taken up the issue only when forced to do so, and then reluctantly. The DPJ's control of the House of Councillors has allowed the opposition to deny the confirmation of three Fukuda administration appointees because the appointments were actually traditional *amakudari* fiefs "owned" by particular ministries.[5] In the past in these *amakudari* fiefs, the ministry chose one of its own members to get the plum appointment and the prime minister simply followed that recommendation. The 2007 denial was the first time in fifty-six years that confirmation had been denied for such an appointment. The LDP has thus been forced to recognize this source of corruption and appoint young reformers to the cabinet with the mandate to develop policy. As one sign of recent change, LDP members have even been heard making stinging criticisms of the bureaucracy on occasion. So far, however, they have stopped short of any serious reform.

Even more damaging than revelations of bureaucratic corruption have been those of incompetence (Scheiner and Muramatsu, chapter 9, this volume). The loss of the pension contributions mentioned earlier is a prime example of this incompetence, which also involves corruption, as significant amounts of money were simply pocketed by low-level bureaucrats who were aware that records were not being properly kept. One of the first major examples of incompetence goes back to 1996, when Naoto Kan, then of Sakigake and currently a leader of the DPJ, was the minister of health. At that time, the ministry was concealing clear evidence that HIV-tainted blood was being given to patients, and especially to those with hemophilia (Feldman 2000, chapter 4). Kan made the information public, apologized to the victims and to the survivors of those who had died, and became something of a national hero. The government's failure in this case, while clearly impermissible, is also virtually identical to tainted-blood scandals in several other countries. The most damning part of the Japanese story is that the government subsequently made little effort to reform the way the administration regulated blood products, and now faces a similar problem with hepatitis-tainted blood.

Bureaucratic corruption and incompetence may well prove—like political reform before them—that the LDP can neither adopt effective reforms under pressure nor avoid responsibility for its failure to do so.

The Future of Japanese Politics

Japanese politics is in flux. Of the recent changes, which are lasting shifts and which are temporary blips on the graph? It is too soon to tell for sure. The authors of this volume offer their current best guesses as they analyze what has happened—and why.

Notes

[1] Many within the party continued to see constitutional revision as their historic mission, but they were forced to wait for another opportunity. Prime Minister Abe's recent effort to put constitutional revision back on the agenda was another failed attempt to accomplish this mission.

[2] *Nihon Rettou Kaizou Ron*, 1972.

[3] The total LDP vote went up in 1972 for the first time ever, but the percentages did not change much and most of the vote increase came from rural districts where the LDP already had most of the seats. Increased votes thus did not produce increased seats, and public support for the LDP quickly declined.

[4] *Asahi Shimbun*, May 21, 1974. This and other cited newspaper articles are available by request from the authors. A more recent series of newspaper articles on the "organizational vote" covered five groups: doctors, agricultural cooperatives, labor unions, big business, and the Soka Gakkai religious group (*Yomiuri Shimbun*, March 12–22, 2003).

[5] "51% Favor the Continuation of Oil to American Ships in the Indian Ocean." *Yomiuri Shimbun*, November 14, 2007.

References

Belloni, Frank, Mario Caciagli, and Liborio Mattina. 1979. The mass clientelism party: The Christian Democratic Party in Catania and southern Italy. *European Journal of Political Research* 7:253–75.

Berton, Peter. 1992. The Japanese Communist Party: The lovable party. In *The Japanese party system*, ed. Ronald J. Hrebenar. Boulder, CO: Westview Press.

Christensen, Raymond V. 2000. *Ending the LDP hegemony*. Honolulu: Univ. of Hawaii Press.

Curtis, Gerald L. 1988. *The Japanese way of politics*. New York: Columbia Univ. Press.

———. 1999. *The logic of Japanese politics*. New York: Columbia Univ. Press.

Feldman, Eric A. 2000. *The ritual of rights in Japan*. Cambridge, U.K.: Cambridge Univ. Press.

Flanagan, Scott C. 1984. Voting behavior in Japan: A study of secular realignment. In *Electoral change in advanced industrial democracies*, ed. Russell J. Dalton, Scott C. Flanagan, and Paul Allen Beck. New Haven, CT: Yale Univ. Press.

George Mulgan, Aurelia. 2000. *The politics of agriculture in Japan*. London: Routledge.

Gerring, John, and Strom C. Thacker. 2004. Political institutions and corruption. *British Journal of Political Science* 34:295–30.

Inoguchi, Takashi, and Tomoaki Iwai. 1987. *Zokugiin no kenkyu: Jiminto seiken o gyujiru shuyakutachi*. Tokyo: Nihon Keizai Shinbun Sha.

Johnson, Chalmers. 1982. *MITI and the Japanese miracle*. Stanford, CA: Stanford Univ. Press.

———. 1986. Tanaka Kakuei, structural corruption and the advent of machine politics in Japan. *Journal of Japanese Studies* 12:1–28.

Kabashima, Ikuo, and Steven R. Reed. 2001. Voter reactions to strange bedfellows: The Japanese voter faces a kaleidoscope of changing coalitions. *Japanese Journal of Political Science* 1 (November): 229–48.

Kato, Junko. 1998. When the party breaks up: Exit and voice among Japanese legislators. *American Political Science Review* 92:857–70.

Kitschelt, Herbert. 2000. Linkages between citizens and politicians in democratic polities. *Comparative Political Studies* 33:845–79.

MacDougall, Terry. 1988. The Lockheed scandal and the high costs of politics in Japan. In *The politics of scandal*, ed. A. S. Markovits and M. Silverstein. New York: Holmes and Meier.

Maeda, Yukio. 1995. *Rengou seiken kousou to chiji senkyo* [Proposed coalitions and gubernatorial elections]. *Kokka Gakkai Zasshi* 108:1329–90.

Mair, Peter, Wolfgang C. Muller, and Fritz Plasser. 2004. *Political parties and electoral change*. London: Safe Publications.

Norgen, Tiana. 2001. *Abortion before birth control: The politics of reproduction in postwar Japan*. Princeton, NJ: Princeton Univ. Press.

Otake, Hideo. 1997. *Seiji kaikaku wo mezashita futatsu no seiji seiryoku* [Two political forces for reform]. In *Seiji saihen no kenkyuu*, ed. H. Otake. Tokyo: Yuuhikaku.

Packard, George R. 1966. *Protest in Tokyo: The security treaty crisis of 1960*. Princeton, NJ: Princeton Univ. Press.

Pekkanen, Robert. 2008. What is Koizumi's legacy? In *Japan's political mess: Abe failed, can Fukuda do better?* ed. Mark Mohr. Washington, DC: Woodrow Wilson International Center for Scholars, Asia Program Special Report.

Pharr, Susan J. 1982. Liberal democrats in disarray. In *Political leadership in contemporary Japan*, ed. Terry Edward MacDougall. Ann Arbor, MI: Michigan Papers in Japanese Studies.

Reed, Steven R. 1988. The people spoke: The influence of elections on Japanese politics, 1949–1955. *The Journal of Japanese Studies* 14:309–39.

———. 1996. Political corruption in Japan. *International Social Science Journal* 149:395–405.

———. 1997. The politics of booms: From the new liberal club to the Hosokawa coalition government. In *Japanese politics today: Beyond karaoke democracy*, ed. Purnendra Jain and Takashi Inoguchi, 108–23. South Melbourne: Macmillan Education Australia.

———. 1999. Political reform in Japan: Combining scientific and historical analysis. *Social Science Japan Journal* 2:177–93.

Reed, Steven R., and Ethan Scheiner. 2003. Electoral incentives and policy preferences: Mixed motives behind party defections in Japan. *British Journal of Political Science* 33:469–90.

Scheiner, Ethan. 2006. *Democracy without competition in Japan*. Cambridge, U.K.: Cambridge Univ. Press.

Shugart, Matthew, and Martin P. Wattenberg. 2001. *Mixed-member electoral systems: The best of both worlds?* Oxford: Oxford Univ. Press.

Yomiuri Shinbun. August 11, 2005. Poll at http://www.yomiuri.co.jp/election2005/news2/el_ne_050811_02.htm [in Japanese].

Watanuki, Jouji. 1991. Social structure and voting behavior. In *The Japanese voter*, ed. Scott Flanagan et al. New Haven, CT: Yale Univ. Press.

White, James W. 1970. *The Sokagakkai and mass society*. Stanford, CA: Stanford Univ. Press.

ELECTORAL POLITICS

AVOIDING A TWO-PARTY SYSTEM: THE LIBERAL DEMOCRATIC PARTY VERSUS DUVERGER'S LAW

Steven R. Reed and Kay Shimizu

In 1994 Japan enacted a new electoral system featuring single-member districts (SMDs). Though the new system includes a proportional representation (PR) tier, many reformers hoped it would lead to a two-party system. This points to Duverger's Law, one of the most powerful generalizations yet produced by political science (Duverger 1964; Riker 1986). Duverger's Law states that SMDs lead to a two-party system, and, in fact, Japan has moved closer to a two-party system in every election since the first under the new system, in 1996 (Reed 2007).

Japan virtually has a two-party system in three important senses. First, in most districts, competition is between two—and only two—viable candidates, offering voters a choice between one candidate from the ruling government coalition and one from the opposition. Second, in the 2005 general election, Japan's two major parties together won 55.6 percent of the vote, a higher figure than Great Britain's Labour and Conservative parties captured in the same year. Third, there is only one alternative to the Liberal Democratic Party (LDP), and that is the Democratic Party of Japan (DPJ). If the LDP were to lose, it would mean a DPJ government. That fact was confirmed by the LDP's losses and the DPJ's gains in the 2007 House of Councillors elections. The two parties now face each other across the Diet building, one ensconced in the Lower House and the other in the Upper House. But Japan has yet to experience the defining characteristic of truly competitive two-party dynamics: an alternation in power between the parties. It is interesting to note that Italy adopted something similar to Japan's new SMD system at almost the same time, and Duverger's Law has worked much faster there (Reed 2001). Italy has seen three alternations in power in three elections, whereas Japan has experienced none in four elections. What explains the difference?

The biggest political difference between Japan and Italy since the 1990s is that the predominant party in Italy, the Christian Democrats, disintegrated following electoral rule change, while the predominant party in Japan, the LDP, remained intact. In Italy both the left and right have been engaged in the difficult process of constructing new parties from the rubble of the old, but in Japan only the left is undergoing this process. The LDP experienced a serious split in 2005 and numerous tribulations in its attempts to adjust to the new system and more competitive environment, but it has managed to maintain a continuous organizational coherence—a strategic advantage over the opposition. The party has expended great effort and displayed exceptional ingenuity in avoiding the outcome of a true two-party system: losing power.

Historically, the LDP has displayed an impressive resourcefulness whenever it has faced a threat to its hold on power. When it was founded in 1955, the party seemed determined to revise the constitution, delete the peace clause, and rearm Japan. When that proved politically disastrous, the party reinvented itself in the early 1960s as the party of economic growth. When economic growth came into conflict with environmental protection and pollution control and the LDP lost control of urban local governments, it reinvented itself again, this time as an environmentally responsible party in the 1970 "Pollution Diet" (McKean 1981). A series of corruption scandals and failure to enact political reform resulted in the party's first experience of opposition, in 1993, but the LDP managed to find its way back into power by allying itself with its historic enemy, the Japan Socialist Party (JSP). We must consider the possibility that the LDP will reinvent itself yet again and find a way to bypass Duverger's Law.

Under the new electoral system, the LDP has used three main stratagems to avoid the implications of Duverger's Law. First, the LDP has been very creative in its use of the PR tier to elect two candidates from the same SMD. The logic of Duverger's Law is based on the fundamental fact that only one candidate can be elected from a district. Under these circumstances, third parties have little chance of winning seats and any candidate who wants to win is virtually forced to choose between the two main parties. The LDP has used the PR tier of the current system to keep candidates who cannot be nominated in an SMD from defecting to the opposition.

Second, the LDP has expended an incredible amount of ingenuity and energy in its attempt to get and maintain the electoral cooperation of its coalition partner, the religious party Komei. To obtain Komei votes in the SMDs, the LDP directs its supporters to vote for Komei in the PR tier. Komei has a solid support base but would be devastated by bipolar competition in the SMDs, coming in third at best and winning no SMD seats. Komei has SMD votes it can direct toward LDP candidates, and, if it receives PR votes in return, it can survive and even prosper as a third party—in direct defiance of Duverger's Law.

Finally, the party selected a maverick, Junichiro Koizumi, as party leader in 2001 (Lin, chapter 6, this volume), and he proceeded to win two landslide victories by running against his own party. Duverger's Law envisions two parties taking opposing positions on salient issues, but Koizumi successfully appeared to be both the government and the opposition in the 2001 House of Councillors elections and in the 2005 general elections. The PR tier again played an important role. Koizumi was able to nominate pro-reform candidates known as "assassins" to run against the antireform "rebels" by promising them safe positions on the PR list, thereby mitigating the risk of running against an established incumbent.

In the following sections, we begin with a short history of the Japanese electoral system and the fundamental implications of the electoral-system change of 1994. We then discuss each of the LDP's stratagems in turn, and assess the probability that they will allow the LDP to avoid a two-party system's inherent alternations in power and reestablish predominance. We conclude the chapter by placing our bets on Duverger's Law.

Party Strategy and Performance before and after Reform

From 1947 through 1993, prior to the 1994 electoral reforms that established the mixed SMD-PR system, Japan used the single nontransferable vote (SNTV) in multimember districts (MMDs) to elect the Lower House of the Diet. Under closed-list PR, voters chose a party but could not choose a particular candidate within that party. Under the SMD system, voters typically have two main choices, each representing a different party. In deciding how to cast their votes, citizens can weigh both the party platform and the characteristics of an individual candidate. SMD seats, however—in a manner similar to that of MMD seats—also give candidates powerful incentives to develop their own personal support (Cain, Ferejohn, and Fiorina 1987). This incentive is even stronger in electoral systems that force large parties to run multiple candidates in each district and force voters to choose among candidates from the same party (Carey and Shugart 1995). Thus, the new, mixed SMD-PR electoral system, while eliminating some of the need to develop personal support present under the MMD system, has preserved some pre-1994 elements.

The phenomenon of candidates competing against other candidates from their own party was particularly evident in Japan's MMDs because votes were not transferable. If votes cannot be transferred, the relationship between votes and seats in a particular district can be warped beyond recognition (Cox and Niou 1994). A party that nominates too many candidates risks splitting the vote too thinly—finishing, for example, fourth and fifth in a three-member district and getting no seats. Similarly, a party that runs two candidates may win seats for both candidates if the votes are evenly divided between them, but also may win only one seat if one of its candidates is too popular and receives the lion's share of the vote. We know of no other electoral system that can punish a party for fielding a very popular candidate. These anomalies drew criticism, of course, but the primary problem with MMDs was that they promoted competition among candidates from the same party.

A democracy based on candidates competing to build a base of personal votes by doing favors for individuals in their geographical constituencies is very different from a democracy based on unified parties competing for votes by proposing coherent party platforms. In the former system, voters may simultaneously have their most concrete demands met and yet justifiably feel that the government is unresponsive. They may come to have strongly negative feelings about the legislature but positive feelings about their own representative.

In Japan voters were often angry at the ruling LDP but continued to vote for particular LDP candidates. The popularity of individual members of the party and the legitimacy of the government aggregates to much less than the sum of its parts. Moreover, campaigning in MMDs cost a lot of money (Cox and Thies 2000). As the largest party, the LDP ran multiple candidates in most districts. Each LDP candidate built up his own personal support organization, a political machine called a *koenkai*, to mobilize his personal vote. Gerald Curtis (1988:177) describes it best:

> The fundamental reason for the high cost of campaigning in Japan is that every LDP politician must build and maintain his own political machine. He can rely neither on party organization, which hardly exists at the local level, nor on party loyalties among the electorate which, to the extent that they do exist, are effectively neutralized by an electoral system that forces candidates from the same party to compete with one another. Maintaining one's own political machine means helping prefectural and local assemblymen with their election campaigns, employing one large staff in the district to look after one's support organization, and another large staff in Tokyo to handle constituent requests and to raise money to make all other activities possible.

The need to develop and sustain one's personal vote led to high campaign costs, which, in turn, were a primary cause of political corruption.

SMDs produce powerful incentives to reduce competition to no more than two candidates per district. The process of reducing candidates is a process of coordination among potential candidates and parties. When one candidate withdraws from a district in favor of another, this implies an alliance between the two candidates and/or their two parties. When more than two candidates compete, it indicates a failure of coordination, which often leads to one-party dominance (Cox 1997). How did the LDP maintain its dominance for so long despite its support falling below 50 percent of the vote? The most fundamental cause, before 1994, was the failure of the opposition parties to work together in order to defeat the LDP, and one reason for this failure lay in the MMD electoral system.

Once LDP predominance was firmly established after 1969, elections tended to turn into referenda on the performance of the LDP government. Voters who wanted to express disapproval were offered the option of several different parties. One secret of the LDP's longevity, then, was the splitting of the anti-LDP vote among several opposition parties. In addition, dissatisfied voters had—and exercised—the option of voting for a different LDP candidate or a conservative independent who would join the LDP if elected. In other words, voters could express their dissatisfaction without depriving the LDP of a seat. While the LDP stayed in power for thirty-eight years, the rate of reelection for incumbents, at around 85 percent, was one of the lowest in the democratic world (Reed 1994).

MMDs served Japan reasonably well from the 1950s through the 1970s by producing a moderate multiparty system and a stable majority in the Diet, but the system also produced several festering problems. It failed to produce alternation in power,because it hindered cooperation among the opposition parties. The flip side of a stable government majority was long-term dominance by the LDP. The opposition could not overcome their coordination problems in order to mount a credible threat to the LDP, and the LDP became skilled at breaking up nascent moves toward effective coordination. A main LDP stratagem was to co-opt the most popular opposition policy positions (Pempel 1975) and to bring up issues that divided cooperation among the opposition. Most clearly, the system fostered expensive personal-vote campaigning, which was a major factor in the rising number of corruption scandals after 1974 and particularly after 1989. Commentators criticized "money politics" and yearned for low-cost, party-centered elections. Despite widespread dissatisfaction with MMDs, there was little agreement on what should replace them. Large parties favored SMDs and small parties favored PR. The resulting compromise was a mixed-member system combining both SMD and PR tiers.

Adapting to the New Electoral System

Japan's new mixed-member system places more weight on the SMD than on the PR tier. The allocation of seats in one tier is independent of the other. In other words, the number of seats allocated to a party in the SMD tier does not affect the number of seats allocated in the PR tier, and vice versa. This makes the Japanese system quite different from the German or New Zealand systems, in which the allocation of seats is dominated by the PR tier, but quite similar to the system used in Italy between 1994 and 2001. Under Japan's new system, voters first cast a ballot for a candidate in their SMD and then cast a ballot for a party in their PR bloc. The 130 old MMDs have been redrawn into 300 new SMDs. The PR votes allocated 200 seats in 11 blocs ranging in size from 7 to 33 seats until the 2000 election, when the PR tier was reduced to 180 seats.

In mixed-member systems, the devil is in the details (McKean and Scheiner 2000). The key details of the Japanese system are the double candidacy and "best loser" provisions. Candidates on the PR list may also be nominated in an SMD. This is known as *chofuku rikkoho* (double candidacy) and is a common provision in mixed-member systems. PR candidates running in an SMD may be ranked by the party, but the key element of double candidacy is the option of ranking several candidates together in a tie. These ties are then broken by reordering the candidates according to how close they came to winning their SMD. The final ranking is thus delegated to the voters. First, SMD candidates who win their district are deleted from the PR list. Second, candidates ranked together in a clump are reordered by calculating the *sekihairitsu*, the number of personal-SMD votes for each losing candidate divided by the number of votes for the winner. This provision gives each SMD candidate an incentive to campaign hard, both for himself and his party, even if he has no chance of winning his particular SMD. The closer he comes to winning his SMD, the more likely he is to win a PR seat. Party popularity, however, is also important to candidates, because the more PR votes a party garners, the more PR seats will be available for distribution among that party's SMD losers.

Three elections into the new system, both the LDP and the DPJ arrived at the same stated nomination policy. First, and most obviously, there should be only one nominee per party, per SMD. The party obviously should not nominate two popular SMD candidates, but neither should it allow any independent candidates to split their vote. Independents were a major problem under the old system and one that the SMDs and several other aspects of the system were designed to solve. Second, all PR candidates should run in an SMD (*Yomiuri Shimbun*, July 8, 2002; July 13, 2003; October 28, 2003). The ideal number of pure PR candidates (those running in the PR tier but not in any SMD) is zero, because such candidates have little incentive to campaign hard for their party. Thus, all SMD candidates should be ranked together in a single clump on the PR list, and only candidates who have campaigned hard and done well in an SMD should be given PR seats. Both parties, however, have been forced to admit exceptions to these principles.

We now turn to the LDP's three strategies for avoiding the implications of Duverger's Law. No party should be able to win two seats in an SMD—thus forcing candidates to choose between one of the two parties—but the LDP has used tag teams to avoid this situation. Third parties should be eliminated by bipolar competition in SMDs, but the LDP has developed a strategy for trading LDP votes to Komei in the PR tier, in return for Komei votes to the LDP in the SMD tier. Finally, the LDP has won two elections by running against itself. Koizumi adopted a strategy similar to that of Tony Blair's New Labour, promising to break up the LDP if it did not reform. Each of these strategies did indeed work, preventing the predicted alternations in power. But each appears to have passed the point of diminishing returns.

Strategy 1: Winning Two Seats in a Single-Member District (SMD)

SMDs virtually force a party to nominate one, and only one, candidate per district. Otherwise the party splits its vote among two or more candidates and loses a winnable seat to the opposition. The LDP, however, has often found itself with two candidates who want the same SMD nomination. If the LDP were to nominate only one of these two, the rejected candidate might choose to run for another party, taking her personal support with her. Even if the rejected candidate were to remain inside the party, she might choose to run as an independent, splitting the LDP vote. The LDP thus wants to keep both candidates in the party while nominating only one in the SMD. The solution to this problem has been to create tag teams (also called "Costa Rica arrangements"). The party nominates both candidates—one in the SMD and one in the PR tier—and the candidates promise to switch back and forth between SMD and PR districts at each election. Under such an arrangement, the candidate who is "sitting out" is guaranteed the first PR seat available to the party, regardless of the total votes she received for the SMD seat.

In an established two-party system like that of Great Britain, a party would simply expel any candidate who dared to run as an independent against the party's nominee, but the LDP has never been able to enforce such party discipline. Although a candidate who violates party discipline may be expelled temporarily, the LDP has always allowed such rebels to rejoin if they win a seat. Traditional nomination policy under the old MMD system was simply *kateba jiminto,* meaning, "If you win, you are LDP" (Reed forthcoming). The party has been unable to change this practice under the new system. The most recent example is the most extreme: the readmission of the winning—but not the losing—postal rebels back into the party.

Ideally, the LDP would choose the best candidate to run in each SMD and expel any candidate who violated party discipline. Because the LDP is incapable of enforcing party discipline, however, it must offer rejected candidates a reward for standing down in the SMD. That reward has often been a guaranteed position on the PR list and a promise of the SMD nomination in a subsequent election. The two candidates in a tag team have usually been traditional rivals under the old MMD system. The standard way of handling the return of a defector to the LDP fold has also been a tag-team arrangement, so one member of the team has often run for another party in the previous election. In the coming election, to be held before September 2009, the LDP may decide to form tag teams between candidates who ran against each other in 2005—one as an independent, because she voted against postal reform, and the other with the LDP nomination as an "assassin" trying to unseat the "rebel" (Maclachlan, chapter 8, this volume). Under such circumstances, it is questionable how much cooperation tag teams will be able to muster. In the past, the first election of a newly formed team sees very little cooperation between members, but the candidates soon learn that they are in the same boat and must paddle hard to keep it afloat. Tag teams have tended to work surprisingly well in second and subsequent elections. Even so, the stratagem has drawbacks.

Even if both candidates on a tag team receive a seat, it does not mean an extra seat for the LDP; it simply means that one of the LDP's PR seats has been used to prevent a defection. Such tag-team strategies will be crucial to the LDP in the upcoming election. The party faced extremely difficult choices in six districts with two LDP incumbents, one who was denied the nomination because she voted against postal reform (but has now rejoined the party), and another who ran in favor of postal reform with the nomination. At the time of this writing, the pattern has generally been for the postal rebels to be given the nomination and for the assassins to be forced to find another district or another post, most often that of a city mayor. In other districts, either the rebel or the assassin failed to win a seat, but both still have strong claims to the nomination. As in the past, candidates denied the nomination threaten to run as independents, though we do not yet know how many will follow through on that threat. Similar problems, unrelated to postal reform, plague the party in other districts. District branches are pleading with the party to make exceptions to the rule against new tag teams in order to solve their particular nomination problems, but the party headquarters has not only held firm but has already dissolved three tag-team arrangements—the first time it has been able to do so.

The main advantage of tag teams is keeping two rival candidates within the party. Without tag teams, a candidate who is rejected by the LDP has a strong incentive to accept a DPJ nomination. The new electoral system has thus changed the calculus of potential candidates. Party nominations have become more valuable because only party nominees can win PR seats. Independents get no PR votes and thus can win no PR seats. Candidates who are unable to get an LDP nomination have powerful incentives to accept the nomination of another party in order to give themselves a chance at winning a PR seat. The overall success rate for LDP candidates who switch to the DPJ is over 70 percent—much higher than the 20 percent for candidates who run as independents against LDP nominees. Yet candidates faced with the choice of (1) running as independents in the hope of winning and joining the LDP or (2) running for an opposition party have generally chosen to follow the traditional practice of running as independents. Only a few have made the leap and accepted a DPJ nomination.

The most important reason for reluctance to run for the DPJ is the expectation that the LDP will continue as the party in power and the DPJ as the opposition (Saito, chapter 4, this volume). This perception is based on long experience as well as recent events. The LDP has a clear advantage, but the party with the more recent victory also finds it easier to recruit candidates. After the 2005 landslide LDP victory, the party found itself swamped by 214 candidates competing for the single nomination to a by-election in Chiba 7th district, even though the opening was caused by the resignation of the LDP incumbent, who had been implicated in election-law violations (*Asahi Shimbun,* March 4, 2006). The DPJ unexpectedly won that election, and when the DPJ began recruiting candidates for the next election, the party was swamped with twelve hundred applications (*Asahi Shimbun,* July 1, 2006). The DPJ won the 2007 House of Councilors elections and is now the largest party in the Upper House. We should thus expect the DPJ to have less trouble attracting good candidates for the next election, including those who have recently run for the LDP. The tag-team stratagem is likely nearing its end, and an alternation of power may be on the horizon.

Strategy 2: Keeping Komei Happy

According to Duverger's Law, in SMD systems, parties other than the top two should disappear or fade into insignificance. Many small Japanese parties have indeed disappeared, and of those that remain, the Communists and Socialists have faded into insignificance. Komei, however, is proving an exception to Duverger's Law by prospering despite its third-party status. It has managed to do so by forming a coalition with the LDP and demanding PR votes in exchange for directing its supporters to vote for the LDP candidate in the SMDs.

Electoral cooperation between coalition partners can take place in a variety of ways. Under the old SNTV system, the most common form of cooperation was a "barter" between two of the smaller parties, which agreed to run only one candidate per MMD yet still had difficulty winning even one of the several seats. To take the most common case as an example, Komei would stand down in one district and support the DSP candidate, while the DSP would stand down and support the Komei candidate in the neighboring district. When Italy was using an electoral system similar to Japan's current system, each party was assigned winnable SMDs on the basis of its contribution to the coalition's vote, as determined by the PR totals. The LDP has proved incapable of replicating the Italian strategy. The party headquarters agreed to stand down and support Komei in SMDs, but LDP candidates have defied the party by running and winning without the nomination. Only where Komei was able to win in an SMD against both the opposition party and LDP competitors has this type of cooperation proved successful.

The LDP ran against Komei in 1996 and allied with it in 2000, just as it had run against the Socialists since 1955 but allied with them in 1994. The LDP needs Komei support to win SMDs but has trouble giving Komei anything in return. The organizational base of Komei is a controversial religious group, the Soka Gakkai (White 1970; Hrebenar 1986). Cooperation with Komei has both advantages and disadvantages for the LDP. On the one hand, the group is very well organized. It is an enthusiastic and effective campaign organization that mobilizes the votes of its own membership with speed and efficiency. On the other hand, the group is widely distrusted and disliked by nonmembers. The combination of these two factors means that Komei is very good at providing votes to allies but very bad at getting votes from those same allies (Christensen 2000, chapter 4; Kabashima and Reed 2001). When Komei campaigns for an LDP candidate, the LDP candidate gets many votes from Komei supporters. When the LDP supports a Komei candidate, however, LDP supporters are much less likely to follow their party's lead. The same asymmetry holds for candidates. A Komei candidate who is asked to stand down for the good of the party, stands down. An LDP candidate in the same situation is more likely to run as an independent than to stand down. In the 2000 election, the problem was exacerbated when the LDP used the fact that Komei was part of the New Frontier Party (NFP) as a major reason to vote against the NFP. Many LDP candidates made "The enemy is Komei" the centerpiece of their campaigns. Now they were being asked to cooperate with their enemy, and many proved unwilling to do so.

Complex negotiations took place between the LDP, Komei, and LDP candidates in districts leading up to the 2000 elections. Originally, the LDP had promised to step down and give Komei a free run in twenty-five districts (*Yomiuri Shimbun,* May 27, 2000). In the end, however, Komei ran in only eighteen SMDs, and in eleven of those districts the Komei candidate faced competition from the LDP, the so-called coalition partner. Komei won only two of these seats, while in the seven districts where it faced no such competition, it won five. Only five LDP candidates agreed to accept a PR nomination in order to allow Komei to run in the SMD, and in one case—Aichi 1st district—an LDP independent ran against both Komei and the LDP candidate who had stepped down. In 2003 and 2005 Komei continued to run in the seven districts where it had won in 2000 and in one where it had lost. It also ran in Tokyo 12th beginning in 2003, the LDP incumbent accepting a PR seat for the sake of the coalition. Komei thus ran in nine districts in both 2003 and 2005, for a total of eighteen races. Successful cooperation was the norm in these second and third experiences with coalition government, though in most of the races the Komei candidate was already the incumbent.

The LDP has expended extraordinary effort to support Komei candidates. For example, in Tokyo 12th district—the one new Komei district in 2003—the party produced a special issue of the party newspaper that featured the Komei candidate and included endorsements by the LDP candidate, the party leader, and the secretary general. It then distributed several hundred thousand copies of the paper to voters in the district (*Yomiuri Shimbun,* January 12, 2004). Such efforts have paid off. Cooperation is visible not only at the party level but also among supporters of the two coalition partners. According to exit polls, Komei supporters voted for LDP candidates in increasing numbers, rising from 61 percent in 2000 to 72 percent in 2003 and 78 percent in 2005 (*Yomiuri Shimbun,* September 12, 2005). The pattern among LDP supporters is similar but started from a lower base. Only 38 percent of LDP supporters voted for Komei candidates in 2000, but that percentage rose to 56 percent in 2003 and to 68 percent in 2005.

Komei cannot expect to get many, if any, more SMD nominations from the LDP. Instead, it has focused on getting LDP votes in the PR tier. The Komei PR vote rose steadily between 2000 and 2005, with LDP supporters providing all the new votes. Komei-LDP cooperation was put under extreme strain, however, during the 2007 House of Councillors elections, as illustrated in figure 2.1. How did the LDP direct its supporters to vote for Komei in the PR tier, and why did cooperation fail in 2007?

Figure 2.1 The Komei Vote in the PR Tier, 2000–2007

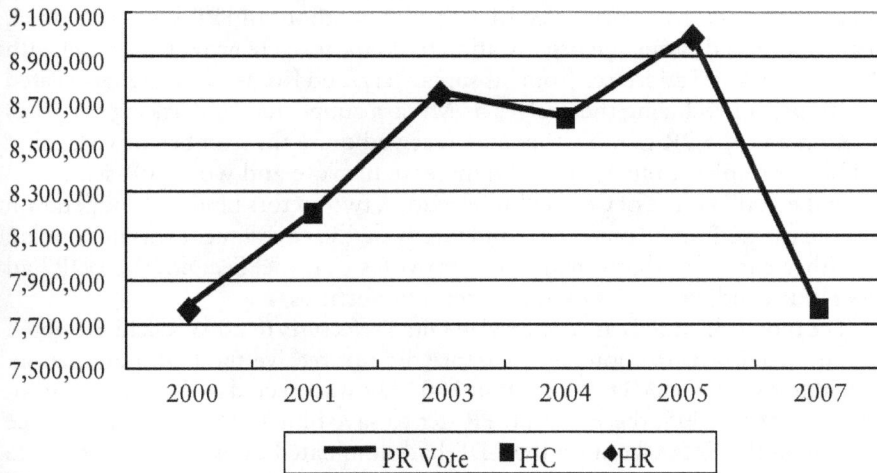

Source: Calculated by the authors from data provided by Steven R. Reed.
Note: HC = House of Councillors election; HR = House of Representatives election.

One of the best-documented examples of an LDP candidate instructing his supporters to vote for Komei in the PR tier is that of Asahiko Mihara of Fukuoka 9th district (*Yomiuri Shimbun,* January 12–15, 2003). Mihara is a second-generation politician who was first elected to the Diet in 1986 from Fukuoka 2nd district under the LDP banner. In 1993 he defected from the LDP and joined Sakigake, one of the three new parties that unseated the LDP in that election. In 1996 he was defeated in the new Fukuoka 9th district by former DSP Diet member Kenji Kitahashi, who was running for the NFP. In 2000 the same two candidates competed, but Kitahashi had joined the DPJ and Mihara had rejoined the LDP. In that election, Komei declared a free vote, endorsing neither candidate. Komei supporters could vote for either candidate, and their decision would be crucial to the outcome. This decision should have hurt Kitahashi, because as a member of the NFP in 1996, he had Komei support but had lost that support in 2000. But Mihara had the support of the anti-Komei religious groups that had been organized into the April Club, and was therefore less attractive to Komei voters. In any case, Mihara lost again and came to the conclusion that the key to getting back into the Diet was Komei support. He and his brother, a councillor in the Kitakyushu City Assembly, began a campaign to win the support of Komei.

In the 2001 House of Councillors elections, Mihara campaigned not for the LDP candidate running in the Fukuoka district, but for the Komei candidate running in the PR tier. When his own election rolled around in 2003, he regularly called for his supporters to vote for Komei in the PR tier. He calculated that

Komei support was worth roughly thirty thousand additional votes and that in a bad year for the LDP, these votes would make the difference between winning and losing. In return he promised to deliver thirty thousand PR votes to Komei, creating a special campaign organization to do the job. He provided Komei with a list of names and addresses from his supporters, and Komei campaigners visited each house, introducing themselves as Mihara supporters and asking for votes for Komei in the PR tier. Neither side received quite the number of votes that had been promised, but Mihara did increase his vote and won a PR seat.

In the 2007 House of Councillors elections, two factors hindered cooperation between the LDP and Komei. First and foremost, the government was unpopular, so neither party felt that it had any extra votes to trade. Second, the LDP had a local PR candidate of its own in several prefectures.

The most celebrated case occurred in Oita Prefecture. In 2005 Seiichi Eto voted against postal privatization and therefore did not receive the LDP nomination. He had not won his SMD (Oita 1st) in 2003 but was elected in the PR tier. As an independent in 2005, there was no PR tier to save him and he had little chance of winning the SMD, because the LDP had nominated an assassin to compete with him. He beat the assassin but not the DPJ candidate. As a result, the DPJ candidate won the SMD, the assassin was awarded a safe PR seat, and Eto was left out in the cold. Under the administration of Prime Minister Shinzo Abe, the LDP welcomed all the winning postal rebels back into the party, which resulted in an immediate drop in the cabinet's approval rating and a moratorium on allowing the remaining—that is, losing—rebels to return. The first losing rebel to be allowed to return to the party was Eto, a close friend of Abe. The LDP then nominated Eto to the PR tier in the 2007 House of Councillors elections, over Komei's objections. Komei feared that LDP supporters who were told to vote for the Komei candidate would instead vote for Eto.

To address Komei's concerns, Eto was required to first change his address to a location outside Oita Prefecture, and, second, to refrain from campaigning in Oita at all. But Komei was not yet satisfied. The party refused to recommend any LDP candidates in Kyushu. Tense negotiations resulted in a bargain in which Komei recommended LDP candidates in Kyushu electoral districts in return for benefits that were not made public. Either Komei got guarantees sufficient to maintain effective cooperation, or the differences between the two parties were papered over and cooperation was in name only. In any event, both Eto and the Komei candidate won seats, but Eto clearly drained Oita votes away from Komei.

It is possible that cooperation between Komei and the LDP may continue, but it appears to have reached its limit. Komei has votes that can be directed to LDP candidates, and those votes have made the difference for many such politicians; but once an LDP candidate captures a high percentage of those votes, she can expect no more. The LDP may well be able to direct more PR votes to Komei, but the balance of costs and benefits for the LDP appears to have reached equilibrium. Neither party can expect much more from the other. This stratagem appears to have passed the point of diminishing returns.

Strategy 3: Running as Both the Government and the Opposition

The fundamental dynamic of two-party politics is that of a government party and an opposition party taking different, if centrist, positions on the issues. Even in functioning two-party systems, party leaders sometimes run against their own party. The most notable example is Tony Blair and his New Labour campaign in Great Britain in 1997. Blair ran against the image of his own party and convinced the voters that Labour had changed. Koizumi used the same tactic in Japan, promising to "change Japan by changing the LDP." But Koizumi differed in two respects from Blair and other such leaders. First, leaders who run against their own party tend to be in opposition when they do so. Second, Koizumi managed to run against his own party twice: once as a candidate for the office of party leader and once as the sitting prime minister. We know of no other leader who has successfully run against his own party two times.

Japanese voters found Koizumi's "new LDP" as attractive as British voters found the idea of New Labour. Japanese voters wanted to kick out the old LDP, but felt that entrusting the government to the inexperienced DPJ was too risky; entrusting it to a new LDP seemed to offer the possibility of change without risk. The effect of running against the old LDP is clearly visible in figure 2.2, which plots the LDP lead over the DPJ in PR voting between 1996 and 2007. There are only two breaks in the downward trend: the 2001 House of Councillors elections and the 2005 general election. In 2001 Koizumi promised to break up the LDP if it failed to reform. In 2005 he refused to nominate the postal rebels and ran assassins against them. It is important to note that Koizumi's electoral record is two wins and two losses. When he ran against the LDP, he won overwhelming victories. When he ran as the LDP prime minister in 2003 and 2004, he lost. Clearly, then, it was not Koizumi who was popular, but the platform of running against the LDP.

In 2001, when the two mavericks Koizumi and Makiko Tanaka led the LDP in the House of Councillors elections, the excitement was palpable. Nevertheless, one often heard voters ask, "How can I vote for Koizumi without voting for the LDP?" The Koizumi cabinet, including Tanaka as the minister of foreign affairs, was greeted with a record 87 percent support according to a *Yomiuri Shimbun* poll, and that support remained high in the 70th percentile throughout the election. The LDP even found a new source of income: selling Koizumi memorabilia. Tanaka, however, turned out to be too much of a maverick. She insisted on publicizing the impressive levels of corruption in the ministry and tried to actually wrest control away from the bureaucrats. She also turned out to be less than competent in managing foreign affairs and was therefore dismissed. Cabinet support immediately fell from 77 to 53 percent, fluctuating between 40 and 50 percent until the 2005 election. During this time the LDP lost two elections: the 2003 general election and the 2004 House of Councillors elections. The Koizumi magic appeared to have been exhausted.

Figure 2.2 The LDP Lead Over the DPJ in PR, 1996–2007

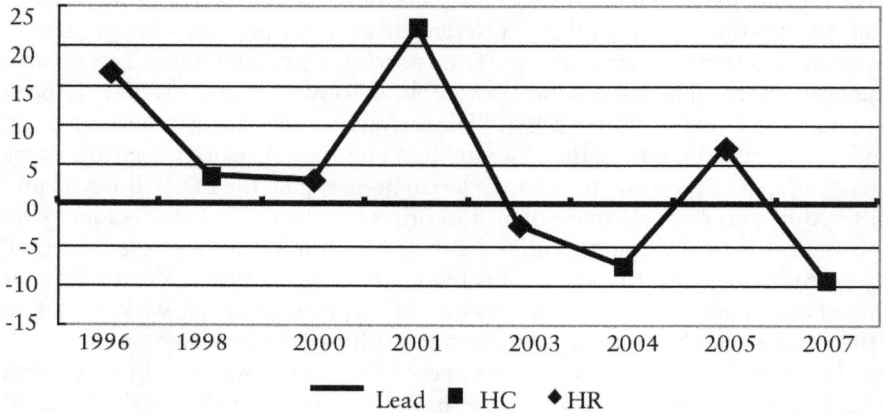

Source: Calculated by the authors from data provided by Steven R. Reed.
Note: HC = House of Councillors election; HR = House of Representatives election.

Koizumi's 2005 election campaign was a media masterpiece. Koizumi had finally pushed his postal-reform bill through the Lower House but watched his own party vote it down in the Upper House (Machachlan, chapter 8, this volume). The LDP had split yet again and seemed headed for certain defeat. Koizumi then proceeded to dissolve the Diet and give what may well be the best speech in Japanese political history. First, he stated the obvious: he had promised to dissolve the Diet if postal reform was not passed. He was merely keeping that promise: "They [the LDP] should have known this was going to happen when they elected me leader." Second, he admitted that the public had little interest in postal reform, but pleaded, "If we cannot pass postal reform, what reform can we pass?" Koizumi understood that while voters cared little about postal reform per se, they did care greatly about reform in general. Third, he said the LDP would not only refuse a nomination to anyone who had voted against postal reform, but would also nominate someone, a so-called assassin, who favored postal reform in each and every district. This was to be an issue election. Voters would be offered a clear choice: do you favor reform or not? Finally, he said, he was disappointed that the DPJ had voted against postal reform, failing even to present an alternative bill. The Democrats, he said, were just like the rebels.

The mass media presented the election as a choice between Koizumi and the rebels. The DPJ was largely ignored. Koizumi made sure that this frame persisted by nominating attractive young assassins to run against the rebels, and by pacing the announcements to maximize press coverage. For a week or so the whole election appeared to be taking place in Hiroshima 6th district between Shizuka Kamei, a rebel leader, and Takefumi Horie, an information technology millionaire who, at the time, personified a young maverick willing to defy the establishment (though he was later arrested on charges of insider trading). The DPJ could not get any coverage until the campaign period had officially begun—that is, after all the regulations on media coverage had come into effect. It was forced to present its case in standard election formats, sitting next to the Communists and flanked by a row of opposition parties, including two new parties formed by the rebels.

Koizumi won another overwhelming victory. In so doing, he had changed the LDP and seemed prepared to change Japan. The *Asahi Shimbun* asked voters if they believed that the LDP had really changed. For most of Koizumi's administration, the percentage agreeing that the LDP had changed was somewhat lower than those of voters who disagreed, dropping to 31 percent after the Tanaka firing; but, as the 2005 election approached, 70 percent agreed and only 22 percent disagreed (Yoshida 2006:185). Yet Koizumi's handpicked successor, Shinzo Abe, decided, with Koizumi's blessing, to abandon every one of the secrets of Koizumi's success.

Abe's cabinet may not have maintained the traditional factional balancing act, but it was filled with traditional LDP faces. More important, Abe squandered most of the Koizumi legacy by allowing the postal rebels back into the party. The result was a disastrous defeat in the 2007 House of Councillors elections. The LDP was "back to normal," meaning that it was again losing elections. But the 2007 loss crossed several new thresholds. Most notably, it was the first time in LDP history that the party was not the largest in the Upper House. Equally important was that the DPJ won in rural areas, which Koizumi had abandoned in the 2005 election in order to win back the urban areas; the LDP lost the rural areas in 2007 in part because of this fact. The LDP could no longer win by being all things to all people. SMDs and the implications of Duverger's Law were forcing them to choose.

If a stratagem works twice, why not use it again? The choice of Taro Aso to succeed Abe and Yasuo Fukuda does not represent an attempt to follow a Koizumi strategy. The problem is credibility. If, for example, the party had chosen a young rebel who had promised to "change Japan by changing the LDP," would voters buy it for a third time? In fact, such a campaign would appear to be tailor-made for Ichiro Ozawa, the leader of the DPJ, to dissect. Ozawa has been saying the same thing since he left the LDP in 1993: "You cannot expect real reform from the LDP. The only way to get reform is through an alternation in power." He could now add, "You believed in Koizumi. How did that work out?" It is very impressive that Koizumi was able to use this strategy twice, but it is very hard to imagine a third attempt succeeding. Although the LDP under Koizumi was on the verge of reinventing itself as a party that could win elections based on policy and leadership instead of clientelism and pork-barrel politics, it did not actually do so, making it harder for subsequent LDP candidates to win by using such promises.

Betting on Duverger's Law

The LDP has been extremely creative and successful in finding ways around Duverger's Law. But the three main stratagems it has used to avoid an alternation in power have reached their limit. Based on figure 2.2, it appears that the LDP will lose the next election unless it comes up with a new stratagem. The figure shows the LDP PR vote minus the DPJ PR vote, so anything above zero indicates an LDP lead and anything below indicates a DPJ lead. The LDP thus lost its lead in 2003 and regained it, though only temporarily, in 2005. The party cannot rely on the same old stratagems to produce another reversal of the trend as it did in 2001 and 2005. Although we can be certain that the party will be as creative as it has been in the past in searching for ways to win, there is no guarantee that another stratagem exists, or, if it does, that the party will find it. Another possibility for avoiding alternation in power exists: the DPJ could somehow make a catastrophic mistake. Now that the DPJ-led opposition has a majority in the House of Councillors, the DPJ's ability to govern will be on public display. If the DPJ fails in its responsibilities, the LDP might win the next election by default. In any case, the forces driving Duverger's Law will continue to function and the options for avoiding an alternation in power will continue to diminish.

Finally, we should discuss the possibility that the PR tier in Japan's MMD system weakens the functioning of Duverger's Law. Each of the LDP's stratagems for avoiding a two-party system has utilized the PR tier, lending credence to this thesis. The PR tier has, in fact, kept the communists and socialists in the Diet, but any party depending solely upon PR seats will have trouble getting more than five or six seats. Thus, the PR tier may weaken the effects of Duverger's Law somewhat, but not by much.

In one respect, the PR tier actually enhances the functioning of Duverger's Law; pure SMD systems tend to produce many safe seats for one party or the other. If one party has many more safe seats than the other, it may prevent an alternation in power. The "solid South" produced Democratic control of the U.S. Congress from 1954 through 1994, two years longer than the LDP dominated the Japanese House of Representatives. Dominance in Quebec also gave the Canadian Liberals an edge over their rivals for many years. In Japan, however, the PR tier gives a party the ability to run good candidates even where it is weak; the party simply promises the candidate either a chance or a guarantee of winning a PR seat. As Robert J. Weiner points out in chapter 5 of this book, we should not expect each and every district to be tightly competitive in Japan, any more than we do in Great Britain. We should, moreover, expect fewer safe seats under Japan's MMD system than under a pure SMD system like Great Britain's.

Given the LDP's past performance, we cannot rule out the possibility that it will reinvent itself yet again and find new stratagems that we have yet to imagine. Nothing in politics is certain. That said, we place our bets on Duverger's Law.

References

Cain, Bruce, John Ferejohn, and Morris Fiorina. 1987. *The personal vote.* Cambridge, MA: Harvard Univ. Press.

Carey, John M., and Matthew Soberg Shugart. 1995. Incentives to cultivate a personal vote. *Electoral Studies* 14:417–40.

Christensen, Raymond V. 2000. *Ending the LDP hegemony.* Honolulu: Univ. of Hawaii Press.

Cox, Gary W. 1997. Making votes count. New York: Cambridge Univ. Press.

Cox, Gary W., and Emerson Niou. 1994. Seat bonuses under the single nontransferable vote system: Evidence from Japan and Taiwan. *Comparative Politics* 26:221–36.

Cox, Gary W., and Michael Thies. 2000. How much does money matter? Buying votes in Japan, 1967–1990. *Comparative Political Studies* 33 (1): 37–57.

Curtis, Gerald. 1988. *The Japanese way of politics.* New York: Columbia Univ. Press.

Duverger, Maurice. 1964. *Political parties, their organization and activity in the modern state.* 2nd ed. London: Routledge & Kegan Paul.

Hrebenar, Ronald J. 1986. The Komeito: Party of Buddhist democracy. In *The Japanese party system,* ed. Ronald J. Hrebenar. London: Westview Press.

Kabashima, Ikuo, and Steven R. Reed. 2001. Voter reactions to strange bedfellows: The Japanese voter faces a kaleidoscope of changing coalitions. *Japanese Journal of Political Science* 1:229–48.

McKean, Margaret. 1981. *Environmental protest and citizen politics in Japan.* Berkeley: Univ. of California Press.

McKean, Margaret, and Ethan Scheiner. 2000. Japan's new electoral system: *La plus ça change . . . Electoral Studies* 19:447–77.

Pempel, T. J. 1975. The dilemma of parliamentary opposition in Japan. *Polity* (Fall): 63–79.

Reed, Steven R. 1994. The incumbency advantage in Japan. In *The victorious incumbent—A threat to democracy?* ed. Albert Somit, Bernhard Boll, and Rudolf Wildenmann, 278–303. Aldershot, England: Dartmouth Publishing.

———. 2001. Duverger's Law is working in Italy. *Comparative Political Studies* 34:312–27.

———. 2007. Duverger's Law is working in Japan. *Senkyo kenkyuu* [Electoral studies] 22:96–106 [in English].

———. Forthcoming. Party strategy or candidate strategy: How does the LDP run the right number of candidates in Japan's multi-member districts? *Party Politics.*

Riker, W. H. 1986. Duverger's Law revisited. In *Electoral systems and their political consequences,* ed. B. Grofman and A. Lijphart. New York: Agathon Press.

White, James W. 1970. *The Sokagakkai and mass society*. Stanford, CA: Stanford Univ. Press.

Yoshida, Takafumi. 2006. *Koizumi naikaku 5-nen 5-kagetsu, seisaku yori kosei de miseta 'gekijou seiji'* [The five years and five months of the Koizumi cabinet: More theater than policy]. Tokyo: *Asahi Shimbun*. (This and other newspaper articles cited in this chapter are available upon request from the authors.)

HAS THE ELECTORAL-SYSTEM REFORM MADE JAPANESE ELECTIONS PARTY-CENTERED?

Ko Maeda

Politics in post–World War II Japan has been characterized by one-party dominance. Except for a short period, 1993–1994, the Liberal Democratic Party (LDP) has governed the country continuously since the party's foundation in 1955. In other words, Japanese politics of the last half-century is largely defined by the LDP and its candidate-centered electoral campaigns (see, for example, Ramseyer and Rosenbluth 1993). LDP candidates focus more on advertising their personal beliefs and achievements than on promoting the party's policies. Once elected, they work hard to bring pork-barrel projects and other benefits to their home districts so that they can claim credit in reelection bids.

The country's 1994 electoral law reform, to be elaborated in the next section, was intended to change such practices. It was argued that Japan's electoral system was creating incentives for legislators to specialize in localized behavior, leading to political corruption and inefficient public spending. The electoral system reform was enacted by the legislature while the LDP was temporarily out of power, and many people hoped that it would transform a one-party-dominated system with candidate-centered elections into a competitive, two-party system with party-centered elections.

Fifteen years have passed since the reform, and four general elections (1996, 2000, 2003, and 2005) have been conducted under the new system. Both scholars and the mass media have been scrutinizing the consequences of the reform, particularly its impact on the number of parties (see, for example, Nishikawa and Herron 2004; Reed 2007). Yet there have been no systematic analyses of whether—and the extent to which—the new system has changed the focus of electoral competition from candidates to parties.

This chapter seeks to empirically assess the impact of the electoral reform on the nature of electoral competition in Japan. This analysis is important not only because it evaluates whether the reform has brought about its intended consequences, but also because the nature of electoral competition will have important implications for the future of Japan's party politics. Some scholars assert that the personal support bases of many LDP politicians are so strong that national electoral issues—such as the prime minister's popularity or the policy platforms of major parties—are not integral to their electoral success. If this is the case, Japanese politics may return to one-party dominance. Yet if

Japanese elections are indeed becoming more and more party-centered, the seats of strong LDP incumbents may not be as secure as they appear to be, and the main opposition—the Democratic Party of Japan (DPJ)—may have a chance to defeat the LDP and win power.

The next section provides details of the electoral-system reform in Japan and its expected implications. With reference to scholarship on the subject, I then discuss how the reform may influence the nature of electoral competition; this is followed by empirical analyses with data from the postreform elections in Japan. I conclude this chapter with some discussion of the future of Japanese party politics.

The 1994 Electoral-Law Reform and Its Intended Consequences

In January 1994, while a non-LDP coalition cabinet was in power, the Diet passed an electoral-reform bill abolishing the single nontransferable vote (SNTV) system and introducing the parallel plurality and proportional representation (PR) system. The SNTV system was used to elect the members of the House of Representatives from 1947 to 1993. Under the SNTV, district magnitude varied depending upon district population but was typically between three and five. Each voter cast one ballot for an individual candidate, and the top n candidates in an n-member district were elected.

Under the new electoral system, the seats of the House of Representatives are divided into 2 groups: 300 members are elected from the same number of single-member districts (SMDs), and 200 (reduced to 180 beginning with the 2000 general election) are from 11 regional PR blocs. Each voter casts one ballot for an individual candidate running in the SMD and one ballot for a political party that registers a list of candidates in the region. Candidates can run in both the SMD and PR tiers (*chofuku rikkoho*); those who secure seats in SMDs are automatically removed from the party lists for the PR seats. Candidates who are defeated in SMD races but win seats in PR are often called "zombie legislators."

The PR tier is operated as a basically closed-list system in which the rank of candidates in party lists is predetermined by parties before the election. But parties can list multiple candidates with the same rank if the candidates are also nominated in the SMD tier. Once the voting is complete, those who are elected in SMDs are removed from the list, and the remaining equal-rank candidates are ordered according to how close their vote shares are to the winners of their respective SMDs (the closeness is measured by *sekihairitsu*, or the percentage of vote share compared with that of the winner).

Most observers maintain that Japan's candidate-centered politics stemmed from the old SNTV electoral system. Since multiple candidates from the LDP competed in each district, the LDP candidates could not simply rely on the party's name for electoral victory but instead needed to differentiate themselves and amass personal supporters. Hence, candidates devoted much money and energy to activities that would enhance their name recognition and reputation in their home districts. Pork-barrel politics and corruption were natural consequences of this incentive structure.

There were attempts to change the electoral system from the SNTV to something else in the 1950s and 1970s, but there was not enough momentum. This changed in the late 1980s, when a major political corruption case and other issues shook the entire political system (Reed and Thies 2001). *Seiji kaikaku* ("political reform") became a key phrase on the political scene, and abolishing the SNTV system was considered an integral component of the reform.

In a parliamentary policy speech given on February 10, 1989, Prime Minister Noboru Takeshita declared that political reform was the "most important agenda" of his cabinet, adding that his cabinet would examine "the way elections ought to be" and carry out drastic reforms.[1]

On April 27, 1989, an advisory committee to the prime minister (Seiji Kaikaku ni Kansuru Yushikisha Kaigi) submitted a report on political reform that listed the realization of "less costly, policy-centered elections" on its agenda, although it did not explicitly argue that the SNTV had to be abolished.[2]

On May 23, 1989, the LDP released a document titled "Seiji kaikaku taiko" (Fundamental principles of political reforms), in which the party announced that it would "seek a transition to a new electoral system," arguing that "many of the principal tasks that are the core of the political reform are in an inseparable relationship with the revision of the SNTV system."[3] The document also contended that "under the SNTV system, elections tend to be personal-based rather than party-based. As long as a party seeks to be a majority party, infighting within the party is inevitable. This facilitates the tendency that the politicians place the emphasis of daily activities and electoral campaigns on non-policy-related things, causing pork-barrel politics and costly elections."

On April 26, 1990, an advisory council to the prime minister on the electoral system (Senkyo Seido Shingikai) submitted a report to Prime Minister Toshiki Kaifu. The proposed electoral system combined the SMD plurality tier and the PR tier, and is quite similar to the new system, which was later enacted into law in 1994. The report contended:

> Elections to the House of Representatives should be contested as competition of policies of political parties that seek to obtain power and implement policies. However, under the current electoral system ... elections inevitably become contests among personal candidates rather than contests among parties and policies. ... These problems that are taking place under the SNTV system can no longer be solved by applications of the current rules, and the current electoral system has to be fundamentally reformed in order to materialize policy-centered and party-centered elections.[4]

To achieve those goals, the report recommended the parallel plurality-PR system, arguing that the plurality portion of the system allows the voters' choice of ruling party to be clearly expressed, while the PR portion of the system allows minor parties to obtain parliamentary seats.[5] It is interesting that the council appears to have believed—perhaps somewhat naively—that by combining two components, the country could enjoy the best of both.

Clearly, the realization of party-centered elections was a key concern of those involved in the reform process. Under the old SNTV system, LDP candidates' electoral campaigns focused on personal appeal and achievements such as pork-barrel projects and casework to win votes. The introduction of the new system was expected to transform the whole electoral structure and create a policy-oriented political competition in which candidates advertise the policies of their parties to the voters, who then vote based on those policies.

The landslide victory of the LDP in the 2005 general election, in which many LDP candidates with very few or no local ties or name recognition were elected, appears to be an example of a party-centered election in which the high popularity of the prime minister overrode local contexts and candidate characteristics. Yet, without a systematic analysis, we do not know whether the drastic national swing for the LDP in 2005 was an idiosyncratic phenomenon or a natural consequence of the electoral system reform. In the next section, I will theoretically consider what can be expected under Japan's new electoral system.

Theoretical Considerations

Political scientists have extensively studied the impact of electoral systems on party politics, both theoretically and empirically (see, as examples, Duverger 1954; Rae 1971; Taagepera and Shugart 1989; Lijphart 1994). There are fewer studies on the impact that electoral systems may have on whether the resulting elections are party- or candidate-centered (for example, Carey and Shugart 1995; Grofman 2005). The fact that Japan's new electoral system is a combination of two separate tiers complicates the issue; we must consider the impact of each and also how the two interact.

In considering the relationship between the two tiers, the fact that Japan's is a parallel system—as opposed to the mixed-member proportional (MMP) system—is crucially important. Under the MMP system used in Germany and New Zealand, the parties' vote shares in the PR tier determine the final allocation of seats, whereas in the parallel system, the results of the two tiers are simply added together to produce the final result. Hence, in the MMP system, the main battlefield of electoral competition is the PR portion, and the races for the SMDs are of secondary concern. Under the parallel system, however, winning an SMD will directly increase the party's total number of seats by one; hence, the relative importance of the SMD portion is higher in the parallel system than in the MMP system (McKean and Scheiner 2000). Further, two characteristics of Japan's system make the SMD races far more important than the PR contests. First, the number of seats allocated to the SMD portion (300) is much larger than the number for PR (180). Second, because of the dual-candidacy rule, the PR seats are often viewed as consolation prizes for SMD losers. In 2005, 117 of the 180 seats (65 percent) allocated to the PR tier were taken by candidates who were defeated in their respective SMDs. It is of course more prestigious for politicians to win an SMD seat than to lose in an SMD race and secure a seat in the PR portion. All these factors make the SMD portion the main component of electoral competition under Japan's mixed system.

What, then, is the impact of SMDs on whether the elections are candidate- or party-centered? Although there has been much research on how the SMD system influences the number of parties, we know much less about its impact on the level of personalization in elections. Also, it appears that there is a wide variation among countries that use the SMD system: the United Kingdom and the United States both use the same SMD plurality system, yet it is well accepted that parties' and party leaders' popularity largely determine the SMD races in the United Kingdom, while individual candidates' qualities are significant in U.S. congressional elections (see, for example, Gaines 1998).

In their widely cited article on the ranking of electoral systems in terms of politicians' incentives to garner personal votes, Carey and Shugart (1995) classify the U.S. and U.K. systems in separate groups. Since primary elections are used in the United States to determine who will receive the party's endorsement, the party leaders do not control candidate nominations in the U.S. system. But in other SMD systems—such as those of Britain and Canada—party leaders have stronger control over who will run under the party's label. The authors argue that the British SMD system is like a closed-list PR election with only one seat available in each district. Since the nomination is determined by the party leader and the candidates' electoral fortunes are dependent on the party's popularity, individual candidates have little incentive to cultivate personal votes. In short, the SMD system does not have a uniform impact, but whether the elections become party- or candidate-centered depends on other factors—in particular, candidate-nomination rules.

The LDP's candidate-nomination rules in SMDs are different from those of both the U.S. and U.K. systems. On the one hand, primary elections have been extremely rare, and even when they have been held, the party's local branches have typically played an active role in screening candidates. Hence, the LDP's practice is quite different from those of the major U.S. parties. On the other hand, the party leadership's power is not as strong as in Westminster parliamentary democracies, because the incumbent LDP legislators basically obtain the party's endorsements automatically. The LDP's candidate-nomination rules thus cannot be easily classified into either category, and the LDP's candidate-selection practices may have a unique impact on the nature of electoral competition.

Since LDP incumbents almost automatically win endorsements in the same districts for the next election, those who keep winning in elections will maintain strongholds in their local districts. In addition, veteran legislators whose careers started during the old SNTV era would have already developed their local support organizations when the new electoral system was introduced. Having stable supporters, they may become self-reliant in their reelection bids, with no need for the party's popularity or resources to stay in office. Since those candidates can be relatively independent from the party leadership, the party may find it difficult to be internally united and to present coherent programs to the public.

This tendency would be particularly strong in rural areas that have been receiving benefits from traditional LDP policies, such as protectionist measures for farmers and small-business owners and massive spending on public-works projects in less populated areas. LDP supporters in those areas have been the beneficiaries of such practices, and they would most likely want to the LDP and its politicians to continue along the same vein. LDP incumbents in those areas would therefore not have felt an imminent need to change their campaign practices when the electoral system changed. The mobility of people in rural areas is low, and LDP politicians have stable support bases. For those candidates, advertising the party's programs instead of their personal achievements would be an unnecessary gamble. Having stable supporters who want LDP politicians to continue working hard to bring pork back to the district, they may simply try to keep winning elections in the traditional way. Hence, party-centered elections may not be observed in rural areas—or at least less so than in urban districts.

At the same time, we should not ignore the recent movement toward party-based elections in Japan. The DPJ released its first manifesto before the 2003 election, arguing that a manifesto is different from traditional electoral promises or slogans in that it is a coherent plan of policies promised by a party—not by an individual candidate—and that voters should choose a ruling party in a general election by comparing manifestos. Since then, it has become common for major parties to publish a manifesto before elections.

Also, the number of parties has been decreasing throughout the postreform era, and the DPJ has arguably established its status as the only alternative to the LDP. The number of SMD candidates from the DPJ has been steadily increasing, reaching 289 in 2005 (96 percent of all SMDs), and the DPJ has been the only opposition party with 10 or more Lower House seats since the 2003 election. Today, the country's political system is—according to a variety of indicators—virtually a two-party system (Reed 2007). It is fundamentally different from what it was like when the LDP was founded in 1955, when the opposition camp was highly fragmented and no opposition party even nominated enough candidates to overtake the LDP. Now it seems the stage is set for party-centered elections and a two-party system.

The next section empirically assesses the extent to which elections in Japan have become party-centered. If the preceding discussion is correct, we should observe party-centered electoral changes more in urban areas and in recent elections.

Empirical Investigation

The analysis in this section consists of two steps. I first provide evidence that the vote share in the PR portion reflects the party's popularity reasonably well. Then, using the PR vote share as a proxy of the party's popularity, I examine the extent to which the SMD vote results of LDP candidates are determined by the party's popularity.[6]

Figure 3.1 plots the LDP's vote share in the PR tier (panel A) and in the SMD tier (panel B) in the four postreform elections against the proportion of the population living in densely inhabited districts (DIDs), as defined by the government's statistics bureau.[7] This is a widely used measure of the level of urbanization, which has been known to be a strong predictor of the LDP's strength. It is clear from the figure that the LDP obtained higher shares of votes in rural areas than in urban areas, although this urban-rural gap is not visible at all in 2005. Table 3.1 shows the winning rate of LDP candidates in SMDs, classified by the DID levels. The LDP's dominance in rural areas, except in the 2005 election, is apparent from the table.

Table 3.1 The Winning Rate of LDP Candidates in SMDs, Classified by DID Level, 1996–2005

DID	1996	2000	2003	2005	Total	Number of districts in 2005	Examples
0.0–0.25	87.8	82.7	85.4	67.4	80.1	43	Iwate 4th (Ichiro Ozawa's district)
0.25–0.50	67.1	80.3	79.7	80.3	76.6	72	Fukushima 1st and Tottori 1st
0.50–0.75	58.6	62.5	63.8	67.7	63.3	62	Tochigi 1st and Kagawa 1st
0.75–1.0	38.2	43.7	37.6	79.8	53.7	123	All districts in Tokyo, Kanagawa, and Osaka

Source: See endnotes 6 and 7.

Comparing the PR and SMD votes in figure 3.1 clearly reveals that the SMD votes are much more varied than the PR votes. This difference may stem from the fact that SMD votes are affected by local contexts, such as the reputation of the incumbent, how many candidates competed, and whether the major parties nominated candidates. PR votes, on the other hand, more directly reflect the voters' evaluation of political parties.[8]

Figure 3.1 The LDP's Vote Share and DID Levels, 1996–2005

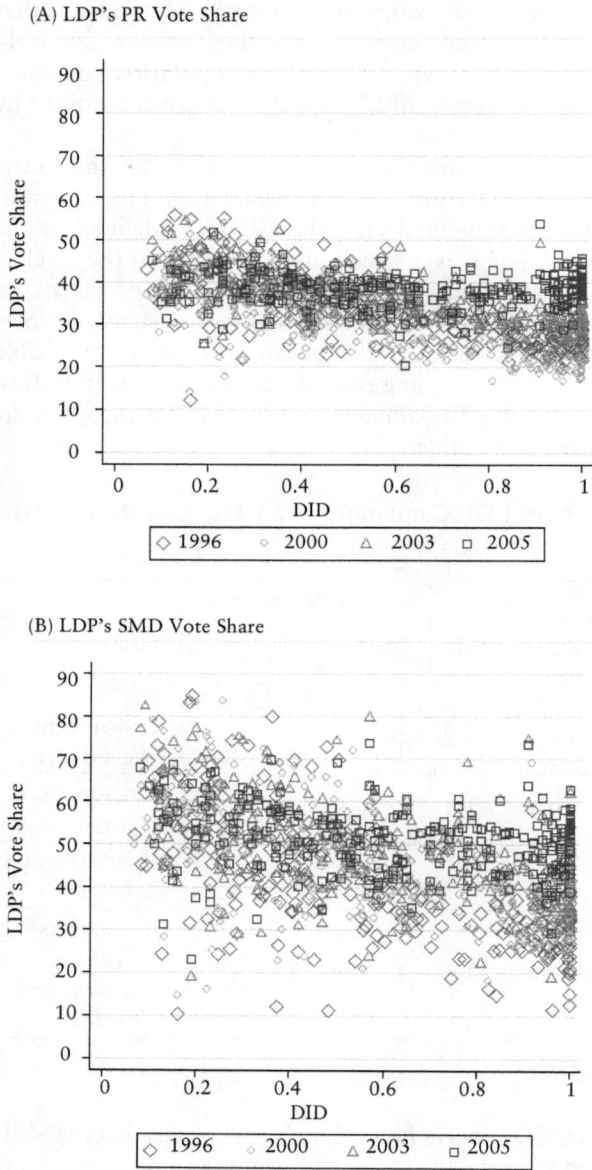

(A) LDP's PR Vote Share

(B) LDP's SMD Vote Share

Source: See endnotes 6 and 7.

This contrast between PR votes and SMD votes is also clear from the pattern of vote changes. The change in LDP vote share from the previous election has a wider variation across districts in the SMD portion (standard deviation: 10.2) than in the PR portion (standard deviation: 6.2). Also, in the 2000 election, in which the unpopular prime minister Yoshiro Mori entered the election with a remarkably low 18.2 percent approval rating (Naikaku Sori Daijin Kanbo 2001), the LDP's average PR vote share indeed declined by 4.3 points; yet the average SMD vote share went up by 4.3 points. Again, it appears that the PR votes reflect an evaluation of the party and/or the government, while the SMD votes are influenced by other factors as well. In the following discussion, I use the change in the PR votes as a proxy of the change in the LDP's (and the government's) popularity.

The differences between the PR and SMD tiers already suggest that Japan's postreform elections are not entirely party-centered. If voters are casting ballots solely based on their evaluation of the political parties and their programs, there should be no difference between the two tiers of the electoral system. Yet no one predicted that Japan's candidate-centered elections would instantly change to purely party-centered elections when the new system was introduced. A more interesting and practical question is when and where people base their votes on parties and national issues rather than on candidates and local contexts.

Figure 3.2 shows the changing patterns of votes for the LDP in the SMD and PR tiers. The 1996 election is not included because it was the first election under the new system (and thus has no previous, similar election to be compared with). The x-axis is the vote swing in PR from the previous election, and the y-axis is the swing in SMDs. Circles that are on the 45-degree line are districts where the LDP gained (or lost) the same amount in SMDs and PR, suggesting a party-centered election. But circles that are far from the 45-degree line are districts where the swings in SMDs and PR were different. In this analysis, only the districts where the LDP nominated the same candidate in the previous and current elections are shown.[9]

The three graphs in figure 3.2 indicate a changing pattern of linkage between the two tiers of the electoral system. In panel A (the 2000 election), almost all the districts are located to the left of the y-axis, indicating a strong tide against the LDP in the PR portion, perhaps largely due to the low popularity of Prime Minister Mori. In terms of the SMD vote swing, however, a large majority of LDP candidates increased their vote share. The linkage between PR and SMDs was weak; the party's (and party leader's) low popularity was directly reflected in the PR vote swing but not in the SMD vote swing.

In 2003, two years after Koizumi became the prime minister, the LDP fared much better than in 2000. In most districts, the LDP increased the PR vote share, as shown by the fact that most of the circles in panel B are located to the right of the y-axis. The SMD swing is still varied, but compared with those in panel A, the circles are now located relatively close to the 45-degree line. This contrast shows an increased likelihood that the fates of LDP candidates in SMDs are influenced by the party's popularity.

Figure 3.2 The LDP's Vote Change in the SMD and PR Tiers

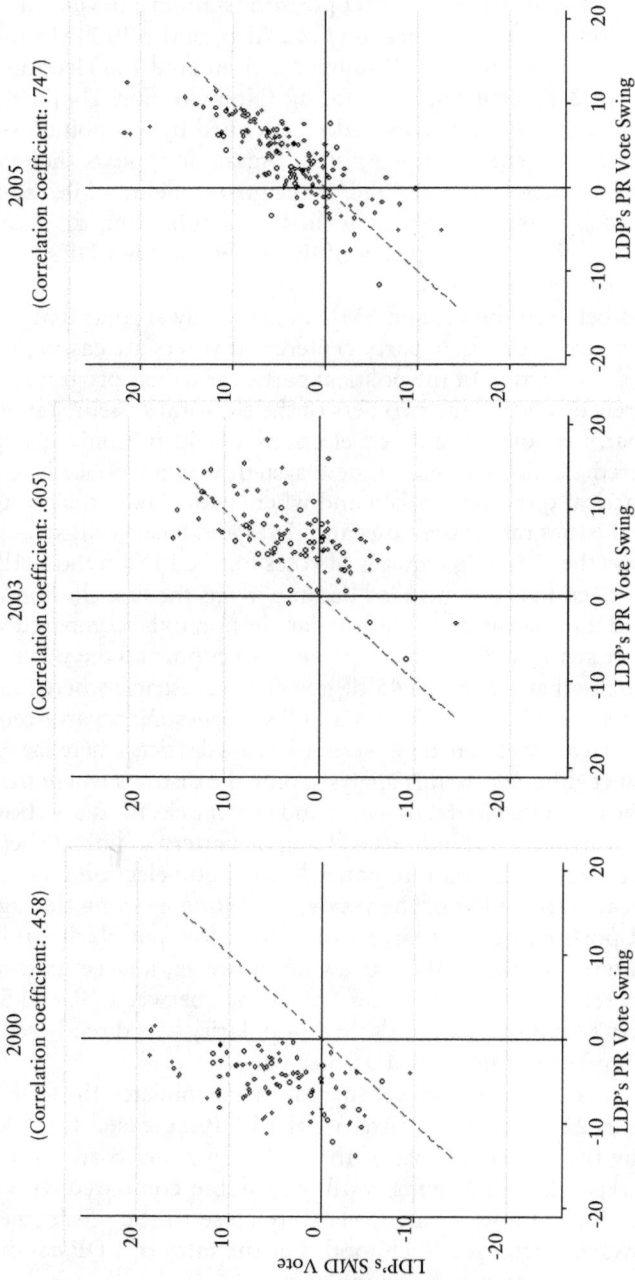

2000
(Correlation coefficient: .458)

2003
(Correlation coefficient: .605)

2005
(Correlation coefficient: .747)

LDP's SMD Vote

LDP's PR Vote Swing

Source: See endnote 6.

Panel C covers the 2005 election, in which Koizumi led the LDP to a historic victory. It is immediately clear that the linkage between PR and SMD is now even stronger: more and more districts are clustered around the 45-degree line, and a large majority had positive swings. Koizumi's high popularity apparently produced increased vote shares in both the SMD and PR tiers.

The trend of a strengthening PR-SMD linkage can also be confirmed by a measure of linear relationship between the two dimensions. The correlation coefficient increased from .458 in 2000 to .605 in 2003 and, finally, to .747 in 2005. These graphs and numbers suggest that the postreform elections in Japan are becoming increasingly party-centered; but perhaps it would be prudent to wait and observe another election before making a definitive conclusion, since the 2005 election was unique in many ways.

We now move on to the next question: in what kind of district is the party's popularity (represented by the PR swing) strongly related to the SMD swing, and in what kind of district is it not? In many districts, especially in 2000 and 2003, the SMD swing and the PR swing seem independent of each another, suggesting the strong impact of local factors. In other districts, the two swings are moving together, implying a party-centered election. What creates this difference? In the previous section, I argued that the urban-rural gap has a strong influence: party-centered elections may be observed in urban districts, while traditional LDP politics still prevails in rural areas. The following regression analysis tests this hypothesis.

Table 3.2 shows the results of regression analyses of the LDP candidates' SMD vote swings in postreform elections. The leftmost column is for the pooled sample, and the rest is for the analyses of individual elections. Since I expect that the PR vote swing and the level of urbanization have interactive effects on the dependent variable, a multiplicative interaction term (PR swing times DID) is included in the model. The inclusion of this term allows the coefficient and the significance of the PR swing to vary depending on the level of the DID variable. If my hypothesis is supported, we will find that the PR swing has a positive and significant impact on the dependent variable in urban areas but not in rural areas.

A number of control variables are included in the model. The SMD vote share in the previous election is a variable that represents the base from which the swing takes place. Where the LDP obtained a large vote share in the previous election, it has a large base of votes to lose. As expected, this variable has a significant and negative impact in all four models. The incumbency status variable takes the value of 1 if the candidate was victorious in the SMDs in the previous election. Those who secured a seat in the PR portion are not considered incumbents here. Yet, since the candidates who are in a "Costa Rica" agreement, may have an advantage, I have included a dummy variable for such candidates (for more on Costa Rica agreements, see Reed and Shimizu, chapter, this volume).

Table 3.2 Dependent Variable: Vote Swing in SMDs from the Previous Election

	All	2000	2003	2005
PR swing	0.362*	-0.027	0.227	0.351
	(0.170)	(0.501)	(0.428)	(0.193)
DID	-1.459	1.571	-5.692	1.237
	(1.267)	(5.190)	(4.245)	(1.606)
PR swing × DID	0.404*	0.881	0.541	0.359
	(0.172)	(0.718)	(0.501)	(0.257)
Previous SMD vote share	-0.247**	-0.191*	-0.240**	-0.358**
	(0.038)	(0.083)	(0.075)	(0.045)
Incumbent	2.203**	3.039*	0.771	3.068**
	(0.631)	(1.446)	(1.256)	(0.758)
"Costa Rica"	2.760**	3.975	1.683	2.419*
	(0.990)	(3.105)	(1.448)	(1.045)
New candidate	-1.342	1.225	-2.071	-2.832**
	(0.730)	(1.849)	(1.381)	(0.764)
Number of candidates	-1.825**	-2.158**	-1.821**	-1.431**
	(0.297)	(0.558)	(0.446)	(0.404)
Multiple conservatives	-3.386**	-1.687	-5.069**	-4.656**
	(0.793)	(1.041)	(1.903)	(1.145)
Komeito support	1.921**	3.166**	0.823	0.854
	(0.480)	(0.961)	(0.814)	(0.578)
By-election	-4.625**	-8.492*	-4.433**	-1.963
	(1.663)	(3.951)	(1.154)	(1.413)
2003 dummy	-8.655**			
	(1.113)			
2005 dummy	-3.111**			
	(0.898)			
Intercept	15.504**	9.634	10.755	15.948**
	(2.157)	(5.487)	(5.738)	(2.220)
n	547	159	170	218
R-squared	0.53	0.34	.055	0.76
Standard error of regression (SER)	4.91	6.03	5.23	3.17

Note: Robust standard errors appear in parentheses.
* Significant at 5 percent.
** Significant at 1 percent.

The new-candidate variable is a dummy variable that takes the value of 1 if the candidate did not run in the previous general election in the same district. New candidates may obtain fewer votes than continuing candidates because of low name recognition.[10] The change in the number of relevant (competitive) candidates in the district is also included in the model. The greater the number of candidates running, the fewer the votes an LDP candidate can expect. Independent candidates or candidates from "other" parties who obtained less than 3 percent of the votes are considered noncompetitive and thus are not counted.

The multiple-conservatives variable is included to control for the impact of the situation in which a candidate with significant ties to the LDP competes against an LDP candidate (*hoshu bunretsu*). This variable measures the change from the previous election, and takes the value of 1 if there was no such candidate in the previous election but there is one in the current election. On the other hand, if such a candidate ran in the previous election but not in the current election, this variable takes the value of –1. If neither or both the previous and current elections have had such a candidate, this variable then takes a 0.

Since the 2000 election, many LDP candidates have received support from the party's coalition partner, New Komeito, in their electoral campaigns, and they should expect higher vote shares.[11] I have included a variable for New Komeito support; like the multiple-conservatives variable, it measures the change and takes the values of 1, 0, or –1. Whether there was a by-election in the SMD since the previous general election or not is also included in the model. Finally, for the pooled sample only, the dummy variables of 2003 and 2005 are specified in the model.

Districts considered anomalous were taken out of the sample. These included districts where either the LDP or the largest opposition party did not nominate a candidate in the current or previous election, where there was a "postal rebel" (a former LDP legislator expelled from the party by Koizumi after opposing the postal-privatization bill in 2005), and where the district boundaries were changed to a non-negligible degree during the 2002 redistricting.[12]

Since an interaction term between the PR swing and DID is included, the impact of the PR swing on the dependent variable must be interpreted with varying levels of DID. For example, the coefficients of the PR swing and PR swing times DID are .362 and .404, respectively, in the pooled model. In that case, the slope coefficient of the PR swing is

$$.362 + .404 \times DID$$

Since high values of DID indicate urban areas (the maximum value is 1), this result shows that the impact of the PR swing on the SMD swing is larger in urban districts than in rural districts. The significance of the slope coefficient of the PR swing also varies with DID, and the standard error of the PR swing's coefficient in the pooled model is calculated in the following way:

$$.029 + (.030 \times DID^2) + (2 \times -.027 \times DID)$$

where .029 is the variance of the coefficient of the PR swing, .030 is the variance of the coefficient of the interaction term, and –.027 is the covariance between these two coefficients (Friedrich 1982; Brambor, Clark, and Golder 2006).

Since both the coefficient and the standard error of the PR swing change with the value of DID, a graphical presentation is useful in evaluating the effect and the significance of this variable. The four graphs in figure 3.3 show the effect and the significance of this variable, and the graphs correspond to the four models in table 3.2. The solid lines represent the coefficient of the PR swing, and the dotted curves show the 95 percent confidence intervals. Hence, where the zero line (the x-axis) does not fall within the confidence interval, the impact of the PR swing is statistically significant.

In all four graphs, the solid line has a positive slope and lies above the x-axis, meaning that the PR-SMD linkage is stronger in urban areas than in rural areas. Furthermore, in 2000 and 2003, the PR-SMD linkage is statistically insignificant in rural areas (where DID is below approximately .45 in 2000 and .40 in 2003). This is consistent with our expectation that the party's popularity is not important for rural LDP candidates' electoral fortunes. In 2005 the PR swing's impact is significant regardless of the level of urbanization, which is not surprising because, as we saw in figure 3.2, the PR-SMD linkage in 2005 was much stronger than the linkage in earlier elections.

Discussion

The evidence provided in the previous section shows that party-centered elections are taking place (1) more in recent elections than in the past, and (2) more in urban districts than in rural districts. The introduction of manifestos in electoral campaigns and the reduction of the number of parties may be facilitating the trend toward party-centered elections, especially in urban areas where the high mobility of the population makes it difficult for legislators to build personal support bases. As discussed earlier, the realization of party-centered elections was one of the principal goals of the 1994 electoral law reform. Thus, it appears that the reform is creating its intended result in Japanese elections.

Not only is creating party-centered elections important because this was a reform goal; it is highly relevant to one of the most important questions in Japanese politics: Will the LDP ever lose power? As noted earlier, if many incumbent LDP legislators have loyal support organizations that are so stable that national political issues have no influence over their electoral fortunes, the LDP government is not vulnerable to problems such as economic mismanagement, corruption scandals, and the like. But the empirical evidence

Figure 3.3 Impacts of the PR Swing on SMD Vote Changes

(A) All Elections

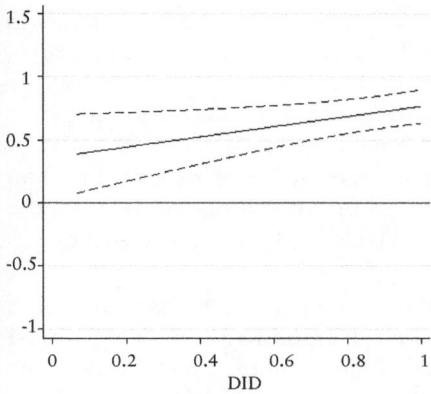

(B) 2000

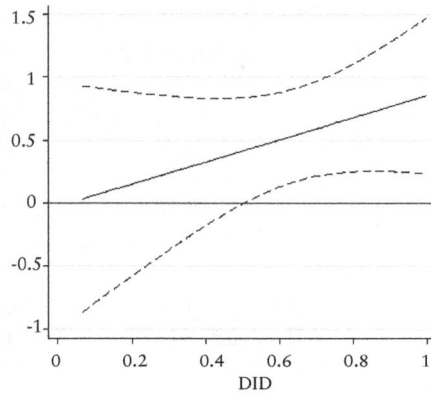

(C) 2003

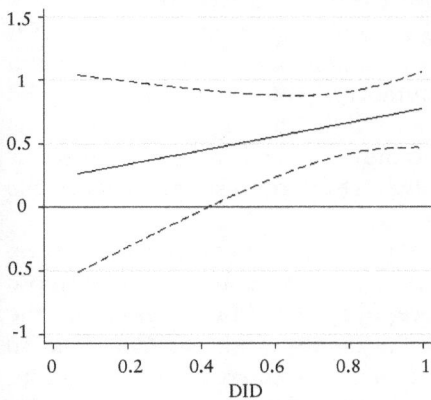

(D) 2005

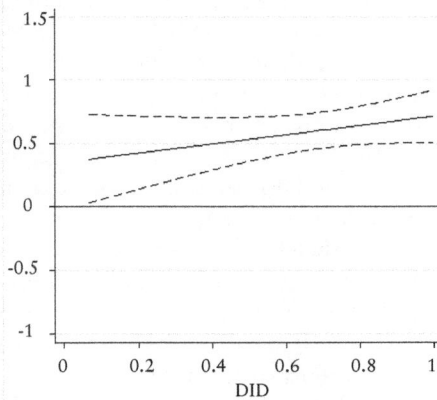

Source: See endnotes 6 and 7.

presented in the previous section indicates that Japanese elections are becoming increasingly party-centered, and thus the incumbents' local strongholds are not as strong as they were in the past.

Does that mean the DPJ has a good chance of unseating the LDP in the near future, or even in the next election? Especially after the 2007 Upper House elections, in which the DPJ won a historic victory and became the largest party in the Upper House, much attention has been paid to the question of whether the DPJ will also be able to defeat the LDP in the next general election and finally end the LDP government. The current DPJ leadership seems committed to making this happen. Will it succeed?

The data show that an alternation in power in the next election is not very likely. This is because of the asymmetric distribution of the vote margins between LDP candidates and DPJ candidates. Figure 3.4 shows the distribution of the differences between the vote shares of LDP candidates and DPJ candidates in SMDs in the last three elections.[13] The districts where the LDP won are on the right side of the graph, and the districts that went to the DPJ are on the left side. It is apparent that many LDP winners won by a large margin over their DPJ opponents, whereas most DPJ winners won close races. In 2005, 14 of the 52 DPJ winners in SMDs (27 percent) were elected with a smaller than 3 percentage point margin over their runners-up. In contrast, only 16 of the 219 LDP candidates (7 percent) who won SMDs in 2005 had margins of less than 3 percentage points.

Since a larger proportion of DPJ legislators are narrow winners compared with their LDP counterparts, the DPJ is more vulnerable to a vote swing against it; this is what happened in 2005, when the DPJ lost half of its SMD seats. Even if the LDP loses votes nationally, many of its incumbents are safe because of the large vote margins they enjoy in their districts. Hence, it will take a rather large swing in votes from the LDP to the DPJ if the latter is to defeat the former. Here are some hypothetical scenarios: In the 2005 election, the average vote share of the LDP candidates in SMDs went up by 3.02 percentage points from 2003.[14] If all DPJ candidates' vote shares increase by 3.02 points in the next election and their strongest contenders lose the same number of votes, the DPJ will win 82 SMDs—not nearly enough to win power. Even if the electoral swing is twice as large, the DPJ's SMD seats would go up to only 137, still short of 50 percent. In short, the DPJ needs an unprecedentedly large electoral swing to defeat the LDP in the next election.

Nevertheless, if the current trend toward party-centered elections continues, incumbents' strongholds will be undermined and electoral results will be more volatile, enabling large swings to take place. In the 1997 British elections, the Labour Party increased its vote share by 8.8 points, while the Conservative Party's support dropped by 11.3 points.[15] In a party-centered political system, gigantic electoral swings such as this can take place if the popularity of parties changes drastically, and a swing of this size is large enough for the DPJ to overtake the LDP in the next general election. Whether Japanese elections have or will become party-centered is a crucially important question to consider if we are interested in the future of party politics and the possibility of an alternation in power in Japan.

Figure 3.4 The LDP's Vote Margin over the DPJ in SMDs

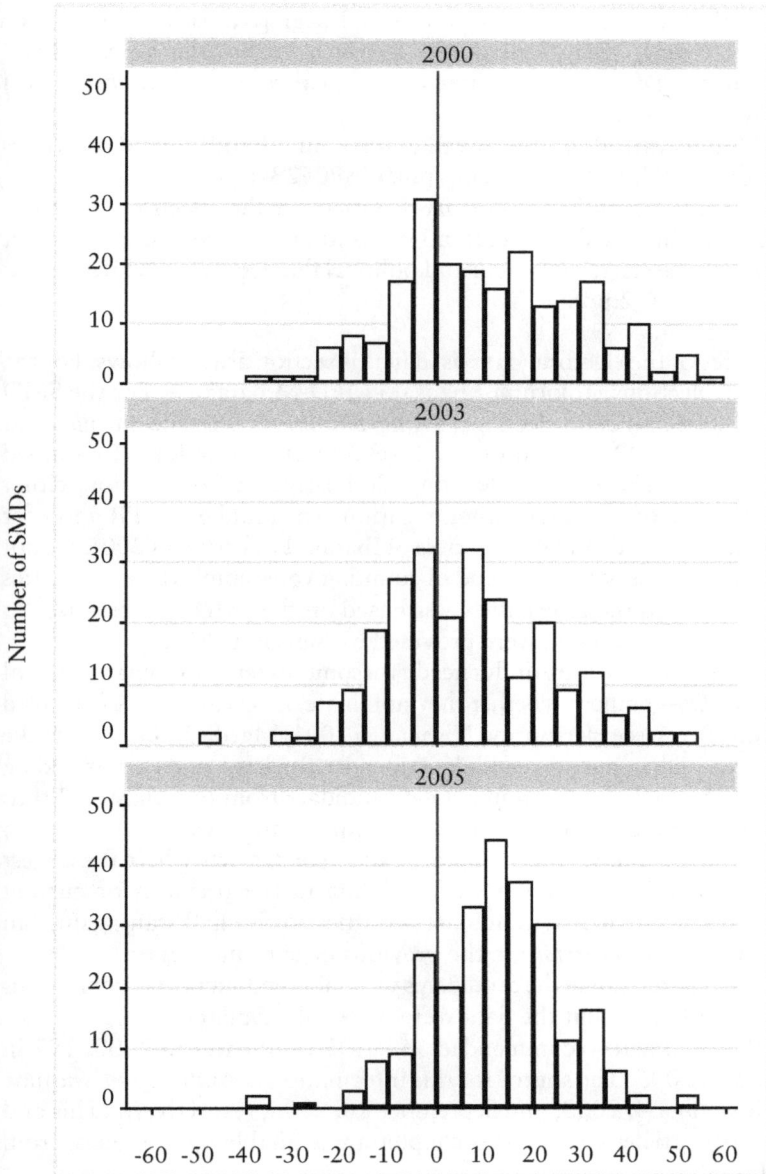

Source: See endnote 6.

Notes

[1] The Ministry of Foreign Affairs of Japan, Diplomatic Bluebook 1989. Available online at http://www.mofa.go.jp/mofaj/gaiko/bluebook/1989/h01-shiryou-1.htm.

[2] Seiji Kaikaku ni Kansuru Yushikisha Kaigi [Advisory Committee on Political Reform], "Seiji kaikaku ni kansuru yushikisha kaigi teigen" [Proposal from the advisory committee on political reform], http://www.secj .jp/pdf/19890427-1.pdf.

[3] Liberal Democratic Party, "Seiji kaikaku taikou" [Fundamental principles of political reforms], http://www.secj.jp/pdf/19890523-1.pdf.

[4] Senkyo Seido Shingikai [Advisory Council on the Electoral System], "Senkyo seido oyobi seiji shikin seido no kaikaku ni tsuiteno toshin" [Report on the reforms of the electoral system and political finance system], http://www .secj.jp/pdf/19900426-2.pdf.

[5] Same as note 4.

[6] The sources of the electoral data used in this section are as follows: For the 1996 and 2000 elections, Tokifumi Mizusaki's JED-M database. For the SMD portion of the 2003 and 2005 elections, *Sankei Shimbun*'s Web site, http://www. sankei.co.jp. For the PR portion of the 2003 and 2005 elections, I obtained the data from every prefecture's Election Administration Commission, either through its Web site or by direct communication. The numbers of PR votes for the parties in the 1st, 2nd, and 4th districts of Ibaraki Prefecture in 2005 are not precisely known because of the method of counting votes employed in two cities in Ibaraki. I estimated the LDP's PR votes based on the SMD vote results.

[7] The data on this variable were provided by Steven R. Reed.

[8] Of course, PR votes are influenced, to some extent, by what political parties do in SMDs—namely, whether they nominate SMD candidates (so-called contamination effects; see Herron and Nishikawa 2001; Maeda 2008). Yet, unlike small parties, the LDP nominates candidates in most districts—and I am excluding districts where the LDP did not nominate a candidate from my analyses. I thus believe that this is not a major issue in the subsequent analyses.

[9] In addition, the following districts are excluded: districts where the largest opposition party did not nominate a candidate in the previous or current election, and districts where a candidate with ties to the LDP ran against an LDP candidate (*hoshu bunretsu*) in the previous or current election.

[10] I wanted to differentiate the candidates who inherited support organizations from retiring candidates, but the data were not easily available.

[11] The New Komeito recommended 156 LDP candidates in 2000, 197 in 2003, and 239 in 2005. The source for this information is *Asahi Shimbun*: June 14, 2000, November 4, 2003, and September 10, 2005, respectively. (This and other newspaper articles cited in this chapter are available upon request from the author.)

[12] I decided that redistricting on the following districts was negligible, and hence they were included in the analysis: Chiba 7, Tokyo 12, Tokyo 13, Shizuoka

7 (formerly 9), Shizuoka 8, Mie 2, Mie 3, Osaka 16, Osaka 17, Kumamoto 1, and Kumamoto 2. Also, Hokkaido 7 is exactly the same as the old Hokkaido 13.

[13] The districts where either party nominated a candidate, the districts where postal rebels ran, and the districts where neither party won are excluded. There were 217 SMDs included in 2000, 243 in 2003, and 249 in 2005.

[14] The LDP candidates who ran against postal rebel candidates are not included in this calculation.

[15] The data are from Wolfram Nordsieck, "Parties and Elections in Europe: United Kingdom," http://www.parties-and-elections.de/unitedkingdom2.html.

References

Brambor, Thomas, William Roberts Clark, and Matt Golder. 2006. Understanding interaction models: Improving empirical analyses. *Political Analysis* 14 (1): 63–82.

Carey, John M., and Matthew Soberg Shugart. 1995. Incentives to cultivate a personal vote: A rank ordering of electoral systems. *Electoral Studies* 14 (4): 417–39.

Duverger, Maurice. 1954. *Political parties: Their organization and activity in the modern state*. New York: John Wiley.

Friedrich, Robert J. 1982. In defense of multiplicative terms in multiple regression equations. *American Journal of Political Science* 26 (4): 797–833.

Gaines, Brian J. 1998. The impersonal vote? Constitutional service and incumbency advantage in British elections, 1950–92. *Legislative Studies quarterly* 23:167–95.

Grofman, Bernard. 2005. Comparisons among electoral systems: Distinguishing between localism and candidate-centered politics. *Electoral Studies* 24:735–40.

Herron, Erik S., and Misa Nishikawa. 2001. Contamination effects and the number of parties in mixed-superposition electoral systems. *Electoral Studies* 20:63–86.

Lijphart, Arend. 1994. *Electoral systems and party systems: A study of twenty-seven democracies, 1945–1990*. New York: Oxford Univ. Press.

Maeda, Ko. 2008. Re-examining the contamination effect of Japan's mixed electoral system using the treatment-effects model. *Electoral Studies* 27:723–31.

McKean, Margaret, and Ethan Scheiner. 2000. Japan's new electoral system: La plus ça change . . . *Electoral Studies* 19:447–77.

Naikaku Sori Daijin Kanbo [Cabinet secretariat]. 2001. *Seron chosa nenkan* [Yearbook of opinion surveys]. Tokyo: Okurasho Insatsukyoku.

Nishikawa, Misa, and Erik S. Herron. 2004. Mixed electoral rules' impact on party systems. *Electoral Studies* 23:753–68.

Rae, Douglas W. 1971. *The political consequences of electoral laws*. Revised ed. New Haven, CT: Yale Univ. Press.

Ramseyer, J. Mark, and Frances McCall Rosenbluth. 1993. *Japan's political marketplace*. Cambridge, MA: Harvard Univ. Press.

Reed, Steven R. 2007. Duverger's law is working in Japan. *Japanese Journal of Electoral Studies* 22:96–106.

Reed, Steven R., and Michael F. Thies. 2001. The causes of electoral reform in Japan. In *Mixed-member electoral systems: The best of both worlds?* ed. Matthew Soberg Shugart and Martin P. Wattenberg. Oxford: Oxford Univ. Press.

Taagepera, Rein, and Matthew S. Shugart. 1989. *Seats and votes: The effects and determinants of electoral systems*. New Haven, CT: Yale Univ. Press.

PORK-BARREL POLITICS AND PARTISAN REALIGNMENT IN JAPAN

Jun Saito

This chapter examines the Japanese partisan realignment of the 1990s and its influences. As discussed in previous chapters, the 1994 electoral reform has produced its intended results. The new system, based on single-member districts (SMDs), strengthened the authority of party leadership and weakened factions. The effective number of parties has shrunk—gradually, but steadily. Although partisan strength is lopsided in favor of the coalition led by the Liberal Democratic Party (LDP) in the Lower House, the Democratic Party of Japan (DPJ) controls a plurality of seats in the Upper House.

Because the new SMD system draws competitors to the center of the ideological spectrum (Cox 1990), the largest opposition party is no longer as ideologically committed as it was under the old system of the single nontransferable vote (SNTV). The DPJ is becoming a pragmatic alternative to the LDP, something that the Japan Socialist Party (JSP) never was. In addition, since Junichiro Koizumi's LDP was electorally successful in urban districts, the LDP incumbents' districts are no longer predominantly rural. Now that the LDP and the DPJ represent large cities and rural areas in both chambers, the partisan schism is ostensibly murky.

Amid the turbulent political climate of the 1990s, when the DPJ emerged as the LDP's main opponent, a dozen new and old political parties disappeared. This realignment, similar to other types of political change, took place at both the level of voter behavior and political strategy. At the first level, we observe increasing numbers of floating voters, now detached from their old partisan identifications (Kawasaki 2007). At the second level, a number of incumbent legislators switched their party affiliation between elections; many local politicians in the same *keiretsu* (national-level candidates' support group) followed suit. Although these two trends are closely interrelated, this chapter focuses primarily on political strategies and provides an explanation of the circumstances under which the incumbents tried to switch parties between elections.

Existing studies of party switching in Japan have focused on generational conflicts inside the LDP (Cox and Rosenbluth 1995; Kato 1998) and legislators' preferences for electoral reform (Reed and Scheiner 2003). While acknowledging that these factors explain some of the important variations in the legislators' choice of parties, I propose an alternative theory that consistently explains the series of party-choice decisions throughout the 1990s. Specifically, constituents' need for infrastructure investment structured the landscape of bipartisan confrontation in Japan. Although pork-barrel politics has long been at the heart of the LDP's regime, *shinkansen* (new bullet-train trunk lines) and highways affected the fate of the parties in a nonintuitive way. Once bullet-train tracks were laid out in a district, the discipline of the party organization eroded and incumbents left the party more frequently.

In order to explicate the pattern of party switching and realignment in Japan, this chapter is organized in the following manner: The second section briefly describes the process of partisan realignment in Japan and compares competing explanations for party switching. The third section presents the hypothesis that the construction of transportation infrastructure altered the political landscape of Japan. The fourth section examines three pairs of comparative case studies. The fifth section provides a statistical analysis based on an empirical measure of infrastructure needs. The chapter concludes with a discussion of the legacy of infrastructure policy reform during the Koizumi administration.

Party Switching in the 1990s: Competing Explanations

On June 18, 1993, a historic no-confidence motion against Prime Minister Kiichi Miyazawa was passed by the Lower House by a margin of 255 to 220, and incumbents in his own party provided pivotal votes. Among the 274 Lower House incumbents who were affiliated with the party, 39 voted in favor of for the motion and another 18 legislators abstained. Miyazawa immediately called an early election by dissolving the Lower House. Within a few days, 48 incumbents had left the LDP to form the Renewal Party (RP) and the New Party Harbinger (NPH).

When the initial defection took place in June 1993, the LDP experienced a gradual decline in its level of popular support. Rampant money scandals—culminating in the Recruit Company scandal in 1989—resulted in Prime Minister Noboru Takeshita's resignation. Public distrust in the political institution was widespread and severe. Morihiro Hosokawa, a former governor of Kumamoto, and his Japan New Party (JNP) entered the national political scene in the 1992 Upper House election, attracting support from urban centrist voters who were dissatisfied with the conventional ways of politics. Despite these undercurrents, there was little indication that the LDP would lose the majority in the Lower House in the next general election. The party's approval rating was still high enough to warrant a majority.[1] Rather, a small but sudden decline in the LDP approval rating followed the defection of the 48 Lower House incumbents who formed the RP and the NPH. If these defectors had stayed, the LDP could have successfully maintained its preexisting level of popular support and could have pursued reform from within, as the party had done in the past.

The LDP obtained a plurality of seats, but the coalition bargaining among the defectors and the former opposition parties eventually forced the LDP out of power for the first time in the party's thirty-eight-year history. After Morihiro Hosokawa became prime minister in August 1993, LDP legislators intermittently left the party. Since the non-LDP coalition government involved as many as eight parties, the government was popular but unstable. After the electoral reform bill was passed in the Diet in January 1994, Hosokawa's coalition gradually lost its cohesiveness. Charged with his own money scandal, Hosokawa resigned in May 1994. The JSP and the NPH left the coalition, and Tsutomu Hata (of the RP) formed a minority government.

While Hosokawa and Hata were heading the non-LDP coalition cabinets between August 1993 and June 1994, 22 of the 227 Lower House incumbents who had been reelected under the LDP label left the party. Although the LDP's clout in the legislature was shrinking, the party still controlled a plurality of seats and was in a position to cut deals with frustrated members of the coalition camp, in particular the JSP and the NPH. By nominating the leader of the party's longtime nemesis, the LDP returned to power after less than a year of interruption. Tomiichi Murayama, then the chairman of the JSP, became prime minister on June 30, 1994.

While Murayama was heading the LDP-JSP-NPH coalition, the new districting scheme was announced. In order to survive under the new SMD proportional representation (SMD-PR) hybrid system, the opposition parties joined forces to form the New Frontier Party (NFP) in December 1994. The NFP was basically an alliance of new entrants into politics, former defectors from the LDP, members of the former Komei Party, and other incumbents backed by private-sector labor unions. The 1995 Upper House elections yielded a favorable result for the NFP, and pundits as well as the public had mixed projections about the results of the first Lower House elections under the new SMD system. During this period, thirteen legislators who had won a seat under the opposition party label switched to the LDP. Apparently, the redistricting done for the new electoral system affected their choice of party.

The first SMD-based election, in October 1996, resulted in a small but decisive victory for the LDP-led coalition. Although the 3 parties in the coalition won a total of 256 seats, the LDP's 239 seats still fell short of the majority requirement of 251. The LDP leadership actively hunted for possible defectors from the opposition. A total of 24 legislators elected under opposition party labels had joined the LDP camp by December 1998.

The flip side of the LDP's expansion was an increasingly fragmented opposition. The NFP was torn apart in late 1997, and it would take several years before the DPJ became a cohesive challenger to the LDP. Ichiro Ozawa was heading the NFP when the party dissolved. His followers formed the Liberal Party and joined the LDP-led coalition in January 1999. Furthermore, the Komei, formerly an organizational cornerstone of the NFP, jumped on the bandwagon in October 1999. The Komei has a loyal electoral support base backed by Soka Gakkai, a fundamentalist sect of the Buddhist order Nichiren Shu. The LDP's electoral support base under the new electoral system was thus significantly strengthened, especially in urban areas, where Soka Gakkai's organizations are solid. But the DPJ was expanding by accommodating stray incumbents who were formerly affiliated with the NFP. Although the DPJ had won a sizable number of seats in the 1998 Upper House elections, its electoral strength was still limited because it held only about one-fifth of the seats in the Lower House.

When the Komei joined the LDP-led coalition, the bargaining clout of Ozawa's Liberal Party was marginalized. The Liberals were no longer pivotal in either the Lower House or the Upper House. Frustrated by the fact that the LDP was reluctant to provide electoral backing for his party, Ozawa decided to leave the coalition in April 2000. But only 19 of the 39 Lower House incumbents in his party followed him. The remaining 20 incumbents formed the Conservative Party and stayed in the coalition. Between the first SMD election, in October 1996, and the second one, in June 2000, a total of 34 former opposition-party incumbents either reverted to the LDP or formed a new party that would become part of the LDP-led coalition.

The basic framework of today's partisan map was completed as Ozawa's Liberal Party left the coalition. Since this equilibrium was reached, opposition-party incumbents have effectively stopped converting to the governing coalition. The Liberal Party joined the DPJ through the 2003 Lower House elections, and Ozawa now heads the DPJ. Komei supporters have provided consistent support for the LDP, and the LDP has successfully maintained its majority party status.[2]

What variables explain this complex series of political interactions, which eventually produced the current partisan structure? Cox and Rosenbluth (1995) were the first to conduct an empirical analysis of the LDP's split in 1993. Building on the theory of coalition politics, they argue that a gradual decline in the LDP's electoral prospects led a subset of legislators to defect. In particular, they found that junior legislators who were electorally vulnerable were the most likely to defect. Drawing upon Hirschman's theory of voice and exit, Kato (1998) argues that the legislators most likely to exit raised their voices first. She also finds that junior legislators, who had a smaller stake in the party, were most likely to leave it.

In addition to these studies, based on the generational-conflict hypothesis, Reed and Scheiner (2003), as well as Tatebayashi (2004), examine the effect of each legislator's policy preferences on the choice of parties. Tatebayashi (2004) investigates whether incumbents' policy specialization (by means of the LDP's intraparty policy committees) was correlated with the probability of defection. He finds that legislators who were sitting on pork-barrel committees were more likely to leave the LDP. Reed and Scheiner (2003) investigate the interaction between the legislators' preferences for institutional reform and electoral vulnerability. In their interpretation, legislators who supported institutional reform defected from the majority party to achieve their policy ideals. Reed and Scheiner measure the legislators' preference for reform by whether the incumbents signed "Chusenkyokusei haishi sengen" (The resolution to ban medium-sized districts) by December 18, 1992.³ This resolution reflected one of the political reform initiatives of the time and attracted substantial support from the business, labor, and academic sectors. Reed and Scheiner find that a disproportionate number of those who signed the resolution eventually left the party. Their empirical analysis also indicates that the effect of seniority is no longer significant once the preference for reform is taken into account.

Although these studies provide useful insights into the working of the LDP's party organization, they are not free of shortcomings. First of all, none fully explains why legislators defected from the LDP in multiple stages. Most of these studies focus on the LDP's historic split in 1993 and ignore the remaining party switches of the 1990s. Second, none has investigated why a significant number of LDP defectors eventually returned to the fold. If legislators' behavior was motivated purely by their desire to establish a competitive bipartisan system, then why would they return to the LDP? Alternatively, if their behavior was driven solely to further their careers and access to government resources, then why would some of the defectors stay in the opposition? Japan's current partisan schism reflects the results of successive rounds of electoral contests as well as party switching. Given the complexity of legislators' behavior, the existing theories fail to account for the pattern of partisan realignment, which was one of the most important developments in Japanese politics in the 1990s.

To understand these remaining puzzles, we need to clarify under what conditions each incumbent values membership in the governing coalition. My explanation is that legislators' choices are constrained by constituents' demand for pork-barrel projects. When incumbents represent underdeveloped districts and seek reelection, they need to be affiliated with the governing coalition. In particular, the availability of bullet-train stations, highways, and airports significantly affects the demand for additional pork-barrel projects and incumbents' choice of party membership.

The Infrastructure Hypothesis

Individual incumbents try to solidify their campaign organizations by appealing to large-externality programmatic policies (such as constitutional revision and national defense debate) and/or narrowly targeted pork-barrel tactics.

Unlike subsidies, which are determined each year, construction of transportation infrastructure is an irreversible process. A significant amount of the construction cost is spent in the locale where the initial investment is made, and asset-price hikes in the surrounding areas follow. Once the locale is connected to the transportation network, it is almost impossible for the government to destroy the existing infrastructure. As empirical studies in growth economics suggest, transportation infrastructure has produced positive economic effects, especially in Japan's high-speed growth period (see, for example, Murata and Morisawa 2003). The initial investment in transportation infrastructure provides local residents with jobs, money for land purchase, and other forms of targeted private goods, but the economic benefit of using existing infrastructure satisfies the defining characteristics of local public goods. This economic benefit does not disappear regardless of whether local residents support the incumbent party. In addition, once the locale is incorporated into the transportation network, further investment provides only a marginal economic benefit—except perhaps the alleviation of congestion. Seen from the perspective of immobile asset owners, both asset and production incomes are significantly affected at the time of initial investment.

In districts where voters have ready access to bullet trains, highways, and airports, additional investment in infrastructure will generate benefits to the district commensurate with construction costs (see, for example, Weingast et al. 1981). In other words, only construction companies and their employees will reap the benefits of the investment. In electoral districts where voters must spend hours driving to the airport and must transfer several times to go to large cities, additional investment can bring in a sizable amount of new benefits (public goods). If the incumbent can credibly advertise his or her platform for new infrastructure projects, local residents might expect a future inflow of construction costs, possible asset price hikes, and a continuous stream of productive income effects. For instance, the business sector would look to widen the range of its market transactions. The tourism industry would anticipate an increased number of visitors to spas and other places of interest. Owners of rice paddies would be excited about possible opportunities to sell their properties.

Construction of new bullet-train tracks and highways, however, is centrally controlled by the LDP's intraparty policy committees. In particular, the Tetsudo Chosakai (Railroad Investigation Panel) and Douro Chosakai (Road Investigation Panel) of the LDP's Policy Affairs Research Council are renowned as the nests of *zoku*, or the pork-barrel tribes in the party. Unless authorized by these panels and the Somukai (General Conference), key infrastructure projects remain up in the air. The party leadership can strategically target when and where highways and bullet-train projects are started.

Thus, when the probability of the LDP's staying in power is high, the incumbent can appeal to infrastructure policy only if he or she is affiliated with the party. But when the probability of an LDP majority declines, legislators whose preferences are distant from those of the leadership are increasingly willing to take a gamble. By splitting the party, they can bet on the possibility that they will be pivotal in forming the next cabinet. Even when toppling the dominant party is difficult, the dissatisfied legislator may hope to get reelected under a non-LDP reformist platform. Thus, the rigidity of reelection constraints systematically ties some legislators to the party.

In conclusion, productive infrastructure is an effective device for buying off the electoral support of local residents *only until* its construction is credibly committed. Once irreversible infrastructure projects are initiated, local residents will lose the incentive to overcome the collective-action problem and to comply with what the governing party wants them to do. When the LDP's electoral strength is solid, incumbents who represent infrastructure-rich districts are more likely to leave the party. Similarly, opposition-party members are lured to convert to the LDP under this circumstance. When the LDP's collective electoral future is uncertain, as in the case of the non-LDP coalition period, legislators are more likely to behave in accordance with their policy preferences.

Shinkansen and Electoral Politics: Comparative Cases

To illustrate how the logic of pork-barrel politics operates in day-to-day political activities, three pairs of comparative cases are provided in this section. Each pair consists of a treatment and a control observation—that is, a municipality with and without *shinkansen* (bullet train) stations. The first pair is Oyama and Ashikaga, in Tochigi Prefecture, intended to explicate how the presence of transportation infrastructure enriches owners of immobile assets and changes the patterns of political transactions. The second pair is Hachinohe and Hirosaki in Aomori; these two cities show how a pending infrastructure project enhances the discipline of the local party organizations. The third case compares Ueda and Tsuruoka, homes of the LDP's former "neo-new leaders" Tsutomu Hata and Koichi Kato. I will explain why Hata was able to defect in 1993, whereas Kato was reluctant to leave the party when he unsuccessfully fomented *Kato no ran* ("Kato's rebellion") in November 2000. I've chosen these three pairs of cases based on similar population size and the political affiliations of those who represent these municipalities. The demographics of these cities are summarized in table 4.1.

A Bullet Train Changes the Business Climate: Ashikaga versus Oyama

Modern economic development entails the transformation of employment structures, and the labor force typically shifts from the less productive agricultural sector to more competitive ones. This process is embodied through the transformation of employment within a fixed geographic domain and the migration of people from less productive regions to more productive ones. Such growth-promoting trends and their electoral consequences are clarified by comparing Oyama and Ashikaga, both about 50 miles north of downtown Tokyo and at the southern end of Tochigi Prefecture.

Both Oyama and Ashikaga developed as industrial cities in the suburbs of Tokyo; textiles, food processing, and machinery were the major components of their local industries in the early postwar period. By the time the bullet-train station in Oyama started operation in 1982, Ashikaga had a larger population and a larger share of the manufacturing sector.[4] What marked a sharp difference between these two cities was their location. Oyama is located between Utsunomiya, the prefectural capital, and Tokyo. It was naturally regarded as an appropriate site for a new bullet-train station. In contrast, Ashikaga is about equidistant from the Joetsu and Tohoku *shinkansen* lines, the two bullet-train lines that started operation in 1982. It takes roughly two hours by local rapid-

Table 4.1 Bullet Trains and Electoral Politics: Case Comparisons

Pair	City (Prefecture)	Incumbent 2005 (Party)	*Shinkansen* (Start of operation)	Population[a] 1980–2005	LDP vote share 1980–2005 (%)
1	Oyama (Tochigi)	Sato (LDP)	Tohoku (June 1982)	127,226	52.6
		Yamaoka (DPJ)[b]		160,150	51.2
	Ashikaga (Tochigi)	Motegi (LDP)	Control	165,756	54.5
				159,756	70.4
2	Hachinohe (Aomori)	Oshima (LDP)	Tohoku (Dec. 2003)	238,179	66.0
		Tanabu (DPJ)[b]		238,428	52.0
	Hirosaki (Aomori)	Kimura (LDP)	Control	175,330	41.8
				173,221	52.7
3	Ueda (Nagano)	Hata (DPJ)	Nagano (Oct. 1997)	111,540	52.0
				123,678	37.1
	Tsuruoka (Yamagata)	Kato (LDP)	Control	99,751	57.6
				98,127	64.2

Sources: Asahi Shimbun 2005, Mizusaki 1993, Sorifu Tokeikyoku 1982, Somusho Tokeikyoku 2007.
Note: [a] Population based on premerger municipal boundaries comparable between 1980 and 2005.
[b] Saved in the PR portion.

train service to commute from either city to downtown Tokyo, but as the bullet train became available to residents of Oyama, the commuting time was shortened to less than an hour. Municipal population sizes along the *shinkansen* lines have grown consistently, but Ashikaga's population has remained stagnant for the past four decades. As the new bullet-train stations drew commercial activities away from Ashikaga, its downtown became a collection of shuttered buildings.

The changing business environment has affected the revenue structure of these two cities and the strategies of incumbent legislators. While Ashikaga's municipal finances have stayed dependent on subsidies from the central government, Oyama has grown out of such dependence. As of fiscal year 2000, only 4 percent of Oyama's municipal budget depended on transfers from the central government, whereas the figure was 30 percent in Ashikaga.[5]

The need for incumbent members of the Diet to serve as the "pipeline of the pork" (Scheiner 2005) is clearly higher in Ashikaga. Both Oyama and Ashikaga belonged to the same district under the old SNTV electoral system, and the LDP's strength in the 1980 election was roughly the same in both cities. But the electoral reform divided Ashikaga and Oyama into two separate SMDs. In Ashikaga, the LDP is much stronger today than it was a few decades ago, and this is not necessarily the case in Oyama. Toshimitsu Motegi, who currently represents Ashikaga, initially ran under the JNP label in the last election, in the old SNTV system. He stayed in the JNP while the non-LDP coalition was in power. In late 1994, soon after the LDP had regained its majority status in July, he switched his party affiliation to the LDP and stayed on. Kenji Yamaoka, who now serves as the DPJ's chairman of the Diet Affairs Committee, obtained the largest number of votes in Oyama in the 2003 election. He was saved in the PR tier even in the turbulent 2005 election. Initially elected from the LDP's Upper House PR list, he converted to the Lower House in the 1993 election. He left the LDP in 1994 and has since followed Ozawa's course of action.

Pending Projects Discipline Local Organizations: Hirosaki Versus Hachinohe

Transportation infrastructure, once its construction is credibly committed, erodes the discipline of local party organizations. Infrastructure investment is an effective method of vote-buying only while its construction is up in the air. The LDP's electoral performance in Aomori provides a prime example: the party's electoral strength waxed and waned in accordance with the progress of bullet-train projects.

Aomori Prefecture is located at the northern end of Honshu, the main island of Japan. Two of the large cities in this prefecture, Hachinohe and Hirosaki, competed to invite bullet-train routes in the early 1970s (both cities are located roughly halfway between Morioka and Hakodate). Construction of the *shinkansen* line between Tokyo and Morioka had already been committed as

75

of 1970, and the underwater tunnel that connects the mainland and Hakodate, the second-largest city on the island of Hokkaido, had been in progress since 1961 with a view to laying *shinkansen* tracks in the future.

When the bullet-train project that would connect the mainland and Hokkaido emerged on the national budgetary agenda in the late 1960s, local governments organized lobbying groups of various kinds. In October 1968, the city council of Hirosaki established Shinkansen Yuchi Tokubetsu Iinkai, a special committee for promoting construction of the new trunk line. Hirosaki later expanded the lobbying organization to include its neighboring municipalities in both Aomori and Akita prefectures. In the summer of 1970, the city of Hachinohe and nearby municipalities in eastern Aomori jointly decided to lobby for construction of the *shinkansen* line along the Pacific coastal route.

In 1970 the Zenkoku Shinkansen Seibi Ho (National Super-Express Construction Law) was enacted, and construction of the bullet-train tracks between Tokyo and Morioka was started in 1971. The law initially provided that about one-third of the existing railroad tracks throughout Japan be replaced by bullet-train tracks.

The political balance at the time was tilted toward the eastern route. Zenko Suzuki was then the chairman of the Executive Council Board of the LDP, and his district was on the southern border of Hachinohe. When the eastern route was finally adopted in the master plan, Suzuki, along with Prime Minister Kakuei Tanaka attempted to assuage the frustration among residents on the western side by promising that the western route would be constructed without a major time lag. They The construction budget for the eastern route was just about to be authorized when the first oil shock hit the Japanese economy. The government announced the suspension of *shinkansen* construction projects, allegedly to keep inflation under control. That was the beginning of Aomori residents' long struggle for the LDP's political favor.

In 1973, when business leaders of Hachinohe met with Tomisaburo Hashimoto (then the secretary-general of the LDP), Hashimoto explicitly remarked: "We would be happy to lay the two routes of bullet-train tracks, one each in the east and the west. But each of them costs 200 billion yen. In order to protect the capitalist market economy and to get the bullet-train project done, we need your stronger support for the LDP."[6]

The LDP's strength in Aomori exhibited a remarkable surge. Prefectural governors were officially endorsed by the LDP through the 1980s, even when nonpartisan governors jointly supported by the LDP and opposition parties became the norm. In the 1986 double election, all nine members of the Diet elected from Aomori for both chambers were LDP incumbents. Throughout the late 1980s and the early 1990s, the prefectural government of Aomori lobbied ardently to start the construction. The central government, however, officially considered downgrading the blueprints to the mini-*shinkansen* standard, in which case the maximum speed would be significantly slower than the standard *shinkansen*. Avoiding the accumulation of yet more government debt was the rationale behind delaying new bullet-train construction, and the plan was still up in the air until late 1991, when construction of the bullet-train tracks was finally started beyond Morioka.

The LDP's fall from power in 1993 did not stop the bullet-train project in Aomori, and a few LDP incumbent legislators defected from the LDP to join new parties. Immediately before the 1993 election, Morio Kimura from Hirosaki left the LDP to form the Renewal Party. Masami Tanabu (then the minister of agriculture) from Hachinohe left the party shortly after the 1993 election. A large number of the prefectural and municipal legislators followed suit.

The ambitious Kimura ran for prefectural governor in 1995 and defeated the LDP incumbent. Now that construction had begun, the LDP's partisan label was no longer a prerequisite for a governorship. His son, Taro Kimura, inherited the support base in Hirosaki and won the SMD seat in the 1996 election. Unlike in the prefectural governor race, which is contested prefecture-wide, the SMD from which the Kimura family is elected is poorly endowed with infrastructure. Shortly after the election, Taro Kimura ended his affiliation with the NFP, the largest opposition party of the time, and joined the LDP in late 1999. He was reelected under the LDP label in 2000.

The choices made by the Tanabu family were different from those of the Kimuras. Masami Tanabu, then running under the NFP banner, was defeated in the first SMD election in October 1996. He ran in the 1998 Upper House elections from the prefecture-wide district and won. His daughter, Masayo Tanabu, has inherited his electoral support base and ran in her father's former district. Masayo was later elected into the parliament by being saved in the PR tier. The Tanabu family has consistently kept its political distance from the LDP. In the 2001 Hachinohe mayoral election, Toshibumi Nakamura, Tanabu's protégé, defeated Akiyoshi Kanari, who was backed by the LDP. Nakamura's electoral platform emphasized decentralization reform, whereas Kanari did the opposite, asserting that he was better suited to serve as the "pipeline" of public works.[7]

Why Kato's Rebellion Failed: Comparing Hata's Ueda and Kato's Tsuruoka

In addition to the behavior of backbenchers, we can consider how the availability of *shinkansen* affected the choices made by faction leaders. Back in the 1980s, Tsutomu Hata and Koichi Kato were regarded as rising stars in the LDP's new generation. Hata was first elected to the Lower House in 1969 and Kato in 1972. Both of them inherited their fathers' firm electoral support bases in the historic castle towns of Ueda and Tsuruoka. They both represented the primarily agricultural districts of Nagano and Yamagata. It was not surprising that they both belonged to the new generation of the *sogo nosei zoku* (comprehensive agricultural policy tribe), who were interested in enhancing the efficiency of agricultural production and were even willing to lift import bans on rice. They were both regarded as "neo-new leaders," or reform-minded internationalists within the party, and their faction leaders treated them well. Masayoshi Ohira was Kato's political mentor, and while Ohira was prime minister, Kato served as the deputy chief cabinet secretary, which is a gateway to a successful political career. Kato was first appointed as a cabinet minister in 1984, when he became the defense agency chief of the Yasuhiro Nakasone cabinet. Similarly, backed by Kakuei Tanaka, the LDP's kingpin at the time, Hata was on a political-career fast track. He was appointed minister of agriculture in late 1985 and played an important role in U.S.-Japan trade negotiations in the late 1980s.

Despite these common characteristics, Hata and Kato differed widely in their preferences for desirable electoral institutions. Hata was a longtime proponent of an SMD-based system and was heading the LDP's project team for political reform during Toshiki Kaifu's premiership. Hata was one of the standard-bearers of the political reform initiative and was especially popular among reform-seeking juniors of the party. In December 1992, Hata split the Takeshita faction to form his own faction, which eventually became the RP in 1993.

In contrast, Kato was an ardent opponent of electoral reform. When Ozawa and Hata tried to push the political reform initiative forward, Kato, together with Taku Yamasaki and Junichiro Koizumi, formed the "YKK" coalition against them. It is not surprising that Hata left the party and Kato stayed in 1993. The preference hypothesis is consistent with the choices they made, but the *shinkansen* also explains several important features of their subsequent careers.

When Hata left the party in 1993, the construction of Nagano *shinkansen* was already under way. Construction between Takasaki and Karuizawa had begun in 1989, with a proviso that tracks between Karuizawa and Nagano would be constructed in accordance with an inexpensive downgraded standard, which would run substantially slower trains. In 1991, however, the International Olympic Committee (IOC) decided that the 1998 Winter Olympics would be held in Nagano.[8] This decision justified upgrading the *shinkansen* to its full standard. As the construction between Tokyo and Nagano was credibly committed, Hata's hometown of Ueda would house a brand-new station for trains that would reach Tokyo in less than 90 minutes—a roughly 70 percent reduction in travel time. Hata's defection did not delay the construction, and the full-standard Nagano *shinkansen* started operation in October 1997.

As promising figures such as Hata and Ozawa left the LDP, Kato's chances of becoming prime minister rose. Unlike Hata's Nagano, Kato's home district in Yamagata had poor transportation infrastructure. After occupying several key executive positions in the party, Kato inherited Kiichi Miyazawa's faction in 1998. Kato ran for LDP president in 1999 but failed to defeat the incumbent, Keizo Obuchi. Still, voters in his district expected that Kato would someday ascend to the position. In the general election of June 2000, Kato garnered 72 percent of the votes in his district. His electoral platform included the construction of bullet-train tracks between Niigata and his district. His constituents expected that his rise to power would put the regional development initiative into practice.

Within several months, frustrated by Prime Minister Yoshiro Mori's economic policy, Kato threatened that his faction members would approve of the no-confidence motion once it was submitted by the opposition. When Kato waged this rebellion, *Kato no ran*, in November 2000, he persistently emphasized that he would not leave the LDP and would seek to reform the party from within. The no-confidence motion was submitted on November 20, but Kato did not show up in the chamber. His faction became the effective prey of political maneuvering and was split into two. As he lost his influence within the party, Kato's supporters in his home district lamented that the failed rebellion might delay the *shinkansen* project.[9] To this day, the bullet-train project remains up in the air, but Kato's electoral strength has not waned.

Empirical Exploration

Although these cases provide qualitative information on how the nature of electoral transactions was altered by construction of bullet-train stations, they may be subject to selection bias. Since these cases are intended to elucidate my main point, the reader may wonder if they represent the overall pattern of the data. To show that the infrastructure hypothesis explains the partisan realignment well, I first lay out the LDP incumbents' hometowns and their party-switching decisions on a map. I then compare the constituents' infrastructure-needs index (INI) of defectors and nondefectors.

Mapping Politicians' Choices

The location of bullet-train stations and LDP incumbents' hometowns are shown in figure 4.1.[10] The incumbents who left the party in June 1993 are indicated by an *x*, whereas those who stayed are represented by small dots. As mentioned in the previous section, the construction of the Nagano *shinkansen* was already committed in this period, and it is for this reason that bullet-train stations committed as of October 1997 are located on the map, although we are analyzing the LDP incumbents' defection in June 1993.

We can see that LDP incumbents were scattered throughout the Japanese archipelago while defectors in June 1993 were clustered along the *shinkansen* lines.[11] Nobody on the island of Shikoku or in the southern part of Kyushu defected. There are a few areas where we see a concentration of *x*s off the *shinkansen* tracks. Several defectors in northern Kyushu were riding Hosokawa's coattails as his JNP was gaining popularity. Hosokawa was once governor of Kumamoto Prefecture and ran for a Lower House seat from Kumamoto in the 1993 election. By the time Hosokawa retired from politics in 1998, most defectors in this area had returned to the LDP. Incidentally, the construction of the *shinkansen* between Hakata and Kumamoto was not started until 2001. The two legislators from Wakayama (Toshihiro Nikai and Keisuke Nakanishi) followed Ozawa's course initially, but they had also returned to the LDP camp by May 2000.

Figure 4.1 Shinkansen and LDP Legislators' Choice of Party Membership (June 1993)

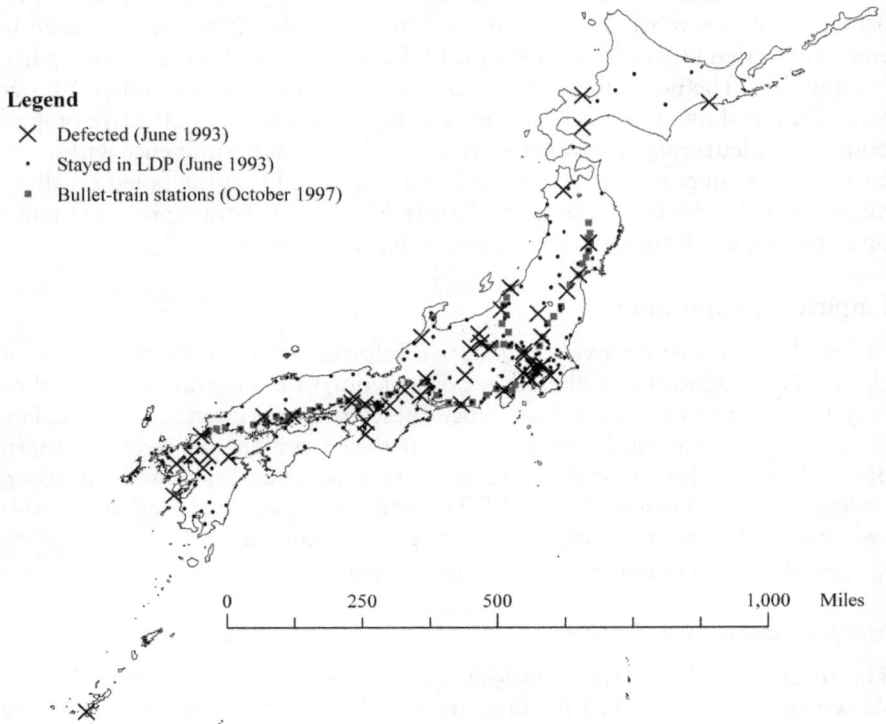

Legend

× Defected (June 1993)
· Stayed in LDP (June 1993)
■ Bullet-train stations (October 1997)

The Infrastructure-Needs Index (INI)

To test whether incumbents from infrastructure-poor districts were tied to the LDP, I operationalized and measured the INI. The variable measures how many key infrastructure projects remain undone in a specific geographic area and was calculated in the following manner: First, I computed the distance between each municipality and three types of key transportation infrastructure: bullet-train stations, highway ramps, and airports with landing strips of 1,500 meters or longer.[12] Second, I assigned dichotomous variables for these infrastructure types, depending on whether the specific municipality was outside the service radius or not. For example, if the closest bullet-train station was more than 40 kilometers away as of January 1, 1998, I assigned the number 1 to the municipality. Similarly, I set the threshold for highways at 20 kilometers and for airports at 100 kilometers. These numbers, while somewhat random, are reasonable since bullet-train stations are located roughly 20 kilometers apart from one another and highway ramps are about 11 kilometers apart. Then I added the three dichotomous variables for each municipality. Theoretically, the municipal INI varies between 0 and 3. If a municipality lacks all three types of key infrastructure, the INI is 3. If the municipality is in the vicinity of all three kinds of infrastructure, the INI is set to 0. Last, I calculated the vote-weighted average of the municipal INIs for each incumbent legislator.[13] This weighting procedure is intended to reflect the infrastructure needs of the incumbent's *jiban* (electoral turf) within the district.

To illustrate how this index behaves, table 4.2 lists the top 20 "needy" LDP incumbents as of April 1993, shortly before the defection. As we can see, only 3 of them participated in the new parties, and all 3 returned to the LDP camp by the year 2000. For instance, Naoto Kitamura is ranked 5th in table 4.2. He left the LDP to join the RP, but he converted to the LDP and provided the party with the pivotal 251st seat in the Lower House in September 1997. The LDP regained the single-party majority by accommodating him. As mentioned previously, Nikai (ranked 15th) initially left the LDP but eventually returned to the nest. Hiroyuki Sonoda (18th) initially joined the NPH and played a key role in the LDP-JSP-NPH coalition. He joined the LDP in December 1999. The current minister of agriculture, Shigeru Ishiba (ranked 20th), joined the NFP after the LDP slipped from power. When the LDP returned to power, however, he left the NFP. He won the first SMD election as a nonpartisan but regained his LDP partisan affiliation in 1997.

But incumbents elected from infrastructure-rich districts have INI values close to zero. Masayoshi Takemura was the head of the NPH and served as the minister of finance in the Hosokawa cabinet. His INI score was 0.04. Ichiro Ozawa's score was 0.34. Although the prefectures they represented are predominantly rural, their infrastructure was already in good shape by the early 1990s.

Hypothesis Testing

I then test whether the INI score is correlated to whether the legislators were loyal to the LDP or not. The simplest method of testing this is to compare the means of the INI, but given that the distribution of INI is skewed to the right, I also conduct Wilcoxon's rank-sum test (Wilcoxon 1945). Table 4.3 provides the statistics.

As we can see, among the Takeshita faction affiliates, those who joined the Hata faction in December 1992 had significantly more infrastructure-rich constituents than those who did not. These Hata faction members later formed the RP. The difference in the mean of the INI across these two groups was 0.3. Not surprisingly, the same pattern is apparent in the LDP's split of 1993: incumbents who were representing infrastructure-rich constituents were more likely to leave the party.

While the LDP was out of power between 1993 and 1994, the political environment was fluid. In this environment, legislators chose parties regardless of district characteristics. We can see that, as far as infrastructure conditions are concerned, LDP incumbents who left the party during this period were not significantly different from those who stayed.

Table 4.2 INI Ranking of LDP Incumbents (April 1993)

Rank	District	Name	Infrastructure-needs index (INI)	Defection (June 1993)
1	Hokkaido 3	Koko Sato	2.65	
2	Hyogo 5	Yoichi Tani	2.24	
3	Kagoshima 3	Susumu Nikaido	1.97	
4	Hokkaido 5	Tsutomu Takebe	1.97	
5	Hokkaido 5	Naoto Kitamura	1.96	√
6	Nagasaki 2	Akira Mitsutake	1.87	
7	Nagasaki 2	Kazuo Torashima	1.85	
8	Ehime 3	Isamu Imai	1.85	
9	Nagasaki 2	Genjiro Kaneko	1.81	
10	Wakayama 2	Chikara Higashi	1.81	
11	Ishikawa 2	Misoji Sakamoto	1.78	
12	Shimane	Hiroyuki Hosoda	1.76	
13	Shimane	Noboru Takeshita	1.76	
14	Ehime 3	Mamoru Nishida	1.73	
15	Wakayama 2	Toshihiro Nikai	1.73	√
16	Ishikawa2	Tsutomu Kawara	1.73	
17	Hokkaido 5	Muneo Suzuki	1.69	
18	Kumamoto 2	Hiroyuki Sonoda	1.67	√
19	Shimane	Hisaoki Kamei	1.65	
20	Tottori	Shigeru Ishiba	1.63	

As the LDP's electoral advantage was consolidated in the new SMD-based system, opposition-party incumbents who represented infrastructure-poor districts tended to revert to the LDP. Among former LDP incumbents who were in opposition as of the 1996 election, 21 returned to the LDP camp by the 2000 election. The difference of mean INI between those who returned to the LDP and those who did not was 0.39, a significant difference at the conventional 5 percent level.

Incumbents who participated in Kato's rebellion were not different from the remaining members of the party. The difference in group mean was only 0.04. In addition to the SMD rule, which made defections unlikely, Kato and his followers had another reason to stay. They were reluctant to leave the party because doing so would have jeopardized their reelection prospects. Since they were representing infrastructure-poor constituents, access to government resources was highly valuable. Although both Kato and Hata were regarded as reform-minded stars of the LDP in the 1980s, they were representing distinct types of constituents, as measured by INI. Their constituents' needs would decide the career paths these candidates pursued.

Table 4.3 Party Discipline and Infrastructure Needs (1992–2000)

Incidents (Date)	Group description (No. of observations)	Mean (Standard deviation)	Group description (No. of observations)	Mean (Standard deviation)	Difference of means (T-value)[a]	Wilcoxon Z-value[b]
Takeshita faction split (Dec. 1992)	Joined the Hata faction (35)	0.466 (0.542)	Stayed in the Takeshita faction (33)	0.768 (0.606)	-0.302** (-2.163)	-2.072**
LDP split (June 1993)	Left the LDP (47)	0.441 (0.558)	Stayed in the LDP (226)	0.653 (0.633)	-0.212** (-2.311)	-2.122**
LDP out of power (July 1993–June 1994)	Left the LDP (22)	0.641 (0.599)	Stayed in the LDP (205)	0.696 (0.623)	-0.055 (0.405)	0.363
Reversion to LDP (Oct. 1996–June 2000)	Stayed in the opposition[c] (21)	0.334 (0.483)	Ran from the LDP camp in 2000[c] (21)	0.725 (0.726)	-0.391** (-2.052)	-1.941*
Kato's rebellion (Nov. 2000)	Did not oppose the no-confidence motion (40)	0.597 (0.648)	Opposed the no-confidence motion (153)	0.554 (0.587)	0.044 (0.388)	0.060

Source: Author's calculation. See endnote 10–13 for definition and data sources.

Note: ** Significant at 5 percent. * Significant at 10 percent.

[a] The t-test is two sided, with an assumption that group variances are different.

[b] The null hypothesis is that the two groups are from the same distribution of the INI.

[c] Former LDP incumbents (as of April 1993) who ran from opposition parties in the 1996 election.

Conclusion

Scholars of Japanese politics observe that providing parochially targeted policy benefits was the key to the LDP's sustained electoral success. However, the empirical findings of this chapter imply that *limiting* the supply of local public goods was the secret behind the LDP's longevity. Despite the exceptional size of the public-works budget, the accumulation of local public goods has long been deficient in Japan (Flath 2000:220). The empirical results suggest that the expedited provision of physical, public capital was detrimental to the discipline of the party. Once infrastructure was built, voters lost incentive to vote for the party and incumbents were more likely to leave. Although *shinkansen* lines and highways were not necessarily the direct cause of partisan realignment, these key infrastructural elements affected legislators' choice of party affiliation.

The empirical results also provide a clue to understanding the electoral politics of the Koizumi reform. While Junichiro Koizumi was the prime minister, highway agencies were privatized and spending on infrastructure curtailed. Subsidies to local governments were reduced without entailing a significant shift of decision-making authority to lower layers of the government. As it privatized highways, the LDP could appeal to urban voters by making the party look like a spending cutter. When it delayed construction, it made the threat of voiding future policy benefits seem imminent to rural voters. For the latter, intermunicipal competition for policy favors grew more severe. Although this strategy could be sustainable only in the short run, we can see why the LDP performed electorally well in both rural and urban districts while Koizumi was in office. Voters' support for the DPJ, however, remained stable in rural prefectures along the *shinkansen* lines. Since the LDP coalition recently decided to lay additional *shinkansen* lines in the Kyushu and Hokuriku areas, the DPJ will perform better in these places.

Notes

[1] According to an opinion poll conducted by the *Asahi Shimbun* (April 28, 1993), the LDP's approval rate before the party's split was 35 percent. This and other newspaper articles cited in this chapter are available upon request from the author. The LDP had managed to return an electoral majority with lower preelection approval rates in the 1970s and the 1980s.

[2] The LDP was split again over the postal-reform bill in 2005, and the People's New Party was formed. Given the limitations of space, this chapter does not discuss this incident. See Imai (2009) for determinants of legislators' attitudes toward the postal-reform bill. His conclusion is that both electoral interests (that is, the number of post offices in the district) and legislators' preferences affected the fate of the bill.

[3] The list of the signatories is from Atarashii Nihon o Tsukuru Kokumin Kaigi (1992).

[4] According to the 1980 census, 15.8 percent of employment in Oyama was in the agricultural sector, compared to 5.6 percent in Ashikaga.

[5] The figures are based on the fiscal-strength index (*zaiseiryoku shisu*), which reflects the formulaic portion of subsidy calculation.

[6] *Deiri Tohoku*, October 22, 2002.

[7] *Deiri Tohoku*, October 29, 2001.

[8] Incidentally, Nagano and Yamagata, the home prefectures of Hata and Kato, respectively, competed for domestic nomination by the Japan Olympic Committee in 1986. Nagano defeated Yamagata and entered the international selection process.

[9] *Asahi Shimbun*, Yamagata edition, November 22, 2000.

[10] For simplicity, I define incumbent *i*'s hometown as the municipality that records the maximum value of the following quantity:

$$h = \sqrt{\frac{v_{ij}}{v_j} \cdot \frac{v_{ij}}{v_i}},$$

where v_{ij} is *i*'s votes in municipality *j*, v_j is the total number of valid votes in *j*, and v_i is *i*'s total votes in the district. Thus, *h* is the geometric mean of *i*'s vote share in *j* and the municipality *j*'s share in *i*'s votes.

[11] The location information for municipalities is based on the longitude and the latitude of city halls and town halls (Takeda 2003). I modified the data set to reflect the municipal borders as of January 1, 1998. Similarly, completion dates of bullet-train tracks are based on Kokudo Kotsusho Tetsudokyoku (2004). Location information for infrastructures analyzed in this chapter is based on a mapping Web site that uses the Tokyo data (http://map.goo.ne.jp/).

[12] In addition to data sources in footnote 11, completion dates for highway ramps and airports are adopted from Zenkoku Kosoku Doro Kensetsu Kyogikai (2004) and Nihon Koku Kyokai (2004), respectively.

[13] Incumbent *i*'s vote-weighted INI x_i is defined as:

$$\bar{x}_i = \sum_j \frac{v_{ij}}{v_i} x_j,$$

where v_i is *i*'s total vote, v_{ij} is *i*'s votes in *j*, and x_j is the municipal INI.

References

Asahi Shimbun. 2005. Asahi.com de miru 2005 sosennkyo no subete. [Everything about the 2005 general election as seen on Asahi.com]. Tokyo: *Asahi Shimbun*. (This and other newspaper articles cited in this chapter are available upon request from the author.)

Atarashii Nihon o Tsukuru Kokumin Kaigi [National Conference to Create a New Japan]. 1992. *Chusenkyokusei haishi sengen* [The resolution to ban medium-size districts]. Pamphlet. Tokyo: Atarashii Nihon o Tsukuru Kokumin Kaigi.

Cox, Gary W. 1990. Centripetal and centrifugal incentives in electoral systems. *American Journal of Political Science* 34 (4): 903–35.

Cox, Gary W., and Frances M. Rosenbluth. 1995. Anatomy of a split: The Liberal Democrats of Japan. *Electoral Studies* 14 (4): 355–76.

Flath, David. 2000. *The Japanese economy.* Oxford: Oxford Univ. Press.

Imai, Masami. 2009. Ideologies, vested interest groups, and postal saving privatization in Japan. *Public Choice* 138 (1–2): 137–60.

Kato, Junko. 1998. When the party breaks up: Exit and voice among Japanese legislators. *American Political Science Review* 92 (4): 857–70.

Kawasaki, Soichiro. 2007. *Senkyo kyoryoku to mutohaso.* [Electoral pacts and nonpartisan voters]. Tokyo: Nippon Hoso Shuppan Kyokai.

Mizusaki, Tokifumi. 1993. *Sosenkyo deta besu: JED-M deta (28–40)* [General election database: JED-M data for the 28th through 40th general elections]. Tokyo: LDB.

Murata, Osamu, and Tatsuya Morisawa. 2003. Bunya betsu shakai shihon no seisanryoku koka [Productivity effects of public capital by sector]. Discussion paper, Toyota Foundation.

Nihon Koku Kyokai [Japan Aeronautic Association]. 2004. *Koku tokei yoran* [Aeronautic statistics almanac]. Tokyo: Nihon Koku Kyokai.

Reed, Steven R., and Ethan Scheiner. 2003. Electoral incentives and policy preferences: Mixed motives behind party defections in Japan. *British Journal of Political Science* 33 (3): 469–90.

Scheiner, Ethan. 2005. *Democracy without competition in Japan: Opposition failure in a one-party dominant state.* New York: Cambridge Univ. Press.

Somusho Tokeikyoku [Ministry of Internal Affairs and Communications, Statistics Bureau]. 2007. *Heisei 17-nen kokusei chosa* [National census 2005]. Tokyo: Nihon Tokei Kyokai.

Sorifu Tokeikyoku [Prime Minister's Office, Statistics Bureau]. 1982. *Shoowa 55-nen kokusei chosa hokoku* [National census 1980]. Tokyo: Nihon Tokei Kyokai.

Takeda, Takashi. 2003. *Zenkoku todofuken shichoson ido keido ichi deta besu* [All-Japan municipality longitude and latitude database]. Tokyo: Vector.

Tatebayashi, Masahiko. 2004. *Giin kodo no seiji keizaigaku* [The logic of legislators' activities: Institutional analysis of LDP dominance in Japan]. Tokyo: Yuhikaku.

Weingast, Barry R., Kenneth A. Shepsle, and Christopher Johnsen. 1981. The political economy of benefits and costs: A neoclassical approach to distributive politics. *Journal of Political Economy* 89 (4): 642–64.

Wilcoxon, Frank. 1945. Individual comparisons by ranking methods. *Biometrics Bulletin* 1:80–83.

Zenkoku Kosoku Doro Kensetsu Kyogikai [National Association for the Promotion of Highway Construction]. 2004. *Kosokudoro binran* [Highway handbook]. Tokyo: Zenkoku Kosokudoro Kensetsu Kyogikai.

DECLINING ELECTORAL COMPETITIVENESS IN JAPAN: POSTREFORM TRENDS AND THEORETICAL PESSIMISM

Robert J. Weiner

The bubble of Japan's political expectations hasn't yet burst. True hopes for policy-driven elections, reduced campaign spending, and frequent alternation in government have cooled since the mid-1990s. But both popular and scholarly observers find that the recent electoral reform and realignment are indeed fulfilling their promise in at least one area: electoral competition. The Liberal Democratic Party's (LDP's) fall from government in 1993 led to a proliferation of new parties more willing and better able to join electoral combat than the previous leader of the anti-LDP opposition, the Social Democratic Party of Japan (SDPJ). These new opposition forces, together with a new Lower House mixed-member majoritarian (MMM) electoral system that combines both single-member-district (SMD) and proportional representation (PR) tiers, stood to encourage some cross between focused bipolar competition and reinvigorated multipolar competition. SMDs, in particular, were promoted by electoral-reform proponents in order to encourage balanced, two-party competition, and most scholarly observers agree that this is the result we should expect, at least eventually (Reed 1990, 2001, 2007; Niemi and Hsieh 2002).[1]

I argue that these conclusions are overly optimistic. Japan has not yet achieved the competitiveness that observers claim, and we have little reason to expect it to do so in the future. As most observers are well aware, the LDP (as of this writing) still dominates the Lower House, possible future victories by the Democratic Party of Japan (DPJ) notwithstanding (see, for example, Scheiner 2006). In this chapter, we examine a more overlooked but similarly important aspect of party competition, one whose prognosis is perhaps even more bleak: district-level competitiveness. As the familiar case of the United States shows, fierce two-party competition in a national legislature may coexist with lopsided and stagnant elections to the legislature—and the latter is no small problem. Legislators, whether they belong to the government or to the opposition, are chiefly kept accountable by electoral-district competition to maintain their seats. This is especially true in candidate-centered systems such as Japan's, where legislators enjoy some measure of genuine individual power and district contests are not simply proxies for choosing a prime minister.

Electoral reform has not energized district-level competition in Japan. If anything, it has made things worse. Electoral reform has helped a set of smaller opposition parties coalesce into a single, focal challenger to the LDP, but district-level competitiveness has only worsened. Competition in Japan's Lower House SMDs has been falling since 1993. Two-fifths of SMDs are already uncompetitive—characterized by a vote split at least as great as 60–40 (or the multicandidate equivalent)—and competition is declining in the most competitive districts.[2] While Japan may have two parties in each district (Reed 2007), it still lacks genuine two-party *competition* in each district.

And we should not be surprised. There was little reason for reformers and analysts to be optimistic in the first place. More than any other type of district, SMDs promote a lopsided balance of party power and uncompetitive elections. They are small enclaves—*not* microcosms of the polity at large—in which one party often enjoys unrepresentative strength. SMDs compound this distortion by conferring advantages upon incumbents and encouraging both voters and parties to abandon lost-cause candidacies. Reformers who cared to look would have seen this pattern in SMD elections outside Japan; indeed, they would have seen it in SMD elections *within* Japan, outside the Lower House. The general competition-reducing tendencies of SMDs, combined with the uncompetitive trends observed in Japan thus far, give us little reason to expect improvement in the future.

Competitiveness Is Low—and Getting Lower

We measure district competitiveness through a straightforward runner-up (RU) ratio—the ratio of the runner-up's vote to the winner's vote.[3] Any SMD's RU ratio must fall between 0 (an uncontested race) and 1 (an exact tie for the seat at stake), inclusive. The higher the RU ratio, the more competitive the district race.[4] We can also take a simpler, binary approach and call districts either competitive or uncompetitive according to whether their RU ratio clears some (necessarily arbitrary) threshold value. Following Niemi and Hsieh (2002), I set this threshold at 0.7. District-level races whose RU ratios exceed 0.7 can be called competitive, and others uncompetitive. That is, a race is competitive so long as the runner-up draws at least 70 percent of the winner's vote.[5] When there are only two entrants—as is the case in many U.S. elections—an RU ratio of 0.7 corresponds to a 59-41 vote percentage split. This is as weak as a runner-up can be without an SMD being considered uncompetitive or "safe" (for the front-runner) by conventional standards (Niemi and Hsieh 2002; Carty, Eagles, and Sayers 2003; Jacobson 2004).[6]

For reference's sake, before examining post-electoral-reform competitiveness patterns, we might briefly look at their prereform counterparts. Figure 5.1 contrasts RU ratios for prerealignment Lower House races from election years 1958 through 1990, which were held in single nontransferable vote (SNTV) districts, with RU ratios for Lower House SMDs over the four election years since electoral reform, 1996 through 2005.[7] The histogram (and others like it, shown later in this chapter) divides election results into eleven possible RU-ratio categories, with the degree of competitiveness increasing from left to right. Leftmost are uncontested races, whose RU ratio is exactly 0. All possible contested-election RU ratio values are then grouped into "deciles" according to their first significant digit: the "0.0s" include all districts with RU ratios above 0 but less than 0.1, the "0.1s" include all districts with RU ratios at or above 0.1 but less than 0.2—and so on, up to the most competitive districts, the "0.9s." Again, when we use an RU ratio of 0.7 as a (perhaps generous) cutoff point to establish a rough distinction between uncompetitive and competitive elections, all districts in the 0.7, 0.8, and 0.9 ranges qualify as competitive.

Figure 5.1 Lower House District Competitiveness (RU ratios)

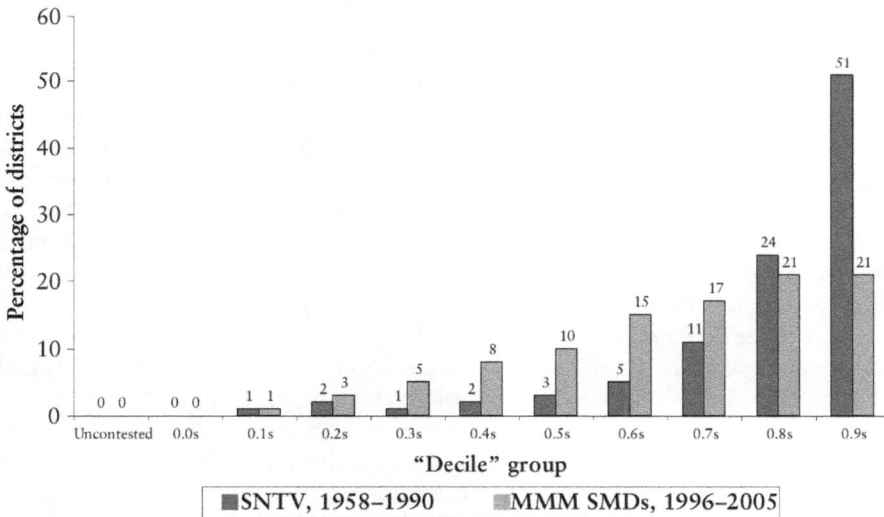

Prereform SNTV districts' high degree of competitiveness—by the RU ratio standard, at least—is immediately apparent.[8] Overall, 86 percent of all districts are competitive and have at least one runner-up gaining at least 70 percent as many votes as the lowest-finishing winner (indeed, in nearly one-third of all prereform districts, two or more runners-up ran this strong a race). The histogram slopes up to the right, with the number of elections in each category increasing (or at least staying the same) as we move from left to right, or from less competitive to more competitive deciles. In other words, higher-competitiveness deciles here always account for more districts than any less competitive decile (the only slight kink in this pattern comes at the 0.2s). Districts with RU ratios in the 0.9s alone make up more than half of all prereform Lower House contests. The average prereform RU ratio is 0.84.

Competitiveness in postreform SMDs is clearly much lower. Only 59 percent of postreform SMDs are competitive by the 0.7 RU-ratio standard, with RU ratios in the 0.7s, 0.8s, or 0.9s. Competitive Lower House districts are no longer much more common than uncompetitive ones. As with prereform districts, the histogram slopes up to the right, but the slope is much less steep. Districts with competitiveness levels in the 0.9s are no more common than those in the 0.8s, and neither is much more common than those in the 0.7s or 0.6s. The average postreform RU ratio is 0.72. In other words, *the average postreform district is just barely competitive by conventional standards.*

Over time, in the four elections held since electoral reform, the average RU has held steady at this barely competitive level from election year to election year (figure 5.2). Though 2000 was especially poor—with competitive runners-up in just over 50 percent of districts—this proportion has hovered at just over 60 percent in each of the other three election years. Similarly, each election year's overall average RU ratio has hovered near the 0.7 competitiveness threshold: 0.73 in the 1996 election, 0.69 in 2000, 0.73 in 2003, and 0.74 in 2005.

The fact that average competitiveness has remained stable since electoral reform need not imply that the number of districts with competitiveness gains has matched the number with declines, but this is roughly what we observe. Districts with competitiveness gains are about as numerous as those with declines. In 2000, 170 of 300 districts declined in competitiveness. In 2003 this number fell to 128 of 295 (ignoring 5 redistricted districts), but it rose to 152 of 300 in 2005.[9] Competitiveness changes also tend to be small. In each of these three years, between 38 and 44 percent of SMDs had RU-ratio changes of less than 0.1 (in either a more or less competitive direction), and between two-thirds and three-quarters of SMDs had an RU-ratio change of less than 0.2.

Exactly where these gains and declines are occurring, though, is of more concern. While overall competitiveness is not sharply declining, the number of *highly* competitive districts is. In figure 5.2, the year-to-year RU-ratio-distribution charts show that the modal-closeness decile has gradually shifted from right to left, or from more to less competitive: the modal-closeness decile was in the 0.9s in 1996 and 2000, the 0.8s in 2003, and the 0.7s in 2005.

Of course, if highly competitive districts are disappearing but overall average competitiveness is holding steady, there must be compensatory gains at the lower end of the RU spectrum. In effect, competitiveness since electoral reform is regressing to the mean. Very competitive districts do tend to grow less so, but very uncompetitive districts tend to grow somewhat more competitive. Closeness ratios tend to shift either down or up toward a value of roughly 0.7—that is, toward borderline competitiveness at best—and tend to do so gradually (as opposed to, say, jumping from 0.95 past 0.7 and down to 0.4, or from 0.4 past 0.7 and up to 0.95).

Figure 5.2 Percentages of Districts in Each Closeness Ratio Category, by Election Year

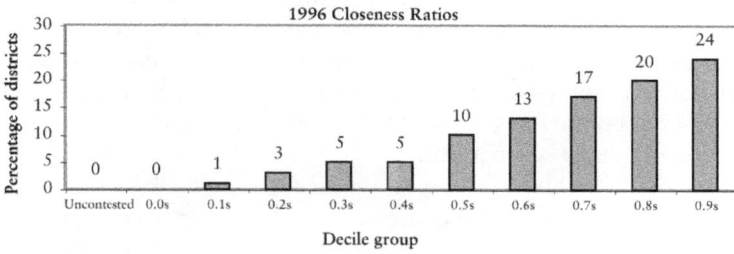

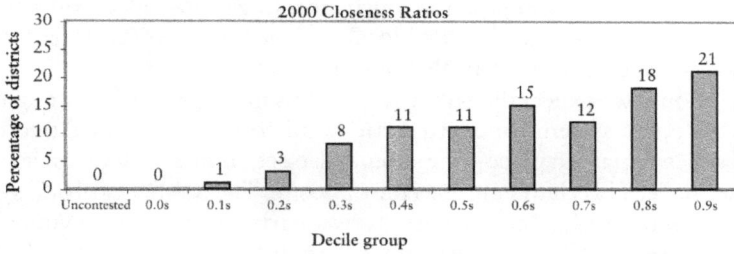

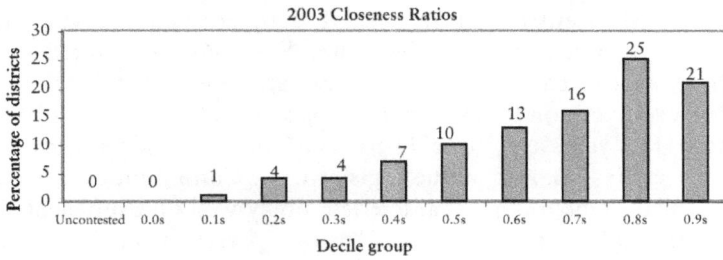

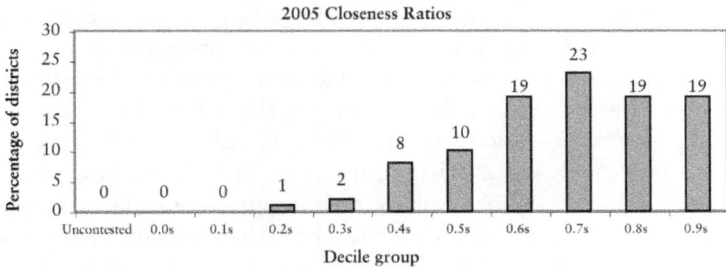

1996 Closeness Ratios

Decile group	Uncontested	0.0s	0.1s	0.2s	0.3s	0.4s	0.5s	0.6s	0.7s	0.8s	0.9s
Percentage of districts	0	0	1	3	5	5	10	13	17	20	24

2000 Closeness Ratios

Decile group	Uncontested	0.0s	0.1s	0.2s	0.3s	0.4s	0.5s	0.6s	0.7s	0.8s	0.9s
Percentage of districts	0	0	1	3	8	11	11	15	12	18	21

2003 Closeness Ratios

Decile group	Uncontested	0.0s	0.1s	0.2s	0.3s	0.4s	0.5s	0.6s	0.7s	0.8s	0.9s
Percentage of districts	0	0	1	4	4	7	10	13	16	25	21

2005 Closeness Ratios

Decile group	Uncontested	0.0s	0.1s	0.2s	0.3s	0.4s	0.5s	0.6s	0.7s	0.8s	0.9s
Percentage of districts	0	0	0	1	2	8	10	19	23	19	19

91

On balance, then, district competitiveness in post-electoral-reform Lower House elections has been discouraging. In each election, two-fifths or more of all districts have seen uncompetitive races. Average competitiveness has remained stable over time, but only at a barely competitive level. Lack of change in average competitiveness masks regression to this barely competitive mean, a trend that involves declines in the most competitive districts. These declines are counterbalanced only by competitiveness gains that push very uncompetitive districts toward borderline competitiveness, not by gains that push borderline districts toward sharp competition.

SMDs Are Uncompetitive Elsewhere

Why has the new MMM electoral system only made things worse? Or, putting aside this apples-and-oranges comparison to prereform SNTV, why is competition in postreform Japan so low in absolute terms? Electoral reform has helped give Japan two parties (or blocs), but genuine two-party *competition* has failed to take root in many electoral districts.

And should we expect the patterns seen thus far to persist? One might argue that as the party system begins to settle—and so long as Japan's two current major parties remain in place—we should also see competitive races develop on a broader scale. This chapter argues the opposite. The MMM electoral system is only four elections old, and the current two-party system is even younger. The future promises even less competition, especially when dealing with SMDs.

Japanese electoral reformers might have been sobered by a look at other, longer-lived SMD-centric polities, where competitiveness levels are even worse. The two-party systems of the United States and the United Kingdom, for example, were often touted as models by Japanese electoral reformers, but district-level competition in both countries is strikingly anemic. As Wildavsky (1959) noted fifty years ago, "local bi-partism" need not and has not developed where two parties coexist in the legislature. "Communities with a wide range of similar demographic characteristics may well find sufficient political expression through a single party. . . . The two-party systems in America and Great Britain are, for the most part, alliances of predominantly one-party areas." Although much of the lopsidedness observed in the United States can be blamed on redistricting plans that construct safe havens for incumbents of both major parties, Great Britain's district competitiveness is nearly as bad, even without partisan gerrymandering (but with a practice of shifting stronger incumbents to safer districts, thus cementing the safeness of those districts). Figure 5.3 presents RU-ratio distributions for House of Commons elections in Great Britain in 2001 and 2005 (and for New Zealand parliamentary SMDs in 2002 and 2005).[10] In Great Britain, only about one-third of all districts are competitive. Most common are districts where the strongest challenger draws only 40, 50, or 60 percent of the winner's vote. Minor realignments aside, this is a party system whose modern incarnation, by any measure, has had at least

Figure 5.3 Great Britain and New Zealand District Competitiveness (RU ratios)

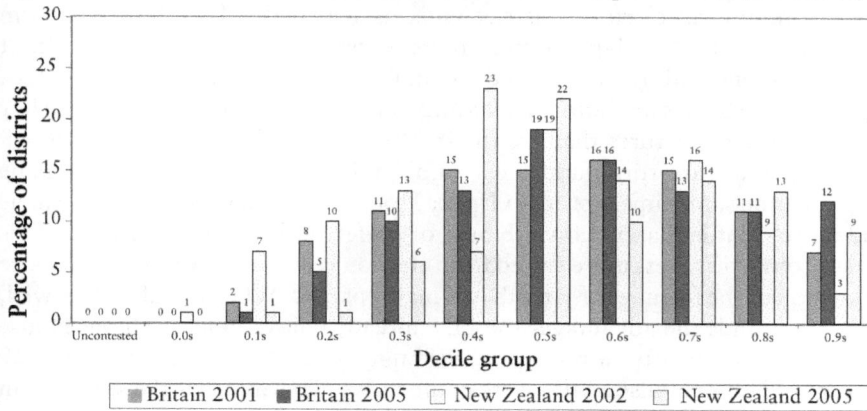

Percentage of districts

Decile group: Uncontested, 0.0s, 0.1s, 0.2s, 0.3s, 0.4s, 0.5s, 0.6s, 0.7s, 0.8s, 0.9s

■ Britain 2001 ■ Britain 2005 ☐ New Zealand 2002 ☐ New Zealand 2005

a half-century's worth of settling into its SMDs. It may well show us the future of SMD competitiveness in Japan.

Of course, both British and American elections are held exclusively in SMDs, while Japan's Lower House SMDs coexist with a smaller PR portion within an MMM system. Party and voter behavior may differ in SMDs when PR elections to the same parliamentary chamber are also held simultaneously, perhaps in a more competitive direction. But, as shown in figure 5.3, results in the SMDs of New Zealand's mixed-member proportional (MMP) system—where the proportional component is even stronger than Japan's—differ little from Britain's.[11]

More important, Japan has its own history of uncompetitive SMD races at other levels of election. Japanese prefectural assembly elections, like prereform Lower House elections, have always used SNTV districts of a variety of seat magnitudes—but unlike prereform Lower House districts, which mostly ranged in size from three to five seats, about two of every five prefectural SNTV districts are as small as one seat; and a one-seat SNTV district is simply a more precise name for an SMD.[12] Competitiveness has been abysmal in prefectural SMDs, both before and since party realignment began in the early 1990s. This is true even if we ignore rural areas, where SMD electorates tend to be the smallest (and where the LDP's strength is greatest, though prefectural races in rural SMDs tend to be intraconservative affairs in the first place), and we focus only on SMDs in regular cities (*shi*) and in government-designated large cities' wards (*ku*), respectively.[13] Between 1985 and 2005, only one-third of regular-city SMDs were competitive. The same was true even in large-city-ward SMDs, where we might expect incumbents to be least entrenched and partisan support to be the most balanced. Among regular-city SMDs, not only were two-thirds uncompetitive, but more than one-third were outright uncontested, with no one running against the eventual winner. Only 5 percent of large-city-ward SMDs went uncontested, but some 60 percent had RU ratios between 0.2 and 0.7—a tepid pattern of competition that matches that of Britain and New Zealand.

93

Japan's Upper House elections also involve SMDs. Each voter casts both a PR vote and an electoral district vote, as with MMM in the postreform Lower House. Each of Japan's prefectures serves as an SNTV electoral district of between one and five seats—and again, one-seat SNTV districts are SMDs. Upper House SMDs are homogenous and not particularly representative. They comprise the prefectures that are the smallest in population (in 2007, the 29 smallest), most are rural, and most rural prefectures are strongholds of the LDP.[14] At the same time, voting in Upper House elections is more party-centric and more volatile than in Lower House or prefectural assembly elections. This makes competitiveness more varied from election year to election year, and more a function of the fortunes of Japan's two major parties. When the LDP does well, this compounds the advantages the LDP already enjoys in most Upper House SMDs, and competitiveness drops accordingly. In 2001, for example, only 29 percent of Upper House SMDs were competitive. This matches the situation in Great Britain and New Zealand, as well as in Japanese prefectural SMDs (but without uncontested elections). When the LDP does poorly, though, its Upper House SMD advantage is neutralized, and competitive races are the result. In 2007, 76 percent of Upper House SMDs were competitive, and none had an RU ratio below 0.4—a competitiveness pattern approaching that seen under the prereform SNTV system. Thus, the Upper House does offer some hope that broadly competitive district elections might be possible in SMDs—but only among a subset of districts in which one party normally enjoys a marked advantage, and only given the double-edged sword of volatile, party-based voting, which makes *uncompetitive* elections just as likely.

SMD Dynamics Only Suppress Competition

District-level competition in Japanese Lower House SMDs is already low, but competitiveness in most other SMD-centric systems is even lower. As (or perhaps, if) Japan's two-party system grows more stable, should we expect more competition to develop? Or should we expect it to go the way of the Anglo-American two-party systems that electoral reformers sought to emulate? We argue that the latter is more likely.

SMDs Are Naturally Imbalanced

Dividing any large polity into smaller SMDs yields variation in each district's balance of party support. Of course, the degree to which districts differ will itself differ from country to country, with the exact pattern dependent on geography, demographics, and party divisions. A significant number of SMDs are likely to start out privileging one party or candidate, and are bound to be uncompetitive no matter what strategies political actors pursue. All else equal, population matters: the fewer residents in a district, the more likely it is that one partisan interest predominates, and the less likely it is that even one strong candidate can be found to stand for the disadvantaged party. This helps explain why prefectural assembly SMDs tend to be less competitive and often go uncontested. But the same principle applies to SMDs as compared to larger districts, whether multimember SNTV or PR: SMDs are by definition the least populous constituencies into which a given polity can be divided.

We might like to think that lopsided party strengths will tend to even out over time—that some basic political force will eventually fill an uncompetitive vacuum. Strong incumbents eventually fail to please all their varied supporters, underdogs adjust their policies to attract more supporters, stronger challengers are unearthed, voters build up sympathy for the underdog, and so on. All of these tendencies are plausible, and all occur from time to time. But none can be counted on as a regular equilibrating mechanism.

On the contrary, parties, candidates, and voters in SMDs in well-institutionalized, "settled" party systems tend to behave in ways that either have no clear effect on competitiveness or tend to decrease it (the one countervailing tendency is the generic regression-to-the-mean effect, in which the most competitive districts necessarily tend to become less so and the least competitive districts necessarily tend to become more so). Parties, candidates, and voters gradually turn competitive districts into uncompetitive ones and keep uncompetitive ones from moving in the opposite direction. In other words, an SMD's starting-point imbalance of party power is the best we can usually hope for. Strong runners-up eventually drop out, other potentially strong runners-up never run in the first place, and voters defect from challengers to incumbents. Partisan vote swings and realignments help entrench front-runners just as often as they lift up challengers. Of course, these processes are messy. Each election year, competitiveness will go up in some districts and down in others; or, on a broader scale, some election years will see most districts grow more competitive and other years will see most districts grow less so. Significant party realignments shake the system up and restart the process from scratch. But, on balance and over time, most dynamics point in only one direction.

Vote Swings Don't Cure Imbalances

We have no reason to expect shifts in voter support to tilt uncompetitive SMDs toward competitiveness any more than they might do the reverse. Take, for example, the 2003 and 2005 Lower House elections: 2005 saw a relatively large vote swing in the LDP's favor, yet numbers of competitive and uncompetitive districts, respectively, remained roughly the same as in 2003, as noted earlier. Also as noted, most SMDs see only small changes in competitiveness levels from election year to election year, especially when the slate of parties fielding candidates remains the same. At the same time, while a uniform nationwide swing by definition helps one party everywhere, the same does not hold for competitiveness. The LDP's favorable swing in 2005 helped LDP runners-up and thereby eliminated some uncompetitive DPJ victories, but it also helped

POLITICAL CHANGE IN JAPAN

LDP front-runners and thereby created more uncompetitive LDP victories. In the aggregate, the number of competitive races remained the same. Nationalized vote swings, even relatively large ones, did not alter basic party-strength imbalances; they only changed each party's ability to profit from those durable imbalances on the margins.

Similarly, even if the DPJ gradually increased its vote support over time—that is, even if the party were to enjoy not only a one-time vote swing but a more durable nationwide shift in its favor—our expectations would be the same. Such a shift would turn some contests in which the DPJ lagged uncompetitively behind the LDP into competitive ones, but it would also turn some contests in which the DPJ closely led an LDP challenger into uncompetitive ones. For overall competitiveness across all SMDs, the results are a wash, so long as both major parties normally win some portion of both competitive and uncompetitive districts. (If only one major party normally wins most competitive and/or uncompetitive districts, we have an uncompetitiveness problem of a different kind, as seen earlier in Upper House SMDs.)

For a nationalized (or at least multiple-district) vote swing to improve competitiveness in Japanese SMDs, it would need to take the form of a durable, nonpartisan, anti-incumbent shift. Competitiveness would also improve, of course, if each major party were to bolster its vote support in its weaker areas—the DPJ in rural regions, for example—but not in areas where the party is already strong. Both developments are theoretically possible, but we have no theoretical or historical reason to *expect* them to occur as party systems mature, as the examples of Britain and New Zealand illustrate.

Major Realignments Sustain Competition, but Are Nearly Complete

The greatest potential for significant jumps in competitiveness can be found in districts in the final throes of party realignment—for example, districts in which the DPJ finally runs a candidate after having ceded victory to the LDP for several elections, or districts where the LDP suffers splits and coordination breakdowns. Large jumps in competitiveness occur disproportionately in districts whose slate of major-party candidates is unsettled and undergoes change. We can define such "major-party-slate-change districts" as those with new entry or exit by the LDP, DPJ, Liberals, Kokumin Shinto—or "postal rebel" independents—or with a change in the number of LDP or DPJ candidates as a result of intraparty splits or their resolution. Such changes in a district's slate of parties—as opposed to simple vote transfers among, say, a consistent slate of LDP, DPJ, and Japan Communist Party (JCP) candidates—tend to produce the greatest competitiveness-level swings. In 2003 major-party-slate-change districts accounted for 44 percent of all SMDs—but 52 percent of those whose RU ratios dropped by 0.2 or more, and 64 percent of those whose RU ratios increased by 0.2 or more. In 2005 major-party-slate-change districts accounted

96

for 33 percent of SMDs, and only 30 percent of those SMDs whose RU ratios fell by 0.2 or more—but 53 percent of those whose RU ratio improved by 0.2 or more.

This implies a decline in overall competitiveness over time. Absent a new bout of fundamental party realignment, unstable, competition-inducing districts will gradually disappear and be replaced by "normal" SMDs—that is, SMDs in which party realignment has largely run its course, where parties have settled on a single candidate, and no redistricting has occurred. Again, major-party-slate-change districts accounted for 44 percent of all SMDs in 2003 and 33 percent in 2005. By the election of 2005, only 20 percent of SMDs (or 61 in all) remained unsettled, with good potential to become major-party-slate-change districts in the next general election: 41 districts with a conservative postal reform maverick, 11 in which the LDP suffered a schism and ran more than one candidate, 4 in which the DPJ ran no candidate, and 5 with some combination of these nonstandard features. By the next election, some of these postal reform and intra-LDP schisms are likely to have been resolved. Meanwhile, by 2005, 214 SMDs had settled into the current party system's "standard" party slate: one LDP candidate and one DPJ candidate, with an additional JCP candidate in most cases. Twenty-five more districts featured this partisan lineup plus one SDPJ candidate. Again, absent significant realignment, the only possible sources of future increases in competitiveness in these 239 settled districts are voting-behavior shifts or further candidate-slate shifts. But neither is a reliable source of competitive energy. If anything, their overall effect over time should be to drag competitiveness even lower.

Minor Realignments Will Be Few and Ineffective

One possible but ultimately unpromising mechanism through which vote shifts might improve SMD competitiveness is strategic voting (see, for example, Cox 1997). In SMDs, strategic voting occurs when two candidates are clearly the only ones viable in a district, with voters able to perceive a gap between expected vote support for them and all other candidates. To avoid "wasting" their vote, supporters of candidates expected to finish in third place or lower may strategically abandon their candidates for whichever of the top two candidates they most prefer. Of course, in districts where even the second-strongest candidate is seen to have no chance, voters who support that candidate must resign themselves to casting a "wasted" vote as well—but since these voters are no better able to affect the outcome of the race by deserting their hopeless runner-up, they have no incentive to do so.

Strategic voting constitutes a kind of minor realignment within individual districts even without any candidate-slate changes. Voters collectively shift the balance of party power within given SMDs, punishing weak entrants and rewarding strong ones. Under some conditions, this might gradually boost competitiveness over time, but it offers little hope of doing so in Japan. First, most strategic voting that is possible under the current party system has already occurred. Most candidates in third place or lower have already disappeared from Japan's SMDs: as noted earlier, by 2005 most districts were contested by one LDP candidate, one DPJ candidate, and one JCP candidate. The only remaining voters with any incentive to abandon their candidates support the JCP or the occasional SDPJ or minor LDP spin-off party candidate—and if these voters have not already strategically abandoned their candidates, they are unlikely to do so in the future.

Second, strategic voting improves competitiveness only if the votes of abandoned candidates regularly flow to the *weaker* of the two top candidates. This is something that neither strategic voting theory (Cox 1997) nor Japanese voting behavior guarantees. Socialist and anti-LDP conservative voters are as open to switching to the LDP as they are to the DPJ. And even if both they and JCP supporters were to redistribute all their votes to, say, the DPJ, this would strengthen both DPJ underdogs and DPJ front-runners. If anything, the one voting-behavior shift we *can* expect to affect competitiveness uniformly across all districts is the tendency for voters in SMDs to gravitate *non*strategically toward incumbents—especially in a political environment as clientelist and candidate-centered as Japan's (see, for example, Scheiner 2006).

A more clear form of minor realignment is further change in the slate of minor candidates and parties running in a given SMD, which offers more potential to shake up competition patterns than voter-driven changes do. Candidate-slate changes might reflect party-system-wide realignments that produce entirely new parties or drive out existing ones, thus adding or removing candidates in all or many districts at once (or causing an existing candidate to switch party labels). Such changes might also reflect an existing party's strategic decision to run candidates in several districts that it had previously ignored as unpromising or to abandon districts that are no longer considered promising. In any given district, such changes occur only intermittently, but they are likely to produce vote-swing changes more volatile than the election-to-election shifts that occur when candidate slates remain constant. In turn, candidate-slate changes are more likely to spark competitiveness changes as well. As with vote shifts, though, the *direction* of competitiveness change promised by candidate-slate changes is either indeterminate or negative. We have no reason to expect these to make Japan's SMDs any more competitive than they are now.

The main systematic component of party-slate change is strategic candidate entry. Strategic entry—a general term covering both strategic entry by new candidates and strategic *exits* by previous candidates—is largely analogous to strategic voting. Its main effect on competitiveness, and on party-system development more broadly, comes when a candidate or party expects to lose in a district and strategically decides *not* to contest it, rather than simply running without any concern for such calculations.[15] As with strategic voting, the effects of strategic entry are often indeterminate. But they carry competition-suppressing potential as well.

We can imagine that a strategic party's (or candidate's) decision whether or not to enter is based on the standard decision-theoretic $pb-c$ expression, where p is the probability of winning a seat, b is the benefits to be gained from winning, and c is a positive cost of entry smaller than b. Entry promises a payoff of $pb-c$, while nonentry promises a payoff of zero. Strategic parties will enter a district race, then, when the likelihood of winning and/or the benefits to be gained from winning outweigh the various costs of running a campaign. When the costs are too great, strategic parties concede the district; when the costs are too great in *all* districts, strategic parties fold. Again, strategic entry is largely analogous to strategic voting: strategic voters abandon candidates who are clearly destined to finish in third place or lower; strategic parties beat them to the punch by abandoning candidacies that are clearly destined to finish in third place or lower.

Japan's version of MMM was thought to dull parties' strategic exit incentives. Simultaneous PR elections could lead parties to sponsor SMD candidacies in an attempt to raise the party's profile and increase its PR vote, even in SMDs that are themselves unwinnable (Cox and Schoppa 2002). The new system also allows SMD candidates to run simultaneously on a PR list (Suzuki 1999; McKean and Scheiner 2000), with their performance in the SMD race directly affecting their PR fortunes by breaking ties with other PR party candidates on the list ranked at the same position. Here again, for some of these dual candidates, running in an SMD may be worthwhile even if the district seems unwinnable.

In fact, Japan's electoral environment makes strategic exit relatively attractive and common, PR "contamination effects" under postreform MMM notwithstanding. Elections are notoriously costly—that is, the c term in $pb-c$ may often be high enough to discourage campaigns. Just as important, election outcomes are comparatively predictable, thanks to incumbency advantages, single-party dominance, and candidate-centered voting. SMDs themselves contribute to this: compared to larger-magnitude districts such as those used in the prereform SNTV system, SMDs require candidates to exceed a higher vote-percentage threshold to win a seat, and they tend to be contested by fewer candidates in smaller geographical areas (Cox 1997 and Reed forthcoming). Potential challengers are better able to forecast their eventual defeat—and as defeat grows more certain, the p term in $pb-c$ approaches zero.

In part as a result, some smaller Japanese parties practiced strategic withdrawals even in prereform multimember districts (MMDs)—something rarely seen among small parties even in SMD-centric countries outside Japan. The JCP, which regularly ran candidates in every national election available, was the exception here. The Clean Government Party (CGP), in contrast, was perhaps exceptional in the opposite direction: ruthlessly strategic under the SNTV system, it cautiously rationed its candidacies and rarely fought a losing battle. But, if anything, prerealignment Japanese parties and candidates acted more like the CGP than like the JCP. In SNTV Lower House elections, the only parties other than the JCP that bothered to stand weak candidates were the Democratic

Socialist Party (DSP), many of whose efforts were concentrated in a few early election years, and the New Liberal Club (NLC), whose electoral activity was geographically limited and short-lived. Crypto-LDP independents accounted for only about as many weak losers as the DSP, and in SMDs they were gradually (if not completely) crowded out by official LDP endorsees. Similarly, under MMM in the prereform Upper House, parties other than the LDP, Socialists, and JCP consistently declined to contest SMDs.[16]

This practice of strategic withdrawal has, in turn, continued under postreform SMDs, despite the extra entry incentives that the MMM system provides. Most small parties do one of several things: ignore most SMDs (in the case of the Socialists and the anti-postal-reform People's New Party), form electoral coalitions with larger parties that constitute mergers for electoral purposes (for example, the CGP with the LDP), or abandon the party system through absorption by larger parties (in the case of most other small parties). Candidacies outside the LDP (and its electoral coalition partners), the DPJ, and the JCP are largely limited to a dwindling number of Socialists, major parties' dissidents and splinters, and very weak genuine independents. This may seem unremarkable given Japanese parties' history of strategic withdrawals, but note again the contrast with other countries using pure-SMD and SMD-centric mixed-member electoral systems, whose minor parties often contest all district elections. The gravitational pull of Duverger's Law is especially strong in Japan.[17]

As with strategic voting, the potential that strategic withdrawals by parties other than the top two will improve competitiveness is small. First, again, the votes of small parties that quit a district may be redistributed to either the front-runners or a challenger—and to either the LDP or the DPJ. There is no reason to always expect small parties to gang up on larger ones in some minimal-winning coalition, or in imitation of prereform opposition alliances against the LDP. Thus far, party realignment has not only seen many smaller political forces coalesce into the current incarnation of the DPJ, but it has also seen the LDP camp benefit from the significant addition of the CGP and the lesser addition of the short-lived Conservative Party. If anything, these strategic withdrawals and subsequent mergers and coalitions have coincided with a *decline* in competitiveness since reform.

Second, as with strategic voting, parties other than the top two have done most of their strategic withdrawing already. Any competitiveness improvement to be gained from strategic withdrawals has mostly been registered.[18]

Perhaps the largest pool of voters that might eventually be liberated through strategic withdrawals belongs to the JCP. The JCP is not immune to strategic calculation. The party withdrew from a small portion of Lower House districts (25 of 300) for the first time in 2005, and as of this writing is exploring further withdrawals for future elections. And in local-level multiseat districts where the JCP's vote-support base is large enough for it to gain more than one seat, the party often expertly runs an optimum number of candidates and engineers any necessary division of bailiwicks. Elections to the special-ward (*tokubetsu ku*) assemblies of Tokyo, conducted in at-large districts with several dozen seats, are one striking example. In this respect, the JCP resembles the CGP: both boast well-organized memberships that allow for precise vote forecasting and coordination of multiple candidacies within a district. But most JCP candidates draw only small percentages of the vote—the party's median SMD vote share in 2005 was 7 percent—and the districts from which the party is considering retiring are precisely those in which it performs *most* poorly. And since many of these are rural districts, the likely effect on competitiveness would only be to turn uncompetitive districts into slightly less uncompetitive ones.

The potential for strategic withdrawal by the SDPJ to improve future competitiveness is even more limited. The party had already abandoned all but 38 SMDs by 2005. In more than half of the remaining 38, its candidate received less than 10 percent of the SMD vote—and, as noted earlier, its supporters in the mostly rural SMDs it contests might well shift their support to the LDP and the DPJ in equal numbers. The LDP independents who quit the party in 2005 over postal reform, on the other hand, by splitting the LDP conservative vote in a number of LDP-heavy districts, provided an injection of competitiveness that will probably fade as the more successful among them gradually but inevitably return to the LDP.

The one way in which strategic entry holds the clear, systematic potential to change the competitiveness of Japanese elections is where it fundamentally differs from strategic voting: strategic withdrawal may be practiced not only by the minor candidates in a district but also by the weaker of the two major ones. That is, while strategic-entry decisions by parties and candidates are most often seen as an engine of minor-party realignment, they may provoke major-party slate change as well. But we have seen no evidence of this in Japan thus far—and to the extent we do observe it in the future, it only stands to *worsen* competitiveness.

As noted earlier, when one of the two major parties' candidates is clearly destined to lose, strategic voters have no particular incentive to abandon that candidate, because doing so has no effect on the outcome of the election. But the weak major-party candidates themselves, as well as their parties, do have an incentive to quit the race. Their strategy is the same as that of smaller parties: running a hopeless campaign may not be worth the expense it entails, and abandoning lost-cause districts frees resources that might be used more efficiently elsewhere. When the weaker of the two major-party candidates withdraws, this *necessarily* lowers competitiveness. The potential runner-up's withdrawal turns what might have been a weakly competitive race, or perhaps a borderline uncompetitive one, into an extremely uncompetitive race, or perhaps an entirely uncontested one. This is the type of strategic withdrawal that produces large proportions of uncontested races in Japan's prefectural SMDs, in which no second major-party (or second independent) challenger finds it worthwhile to mount a campaign against the eventual winner. It is worth noting that in both rural and regular-city prefectural elections, uncontested races are two to five times more common in SMDs than they are in three-to-five-seat SNTV districts such as those used in the prereform Lower House.

Might either the LDP or the DPJ eventually begin to withdraw its weaker candidates from Lower House SMDs? Thus far, neither has done so. The DPJ, as it has matured, has gradually increased its district coverage. By 2005 it ran candidates in 291 of 300 SMDs, including many it must have expected to lose. The LDP and its electoral coalition partners fielded an *over*-full slate of candidates in 2005—at least one in every SMD, and 314 in all, once we include unendorsed but LDP-affiliated independents. But a shift to a more strategic approach is not unthinkable, for the DPJ in particular. The DPJ is a young party. It is unclear whether its current pattern reflects the early stages of a long-term commitment to run candidates everywhere or a preliminary stage of "testing the electoral waters," after which the party will begin to abandon weaker districts (or after which its stronger, "quality" candidates will begin to abandon such districts and cede them to weaker challengers). This is the long-established practice of major parties in the United States: in Massachusetts, for example, the Republicans often bypass half of all Congressional races. And the DPJ itself already takes this strategic approach at the prefectural level. In prefectural assembly elections in 2006 and 2007 (held in all but two prefectures), the DPJ fielded candidates in only 14 percent of SMDs, less than half of which were rural. This compares to 74 percent on the LDP's part. Indeed, in those years the DPJ accounted for only 13 percent of all prefectural candidates across all districts, both SMDs and MMDs. Perhaps the DPJ is strategically forgoing local races precisely in order to save its resources for national contests, but its local strategies might also be setting a precedent for later Lower House selectiveness as well. Either way, any step toward greater willingness to strategically withdraw weak candidates on either major party's part would only decrease competitiveness to a new low in the future.

Conclusion

In 1993 many observers expected postreform Lower House SMDs to improve electoral competitiveness in Japan. But whether the chaos of party realignment and the effects of electoral reform were enough to rekindle electoral competition in Japan should have been a toss-up at best. And as it turns out, they weren't. Competitiveness in Japan's SMDs has been low since electoral reform and is only falling.

As in the United States and Great Britain, and contrary to reform-era optimism, SMDs do little to produce vibrant two-party competition at the district level. In fact, they do quite the opposite. Cutting a country into small districts produces uncompetitive balances of power. Compounding this, a number of phenomena found in established party systems and especially in SMDs— incumbency advantages and strategic district withdrawals, in particular—tend only to depress competition over time. They gradually but predictably turn competitive districts into uncompetitive ones and keep uncompetitive districts uncompetitive. Nothing predictably does the reverse. Other phenomena that one might expect to provoke competition—party realignments, nationalized vote swings, strategic voting—actually have either indeterminate or intermittent and short-lived effects. On balance, then, SMD competitiveness tends only to decline as party systems mature. We can already see this in older SMD-centric systems elsewhere, and we should expect the same in Japan.

Notes

[1] These observers have acknowledged the persistence of uncompetitive elections (Reed 2001, 321; Niemi and Hsieh 2002, 88–89) but continue to maintain that a two-party result should ultimately emerge in equilibrium. For a dissenting view, see Weiner (2003).

[2] Analysis of Lower House elections is based on raw data collected by Matthew Carlson, Ross Schaap, and the author for the 2003 election; and on data collected and generously provided by Steven R. Reed and Ethan Scheiner for the 1996 and 2000 elections and by Scheiner for the 2005 election.

[3] I use the term "RU ratio" to highlight the analogy to Gary W. Cox's (1997) "SF ratio," the ratio of the *second* runner-up's vote to the *first* runner-up's vote. Some call this ratio the *closeness ratio,* especially in reference to SMDs (Weiner 2008). In Japanese Lower House elections, the RU ratio is also equivalent to the first runner-up's *sekihairitsu*, the quantity used to break ties among copartisans who are made to share the same ranking on a regional PR list and simultaneously run in SMDs—and who lose in those SMDs.

[4] I pointedly avoid measures based on "effective" numbers of electoral candidates (the most common such measure, developed by Marku Laakso and Rein Taagepera [1979], is the Hirschman-Herfindahl index of industrial concentration as applied to candidates instead of firms). Larger numbers of effective candidates (or parties) are often taken to indicate greater district competitiveness (Strom 1989, Wilkinson 2004), but effective numbers are not well suited to measure this. They assess the total strength of the runner-up field but cannot distinguish between one strong runner-up and several weak ones (Niemi and Hsieh 2002; see also Reed forthcoming).

[5] We might create a separate "hypercompetitive" category for races in which *more* than one eventual loser gains at least 0.7 of the winner's vote. But such races are not common in Japan; there were twenty-eight in 1996, sixteen in 2000, four in 2003, and six in 2005, out of three hundred district races each election year.

[6] Steven R. Reed (forthcoming) argues that a proper measure of competitiveness should account not only for closeness in the immediate election, but also for vote volatility. If voting patterns in a district are volatile, then even a runner-up with much less than 0.7 of the winner's vote might stand a chance of winning next time. But the 0.7 RU-ratio threshold seems consistent with this

alternative approach. In election years 2000, 2003, and 2005, in the 477 cases in which runners-up in previous election years ran again (in the same district), almost none who had previously fallen short of 0.7 of the winner's vote went on to win in their next attempts. Nearly all previous-election runners-up who did succeed in their next attempts had previously exceeded 0.7; on average, they had gained 0.89 of the winner's vote. Results based on a threshold as low as 0.7 thus may *overstate* competitiveness in Japan, if anything.

[7] This excludes the unusually volatile SNTV elections predating the formation of the LDP and institutionalization of the "1955 system" parties, as well as the 1993 election triggered by the split of the LDP. Since volatility usually implies competition, this likely understates competitiveness across the entire prereform period—and thus understates, if anything, the drop in competitiveness seen since electoral reform. Analysis of pre-1993 Lower House election results is based on raw data drawn from the Lijphart Election Archive (http://ssdc.ucsd.edu/lij) data set, downloaded in January 1996, with slight subsequent corrections by the author.

[8] The RU measure looks only at gaps between the highest loser and the lowest winner, and ignores gaps among winners and among losers. Reed and Shimizu (chapter 2, this volume) rightly propose a more subtle measure of closeness than this for MMDs.

[9] Here and in all analyses addressing year-to-year change, cases from 1996 are omitted, since they were the first held under MMM.

[10] British election analysis is based on data collected by Pippa Norris and was downloaded from http://ksghome.harvard.edu/~pnorris/Data/Data.htm, version 1.3, released June 13, 2005.

[11] Analysis of New Zealand elections is based on raw data collected by the New Zealand Ministry of Justice's Chief Electoral Office and downloaded March 10, 2008, from http://www.electionresults.govt.nz.

[12] Analysis of Japanese prefectural elections is based on raw data drawn from the Japanese Local Democracy Project data set, which was constructed from official prefectural government election reports and newspaper reports by Yusaku Horiuchi, Ryouta Natori, Jun Saito, Ethan Scheiner, and the author.

[13] A small number of districts in the regular-city category also encompass some rural towns (*machi*) or villages (*mura*), but rural voters are always vastly outnumbered in these.

[14] Analysis of Upper House elections is based on raw data drawn from Saitou (2003) for the 2001 election, and from raw data collected from http://www.jiji.com and generously provided by Ko Maeda for the 2007 election.

[15] Strategic entry usually implies that parties or candidates consider only the likelihood of their winning the *immediate* district election and the costs and benefits involved. Of course, even unpromising and/or highly costly campaigns could be justified for more forward-looking reasons that are "strategic" in an everyday sense, even if they fall outside the narrower definition of "strategic" used here.

[16] Note that any candidates who *do* enter SMDs solely with PR considerations in mind are themselves uncompetitive by definition, since the MMM's "contamination" effect is to encourage SMD entry by parties that fully expect to lose the SMD race and would otherwise abstain or withdraw. Entry by such candidates would increase competitiveness only to the extent that they draw votes away from the district front-runner.

[17] The term is borrowed from Cox and Schoppa (2002).

[18] The same holds true for analogous candidate-slate changes in the other direction, as when the LDP stands a candidate in one of the few SMDs it had previously ignored.

References

Carty, R. Kenneth, D. Munroe Eagles, and Anthony Sayers. 2003. Candidates and local campaigns: Are there just four Canadian types? *Party Politics* 9 (5): 619–36.

Cox, Gary W. 1997. *Making votes count: Strategic coordination in the world's electoral systems.* Cambridge: Cambridge Univ. Press.

Cox, Karen, and Leonard J. Schoppa. 2002. Interaction effects in mixed-member electoral systems: Theory and evidence from Germany, Japan, and Italy. *Comparative Political Studies* 35 (9): 1027–53.

Jacobson, Gary C. 2004. *The politics of congressional elections.* 6th ed. New York: Pearson/Longman.

Laakso, Marku, and Rein Taagepera. 1979. Effective number of parties: A measure with application to west Europe. *Comparative Political Studies* 12 (1): 3–27.

McKean, Margaret, and Ethan Scheiner. 2000. Japan's new electoral system: *La plus ça change* . . . *Electoral Studies* 19 (4): 447–77.

Niemi, Richard G., and John Fuh-sheng Hsieh. 2002. Counting candidates: An alternative to the effective N (with an application to the $M+1$ rule in Japan). *Party Politics* 8 (1): 75–99.

Reed, Steven R. 1990. Structure and behaviour: Extending Duverger's law to the Japanese case. *British Journal of Political Science* 20 (3): 335–56.

———. 2001. Duverger's Law is working in Italy. *Comparative Political Studies* 34 (3): 312–27.

———. 2007. Duverger's Law is working in Japan. *Electoral Studies* 22: 96–106.

———. Forthcoming. Party strategy or candidate strategy: How does the LDP run the right number of candidates in Japan's multi-member districts? *Party Politics.*

Saitou, Kyouko, ed. 2003. *Seikan youran* 21 (Spring), Tokyo: Seisaku Jiho I.P.

Scheiner, Ethan. 2006. *Democracy without competition in Japan: Opposition failure in a one-party dominant state.* New York: Cambridge Univ. Press.

Strom, Kaare. 1989. Inter-party competition in advanced democracies. *Journal of Theoretical Politics* 1 (3): 277–300.

Suzuki, Motoshi. 1999. Strategic parties and strategic voters under Japan's new electoral law. Paper presented at the annual meeting of the Japan Election Studies Association, Akita, Japan.

Weiner, Robert J. 2003. Anti-competition in competitive party systems. PhD dissertation, Univ. of California at Berkeley.

———. 2008. Prefectural politics: Party and electoral stagnation. In *Democratic reform in Japan: Assessing the impact*, ed. Sherry L. Martin and Gill Steel, 151–73. Boulder, CO: Lynne Rienner Publishers.

Wildavsky, Aaron. 1959. A methodological critique of Duverger's political parties. *Journal of Politics* 21 (2): 303–18.

Wilkinson, Steven. 2004. *Votes and violence: Electoral competition and ethnic riots in India.* Cambridge: Cambridge Univ. Press.

Koizumi

How Koizumi Won

Chao-Chi Lin[1]

In April 2001, Junichiro Koizumi won the Liberal Democratic Party (LDP) presidency and so became Japan's prime minister. That the LDP picked him for president is puzzling. Koizumi held policy positions that diverged from the party mainstream. For example, he advocated postal privatization, which had little support in the LDP, and hoped to transform the party by dismantling factions. One would expect a party president to share the party's values, whether in matters of substantive policy or party management. Instead, intense conflict between Koizumi and the party mainstream became a hallmark of the Koizumi cabinet. Why and how was a maverick like Koizumi elected party president in the first place?

Not only did Koizumi stray from the party mainstream, but he lacked the support of a large faction. Before his election, factional support had determined the LDP presidency. Winners were supported by a majority of Diet members only after strategically building a coalition of factions. From the 1970s, nobody would have dreamed of becoming prime minister without the support of the largest faction. Yet, in 2001, Koizumi defeated that faction's favored candidate, Ryutaro Hashimoto, and won the LDP presidency.

How did Koizumi win? It is widely agreed that he ascended to the post as a direct result of changes to the LDP's presidential electoral rules. To dispel its image as a haven of backroom politics and improve the party's popularity, in 2001 the LDP decided to give each prefectural chapter three votes rather than one, as was traditionally the case. Most of the prefectural chapters held primaries to decide how the three votes would be allocated to candidates. This allowed Koizumi to run a public-opinion campaign. In the end, his landslide victory at the local level left Diet members no choice but to support him. In retrospect, the change from one to three local votes and the establishment of primaries were key to Koizumi's victory.

Why did these changes occur? Scholars have emphasized the role of junior members (Shinoda 2003) and several local chapters (Otake 2003). It is true that, without their demands, the party presidential rules would not have been revised. But any change related to the LDP's status quo requires the consensus of powerful LDP leaders, especially those from the largest faction. Even though the party mainstream might not have actively wanted to change the rules, the decision to give three votes to local chapters was made by party executives. In general, dominant actors change rules only when they believe such change will be in their interests. Given the largest faction's power, it should have been able to structure the rules for its own benefit. But the expected Hashimoto victory did not occur. Why and how did party leaders miscalculate?

This chapter examines the 2001 changes in the LDP's presidential electoral rules; in particular, it grapples with the question of why the LDP mainstream agreed to such changes. The following section identifies the characteristics of past LDP presidential elections, because the significance of Koizumi's rise cannot be understood without an understanding of past political trends. This is followed by an analysis of why and how LDP heavyweights decided to revise party electoral rules. I then analyze why the expected Hashimoto victory did not materialize. And, finally, I connect Koizumi's victory to broader trends in Japanese politics.

Factions and the Selection of LDP Presidents

The LDP dominated Japanese politics from its establishment in 1955 until 1993. Then, after a short stint in the minority, it regained its ruling status by joining forces with coalition partners in 1995. All LDP presidents, except Yohei Kono,[2] automatically became Japan's prime minister. According to Article 6 of the LDP Constitution, party leaders shall be elected by the party convention, consisting of all Diet members of the two houses and delegates from each prefectural chapter. Usually, LDP members have accounted for 300–400 Diet member votes. The 47 prefectural delegate votes,[3] which account for only a minority, have meant that the choice of party president is mainly in the hands of Diet members. Since LDP Diet members have been divided by factions since the LDP's inception, faction leaders naturally have incentives to mobilize votes, and LDP presidential elections have been run along factional lines.[4]

According to party rules, a majority of votes is needed to win the presidency. Faction leaders may have wanted to recruit as many followers as possible, but prior to the electoral reform of 1995, the single nontransferable vote (SNTV) limited the size of any one faction and none could obtain a majority (Kohno 1997). Thus, cooperating with other factions to build a coalition was vital. In fact, based on past election outcomes, an alliance of at least three factions was needed to obtain a majority and win the presidency (Hayao 1993).

How was a coalition of factions formed? In the years when there was no viable alternative to the LDP, the selection of party leadership was not expected to have a strong impact on elections. Since the LDP president automatically became the prime minister, factions fought hard for the right to form a government. Factional interests—not policy positions or an individual politician's popularity—decided party leaders.[5] Assuming that faction members would vote collectively,[6] leaders bargained in light of their known bloc of votes. Coalition deals were based mainly on promises of cabinet and party posts that faction members would receive, with the faction of the winning coalition—or the party mainstream—receiving the most important posts. Obviously, this favored a type of party leader who was able to build up the size of his or her faction and make deals with others. Under these circumstances, mavericks were very unlikely to reach the top.

Despite the rise and fall of other factions, the largest faction has retained its status since the 1960s. By the late 1970s, it led all others by a significant margin. After Eisaku Sato (1964–1972), the largest faction was successively led by Kakuei Tanaka and Noboru Takeshita. Both Tanaka and Takeshita became prime ministers, and both resigned because of scandals. After they resigned, the faction did not field a presidential candidate but still played a crucial role. As mentioned earlier, to win the presidency, a coalition of at least three factions is generally needed to obtain a majority. Given the size of the largest faction, a prospective leader with the support of that faction would need only to find another faction to secure a comfortable majority. In turn, if the largest faction decides to withdraw its support, this spells the end of the cabinet; establishing an alternative coalition would be difficult, if not impossible.[7] Although some leaders have tried to challenge the largest faction, it has been difficult to establish a winning coalition without it. In fact, since the late 1970s, when Masayoshi Ohira became the party president, all prime ministers have either been picked from or backed by the largest faction. It was accepted that no one could become prime minister without the largest faction's support.

Factional interests came to overshadow those of the party; money was spent in excess. Even though it was widely agreed that factions should be dissolved, changes did not materialize. No aspiring leaders had the incentive to abandon their existing power base. In response to criticism following Tanaka's Lockheed scandal, the LDP decided to amend the presidential election rules to be more democratic. The party introduced a primary, thereby allowing party members to vote.[8] It was expected that nonfactional votes would supersede the limits of factional bloc voting. But all candidates worked hard to enroll supporters as party members in order to increase the possibility of finishing in the top two and going on to the second stage of voting (Tsurutani 1980; Reed 1984; Kosakai 1986). As a result, membership in the LDP grew dramatically—from 500,000 to 1.5 million members in 1978 (Hrebenar 2000), reaching 3.2 million in 1982 (Z. Tanaka 1986). Since most new members were brought into the party by faction representatives—and much of their party membership fees were paid by the factions—they maintained attachments to particular Diet members and affiliated factions, and tended to vote accordingly. In 1978 and 1982, the candidates supported by the largest faction, Masayoshi Ohira and Yasuhiro Nakasone, won the presidency. Far from eliminating factional maneuvering in the presidential election, the introduction of the primary ended up factionalizing the grass roots of the party.

In 1993 the LDP lost party dominance. Intraparty dynamics began to change and factions became more fluid (Cox, Rosenbluth, and Thies 1999; Park 2001). The LDP amended the party presidential electoral rules in 1995 and extended the electorate to party members. A bundle of 10,000 votes by party members counted as one Diet-member vote. Despite these changes, competition was still along factional lines, because the supporters of the elected presidents could be identified by faction.[9] The largest faction's status remained unchallenged.[10]

Posts were still the major bargaining tools. In 2001 Koizumi ran for the LDP presidency. Coming from a smaller faction and opposing the party's dominant values, he should have been the last person to be selected party leader. But Koizumi unexpectedly beat the largest faction's candidate and assumed the prime ministership.

The Rise of Koizumi to the Prime Ministership

This section examines the background to Koizumi's ascent. By reconstructing the process of how competing actors bargained for new party presidential electoral rules, I specifically look at the largest faction's strategy for securing a favorable electoral outcome—and why this did not work out as expected.

Pressure for Prime Minister Mori's Resignation

In April 2000, when Prime Minister Keizo Obuchi suddenly fell into a coma, a group of five party heavyweights[11] privately decided to appoint Yoshiro Mori as the party president. Because Mori was not chosen through an open process, his legitimacy was questioned from the beginning of his prime ministership. Some 45 percent of the Japanese public responded by suggesting that the way Mori was selected was improper (*Asahi Shimbun,* April 11, 2000).

Demands for Mori's resignation principally resulted from the LDP's fear of losing the upcoming Upper House elections. According to a survey conducted in late January, the LDP was the least favored party in Japan, with a 44.4 percent disapproval rate (Kabashima 2001a). Furthermore, only 23.3 percent of those surveyed said they would support the LDP in the upcoming Upper House elections, while 28.5 percent stated their support of the major opposition party, the Democratic Party of Japan (DPJ). Since the LDP did not do well in the Lower House elections of 2000 under Mori's leadership and support for the Mori cabinet was continuing to fall (see figure 6.1), it was obvious that if the trend continued, the LDP would be unable to win the forthcoming Upper House elections in July 2001. Meanwhile, at the local level, metropolitan assembly elections were to be held in June. Since the LDP had successively lost several gubernatorial elections in Chiba, Nakano, and Tochigi—regarded as solid LDP support bases—local politicians were greatly concerned about their electoral performance and pushed for Mori's resignation. Under strong pressure, Mori announced on March 13 that he would resign (*Yomiuri Shimbun,* March 11, 2000). A party presidential election was to be scheduled.

Figure 6.1 Changes in Popular Support for the Mori Cabinet, April 2000–February 2001

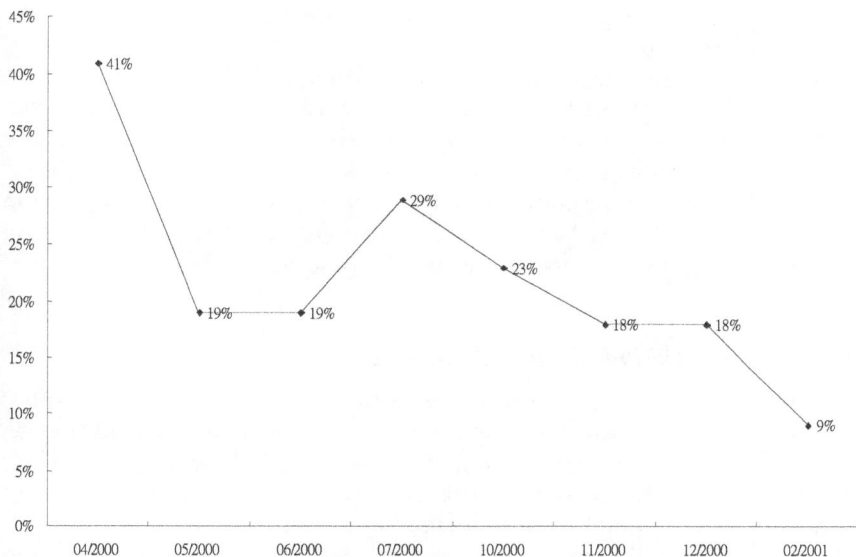

Source: Asahi Shimbun, various issues, compiled by the author.

Debate over How a New Leader Should Be Elected

Since Mori had become the prime minister through informal negotiation, the LDP was criticized for engaging in backroom politics. To rid the party of this negative image, there was a consensus that the new leader should be elected by a vote. But Diet members disagreed as to what constituted an open-party presidential election. Since 1995 Diet members and mass party members had selected party leaders together, with each group of 10,000 party-member votes counting as one Diet-member vote. Since Mori had vacated his seat during his term, according to Article 6 of the LDP Constitution, his successor would be elected by all Diet members and one representative from each prefectural chapter. For party executives, the priority was to stabilize the political chaos and select a new party leader with due process. But those junior members and local chapters who urged Mori to resign did not think it was an open-party election, because such a selection method would eventually leave the choice of the party leader to faction leaders as usual. They feared the public would take this as evidence that the party still made decisions behind the scenes and requested that the LDP revise the rules, lowering the required number of signatures for nomination and allowing party members to participate in selecting their leaders.[12] In response, party executives agreed to lower the number of endorsements from thirty to twenty, allowing more people to run for the presidency. With regard to the

113

electorate, they did not agree to open elections to rank-and-file party members[13] because such elections, they argued, would take more than a month to organize, leaving too little time to prepare for the Upper House elections.

In general, party presidential electoral rules consist, at a minimum, of three aspects: (1) who is eligible to run for the presidency, (2) who can vote, and (3) how votes are totaled (Lin 2007). Since the first two issues were already decided, the only one left to bargain over was how votes should be totaled—that is, how many votes to assign to local party chapters. Within the LDP, any significant issue normally received the approval of top party executives, including faction leaders or representatives. Factions had their own interests, and understood that changes in party presidential elections would affect their influence and resources.

Preferences over LDP Presidential Election Rules

Each faction's main concern was its influence in the subsequent administration. Simply put, factions of the mainstream camp wanted to maintain their advantage, and those outside the mainstream wanted to reverse the balance of power. Their preference of party presidential electoral rules can be easily illustrated by their strength—that is, the number of each faction's Diet members.

Two camps had already emerged before the electoral rule revisions and the election schedule were finalized. One camp was formed by combining the Hashimoto faction, the largest faction, with the Horiuchi faction; thereafter, this faction was the party mainstream, with 145 members. Given its numerical advantage under the existing system, the chances of other candidates getting elected were slim. Therefore, this faction preferred to keep the rules much as they were. An opposing coalition was formed by the Mori faction, the Kato faction, and the Yamasaki faction, with a total of 98 members. But the motives of the three factions varied. Outside the mainstream,[14] the Kato and Yamasaki factions wanted to reverse the existing power structure and establish a system that would allow them to usurp the largest faction's dominance. The motives of the Mori faction, on the other hand, were more complex. It wanted to maintain mainstream status but was not happy with the way that the largest faction had pushed Mori to resign. More than that, it had a potential candidate: Koizumi. Many Mori faction members were inclined to revise the rules to increase their chances of getting Koizumi elected (*Yomiuri Shimbun*, March 15, 2001). Overall, because of their lack of a numerical advantage, the Mori-Kato-Yamasaki[15] coalition preferred to increase nonfactional votes. The other factions did not express their preferences, but some of the 26 unaffiliated Diet members who urged Mori to resign were against factional dominance and preferred to extend the electorate.

Various factions had their own preferences, but their bargaining power was structured by existing institutions. Discussions of the selection methods were supposedly the responsibility of the Headquarters for Political Reform but, in reality, were dominated by Secretary General Makoto Koga (of the Horiuchi faction) and former secretary general Hiromu Nonaka (of the Hashimoto faction). That is, the party mainstream (the Hashimoto and Horiuchi factions) had more influence over party affairs. But this did not mean that they could simply veto other proposals. Mori, as the party president, enjoyed some bargaining power. He agreed that there was no time to prepare for an election in which all party members would vote, but he requested that local votes be increased so as to better reflect public opinion (*Yomiuri Shimbun*, March 14, 21, and 25; 2001). In the end, Koga negotiated with Mori and agreed to give three votes to each prefectural chapter (*Yomiuri Shimbun*, April 5, 2001), tripling the nonfactional allotment of votes. The party presidential election was scheduled for April 24 (*Yomiuri Shimbun*, April 6, 2001). There would be 347 Diet member votes and 141 prefectural representative votes.

Why did the party mainstream agree to give three votes to each prefecture? On the surface, tripling the nonfactional votes did not seem good for the party mainstream, but based on the mainstream's strength, it is reasonable to conclude that such votes were not really nonfactional votes. In the past, prefectural representative votes were determined by local chapter officers, all of whom were also local politicians. Many studies have shown that local chapters are ensembles of individual Diet members' support groups, or *koenkai* (Reed 1984; Curtis 1983). For many years, local politicians had gathered votes on behalf of particular Diet members and were attached to particular factions through those Diet members. Factional affiliations were vertical; that is, the more Diet members a faction had, the greater its influence at the local level. Since the party mainstream had more Diet members, it was expected to have a stronger affiliation with local party executives and more influence over local chapters. This arrangement ensured that the candidate it supported would have a much higher probability of getting elected. In other words, the party mainstream believed that it would benefit from the changed rules. And past election outcomes confirmed this expectation. In 1998 Obuchi, the leader of the largest faction at that time, was also selected by Diet members and prefectural representatives—with one difference: each prefectural chapter had only one vote. It was believed that local party executives would support the party mainstream's candidates.

After the schedule was finalized, four candidates decided to run for president. They were Hashimoto from the Hashimoto faction, Koizumi from the Mori faction, Shizuka Kamei from the Eto-Kamei faction, and Taro Aso from the Koho faction. Because Kamei and Aso did not build any alliances with other factions, it was unlikely that they would win.[16] Therefore, the main competitors were Hashimoto and Koizumi. The Japanese economy remained in recession, so all candidates focused on economic problems—but Koizumi's approach was different. He was against the idea of increasing government spending to stimulate the economy and instead proposed fiscal reconstruction, including privatizing the postal services system. Moreover, he called for the dissolution of party factions.

In 1998 Prime Minister Hashimoto suddenly resigned. A new party president was to be selected by Diet members and local representatives.[17] Although Koizumi was the most popular of the three candidates (Koizumi, Obuchi, and Seiroku Kajiyama) (*Asahi Shimbun*, July 15, 1998), he received only 84 votes—even fewer than the number of his faction members (*Asahi Shimbun*, July 25, 1998).

Table 6.1 LDP Presidential Election Outcome, 1998

Candidate	Votes
Obuchi	225
Kajiyama	102
Koizumi	84

Source: Asahi Shimbun, July 25, 1998.

The outcome of the 1998 LDP presidential election had confirmed the conventional wisdom that popularity is not the most important factor in selecting party leaders. Later, in 2001, when Koizumi was more popular among the public (*Asahi Shimbun*, March 27, 2001), past election outcomes made people doubt that even strong local support of Koizumi would be significant. It was believed that Hashimoto, backed by the party mainstream, had a clear advantage over Koizumi, who was backed by the Mori-Kato-Yamasaki alliance.

Unofficially Regulated Primary

Before the party executive decided to increase the number of prefectural votes, some urban chapters had already decided to let party members determine which candidate their representatives would vote for, regardless of whether the party executive agreed (*Yomiuri Shimbun*, March 24, 2001). In fact, these urban chapters also happened to be the local chapters that demanded Mori's resignation and requested that elections be opened to party members. The party executive thought only a few chapters would have primaries, and assumed that, for most prefectures, three votes would be decided by the local chapter officers, as before. In the end, the party executive decided to allow prefectural chapters to decide whether or not they wanted to hold a primary (*Yomiuri Shimbun*, March 29, 2001) and did not stipulate how the three votes would be allocated to candidates. The party executive even officially admitted the legitimacy of having primaries at the last minute by stipulating that those who registered themselves as party members by the end of the last fiscal year could vote (*Yomiuri Shimbun*, April 5, 2001).

Opening elections to party members seemed to increase uncertainty and dilute the party mainstream's influence. So why did the party mainstream agree to have primaries? The reason is simple. LDP party membership was by and large nominal. As mentioned earlier, people joined the party mainly to support particular Diet members. Many LDP members LDP to Diet members' personal support groups, or *koenkai*, better known as LDP *regional* members. If a prefecture had a higher percentage of Diet members from a given faction, it was expected to provide more votes for that faction's chosen presidential candidate. In other words, primaries would reflect the factional balance of Diet members in the prefecture.

The nominal party membership was also promoted by the Upper House electoral rules. From 1983 onward, the closed-list system was used for the Upper House's proportional representative (PR) voting, in which the party decided the order in which the candidates would be listed and elected. The LDP required any prospective PR candidate to bring in at least twenty thousand party members. Because elections were run in the nation at large (in national districts), the elected candidates were either celebrities or representatives of nationally organized interest groups (Curtis 1983; Koellner 2002). PR candidates worked hard to enroll their constituents as members of the LDP in order to be at the top of the list. As a result of intraparty competition for a good list position, by the mid-1980s, industrial group members—that is, LDP *occupation* members—outnumbered regional members and accounted for more than two-thirds of LDP party members.[18]

In 2001 regional members accounted for one-third of LDP party members (*Yomiuri Shimbun,* April 13, 2001). Since more prefectures had a higher percentage of Diet members from the party mainstream, the mainstream was expected to have more influence over regional members. The outcome was expected to reflect the factional balance of Diet members in particular prefectures. The remaining two-thirds of party members went to LDP occupation members, who collectively joined the LDP through their occupation associations in order to help particular Upper House PR candidates stay at the top of the PR list. Based on the Upper House PR members' factional affiliations and supporting industrial groups (see table 6.2), the Hashimoto faction not only accounted for a bigger share of LDP Upper House members but also had a very strong affiliation with major pro-LDP groups. Accordingly, the Hashimoto faction was expected to mobilize votes more easily than the other factions.

On April 12, when Hashimoto officially announced his intention to run for party president, eighteen heads of industrial groups showed up to demonstrate their support (*Yomiuri Shimbun,* April 13, 2001). In particular, the Former Special Postmasters League, Taiju, with almost 240,000 members—accounting for one-tenth of party members—emphasized that it would mobilize its members to ensure that Hashimoto won. By contrast, Koizumi did not have such a strong affiliation with industrial groups.[19] In fact, his policy opposed interest groups. Since he specifically proposed privatizing the postal system, the special postmasters made it very clear that they would not support Koizumi (*Yomiuri Shimbun,* March 19, 2001). It was expected that Koizumi would have difficulty garnering party-member votes.

Table 6.2 Major Industrial Associations' PR Representatives, April 2001

Industrial group	Number of members	Percentage of LDP party members	Representatives in the Upper House (factional affiliation)
Taiju (Former Special Postmasters)	239,651	10.1	Yutaka Okano (Hashimoto)
Zenkoku Kensetsugyou Kyoukai (Construction)	182,526	7.7	Kuniomi Iwai (Hashimoto), Masashi Waki (Hashimoto)
Gunon Renmei Zenkoku Rengoukai (War Veterans)	154,592	6.5	Yoshihiko Ebihara (Eto-Kamei)
Nihon Kango Renmei (Nurses)	124,056	5.2	Kayoko Shimizu (Mori), Chieko Nohno (Mori)
Nihon Ishi Renmei (Doctors)	115,189	4.9	Keizo Takemi (Hashimoto)
Nihon Izokukai (War-Bereaved)	110,277	4.7	Hidehisa Otsuji (Hashimoto), Tsuguo Morita (Horiuchi)
Zenkoku Tochi Kairyou Seiji Renmei (Local Construction Industry)	93,488	4.0	Ryotaro Sudo (Hashimoto), Akio Sato (Hashimoto)
Zenkoku Takuken Kyoukai Rengyoukai (Real Estate)	92,488	3.9	Tatsuo Shimizu (Hashimoto)
Tokiwakai (Former Japan Railway Employees)	79,287	3.3	Hiro Nakashima (Mori), Daizo Nozawa (Mori)
21-Seiki Wo Tsukuru Kai (Society for the 21st Century)	46,037	1.9	Morishige Naruse (Mori), Issei Anan (Hashimoto)
Nihon Yakuzaishi Renmei (Pharmacists)	39,658	1.7	Yoshihisa Oshima (Hashimoto), Yutaka Mizushima (Hashimoto)*
Nihon Shika Ishi Renmei (Dentists)	29,638	1.3	Soh Nakahara (Hashimoto)
Other groups	303,317	12.8	

Sources: Yomiuri Shimbun, April 13, 2001, and Kokkai Benran, a directory of Diet members and government officials, compiled by the author.

Note: * When Mizushima Yutaka was selected in 1995, he was a representative of the New Frontier Party, Shinshinto. He joined the LDP and the Hashimoto faction later.

As previously stated, past party presidential elections proved that candidates picked from or backed by the largest faction consistently received the majority support of party members. In addition to the elections of 1978 and 1982, in 1991, Miyazawa received 77 percent of local-representative votes (Lin 2007).[20] In 1995 Hashimoto won 80 percent of party-member votes (Cox, Rosenbluth, and Thies 1999), and in 1999 Obuchi received nearly 68 percent of party-member votes, as illustrated in table 6.3 (*Asahi Shimbun,* September 22, 1999).

Table 6.3 LDP Presidential Election Outcomes, 1995 and 1999

Candidate	Diet member votes	Party member votes*	Total
1995			
Hashimoto	239	65	304
Koizumi	72	16	88
1999			
Obuchi	253	97	350
Kato	85	28	113
Yamasaki	33	18	51

Source: Asahi Shimbun, September 23, 1995, and September 22, 1999.
Note: *10,000 party-member votes = 1 Diet-member vote.

At both the central and local levels, there was reason to believe that the Hashimoto faction would win. Meanwhile, the Hashimoto faction looked on the electoral rule changes optimistically. The media's analyses also confirmed Hashimoto's expected victory; pundits didn't think Koizumi would be able to break through the factional blocs easily (*Asahi Shimbun,* March 17 and 28, 2001; *Yomiuri Shimbun,* April 13, 2001). The situation seemed to be politics as usual: the largest faction's candidate would win.

Koizumi's Unexpected Victory

All prefectures, except for Hiroshima and Yamaguchi, held primaries. Quite unexpectedly, Koizumi received 58 percent of party-member votes, and Hashimoto received only 30 percent. Most of the prefectural chapters adopted the "winner-take-all" system to cast all three votes for the candidate who won the primary in the prefecture.[21] Koizumi won 42 out of 47 prefectural chapters and received 123 votes, nearly 90 percent of local-representative votes. After seeing Koizumi's overwhelming victory in the local preliminary elections, Kamei withdrew his candidacy to support Koizumi, and the Horiuchi faction reversed its decision to support Hashimoto prior to the vote at the LDP headquarters (*Yomiuri Shimbun,* April 23, 2001). As a result, Koizumi won an absolute majority, with 298 votes against Hashimoto's 155 and Aso's 31. Table 6.4 summarizes the election outcome.

Table 6.4 LDP Presidential Election Outcome, 2001

	Diet member votes	Local representative votes	Total
Koizumi	175	123*	298
Hashimoto	140	15	155
Aso	31	0	31
Total	346	138 [141]**	484 [487]

Source: Asahi Shimbun, April 25, 2001.
Note: * Osaka and Tottori adopted the d'Hondt system. Koizumi received two votes from Osaka and one vote from Tottori. Hashimoto received one vote from Osaka and two votes from Tottori.
** The total for local representative votes was 141. Kamei received 3 local votes but withdrew his candidacy prior to the vote at the LDP headquarters.

Why Did Hashimoto Lose and Koizumi Win?

What factors explain Hashimoto's defeat and Koizumi's victory? We can partially attribute Hashimoto's defeat to the declining faction discipline resulting from the new electoral rules, as Cox, Rosenbluth, and Thies (1999) would have expected. Indeed, when Hashimoto officially announced his intention to run for party president, 20 members, including 6 Lower House members and 14 Upper House members, absented themselves (Yomiuri Shimbun, April 13, 2001). But a closer look shows that Hashimoto had 140 Diet-member votes, only 5 fewer than the combined membership of the party mainstream of 145. It was very unlikely that many members from other factions supported Hashimoto when he had been defeated in the popular vote. Accordingly, faction discipline in the Hashimoto and Horiuchi factions must have remained at a certain level to keep so many votes.

Park (2001) argues that Koizumi successfully established an alliance with the Eto-Kamei faction against the Hashimoto faction; establishing an alliance by building a factional coalition is a traditional strategy for running for the presidency. But this explanation ignores the fact that the Eto-Kamei faction switched to support Koizumi and the Horiuchi faction reversed its decision to support Hashimoto at the last minute. If Koizumi had not won a landslide victory at the local level, the Eto-Kamei faction and the Horiuchi faction would not have been under such strong pressure to change their original decisions. Koizumi's victory resulted mainly from the support he received at the local level. If Koizumi had won with a smaller margin, say, 60 percent of the prefectural representative votes (that is, if 40 percent of the votes had been for Hashimoto), then neither Koizumi nor Hashimoto would have obtained a majority and needed to enter a run-off. In that case, only Diet members would have been eligible to vote. The result could have been very different.

The party mainstream expected that, with its larger membership, it would swing the vote in Hashimoto's favor. Unexpectedly, only four local chapters supported Hashimoto: Oakayama, Shimane, Kyoto, and Okinawa. Even the Hashimoto faction's strongholds, such as Saga and Tokushima, did not support Hashimoto. Why did the expected victory not materialize?

As macroeconomic conditions were not good, the Hashimoto faction's defeat could be attributed to its wrong choice of candidate. Hashimoto had failed to deal effectively with Japan's political economy as a prime minister. He was the one who raised taxes and made policy mistakes that led Japan toward economic crisis. Macroeconomic conditions were very different from what they had been in the past and the public, not surprisingly, did not want to support him. But this only partially explains Hashimoto's defeat. In December 2000 Hashimoto still ranked first among presidential candidates; Koizumi ranked fourth (*Nikkei Shimbun*, December 12, 2000). Not until March did Hashimoto's support rate decline to such an extent that he was ranked below Koizumi (*Yomiuri Shimbun*, March 10, 2001). I would argue that it was the way in which party heavyweights engaged in politics that made Hashimoto even more unpopular. Behind Koizumi's victory were a number of decisions—relatively small in and of themselves—that culminated in a sea change leading to the selection of Koizumi.

The Public's Desire for Change

The process that made Mori prime minister also made him unpopular from the first day of his tenure. Yet, despite strong public dissatisfaction, the LDP's mainstream continued supporting the Mori cabinet, leading to stronger public distrust. In 2000, when the Kato and Yamasaki factions planned to participate in the DPJ's no-confidence vote, nearly half of the respondents supported it (*Asahi Shimbun*, November 21, 2000). After the no-confidence bill was rejected, support for Mori's cabinet fell to 18 percent (*Asahi Shimbun*, November 22, 2000). A survey showed that among those who did not support the LDP, only 6 percent cited Mori as the top reason. More than 66 percent cited the way the LDP did politics as the main reason they did not support the party (Kabashima 2001a). It is fair to conclude that public distrust resulted not only from the Mori cabinet's lack of legitimacy, but also from the way in which the LDP engaged in politics. Obviously, the public desired a change.

Urban Chapters Push for Primaries

Since the metropolitan assembly elections would be held in June, urban chapters were more concerned about their electoral performance. The LDP had lost urban support in past general elections. In the Upper House elections of 1998, for instance, the LDP did not obtain any seats in Japan's major cities, and in the Lower House elections of 2000, the LDP was defeated by the DPJ in many urban districts (Kabashima 2001b). Moreover, at the local level, the LDP had successively lost several gubernatorial elections in Chiba, Nagano, and Tochigi, all regarded as support bases.

These developments gave local politicians pause. But they found that the party headquarters cared more about how it would maintain its own power. Local chapters insisted that instead of letting national politicians—that is, Diet members—dominate party affairs, local politicians should also have a chance to express their opinions. The chapters called for open elections.

It has been widely agreed that the LDP's successive defeat was related to increasing numbers of nonpartisan voters, who are usually more policy-oriented and less accepting of pork-barrel politics (Tanaka and Martin 2003; Scheiner 2005). If urban chapters wanted to win elections, they should have found a way to attract these voters. By letting party members choose the candidates they liked, urban chapters hoped that they might be able to win over those independent voters and improve their chances of reelection. Therefore, some urban chapters pushed hard for primaries.

Other Chapters Follow Suit

Initially, only some urban chapters decided to hold primaries. But pressure mounted on those chapters that did not. Holding primaries created the impression that people were able to elect the prime minister directly, since people knew that the selected leader would become the prime minister. The public was angry at the way Mori had ascended to the post, and 63 percent stated that they preferred to select their prime ministers through direct elections (*Yomiuri Shimbun*, April 18, 2001). In the end, although it was not mandatory to have primaries, forty-five out of forty-seven prefectural chapters decided to do so.

This decision implicitly invited the public to enter into intraparty dynamics, and it gave candidates a chance to run a popular-opinion campaign. In 2001 the Japanese economy remained in recession. The unemployment rate had reached a record high. In February 2001 both the stock market and the real-estate market fell and entered their tenth year of recession. The growing accumulation of nonperforming loans was expected to give rise to another round of financial troubles. The public feared a crisis, but the Japanese government was unable to turn the economy around. People had become increasingly skeptical of the effects of economic stimuli and were worried about the increasing government deficit. When everyone demanded leadership[22] and change, however, the party mainstream's priority was still to name a new leader without affecting the existing power structure. In contrast, Koizumi proposed dissolving factions and reshuffling the new cabinet without considering whether the factional balance could seek support more easily. His attack on the LDP's core values, pork-barrel politics, and factional politics helped him to cultivate a reform image. Of course, we cannot ignore the truth that those urban chapters pushing for primaries were inclined to support Koizumi. Their efforts to push primaries and attack the party headquarters at the same time promoted Koizumi's popularity.

They supported Koizumi because Koizumi's policy position might attract urban independent voters more easily than Hashimoto and increase local politicians' chances of reelection.

Votes for Hashimoto Not Effectively Mobilized

The impression that people were able to elect the prime minister directly made it difficult to mobilize party members to support a particular candidate. This was true not only in the case of Hashimoto. In Kagawa Prefecture, when the Yamasaki faction's members wanted to mobilize votes for Koizumi, local party members refused and argued that they should vote independently (*Yomiuri Shimbun*, April 18, 2001).

The heads of the industrial associations clearly supported Hashimoto,[23] but their mobilization efforts did not reach down to local branches. On April 15, just before the primaries, the LDP lost the gubernatorial election in Akita, an LDP stronghold[24] where the party had already lost two gubernatorial elections. This time, however, the LDP candidate was defeated by a significant margin of 200,000 votes (*Yomiuri Shimbun*, April 16, 2001). This showed just how unpopular the LDP had become and cast doubt on an imminent LDP victory.

Meanwhile, according to one survey (*Asahi Shimbun*, April 16, 2001), 12 percent of the public supported Hashimoto, and among unaffiliated voters, only 9 percent supported Hashimoto. In contrast, 51 percent of the public and 49 percent of unaffiliated voters supported Koizumi. Accordingly, the possibility of a Hashimoto victory was interpreted as an LDP defeat in the upcoming election. Hashimoto's unpopularity made interest groups worry; if the LDP lost power, their interests would be affected. Meanwhile, the DPJ criticized the LDP for its collusive relationship with interest groups. Although Koizumi seemed able to help the LDP win elections, he proposed undercutting the interest groups. Since they could not decide which candidate they should support, many associations decided to let their members choose whatever candidate they liked (*Yomiuri Shimbun*, April 21, 2001). Even the Special Postmaster Association's local branches, such as Iwate Prefecture, decided to let their members vote independently (*Yomiuri Shimbun*, April 18, 2001), and some members even showed their willingness to vote for Koizumi (*Yomiuri Shimbun*, April 23, 2001).

Timing of Primaries and Voting Sequence

The party executives let prefectural chapters decide whether, how, and when they would hold primaries. Since primaries in various prefectures were not held at the same time, they were not independent events. The early results would influence the voting decisions of those who voted later. Plus, the winner-take-all rule created an impression that most voters supported Koizumi (or that Hashimoto was completely crushed). In particular, the media[25] repeatedly highlighted that

Koizumi was ahead, further promoting support for Koizumi and weakening support for Hashimoto.[26] Counterfactually, if the first seven prefectural chapters to have primaries had supported Hashimoto, or if all chapters had primaries on the same day—that is, if everybody had voted on the same day without knowing other voters' preferences—the situation could have been different.

More important, the primaries were held over the several days (April 19–23) just prior to the vote being taken at the LDP headquarters (April 24), and the outcome of the preliminary elections at the LDP chapters was officially confirmed on April 23, one day before the party presidential elections. Koizumi's overwhelming victory left Diet members no choice but to support him. Otherwise, they would have been criticized for ignoring popular opinion and might have damaged the LDP's electoral performance in the Upper House elections. This voting order caused primaries to have binding effects on Diet-member votes.

In retrospect, Koga and Nonaka's failure to consider local chapters' proposals to increase the participation of local cadres and party members turned out to be a huge mistake. They just assumed that local politicians relied on them to channel money and resources from Tokyo. They forgot that they also relied on local politicians to gather votes for them. Had they responded more efficiently to local chapters' demands—such as how votes should be totaled and when the outcomes of preliminary elections should be announced—the result might have been in their favor.

Conclusion

Either from the position of policy or intraparty power structure, Koizumi should have been the last person selected as LDP leader. His victory was a consequence of changes to the party's electoral rules. These changes should be understood as the LDP's survival response to a changing environment. Conventionally, LDP presidents were determined by factions. It was very rational for the party mainstream to restructure the rules based on the electoral history of party factions. The mainstream believed that by restructuring the rules as they did, their factional interests would not be hurt and the party's popularity would be improved. But their plan did not work as expected. First, they assumed that they could rely on local politicians' support and did not expect that almost all local chapters would decide to implement primaries instead. Second, they expected that local politicians and industrial groups would mobilize votes on their behalf as they had in the past, and did not expect that, in the end, these groups would leave the party members to decide by themselves which candidate they wanted to support.

Overall, it is fair to conclude that the subsequent selection of Koizumi was due to the party mainstream's misjudgments. It overestimated its strength by assuming that the voting behavior of its supporters would not change when the LDP's victory was not assured. In the past, the incentives of LDP supporters played only a marginal role in explaining changes in intraparty dynamics. For a long time, it was assumed that the people and groups that supported faction X in general elections would also support faction X in party elections. This was because supporting faction X would increase the faction's strength, which would in turn help advance local interests. In such circumstances, candidates' policy positions and popularity were secondary. In taking the LDP's victory for granted, interest groups chose individual candidates and factions that could provide better benefits; in other words, their expected benefits were associated with individual LDP candidates, not with the party. If the LDP were not the ruling party, the expected benefits associated with individual Diet members would be uncertain. The LDP presidential election of 2001 showed that when the LDP's victory was not assured, supporters cared more about party differentials.[27]

Not only LDP supporters but also LDP politicians had different strategies when the environment changed. When the LDP dominated the government, the selection of party leadership—and thus of the prime minister—was not expected to have a strong impact on elections.[28] But when the LDP's victory was not assured, the party leader's popularity became increasingly important.[29] Research on the Lower House in 2000 confirmed that the party image and personal appeal of the party leader was exerting a growing influence on voting behavior (Kabashima and Imai 2002). As the environment became more competitive, LDP politicians became more sensitive to the impact of leadership selection on their own reelection and also the party's electoral performance. Independent voters grew to outnumber any group of party supporters (*Yomiuri Shimbun Sha Yoron Chousabu* 2004). Reliance on traditional voters was not enough to secure the LDP's electoral fortune, and the LDP needed to find a way to attract nonpartisan votes.

In 2001 the impact of leadership selection on elections was felt by junior Diet members, who were more electorally vulnerable. In 2003 consideration of the impact of leadership selection on the reelection of candidates became more obvious in the party presidential election.[30] Despite consistent conflict with Koizumi, the Hashimoto and Horiuchi factions split over which candidate they should support[31] and were not able to hold together against Koizumi, not least because they thought he would help them win. As I noted earlier, in April 2001 the LDP was the least favored party. After Koizumi assumed office, a subsequent survey showed that an increasing number of people changed their mind and thought the LDP had a strong reform image (Kabashima 2001b). For the first time since 1993, the LDP's support rate exceeded the percentage of independent voters (*Yomiuri Shimbun Sha Yoron Chousabu* 2004). Furthermore, the LDP did well in the metropolitan assembly elections of June 2001 and in the Upper House elections of July 2001. The LDP's popularity increased because of Koizumi, and his popularity meant that the LDP performed well in metropolitan and Upper House elections. Therefore, in 2003 some Upper House PR members supported Koizumi—even though their constituency

125

groups did not support him—because they thought he would help them win the election scheduled for 2004. For example, the Dentists' Association was against Koizumi. But Soh Nakahara, who represented the Dentists' Association, supported Koizumi (*Asahi Shimbun,* September 10, 2003). For the LDP to win elections, members had to take popular opinion into account when selecting their new party leader.

How Koizumi was elected is even more crucial than his victory. When the right to select the president was limited to LDP Diet members, who also constituted a parliamentary majority—regardless of whether it was in terms of intra-LDP dynamics or the relationship between the legislative and executive branches—the prime minister was answerable to those LDP Diet members and to the factions within them. But when the selection of the president was opened up at the local level, the party leader/prime minister could claim that he was accountable to rank-and-file members over party heavyweights. Moreover, with supporters from across the country, the prime minister now could claim a popular mandate. As Koizumi defeated his rivals in the primaries, he argued that his policy was more popularly supported than that of the old guard.

Then, by being selected by party members, Koizumi acquired a power base that was independent of Diet members. Implicitly, he would not be so vulnerable to factions and would thus reduce the need to compromise with them. A challenge to Koizumi could be triggered only by an explicit vote of no confidence and the recall rule. The incumbency would not end just because one faction threatened to withdraw its support. The revised rule thus made it harder to depose incumbent leadership.

Does the Koizumi phenomenon represent a one-time or an ongoing trend? In other words, are these changes within the LDP easily reversible, or do they have long-term consequences? In 2002, at the Hashimoto faction's behest, the LDP amended the way in which it calculated local-representative votes in proportion to the votes that candidates receive in primaries. This was done to prevent a candidate from winning an overwhelming percentage of local votes like Koizumi did. Now votes cast by Diet members and rank-and-file members are counted simultaneously. Thus, the results of the voting by rank-and-file members cannot affect Diet members' voting, as happened in 2001. At the same time, however, the total number of local votes was increased to 300 from 141, accounting for 46 percent of the total votes—and further diluting Diet members' influence.

Since the election of 2001 gave rise to the impression that people were electing their prime minister, no future elections will be considered fully legitimate unless the head of the party reflects the public opinion. Although the old guard wanted to restore its influence, primary elections for LDP presidents are likely to become institutionalized. In fact, for the LDP presidential election of 2006, the party continued the same rules it used in 2003 to select its new leader. And in 2007, when Shinzo Abe suddenly resigned and Yasuo Fukuda was selected LDP president, 35 out of 47 prefectures held primaries to decide how votes were allocated to candidates.

There is no way the LDP can reinstitute the closed nature of the competition. Now that the public plays a larger role in leadership selection, public opinion is more important and candidates' personalities have become a salient factor.

Notes

[1] The author would like to thank Jennifer Amyx, Martin Dimitrov, Greg Noble, Steven Reed, Yves Tiberghien, and Maria Toyoda for comments on early drafts.

[2] When Yohei Kono was the LDP president, the LDP, the Social Democratic Party of Japan (SDPJ), and the Sakigake Party formed a coalition government and Tomiichi Murayama, from the SDPJ, assumed the prime ministership.

[3] In 1962 the number of representatives from each local prefectural chapter was reduced from two to one.

[4] Another factor that promoted faction-centered competition was the endorsement requirement. Since 1972 the party rules have required that candidates obtain the endorsement of a certain number of fellow Diet members. This requirement encourages politicians to develop a personal power base in order to be nominated, as well as implicitly excluding candidates without any factional affiliation from the contest as a preselection mechanism. For example, in 1981, the endorsement requirement was raised to fifty fellow Diet members, and only major factions would be able to nominate candidates (Z. Tanaka 1986; Lin 2007).

[5] For example, Noboru Takeshita was not popular but became the party president and the prime minister. Toshiki Kaifu was still very popular but was forced to resign.

[6] As to why individual politicians joined factions and how the exchange relationship between leaders and followers was formed and persisted, see Fukui (1976) and Cox, Rosenbluth, and Thies (1999).

[7] For example, in 1991, the largest faction, led at that time by Takeshita, did not support Kaifu's political reform programs and decided to withdraw its support and create another coalition to support Kiichi Miyazawa. Even though Kaifu was still popular with the public, he could not establish an alternative coalition and was forced not to run for reelection.

[8] Party members include associate members, members of the LDP's official support organizations, the Liberal National Congress, and the People's Political Association, better known as "party friends."

[9] For example, in 1998, Keizo Obuchi was supported by the Kiichi Miyazawa faction and the old Michio Watanabe faction, together with Obuchi's own faction. Furthermore, in 1999, Obuchi was supported by all factions except for the Kato and Yamasaki factions.

[10] The largest faction temporarily became a smaller faction, due to a split led by Ichiro Ozawa and Tsutomu Hata in 1993, but it quickly regained its lead later.

[11] They were Hiromu Nonaka (then deputy secretary general), Mikio Aoki (then chief cabinet secretary), Shizuka Kamei (then chair of the Public Affairs Research Council), Masakuni Murakami (then head of the LDP's Upper House caucus) and Yoshiro Mori (then secretary general).

[12] In addition to the "one party member, one vote" proposed by some local chapters (*Yomiuri Shimbun*, March 12, 2001), some junior members, including Ishihara, proposed extending the electorate to local assembly members, giving them the same weight as Diet members (*Yomiuri Shimbun,* March 7, 2001).

[13] Makoto Koga, the party general, made it clear that since the prime minister is selected by Diet members, the right to select party presidents should also be limited to LDP Diet members (*Yomiuri Shimbun*, March 13, 2001).

[14] The mainstream and nonmainstream camps of 2001 could be traced to the presidential election of 1999, when Obuchi, then leader of the largest faction, ran for reelection. Except for the Kato and Yamasaki factions, all factions supported Obuchi. The Kato and Yamasaki factions were therefore nonmainstream.

[15] Yamasaki, Kato, and Koizumi had established a cross-factional alliance, better known as the YKK alliance, over a long period of time.

[16] Neither camp accounted for a majority. With fifty-five members, the Eto-Kamei faction's choice received much attention. If the Eto-Kamei faction would support Hashimoto, then he would have a majority of Diet member votes, virtually meaning that Hashimoto would win. But if the Eto-Kamei faction would support Koizumi, then Hashimoto and Koizumi would tie and need to enter a run-off. Given his faction's critical role in affecting the electoral outcome, it was believed that Kamei wanted to increase its strength by fielding candidacy and bargaining in order to continue serving as the chair of the Policy Affairs Research Council (PARC) or as the secretary general.

[17] In 1998 each prefectural chapter had only one vote.

[18] Usually, when party support declines, so does the number of party members (Scarrow 2000). But in the case of Japan, even though the LDP's partisan support had declined since the 1970s, party membership kept on rising and reached a peak in 1994. It is evident that LDP members were by and large nominal. They did not voluntarily join the party to support the LDP.

[19] Koizumi tried to get support from the Bereaved Society of Japan, Nihon Izokukai (*Yomiuri Shimbun*, April 18, 2001).

[20] In 1978 and 1982, a two-stage vote was held, and the top two nationwide vote-getters in the primaries entered the second stage, in which the LDP Diet members elected the president by a majority vote. In 1995 and 1999, ten thousand votes by party members counted as one Diet-member vote. Different from the primaries of 1978 and 1982 and the leadership selection of 1995 and 1999, in 1991 Diet members and party members voted on the same day but were counted separately. Each prefecture was given one to four votes, depending on the number of party members in each prefecture.

[21] Party executives did not stipulate how votes in primaries should be totaled. Most chapters adopted the "winner-take-all" system. Only Tottori, Osaka, and Tochigi adopted the d'Hondt system to allocate votes.

[22] Sixty-seven percent of the respondents expected the next prime minister to exercise leadership (*Yomiuri Shimbun,* March 27, 2001).

[23] It was reported that the special postal workers were asked to return blank ballot papers on which Hashimoto's name would then be written (*Yomiuri Shimbun,* April 18, 2001).

[24] In 2001 all Diet members in Akita were from the LDP.

[25] Many analysts attributed Koizumi's victory to his skillful use of the media to promote his popularity, as well as to the role of Makiko Tanaka.

[26] This dynamic is very similar to the U.S. presidential nominating process. The states whose primaries occur early exhibit a demonstration effect and enjoy disproportional influence. See Bartels (1988).

[27] The similar dilemma that industrial groups faced in 2001 was apparent also in the 2005 election, when Koizumi dissolved the Diet and campaigned for postal privatization. Industrial groups were also split over which candidate to vote for.

[28] The lower electoral importance of party leaders was also related to the defunct electoral SNTV system.

[29] In 1995 the LDP chose Hashimoto over Kono because Hashimoto was popular with the public and had a better chance of leading the party to victory (Cox, Rosenbluth, and Thies 1999). In addition, Hashimoto's faction promised to offer the post of secretary general to get the support of Kato, who came from the same faction as Kono and was supposed to support Kono.

[30] Leadership selection has been more sensitive to public opinion since the Upper House's PR system changed to an open list in 2001. The reelection of Upper House members is no longer guaranteed even if they're at the top of the list. Rather, it depends on how many votes they get. This change in rules makes candidates more sensitive to popular opinion.

[31] The Hashimoto faction's forty out of forty-two Upper House members and ten Lower House members supported Koizumi instead of their faction's choice, Fujii. We cannot ignore the important role that Aoki—the leader of the Diet members in the Upper House from the Hashimoto faction—played in mobilizing his faction's Upper House members to support Koizumi.

References

Asahi Shimbun. Various issues. (This and other newspaper articles cited in this chapter are available upon request from the author.)

Bartels, Larry. 1988. *Presidential primaries and the dynamics of public choice.* Princeton, NJ: Princeton Univ. Press.

Cox, Gary, Frances M. Rosenbluth, and Michael F. Thies. 1999. Electoral reform and the fate of factions: The case of Japan's Liberal Democratic Party. *British Journal of Political Science* 29 (1): 33–56.

Curtis, Gerald. 1983. *Election campaigning Japanese style*. New York: Kodansha International.

Fukui, Haruhiro. 1970. *Party in power: The Japanese liberal-democrats and policy-making*. Berkeley: Univ. of California Press.

Hayao, Kenji. 1993. *The Japanese prime minister and public policy*. Pittsburgh, PA: Univ. of Pittsburgh Press.

Hrebenar, Ronald J. 2000. *Japan's new party system*. Boulder, CO: Westview Press.

Kabashima, Ikuo. 2001a. Mutouha ga houkisuru [The uprising of independent voters]. *Ronza* (April): 14–35.

Kabashima, Ikuo. 2001b. Koizumi baburu no nazo wo toku [Explaining the myth of the Koizumi bubble]. *Ronza* (July): 40–59.

Kabashima, Ikuo, and Ryosuke Imai. 2002. Evaluation of party leaders and voting behavior—An analysis of the general election of 2000. *Social Science Japan Journal* 5 (1): 85–96.

Kohno, Masaru. 1997. *Japan's postwar party politics*. Princeton, NJ: Princeton Univ. Press.

Kokkai Benran. Various issues. Tokyo: Nihon Seikei Shimbunsha.

Koellner, Patrick. 2002. Upper house elections in Japan and the power of the organized vote. *Japan Journal of Political Science* 3 (1): 113–37.

Kosakai, Shozo. 1986. *Jiminto sosaisen* [LDP presidential elections]. Tokyo: Kadokawa Shoten.

Lin, Chao-Chi. 2007. Does the method of selecting leaders matter? The case of Japan's Liberal Democratic Party. Paper presented at the annual conference of the American Political Science Association (APSA), Chicago, August 30–September 2.

Nikkei Shimbun. Various issues.

Otake, Hideo. 2003. *Nihon gata popyurizumu* [Japanese style of populism]. Tokyo: Chuo Koron Shinsha.

Park, Cheol-Hee. 2001. Factional dynamics in Japan's LDP since political reform. *Asian Survey* 41 (3): 428.

Reed, Steven R. 1984. Factions in the 1978 LDP presidential primary. *Journal of Northeast Asian Studies* 3 (1): 31–38.

Scarrow, Susan. 2000. Parties without members. In *Parties without partisans*, ed. Russell Dalton and Martin Wattenberg. New York: Oxford Univ. Press.

Scheiner, Ethan. 2005. *Democracy without competition in Japan*. New York: Cambridge Univ. Press.

Shinoda, Tomohito. 2003. Koizumi's top-down leadership in the anti-terrorism legislation: The impact of political institutional changes. *SAIC Review* 23 (1): 19–34.

Tanaka, Aiji, and Sherry L. Martin. 2003. The new independent voter and the evolving Japanese party system. *Asian Perspective* 27 (3): 21–51.

Tanaka, Zenitirou. 1986. *Jiminto no doramaturugii* [The LDP's dramaturgy]. Tokyo: Tokyo Daigaku Shuppankai.

Tsurutani, Taketsugu. 1980. The LDP in transition? Mass membership participation in party leadership selection. *Asian Survey* 10 (8): 844–59.

Yomiuri Shimbun. Various issues.

Yomiuri Shimbun Sha Yoron Chousabu. 2004. *Nidai seito jidai no akebono: heisei no seiji to senkyo* [The beginning of a two-party era: Politics and elections in the Heisei era]. Tokyo: Bokutakusha.

HOW LONG ARE KOIZUMI'S COATTAILS? PARTY-LEADER VISITS IN THE 2005 ELECTION

Kenneth Mori McElwain[1]

On August 8, 2005, Prime Minister Junichiro Koizumi called for snap elections for the House of Representatives. The precipitating cause was the intra-LDP (Liberal Democratic Party) division over Koizumi's aggressive push to privatize Japan Post. Although Koizumi had threatened to dissolve the Lower House should the cabinet bill fail, Shizuka Kamei—an LDP faction boss and one of the most vocal critics of privatization—called his bluff. While the reform plan squeaked through the Lower House despite significant LDP defection, postal privatization was blocked in the Upper House when thirty LDP members voted against the measure (Maclachlan, chapter 8, this volume). True to his word—and to the surprise of many observers, including the "postal rebels"—Koizumi followed on with his threat and vowed to put the issue to the voters.

The Lower House election on September 11, 2005, was dubbed "Koizumi theater," due to the media's extensive coverage of the pitched battle between the incumbent "postal rebels," who had been kicked out of the LDP, and Koizumi's handpicked "assassins," who were selected to represent his reform initiative. When the election campaign kicked off on August 30, even entertainment programs spent hours dissecting the Shakespearean intersections of loyalty, betrayal, and conflict among these former copartisans (opinion was split on who betrayed whom). Somewhat absent from the public debate were the actual opposition parties, notably the Democratic Party of Japan (DPJ), which had also voted against the postal-reform bill but was left outside of Koizumi's theater, looking in. When the votes were finally tabulated, Koizumi had carried the day: the LDP won 296 seats (a +60-seat swing)—its largest share ever—while the DPJ won only 113 seats (a −64-seat swing).

While these events offer insights into a number of interesting phenomena, such as how (not) to bargain in parliament or how (not) to maintain party cohesion, this chapter focuses on one question: how important were Koizumi's coattails to the LDP's victory? When Koizumi was first elected as LDP president and Japanese prime minister in 2001, his lionesque hair, telegenic style, and reformist aura propelled him to support ratings of over 80 percent. While these stratospheric numbers fell over subsequent years, Koizumi's approval rating three weeks before the 2005 election was a still-robust 53 percent (*Asahi Shimbun*,

August 20, 2005). Koizumi's popularity gave him political leverage that few of his predecessors possessed. To the extent that an association with Koizumi bestowed some reflected glory, the LDP could use Koizumi's popularity as a tactical tool to boost the electoral prospects of its candidates.

I analyze Koizumi's "coattail effects" in the 2005 election in two related ways. The first half of this chapter deals with *strategic resource allocation*: which electoral districts did Koizumi, the LDP president, and Katsuya Okada, the DPJ president, visit leading up to the election? Because the legal campaign period in Lower House elections is only twelve days long, leader visits are scarce resources that parties must distribute discriminately to win the maximum number of seats. The second half of this chapter analyzes the *effects* of leader visits, disaggregating two types of coattail effects: *collective* (the candidate belongs to the same party as a popular leader) and *selective* (the leader visits the candidate's district during the campaign).

Combining local polling data, newspaper reports on party-leader visits, and a variety of statistical tests, I demonstrate that the LDP adopted an aggressive swing-voter approach while the DPJ pursued a defensive, incumbent-protection strategy. Although both Koizumi and Okada focused their visits on districts with narrow predicted margins of victory, Koizumi favored new candidates or previous runners-up in regions where his personal popularity was high. On the other hand, Okada campaigned on behalf of incumbent candidates irrespective of his own popularity in their districts. As for the substantive effects of these visits, I find no evidence of electoral coattails for Okada, but Koizumi's overall popularity and targeted visits produced consequential improvements in the LDP vote share. Compared to the mean, a one-standard-deviation (3 percent) increase in Koizumi's local popularity raised the LDP candidate's vote share by about 1 percent. If Koizumi actually visited a district, then the LDP candidate received an *additional* boost of 2.4 percent. Approximately 15 percent of electoral races in the 2003 and 2005 elections were decided by margins smaller than 3 percent, suggesting that Koizumi's coattails were critical to the LDP's success.

In the next two sections, I review the literature on strategic resource allocation, coattail effects, and party-leader visits in greater detail. A description and analysis of the statistical methods and findings follow. The final section consists of a discussion of this study's implications.

Party Effort, Resource Allocation, and Coattail Effects

A variety of factors explain election outcomes, some of which deal with national trends and others with local conditions. An example of the former is public perceptions of leader competence: better macroeconomic performance yields higher vote shares for parties in power (Lewis-Beck 1988; Inoguchi 1982; Powell and Whitten 1993). An example of the latter is the importance of candidate quality: research conducted by Jacobson (1989) and Scheiner (2005) indicates that "strong" candidates, especially former local officeholders, are better equipped to win national races than those with no political experience.

An important component of electoral success is strategic party behavior, particularly nomination coordination. Under the pre-1993 electoral system of multimember districts (MMDs) under a single nontransferable vote (SNTV), Japanese parties needed to optimize candidate nominations in order to avoid splitting their votes among too many copartisans (Browne and Patterson 1999; Christensen 2000). The 1994 introduction of the *heiritsu-sei* system, with parallel single-member district (SMD) and proportional representation (PR) tiers, simplified coordination efforts. Because only one candidate can win outright in the SMDs, Duvergerian pressures have taken hold, and Japan has been moving toward a two-party (or at least a two-camp) system (Reed 2007).[2] In recent years, the LDP has coordinated nominations with its coalition partner, the Komeito (or Komei), while the DPJ has taken steps to avoid overnomination with other progressive parties.[3] The primary explanation for nomination coordination is strategic resource allocation: in the short run, parties will only compete where their prospects are strong, and voters and activists should only support candidates with some hope of winning (Cox 1997; Duverger 1954; Reed 1991). As Weiner points out (chapter 5, this volume), resource allocation based on short-term horizons should result in incumbents running unopposed where their support base is strong, and two-party competition where victory margins are smaller.

This chapter focuses on a second side of the resource allocation problem: party effort. An implicit assumption of the strategic entry/coordination literature is that running for office is actually costly for political parties. But entering an election race is relatively cheap; the true costs accrue from trying to *win*. Parties can nominate candidates where they have no hope of winning and spend very little money on the campaign. They may do so to build a foothold in districts with little current following, or they may simply allow a rich, independent candidate who needs no financial support to wear the party's mantle. In measurement terms, candidate nominations are an imperfect way of assessing strategic behavior, because this does not take into account how much effort parties put into winning each seat. To accurately capture party strategy, we need a more precise measure of how much and where parties expend scarce resources.

The standard metric of party effort in political science literature is campaign expenditures. Damore and Hansford (1999) find that the campaign committees of American political parties allocate disproportionately more money to marginal districts in House of Representatives elections. Parties can also influence campaign war chests indirectly: Jacobson, Kernell, and Jeffrey (2004) show that presidents can help candidates raise money through targeted fund-raising efforts.

While money is undoubtedly one of the most revealing signs of campaign effort, a similar analysis is difficult to conduct in Japan because of rigid legal constraints. On the one hand, running in Lower House elections is not free: candidates need to pay a 3 million yen deposit to run in SMDs and 6 million yen for the PR tier. These deposits are meant to discourage frivolous competition, since candidates forfeit their money if they fail to win a minimal number of votes. While these sums are nonnegligible, particularly for independent candidates, they constitute a relatively small share of total campaign expenditures for the major political parties. The bulk of electoral spending is for the campaign process itself, particularly wages for staffers, office rental fees, and other administrative costs. The maximum spending limit for individual candidates is set by law, and in the 2005 election, varied by district between 22 and 28 million yen.[4] Restrictions on political *parties*, however, are much more lax: parties can hire as many staff members as they want, and TV advertisements and transportation costs for campaign speeches do not count toward the legal spending ceiling. While parties are required to file reports on direct monetary transfers to politicians, these ancillary expenditures are not itemized, making it difficult to gauge how much money was spent per candidate during the campaign.

Instead, I use a different metric to assess party effort and resource allocation: campaign visits by party leaders, or *yuuzei*. The electoral salience of leader visits plays a prominent role in the expanding literature on the "presidentialization of parliamentary politics" (Poguntke and Webb 2005). Because prime ministers are selected by other legislators, not elected directly by voters, the individual appeal of party leaders has received less attention in parliamentary regimes than under presidentialism. Over the last 20 years, however, media coverage of parliamentary leaders has grown rapidly. Party leaders receive increasingly more news coverage, and it has become commonplace to see telegenic leaders featured prominently in television advertisements. Japan has been no exception: Krauss and Nyblade (2005) report a steady increase in the number of newspaper articles on the prime minister, the number of prime ministers' campaign visits, and the share of voters who rely on TV news to make ballot choices.

This newfound "cult of the party leader," of which Koizumi is an exemplar, has profound electoral implications. Specifically, party leaders should be able to generate coattail effects—defined as the extent to which the popularity of the party leader affects the electoral fortunes of that party's candidates. A prime minister's coattails have two types of effects, which I term collective and selective. *Collective* benefits are the marginal added value of the party leader's popularity relative to the party's overall popularity. A voter who has little affection for the LDP or for his district's LDP candidate may still vote for the LDP because he wants Koizumi to stay in power. The narrower, *selective* effect is derived from the strategic allocation of party-leader visits. In addition to the collective gains from being part of "Koizumi's LDP," an LDP candidate may benefit from having Koizumi visit her district, give a stump speech at her side in front of a crowded train station, and otherwise impress voters with the visual image of Koizumi and the candidate linked together.

Much like campaign expenditures, the allocation of leader visits is subject to strategic decision-making. For Lower House elections, the Public Office Election Law (POEL) restricts stumping on behalf of candidates to the official twelve-day campaign period (McElwain 2008). Accordingly, the LDP should ration visits to those districts where the marginal, selective effects of a Koizumi visit would generate the highest returns. Even in a relatively small country such as Japan, party leaders are hard-pressed to travel to all three hundred SMDs in this short time frame. An examination of which districts were visited by party leaders allows us to analyze how much and where parties decide to expend the most effort in winning electoral races.

The Logic of Party-Leader Visits

To analyze the allocation of party-leader visits, information was gathered from a variety of media sources. While all political parties initially listed leader visits on their Web sites, this practice was quickly blocked by the Ministry of Internal Affairs and Communication, which informed the DPJ and LDP on September 2, 2005, that updating party or candidate home pages "was most likely in violation of the Public Office Election Law" (*Yomiuri Shimbun,* September 3, 2005).[5] As such, the bulk of campaign-visit data is gathered from the national and regional editions of the *Yomiuri* and *Asahi* newspapers, especially the *Asahi*'s daily reporting of the prime minister's movements. In practice, it is extremely difficult to compile complete data on the precise visit locations of all party leaders, much less lower-ranked officials, because of the aforementioned proscription on self-advertisement by parties and the vague way that most visits are described in the news (for example, "Koizumi traveled around central Tokyo today . . ."). Therefore, this chapter focuses only on the district-level visits of the two major party leaders—Koizumi of the LDP and Okada of the DPJ—for which I have complete data.[6]

Allocation of Party-Leader Visits

Table 7.1 lists some descriptive information on party-leader visits.[7] Koizumi—despite not campaigning on September 1 due to a state visit by the Thai prime minister—visited 72 politicians in 18 prefectures. Okada focused on metropolitan areas, visiting 75 separate districts in 16 prefectures, although 12 districts received an additional, second visit. In the last 3 days of the campaign period (September 8–10), Koizumi and Okada visited 24 and 26 districts, respectively. Koizumi traveled a total of 10,800 kilometers over the 12-day campaign period, approximately 1,700 kilometers more than Okada (*Asahi Shimbun,* September 11, 2005). The most active party bosses were Mizuho Fukushima of the Socialist Democratic Party of Japan (SDPJ) and Takenori Kanzaki of the Komeito, both of whom accumulated extra kilometers visiting candidates in Okinawa. The total distance traveled by party leaders was less than in the 2003 Lower House elections, due to a typhoon that hit Japan between September 5 and September 7, grounding most airplanes and forcing many candidates to halt campaigning for at least one day.

Table 7.1 Party-Leader Visits, August 30–September 10, 2005

Leader (Party)	Koizumi (LDP)	Okada (DPJ)	Shii (JCP)	Fukushima (SDP)	Kanzaki (Komeito)
Total SMD candidates	290	289	275	38	9
No. of districts visited	72	75			
Visited twice	1	12			
Visited in last 3 days of campaign	24	26			
Head-to-head districts visited*	47	53			
Incumbents visited	28	63			
Prefectures visited	18	16	17	20	8
Total kilometers traveled**	10,800	9,100	8,100	16,500	12,100

Source: Asahi Shimbun and *Yomiuri Shimbun*, various editions.
Note: * Head-to-head: LDP vs. DPJ only or LDP vs. DPJ vs. JCP only; $n = 203$.
** From *Asahi Shimbun*, September 11, 2005.

We can tease apart the data to get at the political context of these visits. Overall, there were 203 "head-to-head" matches between the LDP and DPJ, defined as a two-horse race between official LDP and DPJ candidates or a three-party competition that also involved the Communist Party.[8] Neither Koizumi nor Okada placed any extra emphasis on these districts, but one distinctive difference was that Okada spent more time with his party's incumbents. This suggests that the DPJ may have been taking the more conservative approach of defending existing seats rather than trying to win new ones.[9]

While the literature on party-leader visits is relatively new, there are roughly two schools of thought on the distribution of scarce resources. The first strategy is *defensive:* parties should allocate assets where their popularity is the strongest. Given that voter choice can be fickle, a bird in the hand is worth more than two in the bush, so parties should solidify their core base rather than overreach by trying to attract independent or weakly sympathetic voters. The second strategy is *offensive:* parties should target districts where the expected margin of victory is the smallest. If the difference between winning and losing a seat is a few percentage points, a party-leader visit may create a large enough swing to capture a marginal seat.

Previous studies have found mixed support for both defensive and offensive strategies. In their analysis of George W. Bush's stump visits during the 2002 House of Representatives midterm elections, Herrnson and Morris (2006) find that the president was more likely to visit competitive districts. On the other hand, Belanger, Carty, and Eagles' (2003) analysis of leaders' tours in the 2000 Canadian elections shows that established parties (the Liberals, Conservatives, and New Democrats) tended to defend their turfs, while the smaller, regional parties (Alliance and Bloc Québécois) tried to expand their national popularity by visiting districts where their support was relatively weak.

Effects of Leader Visits

Estimating the selective coattail effects of party-leader visits can be tricky, as there are three plausible benefits from leader visits—advertising, mobilization, and association—not all of which deal with coattails per se. *Advertising* effects are media-coverage externalities generated by the activities of party leaders. Because reporters and TV cameras follow party leaders during the campaign period, public speeches by Koizumi or Okada may receive TV airtime that evening and a brief write-up in the next day's newspapers. Even if explicit support for the candidate is not included in the media's coverage, any mention of that candidate's name and party affiliation serves as free advertisement. *Mobilization* effects are psychological rewards for party activists that generate indirect benefits to candidates. From an instrumental perspective, an undecided voter may not learn anything new from listening to a brief stump speech by Koizumi from one hundred meters away. Party volunteers who spend hours walking around with leaflets and making cold calls to voters, however, are more likely to be energized by seeing their party's star. This can, in turn, generate benefits, as enthusiastic campaign volunteers may work harder on behalf of the party, thereby increasing the candidate's vote share.

Technically speaking, neither the advertising nor mobilizational elements are functions of party-leader coattails, since the former is an epiphenomenal externality while the latter is conditional on the behavior of local activists. *Association* effects, however, are direct coattail benefits derived from the explicit linkage between the candidate and the party leader. When Koizumi or Okada claim that the candidate he is stumping for is valuable to the party and to the future of Japan, voters who have warm feelings toward either leader may transfer those sentiments to the local candidate.

The three effects—particularly advertising and association—can be difficult to disentangle. A TV report that shows Koizumi giving a speech in front of a major train station with candidate A at his side generates both airtime for that candidate (advertising) and a visual association between Koizumi and candidate A (association). Media tendencies and campaign regulations in Japan, however, suggest that associational effects outstrip advertising benefits. First, TV coverage of leader speeches tends to be very short and focuses narrowly on the leaders themselves, making it unlikely that voters will even see the candidate's face. Second, Japanese newspapers are required to remain neutral in how they cover electoral campaigns. In practice, this means that many articles omit the candidate's name—sometimes with awkward phrasing—when covering a leader's visit.[10] Take, for example, the following snippets from newspaper articles (the author's own translation from Japanese editions):

> On the second day of the Lower House elections, DPJ president Okada gave a stump speech at JR Kokura Station in the North Kokura Ward of Kita-Kyushuu City. . . *President Okada had come to support the DPJ incumbent in Fukuoka District 10* . . . (*Yomiuri Shimbun,* "Shuuinsen: Minshu Okada Daihyo ga Kitakyushuu Iri," August 31, 2005, emphasis added)

> The two coalition partners' leaders, Prime Minister Koizumi and Chief Representative Kanzaki Takenori of the Komeito, arrived back-to-back in Fukuoka on [September] 2 . . . *Just before 3 PM, Prime Minister Koizumi, who had visited Kurume to support the LDP's official candidate in Fukuoka District 6, stood on the campaign car* . . . (*Asahi Shimbun,* "Koizumi Shushou, Yuusei Tsuyoku Uttae; Komei Kanzaki mo Fukuoka Iri," August 30, 2005, emphasis added)

The other plausible effect of leader visits—mobilization—is also likely to be small. The benefit of seeing the party leader is greatest for activists whose primary allegiance is to the party organization. Japanese campaign activists, however, are mostly members of the *koenkai,* or personal support networks, of individual politicians. While one can love the politician and the party simultaneously, the postal-reform conflict in the Diet tested the relationship between the LDP in parliament and the LDP on the ground. Thirty-seven Lower House politicians were expunged from the LDP for voting against the reform bill, and many others were embittered by Koizumi's decision to force a legislative vote without first ensuring intraparty consensus. At the same time, numerous local LDP politicians in prefectural and municipal assemblies defied the LDP's dictum to withdraw support from the purged politicians, choosing to back the postal rebels' independent candidacies instead. In the best of times, the mobilization effect of a Koizumi visit on local activists would have been small; in the 2005 election, it was most likely minimal.

Given the lack of consistent advertising and mobilization externalities, campaign visits are most likely to produce associational effects: the physical presence and popularity of the leader directly alters how voters perceive that party's candidate. As a result, any vote boosts from leader visits can be ascribed to coattail effects, which are the primary theoretical concern of this chapter.

Testing the Determinants of Party-Leader Visits

I analyze the allocation of party-leader visits using an original data set of district-level visits by Koizumi (LDP) and Okada (DPJ). Each case is one SMD, although the four SMD districts in Okinawa are omitted due to the lack of consistent survey data. The total sample size is *n* = 296.

The statistical tests are based on two related sets of dependent variables. First, I examine whether each party leader visited a given district during the entire twelve-day campaigning period. The dependent variables take the values [0, 1]: as shown in table 7.1, Koizumi traveled to 72 districts, while Okada traveled to 75 districts. Second, I adjust the dependent variable to measure whether Koizumi and Okada visited that district in the last three days of the campaign. On September 6, the *Asahi* and *Yomiuri* newspapers reported district-level results from their respective 150,000-person surveys, which included prefectural-level data on the popularity of different political parties, their leaders, and, most crucially, assessments of which districts were still competitive. That evening, the DPJ and LDP leaders met in Tokyo to review their campaign strategies for the homestretch. With each party armed with up-to-date information, I expect leader visits in the last three days to represent an intensified version of their earlier resource allocation strategies.

The statistical models incorporate independent variables that operationalize recent popular sentiment, past electoral performance, and district characteristics. Descriptive statistics are provided in appendix 7.A. Three of the explanatory variables are based on surveys. *Koizumi popularity* and *Okada popularity* measure the difference between the popularity of each party leader and their respective parties. The *Asahi Shimbun* (September 6, 2005) reports prefecture-specific survey responses to a variety of questions, including: (1) "Thinking of the future of Japanese politics, who do you expect more from: Prime Minister Koizumi or DPJ president Okada Katsuya?" and (2) "Which political party do you support?"[11] The two factors are related, but by subtracting DPJ support from Okada support (*Okada popularity*) and LDP support from Koizumi support (*Koizumi popularity*), we can estimate the coattail "length" of each party leader.[12] I expect both Koizumi and Okada to visit districts where their coattail effects will be strongest—that is, where the values of *Koizumi popularity* and *Okada popularity* are high. I also include *no party preference* to measure the electoral salience of political independents. Ceteris paribus, the preferences of independent voters are more likely to be swayed by small cues, and I expect party leaders to favor districts where *no party preference* is high.

Four independent variables capture the structure of competition in each district. *Assassin* is a dichotomous variable that equals "1" when the race involves an ex-LDP postal rebel *and* one of Koizumi's handpicked assassins. There were thirty-three assassin districts, and these races received the greatest television exposure during the campaign period. Because of their high profile, I expect the party leaders—particularly Koizumi—to favor these districts.

POLITICAL CHANGE IN JAPAN

The variable *2003 margin* is the difference in vote share between the winner and the first runner-up in the 2003 Lower House elections. To the extent that future electoral performance correlates with past performance, the margin of victory in the last election is a good proxy for competitiveness in 2005.[13] As such, the *2003 margin* allows us to estimate whether the LDP and DPJ used an offensive or defensive resource allocation strategy. *Incumbent* is a dichotomous variable that equals "1" where the party's candidate is an incumbent. Similarly, the variable *new* tabulates whether the party's candidate is a new challenger, defined as not having run in the 2003 election. For the DPJ analysis, *incumbent* and *new* measure only official DPJ candidates. For the LDP regressions, they include both LDP and Komeito candidates to better reflect the strong electoral coordination between the two parties.

Finally, I include geographical control variables that measure nonpolitical determinants of leader visits. Given the twelve-day limit on campaigns, the total time it takes to travel from party headquarters to a given district should affect the propensity of visits; party leaders should be less likely to visit remote districts, all things being equal. While measuring travel time can be tricky, I use two related variables: *distance_log*, which is the logged distance in kilometers between Nagatacho, the area of Tokyo where the Diet and many party headquarters are located, and the main city or township of each electoral district; and *distance_sq*, the square of *distance_log*. Given the geography and transportation options available in Japan, I hypothesize that those districts close to Tokyo (which one can travel to quickly by train) or those very far from Tokyo (reachable by airplane) require shorter travel time than districts that are at an intermediate distance.[14]

In models 1A and 1B, I use a logistic regression model to predict the incidence of Koizumi and Okada visits over the twelve-day campaign period. Table 7.2 reports the coefficients and standard errors from the statistical analysis.[15] Since these coefficients are in log odds-ratios, and thus cannot be interpreted in a straightforward fashion, I will discuss the model results in terms of predicted probabilities.

One notable point of similarity is that both party leaders avoided districts where the margin of victory in the 2003 election was large. Holding all other variables at median values, a 1 percent increase in *2003 margin* reduces the probability of a Koizumi visit by 1.1 percent, and that of an Okada visit by 0.6 percent. A 5 percent increase in *2003 margin* reduces the probabilities of Koizumi and Okada visits by 5.4 percent and 2.5 percent, respectively.

On other measures, however, leader strategies diverged. Koizumi avoided shilling for LDP incumbents (-17.7 percent predicted probability), while Okada was much more likely to visit DPJ incumbents (+21.7 percent). Instead, Koizumi focused on areas where his personal popularity was high. A 1 percent increase in *Koizumi popularity* increases the predicted probability of his visit by 5.2 percent, while a 5 percent increase raises the probability of a visit by 32.4 percent. Surprisingly, Okada was *less* likely to visit districts where his popularity was strong, although the coefficient is small and not statistically significant. An

Table 7.2 The Location of Party-Leader Visits

Model: Logistic regression with robust standard errors (in parentheses)
DV: Visit by LDP and DPJ party leader prior to 2005 election

Variable	Entire campaign period		Last 3 days of campaign	
	1A: Koizumi	1B: Okada	2A: Koizumi	2B: Okada
Constant	12.55** (4.81)	4.74 (5.85)	7.65 (6.86)	-24.51*** (6.72)
Distance_log	-0.54 (0.28)	-0.09 (0.29)	-1.59** (0.53)	-0.16 (0.40)
Distance_squared	0.07 (0.04)	-0.03 (0.04)	0.25** (0.09)	-0.04 (0.06)
Assassin	0.90 (0.50)	-0.11 (0.61)	-0.37 (0.93)	-0.65 (1.14)
Incumbent	-1.02** (0.36)	1.64** (0.60)	-1.97*** (0.51)	
New	0.20 (0.46)	1.44 (0.76)	-1.16 (0.68)	
2003 margin	-5.27** (1.87)	-7.07*** (1.80)	-5.67 (3.69)	-9.10* (3.79)
Koizumi popularity	0.23*** (0.07)		0.42** (0.13)	
Okada popularity		-0.17 (0.19)		-0.59* (0.27)
No party preference	-0.33** (0.11)	-0.09 (0.16)	-0.28 (0.17)	0.68*** (0.19)
N	296	296	296	166
Pseudo-R²	0.185	0.227	0.274	0.208

Note: * = p<0.05; ** = p<0.01; *** = p<0.001.

interesting finding is that Koizumi favored districts where assassin candidates were running (+21.6 percent predicted probability), while Okada treated these districts like any other. Since the assassin districts were noted principally for the media's attention on the horse race between postal rebels and Koizumi's handpicked acolytes, it is not surprising that Koizumi viewed these areas as politically crucial. Okada, however, may have judged it inefficient to campaign in districts where his own candidates were the third wheel, as the *assassin* coefficient in model 1B is not statistically significant.

The most counterintuitive result is that neither leader focused on districts with a large proportion of political independents. A 1 percent increase in *no party preference* reduces the probability of a Koizumi visit by 6.6 percent, while a 5 percent increase reduces it by 22.9 percent. *No party preference* was neither substantively nor statistically significant for Okada in model 1B.

The determinants of party-leader visits vary slightly when we focus on the last three days of the campaign period (models 2A and 2B). The regression equations are different for Koizumi and Okada's visits, because Okada visited only incumbents between September 7 and September 10, suggesting that he intensified his earlier strategy of favoring sitting parliamentarians. To avoid statistical overdetermination, I run model 2B with only the districts where DPJ incumbents were involved ($N = 166$). Koizumi followed his earlier strategy of avoiding incumbents (–11.3 percent predicted probability), although he began to avoid new candidates as well (–8.3 percent predicted probability). Both leaders still favored districts where the vote margin in the last election was smallest, and this was particularly pronounced for Okada: a 5 percent increase in *2003 margin* reduced the predicted probability of an Okada visit by 3.4 percent.

The two leaders continued to diverge on the question of personal popularity. A 1 percent increase in *Koizumi popularity* generated a 5.3 percent increase in the likelihood that Koizumi would visit, while the same increase in *Okada popularity* lowered the probability of an Okada visit by 2.6 percent. Okada did, however, place greater emphasis on districts with more independents. While *no party preference* is statistically insignificant for Koizumi visits, a 1 percent increase in model 2B increases the likelihood of an Okada visit in the last three days by 5.6 percent.

Referring to the theoretical distinction in resource allocation strategies, the statistical findings suggest that Koizumi employed an offensive strategy while Okada was more defensive, and neither candidate radically changed his travel patterns over the course of the campaign period. Koizumi's visits were concentrated in the politically important assassin districts, and he avoided safer districts where LDP incumbents were running. Koizumi's travel schedule reflects an explicit attempt to take advantage of coattail effects, as his visits focused on areas where his personal popularity was higher. The DPJ, however, allocated leader visits to help protect the seats it already held. Instead of trying to win new seats, Okada spent most of his time supporting incumbents, and he displayed a surprising tendency to visit areas where his own popularity was relatively low.

Two interpretative points are in order. First, given the diminished media attention on the DPJ in this election compared to the last, Okada's defensive strategy may have been appropriate. Leading up to the previous 2003 Lower House elections, a *Yomiuri* survey (October 25, 2003) showed that 12 percent of voters intended to vote DPJ in SMDs (37 percent for the LDP), while 14 percent would do so in the PR tier (35 percent for the LDP). In a *Yomiuri* poll conducted before the 2005 campaign period (August 20, 2005), 14 percent of voters responded that they would vote for the DPJ candidate in the SMDs

(39 percent for the LDP), while 16 percent claimed the same in the PR tier (37 percent for the LDP). Although the LDP-DPJ gap in the two polls is similar, the increased attention on Koizumi's theater in 2005, particularly the fight of postal rebels versus assassins, meant that the DPJ was unlikely to create an upsurge in popularity during the campaign period, regardless of how many districts Okada visited.

Second, Okada's tendency to ignore his own regional popularity when picking visit destinations may be a function of his lower profile relative to Koizumi, which prompted the DPJ to adopt a tag-team strategy. Nationwide, the proportion of voters who trusted Okada to lead Japan was only 25 percent, compared to Koizumi's 42 percent support (*Asahi Shimbun,* September 5, 2005). Although he had been president of the DPJ since May 2004 and had led his party to electoral victory in the 2004 Upper House elections, Okada was a newcomer relative to party stalwarts such as Naoto Kan and Yukio Hatoyama. Indeed, the DPJ explicitly prioritized teamwork over Okada's personal appeal, as Kan, Hatoyama, and Ichiro Ozawa (whose Liberal Party had recently merged with the DPJ) were sent out to canvass as many districts as Okada. Whether this tag-team strategy worked is hard to judge without comprehensive visit data for the other party bosses, but when it came to Okada, the DPJ did not display any strategic effort to market their leader to generate selective coattail effects.

Testing the Effects of Party-Leader Visits

Having analyzed the determinants of leader-visit allocation, I now turn to the electoral impact of these visits. Here, I use a standard ordinary least squares (OLS) regression, where the dependent variable is each candidate's fractional *vote share* in 2005, ranging from 0 to 1. As with the previous section, I run separate regressions for LDP and DPJ candidates ($N = 286$ and 288, respectively). In addition to the independent variables from the previous section, I include some new measures that better capture baseline electoral outcomes.

First, I disaggregate *incumbent* into SMD winners and PR zombies. PR zombies are candidates who lost in the SMD race but were also listed in the PR tier and "resurrected" by virtue of having a close winner-to-runner-up vote ratio. *SMD incumbent* equals 1 for true incumbents who won the SMD race, while *PR zombie* equals 1 for resurrected PR incumbents. This distinction allows us to implicitly capture the past performance of incumbents, and hence their predicted vote shares in the current election. *Koizumi visit* and *Okada visit*, which were dependent variables in the previous section, are now included as independent variables. While I expect individual visits to improve candidate vote share, I also interact these visit variables with party-leader popularity to generate *Koizumi visit * Koizumi popularity* and *Okada visit * Okada popularity*. The additive popularity variables (*Koizumi visit, Okada visit*) capture the collective coattail effects that candidates obtain from belonging to the same party as their party leaders. The interaction term, however, allows us to tease out the selective coattail benefits of association—that is, of being seen with a popular party leader. Finally, I include the control term *total candidates*, which counts the number of candidates competing in that district. Since the proliferation of candidates—even minor ones—can depress the winning vote share, I expect the coefficient for this variable to be negative.

Table 7.3 reports the results from the OLS regression of candidate vote share. The baseline category in these models is each party's returning challenger—candidates who competed but lost in the last election. Model 1 focuses on LDP candidates exclusively, while model 2 runs the equation for DPJ candidates. Almost all the control variables conform to stated expectations. For both LDP and DPJ candidates, *SMD incumbents* did better in the 2005 election, winning 10.1 percent and 11.1 percent more than their respective returning challengers. *PR zombies* also tended to win more votes, although the coefficient is statistically significant only for DPJ zombies (+4.5 percent). *New candidates* tended to do a bit worse for both parties, and as expected, the variable *total candidates* is statistically significant and negative in both models.

The theoretically interesting result concerns the coattail effects generated by party-leader visits. Unfortunately for the DPJ, Okada's visits generated no boosts in vote share, nor did the candidates benefit from Okada's collective coattails. *Okada visit, Okada popularity,* and the interaction term between the two are all substantively and statistically insignificant. To some extent, this could be an artifact of Okada's poor choice of districts to visit, analyzed in the previous section. By focusing on incumbent candidates, Okada may have missed out on opportunities to convert independent voters to his cause.

Model 1 shows, however, that Koizumi's visits generated substantial increases in the vote shares of LDP candidates. The three key variables—*Koizumi visit, Koizumi popularity,* and the interaction term—are all statistically significant. Because interpreting the value of the collective effects of Koizumi's coattails (*Koizumi popularity*) and the additional selective effects generated by his visits (*Koizumi visit + Koizumi visit * Koizumi popularity*) requires some tricky disentangling of the component and interaction terms, I display their predicted effects in figure 7.1.

The baseline case in figure 7.1 is a returning LDP challenger (*SMD incumbent, PR zombie, new* = 0) competing in a district with two other candidates (*total candidates* = 3). The horizontal axis is *Koizumi popularity*, or the difference between Koizumi's personal support rating and the LDP's collective popularity in each prefecture. The dotted line depicts collective coattail effects from belonging to the same party as Koizumi, while the solid line incorporates the selective effects of party-leader visits. Not surprisingly, LDP candidates did better where

Table 7.3 The Effects of Party-Leader Visits

Model: OLS with robust standard errors (in parentheses)
DV: Candidate vote share

	Model 1: LDP	Model 2: DPJ
Constant	0.551*** (0.029)	0.517*** (0.035)
SMD incumbent	0.101*** (0.009)	0.110*** (0.010)
PR zombie	0.015 (0.013)	0.045*** (0.011)
New	-0.054*** (0.010)	-0.015 (0.013)
Koizumi popularity	0.003* (0.002)	
Koizumi visit	-0.100** (0.033)	
Koizumi visit*popularity	0.009*** (0.003)	
Okada popularity		0.002 (0.003)
Okada visit		0.038 (0.076)
Okada visit*popularity		-0.007 (0.009)
Total candidates	-0.041*** (0.007)	-0.062*** (0.008)
N	286	288
R²	0.584	0.509

Note: * = p<0.05; ** = p<0.01; *** = p<0.001

Koizumi's popularity was higher. Where Koizumi had a popularity level of 9 percent (the mean), LDP candidates had a predicted vote share of 46.1 percent. An increase in Koizumi's popularity of 5 percent raises the LDP candidate's vote share to 47.8 percent. While these coefficients are statistically significant, the actual substantive effect appears to be fairly small, as the difference between the maximum and minimal levels of Koizumi's popularity (12 percent) yields only a 4.2 percent vote swing.

Figure 7.1 Koizumi's Coattails and the LDP Vote Share

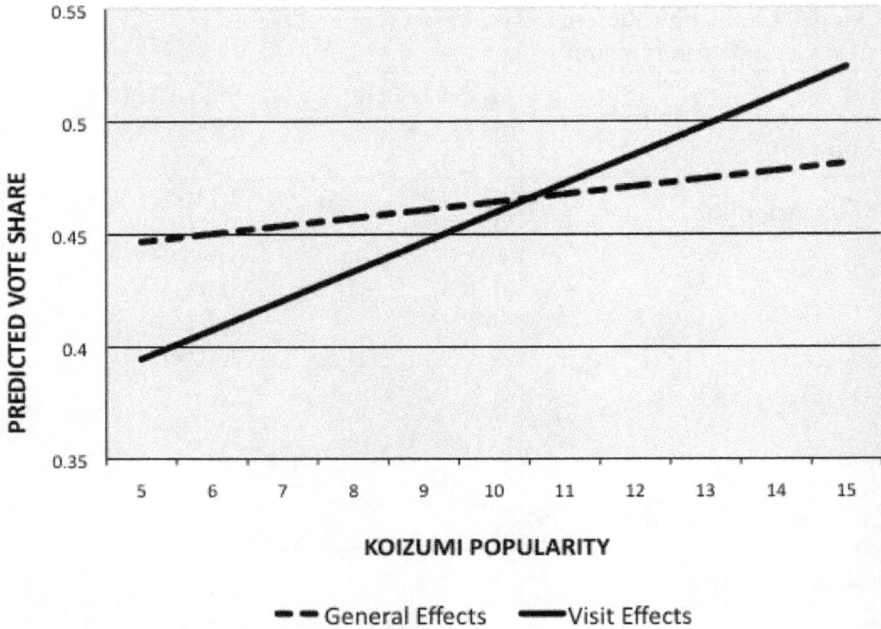

KOIZUMI POPULARITY

- - General Effects ——Visit Effects

The more interesting finding, however, is the effect of *Koizumi popularity* when Koizumi actually visits the district (figure 7.1, solid line). As Koizumi's popularity rises, we see the predicted vote shares of LDP candidates improve rapidly. A 1 percent increase in Koizumi's popularity raises the vote share of LDP candidates who host Koizumi during the election campaign by approximately 1.3 percent. Given an average turnout of 343,192 voters per district, a 1.3 percent increase in vote share equates to approximately 4,460 voters who changed their ballot choice by virtue of a Koizumi visit. As indicated earlier, Koizumi tended to visit districts where his own popularity was higher, and thus was more likely to affect election outcomes. Koizumi's median popularity in visited districts is 11 percent, compared to 9 percent in areas he did not visit; this difference alone generates a 2.6 percent swing in predicted vote share. While the average margin of victory between the SMD winner and the first runner-up in 2005 was 12.4 percent, approximately 15 percent of districts had margins smaller than 2.6 percent, suggesting important opportunities for Koizumi to leverage his popularity through leader visits.

To statistically minded readers, model 1's finding that Koizumi's visits reduced the vote shares of LDP candidates at low levels of *Koizumi popularity* may trigger concerns about endogeneity bias. As covered in the previous section on strategic resource allocation, the locations of Koizumi's visits are predicated on assumptions about their effects. Koizumi was more likely to visit districts where his presence would generate the highest marginal benefit—that is, where the predicted margin of victory was the smallest. Accordingly, the causal arrow between Koizumi's visits and the 2005 election outcome could theoretically go in either direction, resulting in a biased coefficient from the OLS model. In formal terms, the primary concern is that the *Koizumi visit* variable is correlated with the error term. Standard endogeneity tests show, however, that this is not the case, suggesting that the OLS model used here is appropriate.[16]

One caveat to note here is that it is difficult to assess the true effects of Koizumi's visits, because *Koizumi popularity*—the key variable driving the preceding results—is a combination of the support ratings for Koizumi and the LDP, which are not theoretically independent values. Some die-hard LDP partisans reflexively support Koizumi because he is the leader of their party, while a different subset of Koizumi fans support the LDP only because of their affection for the politician. If there are more intrinsic Koizumi supporters than intrinsic LDP supporters in reality, then our measure underestimates the length of Koizumi's coattails. If the opposite holds true and Koizumi supporters are LDP supporters first, then the *Koizumi popularity* variable overestimates the coattail effects. I am inclined to believe the first interpretation—that affection for Koizumi drew people to the LDP—over the second, because Koizumi's support rating was 7 to 11 percent higher than the LDP's in almost every district. Thus, the statistical findings most likely *under*estimate the true magnitude of Koizumi's coattails and how they paved the way for the LDP's stunning electoral victory in 2005.

Conclusion

Observers of European elections have noted the increasing "presidentialization" of parliamentary politics for close to two decades. The media focus on party leaders is unsurprising in presidential systems, where the chief executive (and putative party leader) competes in an election separate from that of the legislature. Parliamentary elections, in contrast, have traditionally been the preserve of the party collective. Yet a host of high-profile party leaders have emerged over the last twenty years—Margaret Thatcher and Tony Blair in the United Kingdom being notable examples. This suggests that charisma may be as important a criterion in picking party leaders as the traditional metrics of policy expertise, seniority, and the ability to forge internal consensus.

Japanese elections have historically been about more than party affiliation, since individual candidate characteristics and the personal vote have been at least as valuable as partisanship (Curtis 1971; Ramseyer and Rosenbluth 1993). If anything, the combination of a parliamentary system and personalistic politics should predispose Japanese elections against the measurable coattail effects of a party leader. This chapter's analysis challenges this view, as Prime Minister Koizumi produced an electoral windfall for his party's candidates by virtue of his overall popularity and the targeted, associational effects of his campaign visits.

In the months after the September 2005 election, Koizumi succeeded in leveraging his electoral coattails for legislative authority. The election left the LDP-Komeito coalition with more than two-thirds of Lower House seats—more than any government had held in the postwar period—and the postal-privatization plan was voted through the Diet with a large supermajority. Importantly, the government had enough seats to enact legislative motions for constitutional amendments, subject to approval in a national referendum. This intensified debates about Article 9 of the Japanese Constitution, which forbids the nation from having a military with offensive-use capabilities. The LDP circulated its proposed draft for a new constitution publicly, and while no changes seem to be forthcoming in the near future, the change in status of the Japan Defense Agency to the Ministry of Defense suggests a more aggressive security posture in the future.

What I do not address here—although it deserves serious analysis in the future—is whether Koizumi's 2005 coattails are unique in Japanese politics. There have been other popular prime ministers in the past, such as Yasuhiro Nakasone in the 1980s and Ryutaro Hashimoto in the mid-1990s, whose campaign visits may have generated an equal or larger electoral benefit. In fact, the effect of leader visits may have been higher when TV news was less dominant, because the novelty of seeing and hearing a party boss was greater.

At the same time, the 2005 election was marked by intense competition among conservative candidates divided by their positions on postal privatization. The opposition parties, particularly the DPJ, were marginalized in the campaign discourse because of the media's extensive coverage of the assassin districts. Given the electoral context, it is not surprising that Okada failed to generate coattails for DPJ candidates, but it is equally unlikely that intra-LDP conflict will continue to upstage the policy positions and stature of opposition party leaders.

Indeed, the size of leader coattails appears to depend on time and context. In the 2004 Upper House elections, Okada—who had just been selected DPJ president—succeeded in rallying voters as the new face of the opposition. In contrast, Shinzo Abe, who followed Koizumi as LDP president and was widely hailed for his populist appeal, led the party during the disastrous 2007 Upper House elections, when the LDP lost its legislative plurality in the Upper House for the first time in its history. Abe was plagued by popular distrust due to his decision to readmit many postal rebels who had beaten Koizumi's assassins, as well as by new revelations that the government had lost millions of pension records. The lesson, perhaps, is that while a popular leader can generate electoral coattails, his or her popularity itself is ephemeral, subject to political maneuvering and unforeseen events.

Notes

[1] Many thanks to Geoff Lorenz for help in gathering the survey data used in this paper.

[2] An important caveat is that the new electoral system allows losing SMD candidates to gain a second life as PR "zombies." Candidates can be listed in both SMD and PR tiers, and the tiebreaker for candidates with the same ranking in the PR tier is their *sekihairitsu*, or their proportion of votes relative to the SMD winner. For more details, see McKean and Scheiner (2000).

[3] The LDP and Komeito do not coordinate completely in all districts. While both sides avoid nominating candidates in the same district, formal cooperation in the form of vote bartering (for example, voting LDP in SMDs, voting Komeito in PR districts) is left to each party's district headquarters.

[4] The expenditure limit in each district in 2005 equaled 19.1 million yen (baseline) plus 15 yen per registered voter. There are also detailed rules about how much candidates can spend on specific items. For example, administrative staff members cannot be paid more than 10,000 yen a day, while food costs are capped at 3,000 yen per person per day.

[5] In practice, the parameters of what constitutes illegal online activities are vague. The POEL enumerates the various mediums that candidates and parties are permitted to use. Because the Internet is not mentioned in the POEL, electoral appeals on Web pages during the campaign period could be interpreted as illegal. While the DPJ argued that the original complaint—the illegality of uploading Okada's first speech after the campaign period started—did not constitute vote canvassing, the LDP, which has generally been lukewarm about electronic media, countered that because voters cast ballots for individual parties in the PR tier, even a collective endorsement of parties was illegal.

[6] Okada's visit data was gathered from his personal Web site, http://www.katsuya.net/report/2005/09/, where visit locations were listed *after* the election ended.

[7] On numerous occasions, Koizumi or Okada visited one particular electoral district and was joined not only by that district's home candidate but also by the candidates of neighboring districts. This was more likely in urban areas, where the party leader gave speeches in front of major train stations. I have coded these joint campaign stops as visits to all participating candidates, not just the home candidate. Voters in urban areas cross multiple electoral jurisdictions over the course of the day, particularly to and from work. The potential audience of a speech at Shibuya Station in Tokyo, for example, is not just the residents of Tokyo District 7, but some subset of the 2.4 million commuters who go through Shibuya daily.

[8] The Communist Party has traditionally been nonstrategic with respect to candidate nominations, running one candidate in each electoral district regardless of the candidate's prospects. The average vote share of a Japan Communist Party (JCP) candidate in 2005 was 2.2 percent.

[9] An important caveat is that party leaders *did* visit electoral districts prior to the beginning of the official campaign period. After the Lower House was dissolved on August 8, party leaders gave policy speeches in front of train stations, department stores, and other commuter hubs. These visits were occasionally accompanied by potential candidates in the next election, but did *not* involve endorsements of these candidates (which would have been illegal under the POEL). Lacking systematic data on these earlier visits, I instead count stops only during the official campaign period.

[10] The omission of candidate names is based on requirements of the POEL, which stipulates that newspapers must remain neutral in their coverage of election news. In practice, this means that newspapers will write down the names of candidates only when all the candidates are included in the article.

[11] There is a small possibility of data contamination in this survey. Because the survey responses were collected over August 31 and September 2—*after* the actual campaign period had started—some respondents may have seen one of the party leaders and changed their opinions before they answered the survey. But since the *Asahi* poll had an average of four hundred responses per electoral district (between one hundred and eight hundred per prefecture), I expect the number of respondents who may have seen the party leaders to be a relatively small proportion of the sample, and hence inconsequential in the final analysis.

[12] The *Asahi Shimbun* did not report responses to the first question (Koizumi versus Okada) for 11 out of 47 prefectures. Here, I used Stata 9's *impute* function to fill in the gaps. *Impute* uses an OLS regression to estimate the predicted value of the missing data. The independent variables used here include (1) prefectural approval/disapproval rates of the cabinet, as reported by the *Yomiuri Shimbun* (June 9, 2005); (2) prefectural support rates for the LDP and DPJ (question 2 in the *Asahi* survey); and (3) the proportion of voters with no party attachment (also from the *Asahi* survey). For each party leader, the imputation regression took the following form:

$$Koizumi = b_0 + b_1(cabinet\ approval) + b_2(LDP\ support) + b_3(no\ party\ preference) + error$$
$$Okada = b_0 + b_1(cabinet\ disapproval) + b_2(DPJ\ support) + b_3(no\ party\ preference) + error$$

[13] Replacing *2003 margin* with similar measures of past performance—difference in vote share between the conservative and progressive candidate, or the average margin of victory over the last two elections—produced no statistically significant differences.

[14] I experimented with various operationalizations—such as whether the district housed the main train station of that prefecture, whether the prefectural capital was located in that district, and the level of population density—but none was statistically or substantively significant.

[15] Predicted probabilities are generated using the Clarify program in the Stata statistics package (King, Tomz, and Wittenberg 2000). I initially explored using event count data (number of times each district was visited) and a zero-inflated negative binomial regression, instead of the logistic regression. However, because the number of double visits by each leader was small relative to the sample (1 for Koizumi and 12 for Okada), I believe that a dichotomous dependent variable is more appropriate.

[16] I first test for endogeneity by rerunning model 1, table 7.3, and including the residuals from model 1A, table 7.2, as an additional independent variable. If the residual term is statistically significant, then we cannot discount endogeneity bias. But I find that this variable is not significant at conventional levels, suggesting that the OLS model is appropriate. In cases of endogeneity bias, the standard approach is to use a Heckman selection model or some related treatment effects model that analyzes the effect of an endogenously chosen binary outcome on another endogenous continuous variable. This method requires us to simultaneously estimate two models: (1) a probit model to predict the location of Koizumi's visits, using the independent variables from table 7.2, and (2) a linear regression that includes the predicted probabilities of the visit from (1) to measure LDP vote share. I test this possibility using Stata 9's "treatreg" function with two-step consistent estimators, as well as a Heckman selection model (Stata 9's "heckman"). I find that the results of the treatment effects and selection models are not statistically different from the OLS used in this chapter. More formally, the correlation of the error terms of the two stages (*rho*) is not statistically significant at conventional levels.

References

Asahi Shimbun, various years. This and other newspaper articles cited in this chapter are available upon request from the author.

Bélanger, Paul, R. Kenneth Carty, and Munroe Eagles. 2003. The geography of Canadian parties' electoral campaigns: Leaders' tours and constituency election results. *Political Geography* 22:439–55.

Browne, Eric C., and Dennis Patterson. 1999. An empirical theory of rational nominating behavior applied to Japanese district elections. *British Journal of Political Science* 29:259–89.

Christensen, Ray. 2000. *Ending the LDP hegemony: Party cooperation in Japan.* Honolulu: Univ. of Hawaii Press.

Cox, Gary W. 1997. *Making votes count: Strategic coordination in the world's electoral systems.* Cambridge: Cambridge Univ. Press.

Curtis, Gerald L. 1971. *Election campaigning Japanese style.* Tokyo: Kodansha International Ltd.

Damore, David F., and Thomas G. Hansford. 1999. The allocation of party controlled campaign resources in the House of Representatives, 1989–1996. *Political Research Quarterly* 52 (2): 371–85.

Duverger, Maurice. 1954. *Political parties: Their organization and activity in the modern state.* New York: Wiley.

Herrnson, Paul S., and Irwin L. Morris. 2006. Beyond coattails: Presidential campaign visits and congressional elections. Univ. of Maryland. Unpublished manuscript.

Inoguchi, Takashi. 1982. Explaining and predicting Japanese general elections, 1960–1980. *Journal of Japanese Studies* 7.

Jacobson, Gary C. 1989. Strategic politicians and the dynamics of U.S. House elections, 1946–86. *American Political Science Review* 83 (3): 773–93.

Jacobson, Gary C., Samuel Kernell, and Lazarus Jeffrey. 2004. Assessing the president's role as party agent in congressional elections: The case of Bill Clinton in 2000. *Legislative Studies Quarterly* 29 (2): 159–84.

King, Gary, Michael Tomz, and Jason Wittenberg. 2000. Making the most of statistical analyses: Improving interpretation and presentation. *American Journal of Political Science* 44 (2): 341–55.

Krauss, Ellis S., and Benjamin Nyblade. 2005. Presidentialization in Japan? The prime minister, media, and elections in Japan. *British Journal of Political Science* 35:357–68.

Lewis-Beck, Michael. 1988. *Economics and elections: The major Western democracies.* Ann Arbor: Univ. of Michigan Press.

McElwain, Kenneth Mori. 2008. Manipulating electoral rules to manufacture single-party dominance. *American Journal of Political Science* 52 (1): 32–47.

McKean, Margaret, and Ethan Scheiner. 2000. Japan's new electoral system: *La plus ça change . . . Electoral Studies* 19:447–77.

Poguntke, Thomas, and Paul Webb. 2005. *The Presidentialization of politics: A comparative study of modern democracies.* Oxford: Oxford Univ. Press.

Powell, G. Bingham, and Guy D. Whitten. 1993. A cross-national analysis of economic voting: Taking account of the political context. *American Journal of Political Science* 37 (2): 391–414.

Ramseyer, J. Mark, and Frances McCall Rosenbluth. 1993. *Japan's political marketplace.* Cambridge, MA: Harvard Univ. Press.

Reed, Steven R. 1991. Structure and behavior: Extending Duverger's Law to the Japanese case. *British Journal of Political Science* 29 (1): 335–56.

Reed, Steven R. 2007. Duverger's Law is working in Japan. *Senkyo Kenkyuu* 22: 96–106.

Scheiner, Ethan. 2005. *Democracy without competition in Japan: Opposition failure in a one-party dominant state.* Cambridge: Cambridge Univ. Press.

Appendix 7.A Descriptive Statistics for Tables 7.2 and 7.3

Continuous variables	Mean	Standard deviation	Min., max.
Distance_log	5.153	1.751	0, 7.575
Distance_sq	29.605	13.938	0, 57.375
Koizumi popularity	9.812	2.849	3, 15
Okada popularity	8.467	1.411	4, 12
No party preference	43.527	1.729	40, 48
2003 margin	0.158	0.147	0.002, 0.791
Vote share (2005)	0.310	0.190	0.022, 0.736
Candidate/district	3.329	0.627	2, 6
Dichotomous variables	Total	LDP + Komeito	DPJ
SMD incumbent	286	144	104
PR zombie	114	39	62
New	264	63	55
Assassin districts	33		

TWO STEPS FORWARD, ONE STEP BACK: JAPANESE POSTAL PRIVATIZATION AS A WINDOW ON POLITICAL AND POLICYMAKING CHANGE

Patricia L. Maclachlan

As recently as 2004, the conventional wisdom was that the Japanese political system had failed to fulfill its potential for change. One scholar opined that the policymaking process—with the Liberal Democratic Party (LDP) at its core—had lost its effectiveness and that democracy in general had become dysfunctional. While Prime Minister Junichiro Koizumi was still widely perceived as Japan's best hope for change, many observers were disappointed that he had failed to carry out his agenda for comprehensive political and economic reform (Kitaoka 2004:6).

Less than two years later, after the passage of Koizumi's postal-privatization bills in October 2005, critics on both sides of the Pacific were hailing the dawn of a new era. The September 11, 2005, general election, which had been fought over issues of policy rather than pork, had severed official ties between the LDP and the influential postmasters' associations. The postal-privatization laws—the product of a new kind of top-down, executive leadership centered on the cabinet office—promised to transform the 130-year-old postal system while weakening the bureaucracy's role in Japanese finances. And the LDP, now cleansed of its antireform elements, was poised to embark on a path of dramatic political and economic reform. For all intents and purposes, it seemed that the "1955 system" (the LDP was eslablished in 1995) had died its last death and that the country was on the threshold of a new "2005 system" (Yamawaki 2005:5).

Or was it? We can now assess Koizumi's achievements in hindsight: what exactly changed under his tutelage and to what extent can we expect those changes to endure? To answer these questions, this chapter analyzes developments in the legislative and electoral processes through the prism of postal privatization, an issue that Koizumi upheld as the most important prerequisite for political and economic change. While I focus more on the processes than on the content of postal privatization, it is important to keep the purposes of privatization in mind. First, Koizumi regarded postal privatization as an essential step toward the reinvigoration of Japan's flagging financial sector. Of particular concern was the Fiscal Investment and Loan Program (FILP), the state's massive "second budget," which was built largely on proceeds from the postal savings and insurance systems. Used to fund a wide range of postwar state projects, including industrial development, public works, and—more recently—support for small and medium enterprises (SMEs) and local infrastructural development, the FILP had long been criticized for contributing to bureaucratic inefficiency and financial wastage, diverting funds from the private banking system, and fueling political corruption. Koizumi and many economists maintained that by privatizing the postal system's financial services and subjecting them to a broader range of incentives to invest in private markets, the FILP would shrink in both size and political significance; these developments would in turn help jump-start the sluggish private banking sector while paving the way for more financial and economic reform in the future (Cargill and Yoshino 2003). Second, Koizumi believed that creating separate companies corresponding to each of the three main postal services (savings, insurance, and mail delivery) and privatizing the first two would weaken the political influence of the postal network—perhaps the largest institutional network in the country (Maeno 1987:163). At the center of that network were two major interest groups: the National Association of Commissioned Postmasters (Zenkoku Tokutei Yubinkyokuchokai) or Zentoku, and Taiju no Kai, a large association of retired postmasters. Together, the associations functioned as a veritable electoral machine, mobilizing votes behind LDP candidates—primarily in Upper House elections—in exchange for policies that preserved the status quo within the postal sector. Koizumi reasoned that by removing their status as public servants and subjecting them to the vicissitudes of private markets, the postmasters' organizational cohesiveness and dependence on the LDP would decline. And as the hold of vested interests over the party loosened, conservative politicians would be more inclined to pursue rigorous financial and economic reform. In sum, Koizumi recognized that the political and economic stakes of postal privatization were high: change the post office and you change Japan.

In this chapter, after briefly chronicling the history of postal privatization during the 1990s, I explore two stages of Koizumi's post-2001 postal crusade: his minimally successful efforts in 2002 to subject the mail-delivery service to competition; and his push to fully privatize the postal system, which culminated in the stunning electoral and legislative events of September and October 2005. In so doing, I show how Koizumi learned from his disappointing performance in 2002 by making creative use of new policymaking institutions, overturning decision-making norms within the LDP, and manipulating the post-1994 electoral rules to pass his postal-privatization bills. But while these actions had a major impact on the postal system and on Japanese politics over the short term, the evidence suggests that Japan is now partially unraveling these changes. After examining these recent developments, I argue in the final section of this chapter that, despite new institutional procedures designed to encourage top-down, executive policymaking and electoral rules that weaken the organized vote, the interest-group machinations that characterized the legislative processes under the old "1955" system have not yet disappeared.

The Road to Privatization

Although postal privatization has been an issue in Japan for decades, it was not until the late 1990s that it assumed a prominent position on the government agenda. In this section, I trace major developments in the privatization saga from the Ryutaro Hashimoto administration through Koizumi's landmark election in September 2005.

The Hashimoto Reforms

When Koizumi assumed the prime ministership in April 2001, the state-owned postal system was being primed for corporatization in 2003 in response to Prime Minister Hashimoto's initiatives of the late 1990s. Although he was linked to the postal lobby through his personal and factional connections to the late Kakuei Tanaka, in November 1996 Hashimoto commissioned the Administrative Reform Council (Gyosei Kaikaku Kaigi) to make recommendations for postal privatization as a stepping stone to broader financial reform. The subsequent decision-making process was a telling illustration of the dynamics of postal politics in late-twentieth-century Japan.

Issued in August 1997, the council's interim report met Hashimoto's expectations to the letter: while the mail-delivery service was to remain under direct government control, the council called for the division of the three services into separate corporate entities, the immediate privatization of postal insurance, and the eventual privatization of postal savings. The report met with vehement opposition from leading members of the political lobby, known informally as the postal family (yusei famirii): LDP politicians in the so-called postal tribe (yusei zoku), bureaucrats in the Ministry of Posts and Telecommunications (MPT; now the Ministry of Internal Affairs and Communications, or MIC), and Japan's network of approximately 19,000 commissioned postmasters as represented by Zentoku.[1] Led by Hiromu Nonaka, the "don" of the postal tribe and an avowed friend of the postmasters, the postal family argued that by eliminating cross-subsidization within the services and subjecting them to market competition, the government plan would push the financially vulnerable mail service deeper into the red and small, inefficient post offices into bankruptcy; this would in turn weaken the network of commissioned postmasters as one of the LDP's most reliable vote-gathering machines.

By October it appeared that the aggressive postal family would force the government to drop its postal-reform plans altogether. Then Koizumi entered the fray, threatening to resign his position as minister of health and welfare if the three services remained under direct state control. Fearing the effects that an unprecedented cabinet resignation would have on his already tarnished reformist image and weak public approval ratings, Hashimoto mustered the wherewithal to cobble together a compromise (Yamawaki 2005:84–85). As the postmasters petitioned the LDP and lobbied local assemblies to adopt resolutions opposing the council's interim report (Kowaguchi 1998:35), Hashimoto and his team resolved to permit the postal savings and insurance programs to invest their funds in private markets rather than channel them directly into the FILP. They then cut a deal with Nonaka. Like other proponents of the state-run postal system, Nonaka recognized the social significance of post offices in rural Japan but worried about the system's future revenue streams.[2] He was eventually persuaded to accept corporatization of the postal system on the grounds that it would both enhance the services' profitability and preserve the interservice synergies that were considered so essential to the survival of individual post offices and hence to the postal network's integrity.

To Nonaka and others in the postal family, corporatization was a tolerable compromise that preserved the institutional foundations of their political power while making them look like bona fide reformers. Koizumi, in contrast, would not be placated. Although the reform plan was by all accounts a step in the right direction, Koizumi was frustrated by the interest-group machinations and consensus-oriented decision-making process that had so diluted Hashimoto's reform vision. He refused to rest until the services had been split up and privatized.

Koizumi's 2002 Legislative Experiment

For a number of reasons, Koizumi was widely known as an anti-postal-system (*han yusei*) Diet member. His grandfather, Matajiro Koizumi, was an early advocate of postal reform; while serving as Prime Minister Osachi Hamaguchi's communications minister for two years from 1929, Matajiro advocated the creation of an independent account for the postal services—an objective that was finally fulfilled in 1934—as well as the privatization of the telephone and telegraph services (Yuseishohen 1971:576). Following in his father's footsteps, Junichiro Koizumi was a loyal member of Takeo Fukuda's faction and a proponent of the Ministry of Finance, which as head of the FILP was in a state of almost perpetual competition with the MPT for control over the proceeds of the postal system's financial services.[3] When Koizumi made his first bid for his deceased father's seat in Kanagawa during the 1970s, he was defeated by a margin of only four thousand votes; many of his supporters blamed the electoral actions of the postmasters for his loss (Yamawaki 2005:46).[4] The postmasters were again a problem for Koizumi during the 1978 LDP presidential primary. While Koizumi stood by his faction boss, Tanaka and his henchmen rallied the party's rank-and-file members—many of them systematically recruited by Zentoku—behind Masayoshi Ohira, the eventual winner (Segawa 2001:15–17 and 64). The postal family also mobilized behind Koizumi's opponents during his two failed attempts in the 1990s to win the LDP presidency.

Although we may never know if Koizumi harbored a personal grudge against the postmasters, he was clearly no fan of state ownership of the postal system. As the minister of posts and telecommunications under Prime Minister Kiichi Miyazawa, he spoke out against the tax-exempt status (*maruyu*) of the postal savings service, was quick to deny the budgetary requests of post officials, and routinely trumpeted postal privatization as a prerequisite for comprehensive banking reform (Yamawaki 2005:23).

One of Koizumi's first objectives as prime minister was to build on Hashimoto's limited postal reforms as a subsequent step toward privatization. Koizumi was skeptical that the flexible management and business accounting system of the new postal corporation—Japan Post (Nihon Yusei Kosha)—would solve the postal system's long-term problems. He was particularly disturbed by projections of rising interest rates, which would have a detrimental effect on the revenue streams of the system's financial services. He also believed that keeping the three services under one corporate roof—one of the postal family's primary demands—would dampen competition and foster management inefficiencies.

In the summer of 2002, Koizumi appointed Masaharu Ikuta as director of the Postal Services Agency (Yusei Jigyocho), which had been launched in January 2001 to administer the postal services until the establishment of Japan Post in 2003. Ikuta defied the consensus-oriented, bottom-up decision-making norms of the postal bureaucracy by imposing top-down leadership procedures on the agency's administrative structure and introducing a host of horizontal organizations to help overcome bureaucratic sectionalism (Yamawaki 2005:25–26). He also weakened the influence of the approximately one hundred "family enterprises" that serviced the postal network by injecting more competition into contract bidding. These steps lowered costs within the services and made the family enterprises less appealing landing spots for retired (*amakudari*, literally "descent from heaven") bureaucrats from the MIC. Meanwhile, Ikuta encouraged product innovation within the postal services and forged a business partnership with Lawson, the nationwide chain of convenience stores. These innovative, cost-cutting steps placed the mail service on sound financial footing after several years of decline.

Koizumi's support for administrative and financial innovation in the Postal Services Agency raised the ire of MIC bureaucrats, many of whom had opposed him since his days as minister of posts and telecommunications. In 2002 post officials were well positioned to score points against Koizumi as he moved to inject competition into the mail service. For, by heeding policymaking custom and delegating the legislative drafting process to the MIC—the ministry in charge of the reform agenda—Koizumi unwittingly opened that process to pressure from the ministry's allies, namely, members of the LDP's postal tribe and the commissioned postmasters, all stalwart opponents of reform in any guise.

In the end, Koizumi defied LDP custom by forcing the cabinet to adopt his postal-reform bills without first securing the party's approval, knowing full well that the LDP was prepared to reject the bills outright. As we shall see, Koizumi's legislative actions grew even more audacious when comprehensive postal reform was on the table. In 2002, however, his maverick behavior failed to subdue the postal family, as evidenced by the very content of the legislation. Put simply, the bills contained enough loopholes to render competition virtually meaningless.

In a blow to price competition between the post offices and the private sector, private entrants into the national mail-delivery market were required to charge uniform delivery fees. New entrants also had to set up approximately one hundred thousand mailboxes (*posuto*) around the country, a prohibitive and needless expense for firms such as Yamato Transport Company that serviced their customers door-to-door or at retail outlets.[5] Not surprisingly, no firms entered the national market between 2003 and 2005.

Koizumi's Postal-Privatization Plan

In 2003 Koizumi put postal privatization at the top of his agenda. Koizumi and his allies maintained that the many prerequisites enjoyed by the services—ranging from corporate and property-tax exemptions to government guarantees of postal savings deposits and interservice synergies—gave the postal services a grossly unfair advantage over private-sector firms. They also hoped that separating the three services and privatizing postal savings and postal insurance would weaken the political functions of the postal network and hence the nucleus of the antireform postal family.

For the most part, Japanese policymaking during the last decades of the twentieth century was centered on the bureaucracy and based on consensus-building between key actors in the relevant ministries and LDP policy tribes. Led by Heizo Takenaka, the post-2003 policymaking process surrounding postal privatization defied tradition by creating institutional spaces for top-down "political" leadership. The most conspicuous expression of this shift was the Council on Economic and Fiscal Policy's (CEFP's) assumption of ultimate authority over the reform process. Lodged in the cabinet office, and led by and answerable to the prime minister, the advisory council consisted of the cabinet's leading economic ministers as well as several high-profile individuals from academia and the private sector. By pulling cabinet ministers out of their bureaucratic bailiwicks, making them directly accountable to the prime minister, and publicizing council minutes on the official CEFP Web site, the council was designed to minimize the influence of special interests. But the council failed to live up to its potential after its establishment in January 2001, meeting only seven times during the Yoshiro Mori administration and accomplishing virtually nothing (Kato 2004; Takenaka 2006:245). Some scholars attribute the council's early failures to the organizational mentality of the bureaucracy, which prevented officials in various ministries from interacting flexibly and effectively with one another (Kato 2004:35). As the early stages of the post-2003 privatization saga suggests, however, interest-group politics were as much—if not more—to blame.

Takenaka took several steps to ensure that the CEFP would follow his (and Koizumi's) lead on postal reform. First, he selected private-sector council members who supported his views on privatization. Second, he and his aides drew up a list of five basic principles that served as the cornerstone for council discussions, which began in the fall (Takenaka 2006:152). Contrary to custom, in which guiding principles were often subject to negotiation at various stages of the decision-making process, Takenaka presented his principles as inviolable at the council's first meeting on privatization and immediately extracted a pledge from council members to respect them. Briefly stated, the principles required that postal privatization (1) invigorate (*kassei*) society and the economy, (2) be consistent with past financial reforms, (3) enhance the convenience of postal customers, (4) make use of the human and infrastructural resources of the postal system, and (5) protect the employment of the greatest possible number of employees within the system. In some ways, these principles acknowledged the concerns of the antireform camp regarding the adverse effects of privatization on the postal network and the employment of the postmasters and postal workers. But they did not, as we shall see, prevent council discussions from sliding into conflict.

Third, to help transcend intracouncil conflict and the fact that no members were experts on the postal system, Takenaka established what was eventually dubbed a guerrilla unit (*gerira butai*)—an inner circle of close aides who fleshed out a game plan for deliberations that would keep the initiative on Koizumi's side. This game plan, which included the division of the postal services into separate corporate entities and the subjection of each service to the same laws that governed comparable private-sector firms, constituted the bottom line for postal privatization (Takenaka 2006:156–57). And to protect that bottom line, Takaneka initiated—and Koizumi approved—the spring 2004 establishment of the Postal Privatization Preparation Office (PPPO, Yusei Min'eika Junbi Shitsu) under the auspices of the cabinet office's secretariat. Consisting of about eighty academics and sympathetic officials from throughout the bureaucracy, the PPPO drew up the September 2004 Postal Privatization Basic Plan (Yusei Min'eika Kihon Hoshin), which served as the blueprint for the 2005 legislation, as well as the legislative bills themselves (Takenaka 2006:122). At an April 26, 2004, ceremony launching the PPPO, Koizumi himself helped write the office's signboard. The event was widely reported by the press, and the accompanying photograph of Koizumi, Takenaka, and two PPPO officials sent a clear message to the public that the prime minister was ultimately in charge of the postal-privatization process (Takenaka 2006:156).

With these supplementary institutions in place, all the CEFP needed to do was approve the handiwork of the PPPO. But this was easier said than done. From the start, Masaharu Ikuta, now president of Japan Post, and Taro Aso, the minister of internal affairs and communications and a friend of the postal family, stalemated the proceedings as they opposed Takenaka's bottom-line requirement that the postal system be divided into three independent services. Meanwhile, key LDP leaders put relentless pressure on Takenaka, threatening to withhold party approval of the privatization plan if Aso's concerns were not addressed. The stalemate dragged on until early September 2004, when Koizumi intervened by meeting personally with Ikuta and Aso. Finally, on September 7, the council adopted the Postal Privatization Basic Plan. A few days later, after

163

Koizumi obtained the LDP's reluctant approval, the cabinet officially endorsed the plan (Takenaka 2006:165–71). Japan Post was to be broken up into four companies, one each for mail delivery, postal savings, postal insurance, and the network of post offices, plus a government holding company that would divest its shares in the postal savings and insurance companies by 2017.[6] Takenaka's basic principles and bottom-line requirements had emerged from the political maelstrom intact, and a fundamental step toward the weakening of the FILP had been reached.

As the PPPO prepared to draft a series of postal-privatization bills, Takenaka, now the minister in charge of postal privatization, launched an all-out campaign to overcome the LDP's lingering resistance by appealing directly to public opinion (Takenaka 2006:174 and 185). Recognizing that most Japanese were befuddled by, or simply not interested in, the complex economic and political motivations behind postal reform,[7] he set out to sell the basic plan in a flurry of town-meeting and television appearances around the country.[8] His message was simple: by expanding the range of services offered by the local post office, postal privatization would improve the lives of consumers and their communities.

Takenaka and Koizumi also offered some concessions to their opponents, knowing full well that the LDP would never vote for the bills without them. These included the establishment of a large government fund to help struggling post offices in rural areas adapt to market forces and continue to provide informal social services to their communities.[9] Takenaka also guaranteed one post office for each town and village, a pledge that helped appease members of the postal family who worried about the possible effects of privatization on both the size and employment levels of the postal network, as well as residents who feared that exposure to competitive market forces would force tiny local post offices into bankruptcy.[10]

While he fought with antireform politicians in the LDP, Takenaka faced opposition from turf-sensitive bureaucrats. In a nod to custom intended to facilitate the smooth implementation of postal privatization, Koizumi instructed Takenaka and the PPPO to invite the input of the relevant economic ministries during the legislative drafting stage, a concession that immediately triggered unwanted interference from the MIC. As Takenaka later revealed, a handful of PPPO bureaucrats remained faithful to the bureaucratic tradition of keeping concerned actors in the legislative loop by leaking information to the MIC and members of the LDP's postal tribe about both the drafting process and Takenaka's personal intentions (Takenaka 2006:176). More dramatically, and in a move that symbolized the bureaucracy's resentment toward its diminishing influence over the policy process, two MIC bureaucrats presented the cabinet with their own set of bills. Tacitly backed by Aso, the bills struck at the heart of Koizumi's ultimate objectives by keeping all three services under a single institutional umbrella, thereby preserving the postal system's susceptibility to pressures from the postal lobby. They also catered to LDP politicians nervous about their electoral fortunes by effectively protecting the postal network and the commissioned postmasters who administered it.[11] Koizumi swiftly rejected the bills and then fired the MIC bureaucrats who had drafted them in collaboration with the LDP's postal tribe.[12] It was an unprecedented move that one angry LDP Diet member described as "a reign of terror" (*Japan Times,* May 18, 2005)—an unwarranted attack by an upstart prime minister against party and bureaucratic prerogatives within the policymaking sphere.

Before the cabinet adopted Takenaka's bills, Takenaka and Koizumi carried out behind-the-scenes meetings (*nemawashi*) with key government ministers, many of whom still had strong misgivings about privatization. As before, Aso was particularly adamant in his opposition, attacking Takenaka personally and accusing him of hating Kasumigaseki (a district in Chiyoda Ward, often used figuratively to refer to the Japanese bureaucracy). Takenaka, for his own part, privately branded Aso a "front" for the postal family (Takenaka 2006:191–92). In the end, first the ministers and then the party leadership cleared the bills, but their support was based on the understanding that the bills would be amended once they reached the Diet. The LDP had authorized the cabinet to submit the bills to the Lower House on April 27 without endorsing their content.

Lower House committee deliberations on the privatization bills began in late May. The proceedings were predictably contentious, with LDP backbenchers voicing their opposition as loudly as the opposition parties. The privatization issues that proved the most troublesome to the LDP were precisely those that had a bearing on the political future of the postal family: the impact of privatization on the size of the postal network, the effects of the separation of the three services on the ability of individual post offices to offer a full range of financial services to their customers, and the future profitability of the privatized services (Takenaka 2006:206–08). Since the Democratic Party of Japan (DPJ) was too divided to sway the proceedings, the debate was largely an intra-LDP affair. Finally, Takenaka and Koizumi granted their opponents several concessions, including the expansion of the government fund from 1 trillion yen to up to 2 trillion yen, and the provision that the government holding company could retain up to one-third of its shares in the postal savings and insurance companies after 2017. After 109 hours of questions—a period, Takenaka claims, that exceeded the committee time devoted to the Mutual Security Treaty in 1960 (Takenaka 2006:216)—the committee approved the bills and submitted them to the chamber for a vote.

On July 5, 2005, the Lower House passed the postal-privatization bills by a 5-vote margin, with 37 LDP members voting against them and an additional 14 either abstaining from or boycotting the vote (*Japan Times,* July 6, 2005). The next challenge was to secure passage through the Upper House, where the LDP did not enjoy a firm majority and its opposition to postal privatization was particularly entrenched. Despite Koizumi's and Takenaka's best efforts to win over individual Diet members, the Upper House defeated the bills by a vote of 125 to 108 on August 8.

The Election

What happened next is now the stuff of political legend. A day after the bills' defeat, Koizumi made good his long-standing threat to dissolve the Lower House and call a snap election, which was to be fought as a referendum on postal privatization. He then withheld the LDP's endorsement for candidates who had voted against the bills, dispatching young, pro-privatization "assassins" (*shikaku*) to run against them. The move, which was made possible by Koizumi's unprecedented control over party nominations, signified once again his willingness to defy party custom as he pushed his reform agenda forward. All the while, he appealed to ordinary Japanese to throw their support behind the pro-reform LDP and against the "rebels" (*zohansha*), the DPJ, and other "forces of resistance," as he called them. By all accounts, it was a masterful manipulation of the voters, most of whom were enthusiastic about reform but apathetic—if not downright confused—about postal privatization.

The short-term effects of Koizumi's gambit on the LDP's ties to the commissioned postmasters were profound. While many postmasters opted to side with the LDP on the assumption that Koizumi was nothing but a passing phenomenon,[13] Zentoku officially abandoned the party during the campaign. Taiju, the association of retired postmasters, viewed Koizumi's attack on the LDP's "forces of resistance" as a betrayal of the postmasters' long-standing exchange relationship with the party. Both associations vowed to back the rebels in constituencies where they were running either as independents or as members of the newly formed Kokumin Shinto or Shinto Nippon; where there were no rebels running, association chapters were given the freedom to back whomever they preferred. For the first time in their postwar history, the postmasters' associations failed to speak with a single voice in an election. Thanks in large part to the postmasters' backing, 15 of the 33 rebels were reelected (Christensen 2006:504), including Seiko Noda, a former minister of posts and telecommunications who had voted against the privatization bills in July.[14] But the LDP ultimately triumphed, securing a landslide victory with 296 of the 480 seats.

On October 11, the Lower House passed the postal-privatization bills by a 200-vote margin; the Upper House followed suit 3 days later with 34 votes to spare. The bills were passed unchanged, save for one small point: to accommodate the delays caused by the election and allow for the reconfiguration of the postal system's computer network, the government agreed to postpone the start date for the privatization process from April to October 2007.

Assessing the Significance of Postal Privatization

The postal-privatization saga appeared to transform Japanese politics on many fronts: the institutional norms of the legislative process; the triangular relations among conservative politicians, bureaucrats, and the commissioned postmasters; and even the manner in which elections were conducted. The remainder of this chapter summarizes some of these changes in an effort to understand not only Koizumi's impact on Japanese politics but also the extent to which we can expect it to endure.

The Financial System

Although the financial prospects of the postal savings and insurance programs are beyond the scope of this chapter, two points warrant attention. First, while privatization is expected to diversify the range of products offered by the two services, it will by no means rid them of the threats of rising interest rates and a liberalized financial system, both of which will complicate the services' efforts to maintain their supremacy in their respective sectors. But the Japan Post Bank enjoys a distinct size advantage that should help offset these challenges. While the private banks are organized at the regional and city levels, the Post Bank has maintained the nationwide scope of its state-administered predecessor, thereby allowing it to subsidize operations in unprofitable regions with proceeds from profitable ones. Contrary to Koizumi's intentions to place postal savings on a level playing field with the private banks, the Post Bank will remain a formidable competitor in private financial markets.

Second, while postal privatization will undoubtedly help shrink the FILP, it will not eliminate it. In FY 1996, the FILP budget reached a historic high of 40.5 trillion yen; after nearly a decade of decreases, projections for FY 2008 stand at 13.9 trillion yen (*Japan Times*, August 31, 2007). These decreases reflect a number of developments, including conservative reactions to the postal system's investment independence from 2001, the reform of government institutions in the wake of Koizumi's 2005 electoral and legislative victories, and efforts over the past decade to reduce Japan's public-works projects. But when all is said and done, there is still significant support for the FILP among politicians, bureaucrats, and even economists; in fact, a government commission has been quietly at work since the passage of Koizumi's postal-privatization package to investigate ways to adapt a smaller FILP to Japan's current needs. Nothing, moreover, will stop the Post Bank from continuing to purchase FILP bonds.[15] In the words of one insider and Takenaka acquaintance, it had long been Koizumi's and Takenaka's wish that postal privatization would help "kill the FILP."[16] This wish is likely to remain unfulfilled, at least for the time being. The political implications of this are profound: as long as the FILP survives, interest groups will continue to pressure the ruling party for a piece of the fund's pie.

The LDP

The postal-privatization process both reflected and contributed to changes within the LDP. Needless to say, the LDP had changed significantly even before Koizumi assumed the presidency, the role of factions and their effects on political leadership being among the more salient cases in point. In the past, career advancement for LDP politicians was heavily dependent on obtaining seniority in the factions; as a result, cabinet members tended to have fairly short tenures and were thus poorly positioned to exercise significant leadership over their ministries (Kitaoka 2004:8). Factions were already on the wane by 2001, thanks largely to the 1994 reform of the multimember district (MMD) system, which had encouraged factional longevity by obliging LDP candidates to run against one another in Lower House electoral districts.

The nature of Koizumi's ascension to the presidency in 2001 both reflected and strengthened these trends. The revival of a primary system for selecting the party president, for instance, increased the power of local LDP chapters and the party rank-and-file relative to that of factions, thereby making the party more attentive to Japan's expanding cohort of urban floating voters (Blechinger-Talcott 2004:24). These developments allowed Koizumi—who from the start was disinclined to follow the party's rule book—to partially transcend what remained of factional power by shuffling his cabinet without consulting faction leaders, disregarding factional wishes, appealing to the public for support, inventing a new cabinet portfolio to enable Heizo Takenaka (who until 2004 lacked a seat in the Diet) to lead key reform projects, and conducting election campaigns on issues of policy rather than factional affiliations. There was perhaps no better proof of Koizumi's leadership skills and the institutional changes that facilitated them than the grudging willingness of the likes of Mikio Aoki, the leader of the LDP Upper House caucus and a vocal critic of postal privatization, to back Koizumi in his successful 2003 reelection to the party presidency on the grounds that he was in a position to lead the party to electoral victory (*Japan Times,* September 23, 2003).

The DPJ

Koizumi's ability to disregard the factions and exercise broad political leadership deepened the long-standing fissures within the DPJ, reducing it to a minor player within the legislative process. In the past, many DPJ members had advocated postal reform; indeed, Japan's largest opposition party was once far more supportive of postal privatization than the LDP, as evidenced by its predominance in a study group organized in 1999 on the issue.[17] But once the privatization process was launched in earnest in 2003, the DPJ's stance on postal privatization was nothing short of confused. In the summer of 2005, DPJ Diet members boycotted most of the Diet committee deliberations on the privatization bills; when they did participate, they focused not on the substance of postal privatization, but rather on unrelated rumors meant to discredit Koizumi and Takenaka (Takenaka 2006:211). In a marked departure from parliamentary custom, moreover, the party failed to put forward a counterproposal for postal privatization until *after* the September 2005 election, when the opportunity to sway the debate had long since passed. The party did, however, produce an eleventh-hour statement on postal reform in its 2005 election manifesto that proposed retaining Japan Post while reducing the size of the postal savings system, but the statement was widely criticized for being financial unfeasible, as well as too little too late.

The DPJ's failure to produce a viable counterproposal on postal privatization was in part due to Koizumi and Takenaka's leadership skills. The two men put the DPJ between a rock and a hard place: opposing postal privatization outright would be the kiss of death for a party that was established on the promise of reform, but quibbling over the specifics of the Takenaka plan would expose the fact that the party had lost the initiative—not to mention any semblance of control over the legislative agenda—to Koizumi and Takenaka. The party's fortunes plummeted even further during the 2005 election campaign, when Koizumi restricted voters' choices to either supporting or opposing privatization—choices that made the DPJ appear even more antireform than it was.

DPJ inertia on postal privatization also reflected its composition as a loose alliance of factions. While some, like the party's former LDP members, were bullish on privatization, others, including supporters of Zentei (the country's largest postal workers-union) were opposed to the idea. Katsuya Okada, the DPJ president in the months leading up to the election, tried in vain to strike a balance between these diverse groups (Yamawaki 2005:165). If he came out in favor of privatization, the left wing balked; if his proposals fell short of Koizumi's recommendations, his reform-minded colleagues complained that he was not going far enough; if he tried to exceed Koizumi's privatization plan by proposing the outright abolition of the postal savings and insurance systems, he was in trouble with the party's Zentei supporters, who were determined to maintain employment levels within the postal system. In short, Okada's efforts to find an alternative approach to postal reform failed because of dissention within the party's diverse membership, as well as the constraints imposed on him by Takenaka and Koizumi. The ultimate irony is that in the past, the DPJ had been quick to attack the LDP for catering to special-interest groups; once Koizumi had distanced himself from the postal family and was pressing forward with comprehensive reform, the DPJ was all but immobilized by special interests (Yamawaki 2005:161).

The Postmasters and Their Relationship to the LDP

Since Tanaka's stint as minister of posts and telecommunications during the 1950s, the commissioned postmasters had functioned as an essential cog in the LDP's electoral machine. In brazen disregard of the 1948 National Public Service Law (Kokka Komuin Ho), the postmasters systematically participated in numerous electoral functions that were collectively dubbed the "fourth service"— after mail delivery, postal savings, and postal insurance. The postmasters, along with their wives and retired colleagues, constituted perhaps the largest cohort of LDP party members, and routinely recruited local residents to join the party and the local support groups (koenkai) of individual politicians. At the height of their influence, Zentoku and Taiju were said to mobilize nearly one million votes behind the LDP, primarily in Upper House elections. Given the almost complete leadership and organizational overlap of Zentoku, the postmasters' voluntary organization (*nin'i dantai*), and Tokusuiren (a national association administered by the MIC to facilitate professional communication between the ministry and the postmasters), postal bureaucrats were also embroiled in these electoral functions. As evident in the 2001 scandal involving the election of Kenji Koso—a retired official from the Kinki Postal Bureau—to the Upper House, it was not unusual for bureaucrats to cooperate with the postmasters and their retired colleagues to mobilize both campaign contributions and votes behind LDP candidates, particularly those who opposed postal reform (see the *Japan Times*, September 1, 2001).[18]

In the past, the LDP rewarded the postmasters' loyalty with protection from Zentei, which had clamored for the abolition of the commissioned postal system from 1946 until the early 1980s, as well as policies to preserve the institutions of the state-run postal system. The postmasters' electoral activities, in other words, held some sway over the policy directions of the party. But the postmasters began to lose ground by the mid-1980s. Population decline in rural areas and the rise of the floating voter made it increasingly difficult to mobilize the vote, as did changes to the electoral system. Even worse for the postmasters, a postal-reform movement was expanding within the LDP, threatening the postmasters' influence over the party. Meanwhile, the media had become increasingly critical of the commissioned post offices, particularly in the aftermath of the Koso scandal.

Koizumi's electoral strategies precipitated a further decline in the postmasters' electoral influence. As noted earlier, his refusal to grant the LDP's official endorsement to candidates who had voted against the postal-privatization bills in July 2005 drove a wedge into the postmasters' loyalties, forcing them to choose between voting for pro-reform LDP candidates or for the rebels. Those split loyalties persisted. As the country prepared for the summer 2007 Upper House elections, the postmasters' associations once again refrained from instructing their local chapters on how to vote. In a few prefectures, the postmasters opted to reward loyalty by throwing their support behind LDP candidates who had voted against the postal-privatization bills in the summer of 2005. In other prefectures, Zentoku and Taiju simply sat out the election for lack of sympathetic candidates, letting individual postmasters vote according to their consciences—even if it meant voting for the opposition (*Tokyo Shimbun*, July 12, 2007; *Asahi Shimbun*, July 25, 2007). In still other prefectures, the postmasters cast their lot with the Kokumin Shinto in the hopes that the party would eventually force an unraveling of some of the more troublesome features of the privatization plan (*Asahi Shimbun*, May 27, 2007). Judging from several local newspaper articles, it appears that the postmasters constituted the largest membership group in local chapters of the party. Following the election—in which it obtained one Upper House seat—the Kokumin Shinto teamed up with the DPJ to submit a bill to the Diet that would delay the start of postal privatization by one year. No action was taken on the bill, and privatization began as planned on October 1, 2007.

The Bureaucracy

Well before the postal-privatization process had moved into its final stages, it was clear that the traditional role of bureaucracy in the policy process was changing. As Muramatsu notes, surveys revealed that bureaucrats—once influenced by politicians through a kind of principal-agent relationship—were losing confidence in the LDP and becoming more and more willing to defy political leadership and policymaking principles (Muramatsu 2004:26 and 29). At the same time, the bureaucracy was steadily losing what remained of its reputation for administrative excellence (Kato 2004). Both trends were apparent during the privatization process. As noted earlier, the now-marginalized MIC tried on numerous occasions to reassert its authority over the policy process by pressuring members of the PPPO and, more dramatically, by fielding alternative legislation—drafted in collaboration with the LDP's postal tribe and reflecting the interests of the postal family. That Koizumi ultimately prevailed in this incident marks a significant victory for his new style of top-down, executive leadership—a style that received the electorate's stamp of approval during the 2005 election.

Meanwhile, the MIC emerged from the postal-privatization process with its influence significantly diminished and its morale low. Unlike the policy process surrounding the privatization of Nippon Telegraph Telecommunications (NTT), which, as Vogel (1996) explains, was centered on the MPT and resulted in an *expansion* of the ministry's regulatory powers over the telecommunications sector, the postal-privatization process effectively sidelined the MIC and drastically reduced its powers—particularly in the postal savings and insurance realms. In October 2007, Japan Post was dissolved and many of its functions assumed by the largely independent government holding company Nihon Yusei.[19] Although the MIC has some oversight over Nihon Yusei, its influence over the savings and insurance systems will shrink. The ministry oversees a special fund (Yucho/Kampo Seimei Hoken Kanri Kiko) that administers savings accounts and insurance policies that were established before the privatization process officially began—a fund that may become a destination for retiring *amakudari* bureaucrats.[20] But as the number of these savings accounts and insurance policies dwindles, so too will the MIC's powers over the postal savings and insurance systems. Meanwhile, its influence over the actual privatization process between 2007 and 2017 will be minimal. In keeping with the top-down leadership endorsed by Koizumi and implemented by Ikuta in Japan Post, broad oversight over the process has been granted to two blue-ribbon committees lodged in the cabinet office. The day-to-day responsibilities of the privatization process will be overseen by the cabinet office's Postal Privatization Promotion

POLITICAL CHANGE IN JAPAN

Office (Yusei Min'eika Suishin Shitsu), the PPPO's successor. Although the MIC has responsibilities for preparing the postal network for privatization and for making recommendations to other bureaucratic organs,[21] its policymaking and administrative powers are a shadow of what they once were. As a result of these changes, the number of MIC bureaucrats in the postal divisions declined in the months leading up to October 1, 2007, as several sought transfer to the more innovative government holding company.[22]

In sum, it appears that the once mighty postal administration has been emasculated. This development can be attributed not only to the new institutions established during the 2001 governmental reorganization, which strengthened the potential for prime-ministerial leadership within the policy process, but also to the leadership skills of both Koizumi and Takenaka. Their decision to concentrate the privatization process within the CEFP partially marginalized the MIC, while Koizumi's decision to appoint Takenaka as postal privatization minister in 2004—and then as MIC minister after the passage of his privatization bills—underscored the prime minister's refusal to submit to interest-group pressure as exercised through the ministry. Takenaka's establishment of the guerrilla unit and the PPPO further reduced opportunities for the MIC and vested interests to influence the policy process. Koizumi's willingness to take drastic steps against bureaucrats who dared to defy the new policymaking procedures drove yet another nail into the coffin of bureaucratic initiative in the postal sphere. Finally, the content of postal-privatization legislation has ensured that the MIC will remain a much smaller player in the overall administration of the postal services.

We can conclude from these observations that Koizumi ultimately succeeded in asserting top-down, executive control over the postal policymaking process and in diminishing the powers of at least one government ministry. When combined with the effects of the 2005 election on the unity of both the LDP's postal tribe and the postmasters' associations, we can also conclude that Koizumi effectively broke up the iron triangle that controlled postal affairs throughout the postwar era—at least for the time being. We cannot conclude, however, that top-down leadership has become an institutionalized fact in the Japanese legislative sphere more generally. The CEFP's relative inertia under Prime Minister Abe Shinzo's watch would seem to underscore this point (*Asahi Shimbun,* April 17, 2007), further suggesting that the council's effectiveness is heavily dependent on the ability of key leaders to take ad hoc steps to buttress the council's authority (see Ito 2006:31–35). More important for our purposes, electoral incentives and developments in the realm of postal privatization itself point to a partial resurgence of the mutual exchange between the LDP and the commissioned postmasters—the most important partnership within the postal system's postwar iron triangle.

The Reemerging Postal Family

While the significance of the electoral and policymaking changes wrought by the Koizumi administration should not be underestimated, there are signs that some of these changes are already unraveling.

First, the LDP and the postmasters have taken steps to patch up their relationship. While the Kokumin Shinto was the party of choice for the majority of postmasters in the July 2007 election, some sided with the party in power—the LDP—on the assumption that this was the safest route toward preserving the commissioned postal system. The LDP, for its own part, tried to woo the rest of the postmasters back into the party's orbit. In the fall of 2006, Prime Minister Abe readmitted eleven of the postal rebels—including Seiko Noda—who had been reelected to the Diet as independents. Although required to take an oath upholding the stipulations of postal privatization, the rebels retained close ties to the postmasters and put pressure on the reform camp to soften the effects of privatization on the postal network. Many in the LDP felt that readmitting the rebels would strengthen the party's position during the Upper House election at a time when it could no longer rely on Koizumi's charismatic personality to attract the floating vote. The fact that the LDP also courted Taiju after the fall of 2006 further underscores this point (*Shukan Asahi,* December 29, 2006). One might safely conclude from these trends that as long as the LDP's electoral fortunes remain uncertain, it will continue to rally the postmasters. And as long as the party rallies the postmasters, it will face pressures to meet at least some of their policy-related demands. As of this writing, it is too soon to determine whether the LDP's loss in the summer 2007 Upper House elections will intensify the party's overtures to Zentoku and Taiju.

Second, although the postmasters have lost much of their influence over postal authorities, steps have been taken to help preserve what remains of that influence. The future of the commissioned postal system and its institutional links to the privatized postal companies are particularly telling in this regard. In 2006 Japan Post president Ikuta declared that in order to carry out a renewal (*isshin*) of the postal services, the commissioned postal system—which, to Ikuta's mind, was as feudal an institution as the old Tokugawa domains (*han*)—would have to be abolished. To that end, he proposed a series of reforms, including lowering the retirement age of the commissioned postmasters from between 65 and 68 to 60; subjecting them to the periodic transfers undergone by their counterparts in ordinary post offices; and most significantly, abolishing Tokusuiren, which had evolved into far more than a mechanism for conveying ministerial directives to the postmasters. Tokusuiren was to be replaced by an administrative structure with centers at the prefectural level that would service both commissioned and ordinary post offices alike. Predictably, the postmasters opposed these proposals, afraid that they would erase most of the features that distinguished commissioned post offices from ordinary ones. Then, after Nihon Yusei assumed ultimate responsibility for reforming the commissioned postal system,[23] a compromise was struck between the corporation's president, Yoshifumi Nishikawa, and Zentoku: while the first two of Ikuta's reforms would stand, Tokusuiren's successor was to consist of local as well as regional administrative units to be controlled by the postmasters (*Shukan Asahi,* December 29, 2006). Although the name would change, Tokusuiren had been saved and would operate under the semigovernmental postal network corporation. When Nishikawa replaced Ikuta as Japan Post president in April 2007 after the latter's abrupt resignation,[24] Nishikawa publicly praised this compromise for maximizing the usefulness of the human resources connected to the old state-run system.

There are several reasons for this retreat from the spirit—if not the letter—of the law. First, since no mention was made of the future of the commissioned postmasters in Koizumi's lengthy (500+ pages) postal-privatization legislation—aside from the stipulation that they would lose their status as public servants—the road was clear for the postmasters to try to leverage some concessions *after* the laws were passed. And leverage they did. Immediately after the 2005 election, a wounded Zentoku regrouped to put pressure on the powers-that-be in order to preserve the institutions of the commissioned postal system.[25] Second, Ikuta's sudden departure from the position of Japan Post president just six months before the privatization process was to begin, and his replacement by the more pro-postmaster Nishikawa, suggested that the Abe government was eager to appease the postmasters in the months leading up to the summer 2007 election.

What does all this portend for the future? First, the lessons of postal privatization suggest that top-down, executive leadership in the legislative sphere is unlikely to succeed within existing institutional structures unless there are innovative leaders in place who are willing to aggressively fend off the inevitable intrusions of vested interests. Prime Minister Abe clearly did not live up to Koizumi's standards in this regard, and neither did his successor, Yasuo Fukuda. Second, and related, the nature of party participation in the policy process has changed in some respects but has remained the same in others. LDP policy tribes now have fewer institutional opportunities to sway the policy process within the new cabinet-led system; at the same time, however, we can expect the LDP to defend the custom of approving policies before the cabinet adopts them. Again, the balance of power between the new top-down policymaking structure and the LDP depends on the presence of strong, risk-taking leadership. Meanwhile, for as long as the LDP's fate at the polls remains tenuous, we can expect the party to continue to court the organized vote, including that of the postmasters. As for the DPJ, the history of postal privatization indicates that the country's largest opposition party is too internally divided to significantly influence the direction of grand policy debates.

Third, the postal divisions of the MIC are a shadow of their former legislative and administrative selves and are likely to remain that way. Fourth, while the MIC's role in the postal family has been diminished, the relationship between the postmasters and their LDP sympathizers is experiencing a partial resurgence as their interests once again converge—albeit partially—on the policymaking and electoral fronts. It is very possible that this resurgence will gather steam in the years ahead. The July 2007 election was, after all, the last time that the postmasters' electoral activities will be deemed illegal; from October 1, 2007, when the postal system embarked on privatization and the postmasters lost their status as public servants, they have been free to engage in political activities to their hearts' content. While their interests are likely to diversify under a privatized system and their internal cohesiveness will no doubt decline, we can expect the postmasters to continue to court special favors from the LDP as they adjust to the changes and insecurities that privatization brings. We must therefore conclude that while Koizumi did much to weaken the power of vested interests in the legislative and electoral spheres, he by no means obliterated it.

Notes

[1] After abandoning its postwar opposition to the commissioned postal system in the 1980s, Zentei, Japan's largest union of postal employees, as well as its supporters in the DPJ, also be counted as members of the postal family. Zentei could not, however, match the political influence of Zentoku, which had intricate institutional ties to both the LDP and the bureaucracy.

[2] In addition to administering the postal services on the ground, the commissioned post offices—which constitute roughly 75 percent of the total number of post offices in Japan—implement informal social services in their communities, most notably assistance to elderly residents.

[3] Koizumi was not a die-hard ally of the Ministry of Finance; his plans for the abolition of the FILP, for instance, met with some resistance from the ministry.

[4] For more on the earlier history of the postal savings system and efforts to reform it, see Rosenbluth 1989, chapter 6.

[5] For more on the 2002 reforms, see Maclachlan 2004.

[6] The holding company will retain its shares after 2017 in the mail and postal network companies, which will be designated *tokushu gaisha* (special corporations that carry out public functions).

[7] According to a Jiji Press public opinion survey conducted in October 2004, six out of ten respondents complained that privatization had not been adequately explained to the public. Only 26.7 percent responded that they understood what postal privatization entailed, and 64 percent claimed that government explanations of privatization had been insufficient (Sadamitsu 2004).

[8] Interview with Naoyuki Yoshino, professor of economics at Keio University and a member of MIC's *yusei shingikai*, Tokyo, July 15, 2006.

[9] The fund depends on proceeds from the sale of the government holding company's shares in the savings and insurance companies.

[10] Interview, Yoshino.

[11] Interview with Nobuyuki Kinoshita, director general of the PPPO (Yusei Min'eika Junbi Shitsu), January 9, 2007.

[12] This may be the first instance in which a prime minister fired bureaucrats over policy differences rather than scandalous behavior.

[13] It appears that many LDP officials also believed that normalcy would return to Japanese politics following Koizumi's departure (Christensen 2006:502).

[14] Noda met frequently with Zentoku—which was desperate to keep her in power—throughout the campaign. She beat her opponent, a professional economist, in a single-member district (SMD) in Gifu Prefecture by 15,800 votes (Yamawaki 2005:177).

[15] Interview with Naoyuki Yoshino, Tokyo, January 8, 2007.

[16] Interview with a Development Bank of Japan executive, Tokyo, January 11, 2007.

[17] Of the seventeen members of the nonpartisan *Yusei min'eika kenkyukai*, organized by Koizumi and the DPJ's Shigefumi Matsuzawa, ten hailed from the DPJ and only two—including Koizumi himself—from the LDP (Koizumi and Matsuzawa 1999:254).

[18] Koso was eventually forced to resign his Diet seat, and more than a dozen posts officials were charged with electoral violations.

[19] The new corporation will continue to be known as Japan Post in English.

[20] Interview with a Postal Administration Bureau official, MIC, Philadelphia, February 8, 2007.

[21] Interview with Postal Administration Bureau officials, MIC, Tokyo, January 10, 2007.

[22] Interview with MIC officials, January 10, 2007.

[23] Nihon Yusei was established in late 2006 to help prepare for privatization. In October 2007, it became a *kabushiki gaisha*.

[24] Nishikawa retained his post as president of Nihon Yusei while serving as Japan Post president.

[25] Interview with four commissioned postmasters, Kitakyushu City, July 10, 2006.

References

Asahi Shimbun, May 27, 2007. This and other newspaper articles cited in this chapter are available upon request from the authors.

Blechinger-Talcott, Verena. 2004. Learning to lead: Incentives and disincentives for leadership in Japanese politics. In *Japanese political reform: Progress in process*. Woodrow Wilson International Center for Scholars, Asia Program Special Report, no. 117 (January): 20–25.

Cargill, Thomas F., and Naoyuki Yoshino. 2003. *Postal savings and fiscal investment in Japan: The PSS and the FILP*. Oxford: Oxford Univ. Press.

Christensen, Ray. 2006. An analysis of the 2005 Japanese general election: Will Koizumi's political reforms endure? *Asian Survey* 46 (4): 497–516.

Ito, Mitsutoshi. 2006. *Kanteishudokei seisaku kettei to jiminto* [The LDP and prime ministerial leadership in the policy process]. *Leviathan* 38 (October): 7–40.

Japan Times. August 31, 2007.

Kato, Junko. 2004. Reforming the Japanese bureaucracy: Perceptions, potential and pitfalls. *Japanese political reform: Progress in process.* Woodrow Wilson International Center for Scholars, Asia Program Special Report, no. 117 (January): 34–37.

Kitaoka, Shin'ichi. 2004. Japan's dysfunctional democracy. *Japanese political reform: Progress in process.* Woodrow Wilson International Center for Scholars, Asia Program Special Report, no. 117 (January): 6–8.

Koizumi, Junichiro, and Matsuzawa Shigefumi. 1999. *Yusei min'eika ron* [A theory of postal privatization]. Tokyo: PHP Kenkyukai.

Kowaguchi, Makoto. 1998. *Yusei no sekigahara* [The postal system's *sekigahara*]. Tokyo: Kubo Shoten.

Maclachlan, Patricia L. 2004. Post office politics in modern Japan: The postmasters, iron triangles, and the limits of reform. *Journal of Japanese Studies* 30 (2): 281–313.

Maeno, Kazuhisa. 1987. *21 seiki wa yuseisho no jidai* [The 21st century is the era of the ministry of posts and telecommunications]. Tokyo: Bijinesusha.

Muramatsu, Michio. 2004. An arthritic Japan? The relationship between politicians and bureaucrats. *Japanese political reform: Progress in process.* Woodrow Wilson International Center for Scholars, Asia Program Special Report, no. 117 (January): 26–33.

Rosenbluth, Frances McCall. 1989. *Final politics in contemporary Japan.* Ithaca, NY: Cornell Univ. Press.

Sadamitsu, Jo. 2004. Yusei min'eika kihon hoshin' ketteuke seron chosa [Public opinion poll on the postal privatization basic plan]. *Jiji TopConfidential* (November 12): 14–16.

Segawa, Kosuke. 2001. *Koizumi Junichiro to tokutei kyokucho no arasoi* [The feud between Junichiro Koizumi and the commissioned postmasters]. Tokyo: Eeru Shuppansha.

Shukan Asahi, December 29, 2006.

Takenaka, Heizo. 2006. *Kozo kaikaku no shinjitsu: Takenaka Heizo daijin nikki* [The truth about structural reform: The diaries of minister Heizo Takenaka]. Tokyo: Nihon Keizai Shimbunsha.

Tokyo Shimbun, July 12, 2007.

Vogel, Steven K. 1996. *Freer markets, more rules: Regulatory reform in advanced industrial countries.* Ithaca, NY: Cornell Univ. Press.

Yamawaki, Takeshi. 2005. *Yusei kobo* [Postal tug-of-war]. Tokyo: *Asahi Shimbun.* (This and other newspaper articles cited in this chapter are available upon request from the author.)

Yuseishohen [Ministry of Posts and Telecommunications], ed. 1971. *Yusei hyakunenshi.* [A 100-year history of the postal system]. Tokyo: Zaidan hojin teishin kyokai.

BEYOND ELECTORAL POLITICS

THE SLOW GOVERNMENT RESPONSE TO JAPAN'S BANK CRISIS: A NEW INTERPRETATION

Ethan Scheiner and Michio Muramatsu[1]

S ince the early 1990s, Japanese bureaucrats have developed a reputation for corrupt behavior and incompetence. The practice of *amakudari* ("descent from heaven"), whereby bureaucrats retire from their government ministries to high-paying jobs in the very industries they once regulated has long concerned the Japanese, but with the worsened economy the problem has attracted additional attention. In the mid-1990s, the Ministry of Health and Welfare admitted to permitting and then covering up the distribution of untreated blood in the 1980s, which led to roughly two thousand hemophiliacs becoming infected with the human immunodeficiency virus (HIV), leading to acquired immune deficiency syndrome (AIDS). And in 2007, the ruling Liberal Democratic Party (LDP) lost the House of Councillors elections in part because of disclosures that the country's Social Insurance Agency had lost the pension records of millions of Japanese. Yet perhaps the best-known misstep is the slow response of bureaucrats to the country's financial crisis in the 1990s.

Until the final decade of the twentieth century, Japan was described as having a "miracle" economy, and Japan's government—most notably the bureaucratic ministries in charge of the economy—was given much of the credit for this success. With an active bureaucracy that developed economic plans and provided "administrative guidance"—in conjunction with the country's tremendous postwar growth, resilience in the face of the 1970s oil crises, and fast action to balance its budgetary books in the early to mid-1980s—the Japanese government developed a reputation for being able to recognize problems in their infancy and develop solutions before problems spiraled out of control. In the 1990s, however, in the face of what turned out to be a dramatic collapse of the real-estate and stock markets and the stagnation of the economy overall, the Japanese government appeared paralyzed. The most glaring example of this was Japan's banking crisis: despite strong signs in the early 1990s that there was a substantial nonperforming loan (NPL) problem in the banking sector, Japan's government took very few steps to address the problem until 1998. Why was the government so slow to respond?

In this chapter, we offer a new approach to understanding this problem. Other political scientists' analyses of Japan's banking system and its problems in the 1990s focus on the increased complexity surrounding financial regulation and instability in the networks linking bureaucrats to financial institutions (Amyx 2004), the bureaucracy's commitment to a particular form of bank regulation (Vogel 2006), and incentives generated by the electoral system (Rosenbluth and Schaap 2003). We do not take issue with the substance of these analyses, but rather argue that they do not address a critical part of the puzzle of the Japanese government's slow response to the bank crisis: politicians' seeming obliviousness to the actions (or inaction) of the bureaucracy. A common explanation for this lack of knowledge and activity in major policy areas in Japan is simply that politicians are not active participants in many complicated policy areas and delegate (or abdicate) discretion over them to the country's bureaucracy. But this does not explain why politicians would behave in this way. In addition, politicians' lack of action on the banking problem was even more puzzling given that many were openly pinning blame for the country's poor economic performance on bureaucrats in the Ministry of Finance.

This chapter focuses on the relationship between Japan's politicians and bureaucrats. Most typically, the literature on politician-bureaucrat relations views the relationship in zero-sum terms, with one side seeking to gain at the expense of the other. But, as noted most pointedly by Muramatsu (1987, 2003) and Kato (2002), under the condition of a longtime, stable relationship between one political party and the bureaucracy, a positive-sum relationship—founded on close cooperation between the two—is likely. Moe's (1989, 1990a, 1990b) analysis of "structural politics" leads us to expect that, in such a context, few structures will be put into place to allow politicians to challenge or constrain the actions of the bureaucracy. But Moe's analysis does not consider what happens if the close ties between such politicians and bureaucrats suddenly break off. We argue that a loss of power—or a loss of the probability of power—by the longtime ruling party will alter the context, shifting the relationship from a positive-sum to a zero-sum.

Political science literature also puts forward the expectation that even when relations between politicians and bureaucrats are less cooperative, politicians can constrain bureaucratic behavior, in part through contacts with interest groups that provide legislators with policy information (see, for example, McCubbins and Schwartz 1987). But the literature gives little systematic attention to when interest groups are more likely to contact politicians with their grievances and information rather than contact bureaucrats directly. We argue that it is in this very area that politicians face a significant problem if they work in a system that shifts from the cooperative to the competitive relationship between legislators and bureaucrats. We argue that because politicians in the cooperative scenario often do not develop structures to help them deal independently with many key policies, bureaucrats have a major advantage in terms of information and legislative capacity in the competitive context. In contrast to "fire alarms" that get tripped and provide politicians with policy information in competitive party structures, bureaucrats in the context that we describe can hide information from the politicians who oversee them.

Speaking specifically about Japan, we argue that single-party dominance—the LDP ruled Japan without interruption from 1955 to 1993—led to an unusually stable and close relationship between the ruling party and central bureaucracy. As a result, Japan's parliament (Diet) never established structures that would allow it to obtain policy information on its own and develop legislative capacity in a number of policy areas, most notably bank legislation. Instead, single-party dominance promoted great bureaucratic discretion, especially in areas such as banking policy controlled by the Ministry of Finance (MOF).

With the LDP's temporary loss of power in 1993–1994, ties between politicians and bureaucrats grew strained. With increasing concerns about the economy, the LDP, once back in power, sought to take away some of the ministry's discretion and jurisdiction, most notably in the area of bank regulation. To combat these efforts, the MOF hid information from the party. At the same time, the uncertainty surrounding what party or parties would control the government made the relevant interest groups less likely to contact politicians, and the troubled banks themselves certainly did not want to notify politicians of their problems. Without structures in place to help it gain information, the LDP had few avenues available to learn more about the problem. Only once the crisis was revealed for all to see in 1998 did the government finally take serious steps to address it.

Japan's Bank Crisis

Throughout much of the postwar era, Japan's banks were noted for their solidity. The staying power of banks was aided by actions taken by the MOF, most notably its banking bureau, which maintained close—although often informal—ties with Japan's banking sector and emphasized minimizing the risk of bank failure. During times of (usually small) bank failure, the MOF coordinated mergers whereby a larger bank rescued the failing one. The result was widely seen as aiding the success of Japan's economy. As Amyx explains, "The implicit MOF guarantee that no bank would fail encouraged individual depositors to entrust their savings with banks, which then could direct funds into investments benefiting the economy as a whole" (2004:108).

Over time, however, problems emerged. In the 1980s, globalization increased the information requirements for doing business. As capital markets liberalized, banks faced greater competition, lost many large corporate borrowers, and were therefore forced to lend to smaller firms outside their established networks. Risk grew, making it particularly important to gain additional information on borrowers. As a result, the MOF sought to impose more formal mechanisms for monitoring banks, but these efforts were rejected both by banks and by the Diet, forcing the ministry to rely—at least as much as before—on informal relations to gain information (Amyx 2004:32). Meanwhile, believing that the ministry's history of finding ways to help rescue failed financial institutions

183

promised something of a safety net, banks extended massive—albeit significantly riskier—loans during the 1980s economic bubble years (Vogel 1996:194), founded in large part on pumped-up real-estate collateral. As the real-estate and stock bubbles burst in the late 1980s and early 1990s, numerous borrowers were unable to repay their loans. Banks also had speculated in real estate, so they too were hit hard by the collapse of the market (Vogel 2006).

Estimates vary on exactly how costly the NPL crisis was, but it is widely considered the most expensive bank-rescue operation in history (Amyx 2004:3), with NPLs totaling at least $600 billion (Amyx 2004:3; Pempel 1998:142). In many ways, this number understates the true impact of the bank failures, because it does not tell the story of how the cost of bailing out the banks harmed the Japanese (and Asian regional) economy in myriad ways, including raising public debt, depressing economic output, weakening consumer demand, and slowing credit flows from Japan.

Throughout the 1990s, the bank problem was frequently noted, but Japanese authorities were exceedingly slow to respond to the crisis: In 1992 LDP prime minister Kiichi Miyazawa explicitly suggested the possibility of using public funds to combat the problem (Amyx 2004:158). And in 1995, Moody's Investors Service downgraded its average rating of the creditworthiness of Japanese banks to "uncertain" (D rating) (Pempel 1998:142–43). But the NPL problem did not take a major place on the public agenda, and the MOF was reluctant to bail out the banks. As a result, with the exception of the controversial home mortgage lending (*jusen*) problem in 1995,[2] no serious steps to address the problem were taken for years. Indeed, it was fall 1998 before politicians finally stepped in, passing legislation that used public funds to help clear the red, and establishing new financial regulatory structures. Most economists argue that Japanese authorities moved far too slowly to get the banks to take care of their NPLs, and Vogel notes that the NPL crisis would have been resolved more effectively and at a lower cost if Japan had acted more quickly and decisively in the 1990s (2006:25–26).

What explains the lack of action? Amyx argues that, when buttressed by government guarantees of rescue, financial institutions have an incentive to hide negative information from regulators in the hopes that high-risk, high-return investments may save them in the meantime (2004:28). Given this context, she argues that it is likely that the MOF lacked information on just how systemic the NPL problem was, and the ministry continued to maintain its ad hoc and informal approach to regulation and rescue (Amyx 2004:161). In contrast, Vogel (2006:49) argues that the biggest reason for the ministry's lack of responsiveness was its overwhelming faith in a long-held model of bank regulation that maintained financial stability without a large-deposit insurance fund or publicly financed bank bailouts (Vogel 2006:49).

Amyx and Vogel present competing views of why the MOF was unwilling to respond to the crisis, but neither tackles the broader question of why no one in the government did. Why did politicians stay out of the fray? True, during the 1990s politicians were focused on other major events, most notably major political reform, shifting party dynamics, the 1995 Kobe earthquake, and the 1995 Tokyo sarin gas attack. Nevertheless, they were not wholly distracted, as they were willing to push other issues such as administrative reform and a hike in the consumption tax. Also, their inaction was not due simply to total faith in the efficacy of ministry policies; the LDP during much of this time actually sought to blame the country's economic problems on the MOF.

Another possibility is presented by Rosenbluth and Schaap (2003), who argue that bank-regulatory regimes are a direct result of the incentives generated by the electoral system. The 1998 bank reform, they argue, was a result of a change in Japan's Lower House electoral system. The implication, therefore, is that the earlier lack of action by Japan's politicians was a result of the incentives created by the prior electoral system. Yet Japan had instituted its new electoral system more than four years earlier and had held its first election under the new system in 1996. It wasn't until a slight shift in the partisan balance of power after an election held for the Diet's less important Upper House, which had not reformed its electoral system, that bank reform was seriously pushed. The electoral-system model can offer no more than a partial explanation why Japanese politicians took so long to deal with the bank crisis.

Perhaps the most straightforward explanation is that politicians never want to engage in the costly and unpopular act of using public funds to bail out banks.[3] Yet it was politicians such as Prime Minister Miyazawa who first pushed for the use of public funds but were talked out of it by the MOF on the basis of "superior" information (driven by the belief that using public funds would create an unnecessary panic when the crisis was likely to be resolved without them).

This last point helps push us toward an answer: it appears that much of politicians' inaction during Japan's bank crisis was due to their reliance upon the MOF for information about the state of the country's banking sector. It turns out that this reliance was tragically flawed, because the ministry actually worked with financial institutions to hide information about the weakened state of Japan's banks (Amyx 2004:258; Vogel 1996:194). For many observers of Japanese politics, this point—that politicians rely heavily upon bureaucrats for important information—is self-evident, but in reality it pushes us toward the real question: why are politicians so reliant upon bureaucrats for information about matters such as the health of the country's banks?

Delegation and Information

To explain the slow response of Japan's government to the bank crisis in the 1990s, we must explain politicians' reliance upon bureaucrats for information. In any complex society, legislators must delegate large amounts of work to the bureaucracy. A central issue for any legislature, therefore, is determining mechanisms that make it possible to trust the information provided by the bureaucracy and to maintain control over the work done by bureaucrats.

Uncertainty is central to delegation, as greater uncertainty over the political environment makes it more likely that legislatures will write detailed, constraining legislation to tie the hands of bureaucratic agents. This last point is similar to Moe's (1989, 1990a, 1990b) discussion of "structural politics," which indicates how the current political context structures legislation and delegation. For example, where uncertainty exists about who will control a particular policy in the future, policymakers may write more specific and detailed legislation to remove the possibility of control by future legislative rivals and to constrain the behavior of bureaucrats. Among parliamentary systems, legislation of this kind is most likely in countries with a coalition or minority governments where those controlling legislation today are very uncertain about their ability to maintain their dominant position in the future (Huber and Shipan 2002; Moe and Caldwell 1994).

Yet a total lack of constraining structures is especially likely in what Moe (1990a) points to as a hypothetical "extreme case," where there is a single dominant and secure majority coalition. We should therefore expect that a party that maintains stable majority control of a legislature for a significant period is especially unlikely to formalize constraints on the bureaucracy. When it is widely assumed that the same political party will be in power for a considerable period, both the party and the bureaucracy are aware that politicians are available to punish current bureaucratic abuses in the future. Longtime single-party dominance should lead politicians and bureaucrats to develop a close relationship in which bargaining and flexibility can be a great advantage. In such a context, strict structures and statutory constraints tie the hands not only of the bureaucrats, but of politicians as well. As a result, there is much less incentive for politicians to establish structures or rules that do so, especially as they—as part of the stable party in power—are most likely able to take necessary steps to fix problems with policy (or with bureaucrats' behavior) in the future.

This discussion stands in sharp contrast to much of the conventional analysis of politician-bureaucrat relations. Much of the classic work emphasizes the competitive side to the politician-bureaucrat relationship, explaining either how bureaucrats can wield power over politicians (for example, Niskanen 1971) or how politicians can use institutional arrangements to influence the behavior of bureaucrats (for example, Kiewiet and McCubbins 1991).

In reality, though, a simple dichotomy does not usually exist in policymaking. For example, as Huber and Shipan point out, "appointment powers, budget authority, monitoring mechanism, and . . . the design of legislation itself provide political actors with considerable opportunities to treat bureaucrats as allies rather than as foes in the policymaking process" (2002:42). Moreover, as Muramatsu (1987, 2003) and Kato (1994, 2002) each show is the case in Japan, when politicians and bureaucrats work together, each can increase the ability of the other to have an impact on the policymaking process. By helping politicians develop greater expertise in areas of concern to the bureaucracy, bureaucrats improve their own chances of passing legislation (Kato 1994). And as bureaucrats share more information with politicians, the views and attitudes of the two groups grow closer together, which makes it easier to pass legislation (Kato 2002). As suggested earlier, however, in the discussion of structural politics, the close relationship and positive-sum context is much more likely in certain scenarios, with the most likely scenario being that of a single party securely controlling the government for a considerable period.

Interest groups are important to the ability of politicians to control bureaucrats, especially in a more zero-sum environment. Without information from interest groups, it is difficult for politicians to judge the behavior and efficacy of bureaucrats. Interest groups provide information by pulling what the political science literature calls "fire alarms" (Lupia and McCubbins 1994; McCubbins and Schwartz 1987; McCubbins, Noll, and Weingast 1987). Upon enacting bills, legislatures do not typically examine a sample of administrative decisions, looking for violations. Such "policing" would be too time-consuming. Rather, legislatures establish a system of rules, procedures, and informal practices that enable individual citizens and organized interest groups to examine administrative decisions (sometimes in prospect), to charge executive agencies with violating congressional goals, and to seek remedies from agencies, courts, and Congress itself (McCubbins and Schwartz 1987:427). At the same time, though, without information from interest groups, it is also difficult for bureaucrats to judge their own efficacy. In many cases, interest groups are more likely to go directly to the policy implementer and therefore serve as "smoke detectors," providing information to the bureaucratic agency rather than to politicians (Brehm and Gates 1997).

Considering Additional Dynamics

There are static elements of previous work that leave important questions unanswered. First, what happens if the level of certainty regarding party control of the government changes? More specifically, what happens to the dynamic between the legislature and the bureaucracy when the party context changes from one in which there is great stability to one in which there is more uncertainty? Second, what shapes interest groups' use of fire alarms? That is, if there is a change in the relationship between the legislature and the bureaucracy, will interest groups change who they contact in the government? The literature notes the presence of both "fire alarms" (interest groups providing information to politicians) and "smoke detectors" (interest groups providing information to bureaucrats). When is one more likely to be present than the other?

We extend the earlier analyses to consider behavior under these circumstances. We argue that a shift away from electoral stability to uncertainty should affect the relationship between politicians and bureaucrats in a number of important ways. More specifically, if a longtime ruling party were to lose power, its relationship to the bureaucratic ministries would undoubtedly change. Even if the party were to return to power, the relationship would likely be less close, with a reduced ability on each side to trust and work with the other. Less certainty would surround the party's likelihood of maintaining office, raising questions about the party's ability to correct future bureaucratic ministerial failures or transgressions. For this reason, a structural analysis would expect the legislature in this situation to establish greater constraints on bureaucratic behavior.

But because of the longtime, close ties between politicians and bureaucrats, as well as the significant grants of discretion given to the administrative branch, the legislature would have never developed structures to help it act more independently, gain information on its own, and stand as a counter to the bureaucratic ministries. No longer as likely to share information with politicians, the bureaucratic ministries in this scenario would maintain a sizeable informational advantage over the legislature.

Where do interest groups fit into the dynamic? To be sure, in a system where substantial discretion is delegated to bureaucrats, interest groups are likely to deal directly with bureaucrats—the people working most closely with most policies—when they want to raise issues about the workings of a particular policy. This is very much the case in Japan, where many groups provide lucrative postretirement careers for bureaucrats and where policy councils (*shingikai*), which play a big part in much of Japanese policymaking, help cultivate ties between interest groups and bureaucrats. But in a situation of longtime single-party dominance, interest groups are also likely to deal with politicians extensively. As Moe and Caldwell note, "Parties and groups, as ongoing organizations, transact with one another again and again over time. All stand to benefit from informal norms and strategies of cooperation . . . that protect political deals from subversion" (1994:180).

We argue that where there is great political uncertainty—such as instability surrounding government control—a shift would likely alter this dynamic. In such a context, interest groups would have much greater incentive to contact the bureaucracy directly, because bureaucrats would likely maintain their position of influence irrespective of the events that follow in the political world.

Considering Japan

Like a significant portion of the literature on American politics, much English-language work on Japanese politics paints the relationship between politicians and bureaucrats in zero-sum terms. The literature is most often characterized by the debate between Johnson (1982), who puts forward a bureaucrat-dominance argument, and Ramseyer and Rosenbluth (1993), who emphasize the dominance of politicians. The debate focuses on the question of whose preferences were being represented in legislation. We should note that irrespective of whose policy preferences are actually put into legislation, it is widely agreed that, in Japan, national-level bureaucrats are extremely active in the policymaking process.

Indeed, relatively few formal restrictions have been placed on bureaucrats' activities in Japan.

Much of the bureaucracy's power stems from the development of Japan as a modern state. Beginning in the late nineteenth century, bureaucrats were the leading actors in the nation's development. Acting within a predemocratic structure, these bureaucrats were able to control state resources and powers. In addition, during the post–World War II occupation of Japan, Western authorities worked extensively through the existing Japanese bureaucracy, further bolstering its power. Nevertheless, under a number of conditions, one would expect national politicians to attempt to restrict the discretion held by bureaucrats. The fact that such efforts were rarely made pushes us to look for reasons other than dependency to explain bureaucrat-politician relations in Japan.

Particularly striking is that Japan matches very closely the "extreme case" laid out by Moe (1990a): perhaps *the* defining feature of postwar Japanese politics has been the longtime state of single-party dominance, which, as Moe predicts, made it more likely for politicians to avoid "hardwiring" policy and the activities of bureaucratic agents. The LDP dominated Japanese politics over 1955–1993, with little serious threat to its control of the government. The close relationship between the LDP and bureaucracy was a major feature of this period (Amyx 2004; Okimoto 1989). Given this relationship and the relative certainty of continued LDP control, LDP governments did not need to develop greater capacity to legislate on their own. Scholars and general observers of Japanese politics frequently point out that bureaucrats acted as legislative support for LDP politicians and that, as a result, Diet members in Japan are allotted only very small staffs and few independent resources to legislate on their own. Given such weak legislative capacity, LDP politicians needed to work all the more closely and cooperatively with the bureaucratic ministries. Indeed, the close relationship between the LDP and the bureaucracy gave the LDP the freedom to reshuffle cabinets regularly without seriously harming overall policymaking expertise. In other words, conditions in Japan encouraged LDP politicians to leave policies vague and to offer substantial grants of flexibility and authority to bureaucratic ministries.[4]

These facts all suggest that it makes much less sense to talk about the power of one occurring at the expense of the other. In fact, either side (politicians or bureaucrats) can create greater power for the other simply by increasing its own ability to influence legislation. Kato's (1994, 2002) analysis makes explicit how an increase in the policy expertise of incumbent politicians by no means runs counter to the influence of bureaucrats. It is often the knowledgeable politicians who most welcome information from the bureaucracy and therefore are most likely to work with bureaucrats. As Kato (1994) points out, by helping politicians develop greater expertise in areas of concern to the bureaucracy, bureaucrats improve their own chances of passing legislation. And Kato (2002) notes that as bureaucrats share more information with politicians, the views and attitudes of the two groups grow closer together, which makes it easier to pass legislation.

How do interest groups fit into the overall policymaking scenario here? The bureaucracy has traditionally held numerous meetings with key interest groups in Japan. Evidence offered by Uriu (1996) suggests that, while Japanese interest groups frequently do tell legislators about problems with the bureaucracy, it has been at least as common for groups in society to deal directly with the bureaucracy. In short, "smoke detectors" may be at least as prevalent as "fire alarms" in Japan.

The LDP lost power in 1993 and did not return to the government until 1994. How did this alter the dynamic described here? To be sure, certain features remained in place even when the LDP was out of power. For example, under Morihiro Hosokawa's brief non-LDP coalition government (1993–1994), the bureaucracy frequently worked with non-LDP politicians who were familiar with the policies under consideration (Kato 2002). Nevertheless, the relationship was clearly changed: the Hosokawa coalition government worked to assert its power over the bureaucracy, most notably taking the unusual step of forcing at least one high-ranking senior bureaucrat from office (Pempel 1998:141).

Japan's Lack of Responsiveness to the NPL Problem

The shift away from the highly stable, positive-sum context dramatically altered the relations of politicians, bureaucrats, and interest groups. Much of the shift was due to the newly competitive relationship between the legislature and bureaucracy. In addition, decreased political certainty and government stability made the bureaucrats an even more inviting contact point than before, increasing the likelihood of "smoke detectors" at the expense of "fire alarms." In turn, the new dynamic hindered Japan's capacity to deal with the banking crisis that emerged.

For years, Japan's MOF maintained close ties with Japan's banking sector. A number of factors contributed to the ministry's ability to gain information about and the cooperation of the banking sector. As a result of its budgeting and taxation role, it had a great deal of information about the economy overall, the banking sector specifically, and changes within both of them. As Grimes notes, "By watching out for the interests of well-placed Diet members in microbudgeting, the ministry can expect cooperation on matters more central to its missions" (2001:43). In addition, as with most policy in Japan, the ministry's decision-making focused in large part on policy councils (*shingikai*), where ministry and industry officials who had been chosen specifically by the ministry met to work out government policy for the sector. As a result, the banking sector usually knew what the MOF was planning to implement even before it acted (Vogel 1996:171–72). Much of the interaction between the ministry and the banking sector worked through informal networks as well (Amyx 2004). Among other things, when the ministry suspected weakness in a particular bank, it would advise the bank on how to proceed and sometimes would even have a retiring official from the ministry take over the management of the bank (Vogel 1996:170).

This created enormously close ties between the ministry and the banking sector and gave each substantial information on the activities of the other. But it is noteworthy that information requirements were lower prior to the 1980s. Japan's insulated financial market reduced a great deal of uncertainty. As Amyx notes, close relational ties between banks and borrowers meant that banks could make loans with relatively little uncertainty about the solvency and activities of those borrowing. And the insulation of the Japanese financial market kept capital scarce and ensured that loans went to relatively high-worth, low-risk projects (Amyx 2004:31).

With capital market liberalization in the 1980s, however, it became much more difficult to monitor and control the banking sector. Larger numbers of banks extended risky loans, founded in large part on collateral that was grossly overvalued given Japan's bubble economy. With the bursting of the bubble at the end of the decade, billions of dollars' worth of loans became unrepayable.

For reasons raised earlier in this chapter, the MOF was reluctant to bail out the failing banks, and the full extent of the problem was largely kept hidden. A few politicians did raise questions about the NPL problem. LDP prime minister Miyazawa was a unique premier in Japan in that he actually had policy experience in the realm of financial politics. In 1992 Miyazawa grew concerned about the NPLs. In August of that year, he became the first politician to explicitly suggest the possibility of using public funds to combat the problem. His suggestion was quickly dismissed by fellow LDP members. Key electoral supporters and construction, real-estate, and especially agricultural cooperatives "comprised many of the clients whose loans had become nonperforming. The party therefore had little interest in seeing a state-backed institution recover delinquent loans" (Amyx 2004:158). Japan's leading business association, Nippon Keidanren, reassured Miyazawa that the economic situation was not dire and convinced him not to take serious action (Amyx 2004:159). In addition, he was persuaded by the MOF's argument that using public funds could evoke panic in the economy, with costs that outweighed the potential benefits.

In 1993 the *Yomiuri Shimbun* alleged that the Nippon Credit Bank (NCB), which the MOF had granted forbearance, had engaged in questionable accounting. In response, a committee in the House of Councillors questioned MOF officials about their NPL policies with respect to the NCB. But the House of Councillors did not push the issue any further after accepting the ministry's explanation that the NCB's financial difficulties would simply disappear when land prices rebounded. The willingness of politicians to follow the ministry's suggestions on the matter seems to result partly from the fact that the problem was not thought to be systemic (Amyx 2004:158–59). Moreover, as Grimes notes, although many doubted the rosy economic forecast offered by the ministry, there was a general unwillingness "to challenge the more knowledgeable

Ministry of Finance on such a sensitive issue, one it had little independent ability to discredit" (2001:160).

Politicians soon became distracted from the problem. As 1993 progressed, scandals—such as that involving LDP bigwig Shin Kanemaru—helped push the Diet to focus on political reform. When reform failed, the LDP split, new elections were held, and an anti-LDP coalition took power, further distracting the political world from the activities of the economy.

When the LDP returned to power, a new dynamic existed between the party and the bureaucracy. Much to the LDP's surprise, during the party's time out of power, the Japanese bureaucratic ministries served their new masters, the anti-LDP coalition, and kept the longtime ruling party at arm's length. As a result, when the LDP returned to power in 1994, there were bitter feelings between the longtime collaborators. In addition, despite its return to power, the LDP—now part of a coalition government—faced substantial electoral uncertainty. Not surprisingly, with more information emerging about the NPL problem, the LDP used the MOF as the scapegoat.

Despite greater awareness of the NPL problem, the government remained slow to act, in large part because the MOF muddied the waters surrounding the issue. The use of public funds to rescue the NPLs would highlight the ministry's failures on the matter. With the Diet looking to punish the MOF for its incompetence, the ministry worked with financial institutions to hide their losses (Vogel 1996:194). As long as it could, it also hid information from the public in order to protect its regulatory autonomy (Amyx 2004:258). As a result, the truth about the banking sector's massive number of NPLs was concealed for a number of years.

Analysis

Given the very high probability that the LDP would continue to dominate Japanese electoral politics throughout the 1955–1993 period, there was little need for it to formally tie the hands of bureaucrats in policymaking. This became problematic when the relationship between the LDP and the MOF became strained following the LDP's return to power in 1994. In fact, much of the LDP's inability to develop a source of information independent of the MOF was due to the lack of formal rules governing the inspections and reporting of the banking sector and the resulting emphasis on informal relations. Amyx explains: "The very opacity of these ties and information exchanged within them meant, however, that the Diet and general public were less than fully aware of the extent of dysfunction present as time went on" (2004:32).

In addition, the party's weak legislative capacity—also undoubtedly a result of the LDP's longtime dominance and, hence, reliance upon bureaucratic service— harmed the LDP's ability to act when its government dominance came into question and it could no longer wholly trust the MOF. This was particularly the case in the highly specialized and technical field of banking policy. According to Amyx, direct oversight of the banking sectors by elected officials—what the political science literature refers to as "police patrols"—is common in most industrialized countries, irrespective of constitutional type (presidential or parliamentary) (2004:29). Yet the work of Amyx and others studying Japanese financial policy makes clear that no such "policing" existed in Japan. It was not unusual for powerful Diet members to establish personal think tanks to deal with important issues, but private-sector finance rarely received much attention in such institutions (Amyx 2004:302, fn. 54). In part, this was due to the lack of electoral incentive for Japanese Diet members to monitor their activities. In general, politicians had tighter links to business sectors other than the banking industry, partly because of "the nation-wide scattering of bank branches and the fact that the business base even of regional banks encompassed numerous electoral districts" (Amyx 2004:56). While finance specialists and committees existed within the LDP, they focused on government revenues and expenditures. Meanwhile, an LDP Financial Affairs Research Council—which focused solely on private-sector finance—did exist, but it held a far more informal position within the party and was given much lower status (Amyx 2004:57).

The failure of the government to respond well to the bank crisis also suggests a great deal about the means by which information was transmitted from society to the government. "Fire alarms" were typically absent in the banking sector. Vogel notes that the LDP generally preferred to have the MOF handle financial policy because of a lack of legislative staff and knowledge of the subject. Politicians would become involved if financial institutions appealed for their help, but such appeals were quite rare in the area of financial policy (Vogel 1996:172). But the lack of "fire alarms" was due to the preferences of the financial sector as much as to weak legislative capacity. Banks preferred to avoid asking politicians for policy favors, because such requests risked drawing political interference in lending decisions (Amyx 2004:57).

"Smoke detectors" were far more common. Grimes notes that "from 1985 to 1997 leadership was often taken by the Ministry of Finance, with politicians' roles usually at the margins, and only occasionally at the center" (2001:221). Moreover, as discussed earlier, a very clear set of ties emerged over the postwar period between the ministry and the banking industry. As a result, banking-sector officials tended to focus their lobbying efforts on the ministry (Amyx 2004:57).

Not only were "smoke detectors" the norm in bank policy in Japan prior to 1997–1998, but the MOF also spent great energy on what one might call "smoke suppressors" as well. In many cases, it was clear that the "smoke detectors were not working as they should; the increasingly complicated nature of financial markets in the 1980s and 1990s made it difficult for the ministry to acquire accurate information on the functioning of the Japanese banking sector. Given the fact that politicians had little means to gain much independent information—since "police patrols" and "fire alarms" were largely nonexistent in the sector—the ministry was able to conceal the true state of Japan's financial markets. In short, the greater contact between bureaucrats and interest groups after the 1970s may have had devastating consequences, because the bureaucracy was able to use this advantage to keep parties in the dark about Japan's fiscal problems in the 1990s (Amyx, 2004).

Surveys of leading Japanese interest groups conducted by Muramatsu and associates (Muramatsu and Scheiner 2007) indicate some noteworthy patterns of group behavior that support the preceding discussion. First, during 1993–1994, when concerns emerged about the state of Japan's banks, there was a dichotomy between which interest groups would contact whom. Much more than in other years, interest groups that did not support the LDP were more likely to contact bureaucrats, whereas those that strongly supported the party contacted politicians. We see this as an indication that the relationship between politicians and bureaucrats had become competitive and strained. And this competitive relationship undoubtedly made it more difficult for politicians to get needed information from the bureaucracy. Second, during this period, interest groups in general were less likely to contact politicians, probably because of the high levels of uncertainty surrounding the stability of the government. As a result, politicians were much less likely to gain important information—for example, about the bank crisis—from interest groups.

In short, it appears that the 1993 decline in the LDP's dominance helped bring about a shift from highly cooperative to competitive LDP-bureaucrat relations—and reduced the likelihood of interest groups contacting politicians. As a result, the LDP had much more difficulty getting reliable information from either the bureaucracy or interest groups about the bank problem. This is all the more problematic, as the surveys show, because economics-related interest groups were less likely to contact politicians in the first place.

Conclusion

This chapter does not seek to explain the successes and failures of Japan's economy. Nor do we seek to answer why the government did or did not respond to any economic problem. For example, we do not try to explain the Japanese government's willingness to accept the growth of the bubble in the 1980s. Rather, we seek to explain the lack of action in the 1990s, when the LDP was in fact looking to blame the bureaucracy for the problems of the economy.[5]

We argue that the inability of the Japanese government to respond to the bank crisis was in large part a result of the loss of power of the long-dominant LDP. The party's multidecade stranglehold on the government made it possible for the Japanese Diet to maintain close ties to the country's bureaucracy and grant substantial discretion to bureaucratic agencies—without creating many structures to counter the ministries' informational advantages. With the LDP's temporary loss of power in 1993–1994, ties between politicians and the MOF weakened substantially and the relationship became more competitive.

And with few formal structures in place to monitor and verify bureaucratic information and behavior, the LDP was in a difficult position to challenge the bureaucracy. Moreover, with the onset of party realignment and unstable cabinet governments in 1993, interest groups looking to provide information on policy to the government had more incentive to contact bureaucrats, whose tenure in power appeared much more secure than that of politicians in the government. The LDP therefore lacked the interest-group "fire alarms" available to legislators in many other contexts.

As a result, when presented with information that did not disclose the true extent of the financial crisis, the LDP was not sufficiently equipped to act against the advice of the MOF. And, not surprisingly, the party took no serious action to address the NPL problem. The outcome was governmental paralysis in the face of a major economic crisis.

In contrast to the most prominent debate on policymaking in Japan, we emphasize the importance of viewing politics throughout much of the postwar period in positive-sum terms, with high levels of cooperation between politicians and bureaucrats leading to particular types of political behavior. And we suggest how policymaking patterns in Japan have been dynamic, with systematic and predictable shifts from a cooperative politician-bureaucrat relationship to a competitive one over time.

This created a difficult situation for the politicians. Interest groups were more likely to contact them when they, the politicians, were less in need of information because of their already close ties to the bureaucracy. But interest groups were less likely to contact them when politicians needed them most, which was the case in the less electorally stable context when politicians and bureaucrats were less likely to cooperate with one another.

We close with some speculations and thoughts on future research. As suggested by the work of Huber (2000), Huber and Shipan (2002), and Moe (1989, 1990a, 1990b), in a more competitive scenario—such as the situation that emerged in Japan after the LDP briefly lost power—one would expect the legislature to create structures to better monitor bureaucrats and access information. Indeed, the reforms enacted by the Japanese Diet in 1998 to finally deal with the NPL and the banking-sector problem were an effort to alter the governmental structures related to financial regulation. As would be predicted by Moe's "structural politics," the new legislation created substantially more formal networks to inspect banks and respond to various financial sector conditions. The ministry's role in inspecting banks was reduced substantially, but gaining information was at the heart of the new rules. Inspectors were given greater latitude than in the past. At the same time, the new structures appeared to promote the use of "smoke detectors." For example, the Financial Reconstruction Agency—created to act as the primary inspecting agent—soon became staffed with a number of officials from the banking sector (Amyx 2004:213), thereby encouraging close ties between bureaucratic inspectors and banks.

Future analysis of the bank-reform legislation would do well to further our understanding of just how much oversight power the Diet gave itself in such matters. Since the mid-1990s, the Japanese government has enacted substantial reform in other areas that affects not merely the substance but the structure of policymaking. In this way, it is possible that the LDP's efforts in the past ten years to enact administrative reform and centralize policymaking in the cabinet were in part a result of the dynamics highlighted in this chapter.

It is also quite likely that the LDP's ability to maintain power again for more than a decade after its 1994 return may have ultimately brought the party and ministries closer together again. But even if so, one might speculate that the events of 2007 could have had a powerful impact on legislators' efforts to rein in the bureaucracy. One wonders whether the LDP's defeat in the 2007 House of Councillors elections, brought on in large part by the Social Insurance Agency's "misplacing" the pension records of millions of Japanese, might push the LDP to establish more formal constraints and oversight.

Notes

[1] We gratefully acknowledge the support of the Institute of International Advanced Studies (Kyoto, Japan), which provided the opportunity to meet and discuss the ideas in this chapter. Great thanks to Steve Vogel, Ellis Krauss, Robert Madsen, Kenneth McElwain, Frances Rosenbluth, Steve Reed, and Mike Thies for insightful comments on an earlier draft of the chapter.

[2] The *jusen* were mortgage-lending companies that received a government bailout after they faced a serious NPL problem.

[3] In many ways, this argument is similar to Yusaku Horiuchi's (2005), that the government was concerned that the bailout would be too costly at the time.

[4] Although not as important as the close relationship between politicians and bureaucrats that emerged from the long and stable period of LDP rule, the Japanese court system no doubt also encouraged greater grants of discretion to the bureaucracy. Japan's court system follows civil (as opposed to common) law practices, and courts in Japan tend to be responsive to the policies of the government and the ruling party (Johnson 2003; Ramseyer and Rosenbluth 1993). Given that Japanese courts tend to act more reliably on behalf of the ruling party as a check on bureaucratic behavior, there was less need for politicians to establish constraining legislation.

[5] This is in contrast to the 1980s, when the LDP and bureaucracy had close ties with one another and politicians had every reason to trust the bureaucracy.

References

Amyx, Jennifer A. 2004. *Japan's financial crisis: Institutional rigidity and reluctant change*. Princeton, NJ: Princeton Univ. Press.

Brehm, John, and Scott Gates. 1997. *Working, shirking, and sabotage: Bureaucratic response to a democratic public.* Ann Arbor: Univ. of Michigan Press.

Grimes, William W. 2001. *Unmaking the Japanese miracle: Macroeconomic politics, 1985–2000.* Ithaca, NY: Cornell Univ. Press.

Horiuchi, Yusaku. 2005. Sakiokuri no kozo: 1992-nen natsu, koteki shikin tonyu wa naze sakiokuri saretaka? [Why was government money not used and postponed in 1992?] In *Heisei baburu: sakiokuri no kenkyu* [Heisei bubble: A study of delayed responses], ed. Michio Muramatsu, 130–57. Tokyo: Toyo Keizai Shimposha.

Huber, John. 2000. Delegation to civil servants in parliamentary democracies. *European Journal of Political Research* 37:397–413.

Huber, John D., and Charles R. Shipan. 2002. *Deliberate discretion? The institutional foundations of bureaucratic autonomy.* New York: Cambridge Univ. Press.

Johnson, Chalmers. 1982. *MITI and the Japanese miracle: The growth of industrial policy, 1925–1975.* Stanford, CA: Stanford Univ. Press.

Johnson, David T. 2003. A tale of two systems: Prosecuting corruption in Japan and Italy. In *The state of civil society in Japan*, ed. Frank Schwartz and Susan Pharr, 257–80. New York: Cambridge Univ. Press.

Kato, Junko. 1994. *The problem of bureaucratic rationality: Tax politics in Japan.* Princeton, NJ: Princeton Univ. Press.

———. 2002. Politicians, bureaucrats, and interest groups in Japan: Transformation from one-party predominance or not? In *Legislatures: Comparative perspectives on representative assemblies*, ed. Gerhard Loewenberg, Peverill Squire, and D. Roderick Kiewiet, 314–28. Ann Arbor: Univ. of Michigan Press.

Kiewiet, D. Roderick, and Mathew D. McCubbins. 1991. *The logic of delegation: Congressional parties and the appropriations process.* Chicago: Univ. of Chicago Press.

Lupia, Arthur, and Mathew D. McCubbins. 1994. Designing bureaucratic accountability. *Law and Contemporary Problems* 57:91–126.

McCubbins, Mathew D., Roger G. Noll, and Barry R. Weingast. 1987. Administrative procedures as instruments of political control. *Journal of Law Economics and Organization* 3 (Fall): 243–77.

McCubbins, Mathew D., and Thomas Schwartz. 1987. Congressional oversight overlooked: Police patrols versus fire alarms. In *Congress: Structure and policy*, ed. Mathew McCubbins and Terry Sullivan, 426–40. Cambridge: Cambridge Univ. Press.

Moe, Terry M. 1989. "The Politics of Bureaucratic Structure." In *Can the Government Govern?* ed. John E. Chubb and Paul E. Peterson. Washington, D.C:. The Brookings Institution.

———. 1990a. The politics of structural choice: Toward a theory of public bureaucracy. In *Organization theory: From Chester Barnard to the present and beyond*, ed. Oliver E. Williamson, 116–53. New York: Oxford Univ. Press.

———. 1990b. Political institutions: The neglected side of the story. *Journal of Law, Economics, and Organization* 6:213–53.

Moe, Terry M., and Michael Caldwell. 1994. The institutional foundations of democratic government: A comparison of presidential and parliamentary systems. *Journal of Institutional and Theoretical Economics* 150: 171–95.

Muramatsu, Michio. 1987. Nihon kanryosei-ron eno wanmoa suteppu [One more step toward a theory of the Japanese bureaucracy]. *Hogakuronso* [Kyoto law journal] 120:60–89.

———. 2003. Seijishudoka no komuin shudan no kongo [The future of public servant groups under the age of political initiative]. *Nihon gyoseigakkai nenpo* [Annual journal of the Japanese Society for Public Administration] 38:3–21.

Muramatsu, Michio, and Ethan Scheiner. 2007. When do interest groups contact bureaucrats rather than politicians? Fire alarms and smoke detectors in Japan. Paper presented at the Modeling Power Relationship in Japanese Democracy conference, Univ. of British Columbia, August 28–29.

Niskanen, William A., Jr. 1971. *Bureaucracy and Representative Government.* Chicago: Aldine-Atherton, Inc.

Okimoto, Daniel I. 1989. *Between MITI and the market: Japanese industrial policy for high technology.* Stanford, CA: Stanford Univ. Press.

Pempel, T. J. 1998. *Regime shift: Comparative dynamics of the Japanese political economy.* Ithaca, NY: Cornell Univ. Press.

Ramseyer, J. Mark, and Frances McCall Rosenbluth. 1993. *Japan's political marketplace.* Cambridge, MA: Harvard Univ. Press.

Rosenbluth, Frances, and Ross Schaap. 2003. The domestic politics of banking regulation. *International Organization* 57:307–36.

Uriu, Robert M. 1996. *Troubled industries: Confronting economic change in Japan.* Ithaca, NY: Cornell Univ. Press.

Vogel, Steven K. 1996. *Freer Markets, More Rules: Regulatory Reform in Advanced Industrial Countries.* Ithaca, NY: Cornell University Press.

———. 2006. *Japan remodeled: How government and industry are reforming Japanese capitalism.* Ithaca, NY: Cornell Univ. Press.

STEALING ELECTIONS: A COMPARISON OF ELECTION-NIGHT CORRUPTION IN JAPAN, CANADA, AND THE UNITED STATES

Ray Christensen and Kyle Colvin

Part of Junichiro Koizumi's appeal as a reformer was his willingness to take on other leaders of the Liberal Democratic Party (LDP) who were widely perceived as corrupt. Koizumi's reform policies directly targeted the supply side of political corruption in Japan by reducing the level of government intervention in the economy. Yet he showed markedly less enthusiasm for strengthening anticorruption legislation. Nevertheless, his efforts seem to have borne fruit; at least the *perception* of corruption in Japan has improved significantly. The index score of perceived corruption in Japan has risen from a relatively mediocre 5.8 on a 10-point scale in 1998 to a 7.6 in 2006, placing Japan ahead of the United States, France, Ireland, Belgium, and Spain.

Though it seems likely that Koizumi's broad reform agenda helped decrease perceived corruption in Japan, it is notoriously difficult to measure the actual occurrence or frequency of corruption in any country. Rather than undertake this Herculean task, we have measured a specific form—election-night corruption—which, in contrast to other forms of corruption, leaves measurable evidence. We compare Japan with Canada and the United States and find, surprisingly, no evidence of election-night corruption in Japan, either under Koizumi or his predecessors. In contrast, we find significant evidence of occasional election-night corruption in both Canada and the United States, a finding that runs counter to conventional wisdom that consistently rates Japan as more corrupt.

Peculiar Characteristics of Election-Night Corruption

Election-night corruption has a long and fascinating history in the annals of U.S. election lore. Most notorious are the stories of Lyndon Johnson's 1941 loss and 1948 victory in Democratic primary races for Texas senate seats. Johnson lost in 1941 because he urged his supporters to release the returns from heavily pro-Johnson precincts early on election night to build up a large margin and discourage his opponent. Meanwhile, his opponent held back the precincts he controlled, saw how many votes were needed for victory, and allegedly manufactured enough votes on election night to defeat Johnson by a slim margin. President Roosevelt is said to have teased Johnson for his mistake in 1941, saying, "Lyndon, up in New York the first thing they taught us was to sit on the ballot boxes" (Dallek 1991:224).

In 1948 Johnson had learned his lesson and was better prepared to ensure his victory over fellow Democrat Coke Stevenson. After Johnson's supporters knew how many votes were needed to turn a narrow loss into a victory, Johnson allies are said to have created enough bogus ballots to provide just that margin. Unfortunately for Johnson, the bogus ballots of Precinct 13 in Alice, Texas, were recorded in alphabetical order. Two hundred additional "voters" not only voted in alphabetical order, but, coincidentally, supplied just the margin needed for Johnson's victory, earning him the nickname Landslide Lyndon. Fortunately for Johnson, both the original and copies of this suspect voting list were lost or stolen before they could be examined by a court, so the legend of the alphabetical voting list in Alice was recorded only in the statements of those who claimed they saw the list in the first few days after the election (Dallek 1991:340; Caro 1991:375–76).

Less obvious, but equally curious, was the 1964 senate election in Nevada. Lieutenant Governor Paul Laxalt challenged the incumbent, Howard Cannon, in a race that went down to the wire. With 90 percent of the vote counted and a six-thousand-vote lead, Cannon declared victory late in the evening. Laxalt, however, refused to concede because most of the uncounted precincts were located in rural counties that strongly favored him. By the next morning, the nearly complete returns gave Laxalt an eighteen-vote lead. Later that morning, two county clerks revised the vote tallies, correcting what they claimed were errors in their previously announced tally for their counties.[1] In a strange coincidence, the only counties to revise their tallies were the home counties of Cannon and Laxalt, and the revisions in each county favored the hometown politician. Cannon won the race, in part because the number of new Cannon votes "found" the morning after the election in the populous Clark County (Las Vegas) swamped the additional Laxalt votes "found" in his much smaller base of Ormsby County (Carson City).

More recently, Fund (2004:78–79) raised questions about Senator Tim Johnson's narrow victory over John Thune in the 2002 South Dakota senate race. Thune held a narrow lead over Johnson until the last returns came in from Shannon County. Those returns gave Johnson just enough votes to win the election. Fund points out that voter turnout—and votes for Johnson—in Shannon County were both disproportionately higher than in other, similarly situated pro-Johnson counties. This anomaly opens the door to questions that perhaps the Johnson vote was altered in Shannon County to give him just enough votes to squeak out a victory over Thune.

All forms of corruption, including election-night corruption, are difficult to identify and prosecute because the participants will not admit their acts to the police (Duggan and Levitt 2002:1594; Kallina 1988:182–93). There is no victim's body or cache of stolen goods to prompt a police investigation. Hence, both generic political corruption and the more specific act of stealing the election on election night typically go undetected and unpunished. In contrast to generic political corruption, however, election-night corruption (the adjustment of the last returns to ensure that a specific candidate has a narrow margin of victory) does leave a distinct trail of evidence. This makes it possible to detect the likely occurrence of such corruption, even without the aid of eyewitnesses.

Election-night corruption is unique because it is based on the knowledge of exactly how many votes are needed to ensure victory. Candidates hold back precincts that they control (colluding with local electoral officials) until they know how many votes are needed to ensure victory. If the candidate is facing sure defeat or sure victory, no further effort is needed; the held-back results are simply released and added to the nearly complete election totals. If, however, the candidate is facing a narrow loss, local electoral officials make last-minute adjustments to ballot totals, creating just enough new votes to win the election for their candidate. Typically only a bare margin of victory is created in election-night corruption—just enough new votes to ensure victory, but not so many as to raise suspicions or to trigger investigations.

It may seem odd that corrupt officials would create only a slim margin of victory; after all, if you are going to cheat in an election, why not give your preferred candidate a convincing win, turning what would have been a narrow loss into a substantial victory? Two factors make slim margins of victory more frequent. The first is the extensive monitoring and record-keeping provisions that surround most balloting. It is actually difficult to create large numbers of bogus votes, because the number of votes that can be created in any given precinct is limited by the numbers of registered voters, the expectations of typical turnout in a given precinct, and the expectations of typical ratios of partisanship in a specific precinct. A corrupt election official may be able to add 50 fraudulent votes to the totals for a precinct in which there were 400 registered voters and 300 actual votes cast, but adding 100 votes to that precinct would certainly call attention to that precinct. Similarly, if a candidate won 200 of the 300 votes cast in that precinct, those totals could be adjusted to 250 of the 300 votes without perhaps attracting attention, but any greater margin is likely to trigger an investigation of the voting returns. Each precinct can produce only a certain number of fraudulent votes without attracting unwanted attention, and the manipulation of each precinct's data requires the corruption of a local election official in that precinct.

The second constraint stems from the vigorous campaign activities, both legal and illegal, that a candidate has engaged in prior to election night. Such activities would have already boosted that candidate's margins to near-maximum levels before the counting begins on election night in precisely those districts in which collusion with a local election official is most likely to occur. When it comes time to find the additional eight or twelve or twenty-five hundred votes needed for victory, the task is already difficult; running up the vote total beyond what is needed for a simple victory makes a difficult task nearly impossible.

For example, in the 1964 Nevada senate election, Laxalt was hobbled by the fact that there were only five thousand voters in his base of Ormsby County. Laxalt had already won 60 percent of those votes. In contrast, Cannon's base of Clark County had more than 64,000 votes cast, with Cannon winning a similar 61 percent of the vote. Cannon could increase his vote share in Clark County by a hardly noticeable 1 percent and create 640 additional Cannon votes, but Laxalt would have to increase his margin of victory in Ormsby County by a much more noticeable 12 percent to create the same number of votes. With both counties adjusting their vote totals upward in the morning after the election, Ormsby County simply couldn't match the vote increase posted by the much larger Clark County.

Similarly, Lyndon Johnson's blatant manipulation of the votes in Alice, Texas, was a mark of his supporters' desperation. Johnson allies had created every additional vote that they could in the areas that they directly controlled, but Coke Stevenson, Johnson's opponent, was still managing to best Johnson's vote totals. In a brazen and ultimately successful attempt to win, Johnson allies reached out of their base to nearby Alice because there still was a large gap there between the number of registered voters and the number of ballots cast, making it possible to create a significant number of additional Johnson votes. Those opportunities had all been used up in more solid Johnson precincts, but by reaching outside their area of direct control, Johnson's allies made themselves vulnerable to claims of cheating by a local official in Alice who was not part of the Johnson machine.

Other forms of electoral corruption are less targeted and relatively uninformed. Ballot boxes may be stuffed or votes may be bought, but these actions occur before anyone knows how many votes are needed to ensure victory. In the absence of such clear information, more bogus votes are better than fewer. Operatives try to create as many votes as they can for their candidate without being caught. These additional votes are obtained even though, ultimately, they might only add to a candidate's already ample margin of victory or be wasted in a losing effort that no amount of corruption is able to reverse.

Thus, election-night corruption is distinguishable from other forms of electoral corruption and all other campaign activities—corrupt or legitimate— that might also affect vote totals. Only election-night corruption affects final vote totals with a precision that comes from knowing how many additional votes are needed to change a loss into a victory. Legitimate campaign efforts and other forms of electoral corruption lack this information and can only affect vote totals bluntly, without precision. For example, a candidate might redouble her efforts in the final days of a campaign because all reports indicate that the race will be very close. She might try to buy more votes, run more advertisements, or enhance her get-out-the-vote effort. Any of these activities should raise her share of the vote over what she would have won if she had not made those last-minute, additional efforts. If, for example, her efforts increase her vote share by 2 percent, do they affect the outcome of the election? The candidate and her advisors know only that the race is going to be very close. Perhaps her additional efforts turn what would have been a 49 percent loss into a 51 percent victory. Or perhaps they turn what would have been a 51 percent victory into a 53 percent victory or a 47 percent loss into a 49 percent loss. All electoral efforts (other than election-night corruption) reverse the outcomes of some races (a 49 percent loss becomes a 51 percent victory), and make other races closer (a 47 percent loss becomes a 49 percent loss) or less close (a 51 percent victory becomes a 53 percent victory). The candidates know only that the race is likely to be close and that additional efforts (legal or illegal) may be needed to secure a victory.

In contrast, all election-night corruption efforts stop at the same place: a slim margin of victory. Thus, it can be identified, at least in the aggregate, by an anomalous number of these ultraclose races. Recent political history in Nevada illustrates this point. Senate races in 1964, 1974, and 1998 were won with 48-, 624-, and 401-vote margins, respectively. Is it just a coincidence that Nevada has had three nail-biter U.S. senate elections in 34 years? Or were vote totals adjusted in one or two of these races to provide a slim margin of victory for a candidate who was otherwise headed for defeat? Unlike with other forms of electoral corruption, it should be possible to trace the existence and frequency of election-night corruption by measuring the number of ultraclose races to see if any or all of the following are present in the data: (1) a disproportionate number of ultraclose races compared with very close races; (2) one political party winning a disproportionate number of ultraclose races compared with very close races; (3) a correlation between the winners of ultraclose races and their party's control of the local electoral machinery.

Predicting Election-Night Corruption

We look for a distinct trail in the electoral records of three separate democracies in an attempt to measure the existence and frequency of election-night corruption. We test the hypothesis that such corruption is more common in countries where the electoral bureaucracy is more susceptible to political penetration and manipulation. Analyzing election results for Japan, Canada, and the United States, we hypothesize that election-night corruption is most likely to appear in the United States, where the election bureaucracy is decentralized and often politicized, and less common in Japan and Canada, which have centralized election rules and a national election bureaucracy. Gerring and Thacker (2004), as well as Treisman (2000), support this hypothesis with their arguments that federal systems tend to have higher levels of corruption.

An alternative hypothesis also exists. Japan has been consistently rated higher than the United States or Canada in measures of perceptions of corruption

(Gerring and Thacker 2005; Anderson and Tverdova 2003). Thus, looking only at perceptions of corruption generally, one might expect Japan to have more frequent occurrences of election-night corruption. We weigh both factors and argue that despite the presence of other forms of political and electoral corruption, election-night corruption should be uncommon in Japan because of the strength, unity, and independence of the electoral bureaucracy. Japan also has a parliamentary system, which Gerring and Thacker (2004) argue tends toward less corruption.

Canada presents an interesting contrast to the Japanese case, having a reputation for significantly less corruption than either Japan or the United States (Gerring and Thacker 2005; Anderson and Tverdova 2003). Like Japan, Canada also has a parliamentary system. But Canada's federal nature opens the door to the possibility of election-night corruption. Nevertheless, given the strong anticorruption reputation of Canada, we predict that election-night corruption should be less common there than in the United States.

Our hypotheses and analysis also add to the growing political science literature focused on corruption by importing significant insights from the study of corruption outside this discipline. With few exceptions, studies of corruption in political science have had two bases: studies of corruption based on perceptions of corruption (Gerring and Thacker 2005; Anderson and Tverdova 2003; Alesina and Weder 2002; Davis, Camp, and Coleman 2004; Xin and Rudel 2004) and on actual prosecutions of corrupt politicians (Meier and Holbrook 1992; Golden and Chang 2001). These excellent studies, though, have their limitations. In contrast, there is a growing literature outside political science that analyzes the telling path left by certain corrupt activities. Thus, Duggan and Levitt (2002) describe how incongruities in the patterns of victories by some sumo wrestlers suggest the existence of deals to throw matches. Similar methods have been used to detect favoritism by soccer referees (Garicano, Palacios-Huerta, and Prendergast 2005), Medicare abuse (Becker, Kessler, and McClellan 2005), and teachers giving illegal help to students taking standard exams (Jacob and Levitt 2003). Duggan and Levitt (2002) also describe the historical example of how there were suspiciously fewer French military conscripts whose height was just above the minimum height, and disproportionately large numbers of those who avoided conscription because their height was just below the minimum. Corruption cannot be confirmed in the case of a specific conscript, a specific exam, or a specific sumo match, but the existence of multiple incidents of corruption can be confirmed. This confirmation comes by comparing the actual distribution of results with a hypothetical distribution that should have existed if there had been no corruption.

Some recent political science work has used related methods to assess the voting preferences of a subset of absentee voters in Florida (Imai and King 2004). Others have similarly applied statistical methods in the study of electoral corruption (Simpser 2005; Mebane 2006), but other than these studies, the comparison of actual and hypothetical results has rarely been done in the study of political corruption. We seek to fill this gap by analyzing the difference between actual election results and a hypothetical distribution of election results if no election-night corruption had occurred.

Measuring Election-Night Corruption by Aggregating Margins of Victory

We test our hypotheses about the prevalence of election-night corruption using two separate methods. The first is the most obvious and compares the number of ultraclose races (those with a victory margin of less than 0.5 percent) with the number of very close races (similar half-percent categories with victory margins of between 0.5 percent and 2 percent). By comparing these two, similar categories, we control for the many factors, legal or illegal, that can affect the closeness of a race generally. Because factors other than election-night corruption cannot distinguish between a very close race (a victory margin of less than 2 percent) and an ultraclose race (a victory margin of less than one-half of a percent), if a distinction occurs between ultraclose races and very close races, it is likely that election-night corruption is occurring.[2]

Thus, in jurisdictions where there is no election-night corruption, the distribution of the margins of victory, plotted according to half-percent increments, should produce a distribution of only incremental changes between half-percent intervals. These incremental changes would reflect the impact of all the factors that generally affect the closeness of races. There might be twice as many 1 percent victories as there are 10 percent victories because races in that jurisdiction are quite competitive. Or there might be twice as many 10 percent victories as there are 1 percent victories because one party dominates races in that jurisdiction or because bipartisan gerrymandering has eliminated all the competitive districts. In either scenario, however, the changes in half-percent categories moving from 1 percent to 10 percent should be incremental. None of the factors (other than election-night corruption) that affect the closeness of races generally can distinguish between victories of 0.5 percent and victories of 1 or 2 percent. Thus, if election-night corruption is not occurring, the difference between the number of races won by 0.5 percent and races won by 1 percent should be consistent with the trend line of incremental differences between, for example, races with a 1.5 percent and 2 percent margin of victory.

In contrast, if election-night corruption is common, there will be a sharp break between the number of ultraclose races and the number of very close races, rather than an incremental change between these two categories. Figure 10.1 reports aggregate totals for Japan, the United States, and Canada.[3]

Figure 10.1 Distribution of Victory Margins in Japan, the United States, and Canada

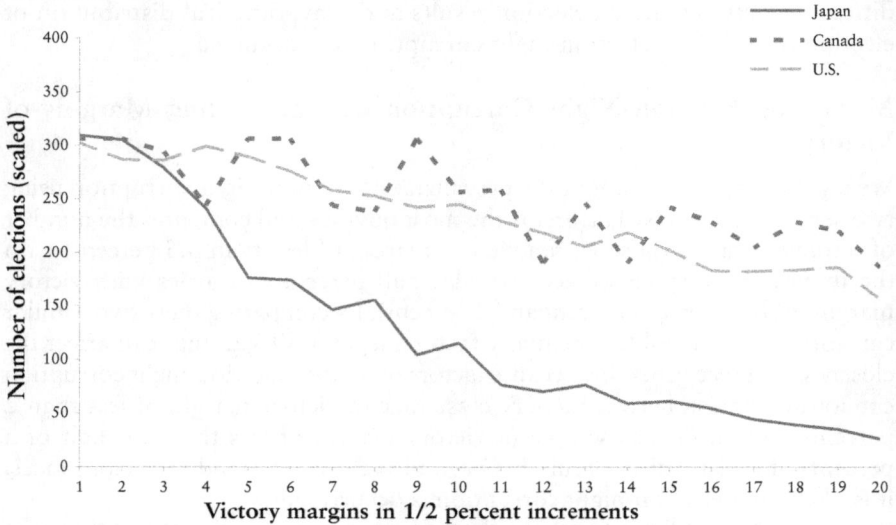

In figure 10.1 we have scaled the results so that all three countries can be placed in comparable positions on the graph, and we have truncated the distribution, showing only the results for the first 20 categories of 0.5 percent increments (all races with a 0–10 percent margin of victory). There is no sharp or disproportionate increase for the ultraclose races (category 1). The overall distribution of Japanese races is skewed in favor of close races, but the biggest increase is in the number of races won by between 2.5 and 1.5 percent—not the ultraclose races. Japan has a distribution skewed toward closer races because most of the Japanese races included in these data sets occurred in multimember districts (MMDs) in which the last-place winner and the first-place loser are much closer to each other in their share of the vote, in contrast to races in the single-member districts (SMDs) used in Canada and the United States.

This first set of data suggests that election-night corruption is not occurring in Japan, the United States, or Canada. It is possible, however, for significant election-night corruption to occur without altering the overall distribution of margins of victory. This can occur if one party disproportionately benefits from election-night corruption. For example, election-night corruption might be disproportionately used by one party to convert what would have been ultraclose victories for their opponents into ultraclose victories for their candidates. It stands to reason that election-night corruption is more likely to be attempted when an opponent's margin of victory would have been small and easy to reverse. If this scenario is correct, then the total number of ultraclose races would not be disproportionately larger, but the party distribution of ultraclose races would stand out in contrast to the party distribution of very close races. Figure 10.2 breaks down the data for Japan reported in figure 10.1 into two groups: LDP victors and opposition-party victors.

Figure 10.2 Japan: Margins of Victory by Party

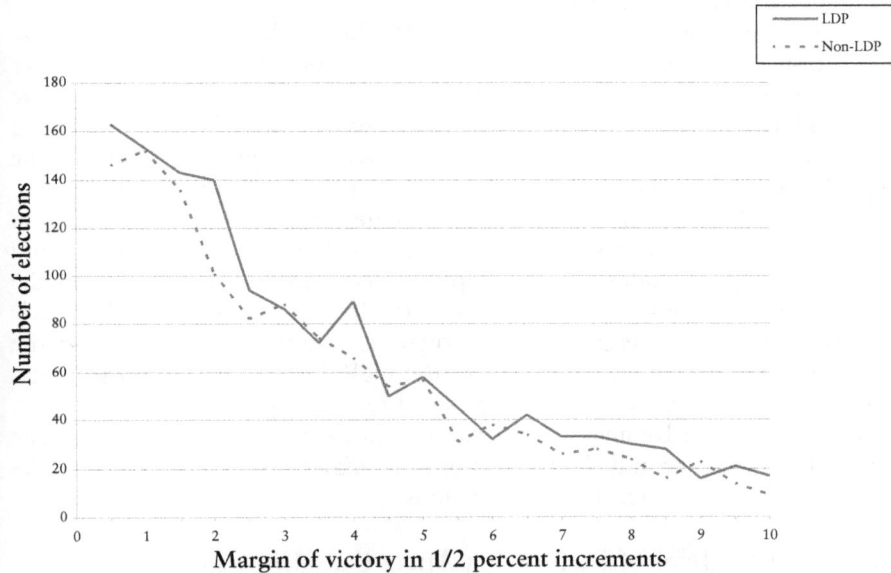

Figure 10.2 is stunning for the near parity of LDP victors and opposition-party victors. There are slightly more LDP victors than opposition-party victors, reflecting the reality that there have been slightly more LDP members of Japan's House of Representatives than there have been opposition-party members of that same house. But the LDP margin over the opposition is no better in ultraclose races than it is in very close, semiclose, or not-so-close races.

In contrast, breaking down the data for the United States by political party shows that the Republicans win significantly more races than the Democrats at every level of victory, from 0.5 percent to 10 percent, except for ultraclose races with victory margins of less than 0.5 percent. Only in this category are there more Democratic victors than Republican victors. The Canadian data is drawn from a much smaller data set, so the results are more volatile and patterns are more difficult to identify.

These same patterns (or their lack) can be analyzed by using the numbers of very close races to extrapolate a predicted number of ultraclose races.[4] This method is similar to that of using the previous year's budget figures as a baseline to predict the following year's budget allocations. There should be a close correlation between both years' numbers, and by using the previous year's figures as a control variable, one can hold constant the many factors that affect budgetary allocations generally and focus on only the factors that incrementally affected the budget in a specific year. Similarly, predicting the number of ultraclose races by using the number of very close races controls for all the factors that affect the closeness of races generally, allowing an isolated analysis of election-night corruption, the only factor that can distinguish between ultraclose and very close races.

When these numbers are calculated for Japan, both the LDP and the opposition have *fewer* ultraclose races than extrapolated trends predicted. We predicted 184 ultraclose races for the LDP, and it had only 163 (21 fewer); we predicted 169 ultraclose victories for the opposition, and they had only 146 (23 fewer). Thus, not only is there no difference between the LDP and the opposition, but both groups show fewer rather than more ultraclose victories. In contrast, the Democrats in the United States and the Liberals in Canada both post significantly more ultraclose victories than were predicted (35 and 12, respectively). In addition, the Republicans in the United States and the Conservatives in Canada also win fewer ultraclose races (17 and 4) than their predicted numbers. It is possible that these net figures could understate the true number of stolen elections on election night because they report the net advantage or disadvantage for each party. If the Republicans stole victories in 40 elections and the Democrats stole victories in 70 elections, the net advantage for the Democrats would show up as only +30, and it would appear that the Republicans were not stealing any elections.

Regression Analyses of Factors that Affect Only Ultraclose Races

We now turn to a second set of statistical tests that analyze each victorious candidate in each election district. Our dependent variable is now whether or not a specific race ended up in the ultraclose margin-of-victory category. This method has the advantage of a larger number of observations for the data set, which allows for the addition of many more control variables into the regression. This method has a disadvantage because the many variables that affect the closeness of a race must be directly controlled for by including those variables in the regression. It is difficult to identify and control for all possible factors that affect the closeness of a race. In contrast, the comparative method used in the previous section had the advantage of capturing the impact of all these factors, identified or unidentified, by using the data for the very close races to calculate the predicted values for the ultraclose races.

To help control for these other factors, we have included several fixed effects variables in the regression for Japan: dummy variables for each of seven regions, and dummy variables for every decade. In addition, we have controlled for incumbency status and the proportion of the district that is urban. There are a total of 3,421 cases in the data set, of which only 79 (2.3 percent) are ultraclose races. Only some of the 15 separate independent variables included in the regression are reported in table 10.1.

Table 10.1 Japan: Binary Logistic Regression of Fixed Effects and Party Variables on Whether an Election Is an Ultraclose Race

2000s	-1.32	(0.46)**
1990s	-0.05	(0.41)
1950s	0.56	(0.38)
Tohoku region	1.73	(1.14)
Kinki region	1.92	(1.06)
Percent urban	0.19	(0.70)
Incumbent	0.25	(0.26)
LDP candidate	0.08	(0.24)
Opposition governor	0.56	(0.29)
N = 3,421		

Source: See endnote 3.
Note: Excluded categories are 1980s, Tokyo, LDP control of a prefecture, and opposition candidates. Standard errors are in parentheses.
* Statistical significance with a p value of <0.05.
** A p value of < 0.01.
*** A p value of <0.001.

Only one independent variable is statistically significant in predicting the number of ultraclose races (decided by less than 0.5 percent) in Japan. There are fewer of these victories in the elections held during the 2000s. This outcome is expected, because these elections used SMDs and had typically wider margins of victory than the margin between, for example, the fourth-place winner and the fifth-place loser that was the basis for calculating of victory margins in Japan's MMDs until 1994.

Having a governor from one of the opposition parties is almost statistically significant, but the sign of this variable is not consistent with a claim of election-night corruption. These data show that if the opposition controls the governorship, an ultraclose race is more likely in that prefecture. When we calculate predicted percentages, however, we find that if a prefecture has an opposition-party governor, an identical 5 percent of LDP candidates and 5 percent of opposition candidates will win by an ultraclose margin. In prefectures controlled by LDP governors, an identical 3 percent of both LDP candidates and opposition candidates are predicted to win by an ultraclose margin. Perhaps the greater number of ultraclose races in prefectures controlled by opposition governors reflects the fact that races between LDP and opposition candidates tend to be closer in areas where the opposition parties have the electoral strength to elect a governor.

These results suggest that no election-night corruption is occurring in Japan, but this simple regression does not distinguish between (1) factors that affect the closeness of races generally and (2) actors related to election-night corruption that would affect only ultraclose races. To distinguish between these factors that affect the closeness of races generally and factors that affect only ultraclose races, we ran 19 additional regressions, changing the dependent variable to each of the other 0.5 percent victory margin categories. There are 19 additional 0.5 percent margin categories located between a 0.5 percent margin of victory and a 10 percent margin of victory. Factors that affect the closeness of elections generally should have a similar impact on both ultraclose and very close races. In contrast, election-night corruption should affect only ultraclose races, not very close races. Thus, if there is a difference between the regression, with ultraclose races as the dependent variable and the other 19 regressions that have very close or close races as the dependent variable, then that difference is likely caused by election-night corruption. The abbreviated results of all 20 regressions are shown in table 10.2.[5]

Very few of the variables included in each regression are statistically significant, and the only variable that is consistently so is that for elections during the period 2000 to 2005. Opposition control of the governorship is statistically significant only in the second and twentieth categories. There are no variables that exert an influence only on ultraclose races, as our hypothesis would suggest. The predicted values also show no evidence of election-night cheating. Where the LDP controls the governorship, the number of LDP candidates winning ultraclose races is not significantly higher; in fact, the distribution of LDP and opposition winners across all 20 categories seems random. Similarly, opposition candidates fare no better than LDP candidates in prefectures in which the opposition controls the governorship.[6]

These results, however, do reveal some factors that affect the closeness of elections generally. For example, the new electoral system has made elections less close than they were under the MMD-based electoral system that Japan used until 1994. Elections held in the 2000 period are statistically significant and are of the expected sign for every category from 0.5 percent to 3.5 percent victories. In some instances, incumbency is correlated with fewer races in a close election category—another finding that is not surprising. Most important for this study is the finding that neither the LDP nor the opposition wins a disproportionate number of ultraclose races when it controls the governorship of the prefecture

Table 10.2 The Impact of Party Control of the Governor's Office on Victory Margins

Dependent variable (%)	Likelihood that an LDP candidate is in victory margin (LDP governor) (%)	Likelihood that an opposition candidate is in victory margin (LDP governor) (%)	Net LDP advantage or disadvantage	Statistically significant variables with direction
Ultraclose (0–0.5)	3.18	2.93	+0.25	2000 - Chubu +
0.5–1	2.72	2.53	+0.19	2000 - Kanto + opp. gov. +
1–1.5	2.90	3.45	-0.55	2000 - 1990 -
1.5–2	3.12	4.20	-1.08	2000 -
2–2.5	3.24	4.30	-1.06	2000 - Inc. -
2.5–3	2.19	3.08	-0.89	2000 -
3–3.5	2.12	2.72	.60	2000 - Inc. -
3.5–4	4.83	4.02	+0.81	None
4–4.5	2.23	3.24	-1.01	1990 +
4.5–5	2.48	1.84	+0.64	2000 -
5–5.5	1.89	1.68	+0.21	None
5.5–6	3.84	3.91	-0.07	2000 - Inc. -
6–6.5	5.37	4.06	+1.31	2000 - Chubu +
6.5–7	1.28	1.39	-0.11	None
7–7.5	0.72	0.99	-0.27	1950 + Kinki -
7.5–8	3.98	3.33	+0.65	2000 -
8–8.5	4.51	3.59	+0.92	1950 - Inc. -
8.5–9	1.22	1.53	-0.31	Inc. -
9–9.5	2.19	1.89	+0.30	None
9.5–10	3.08	2.07	+1.01	Urban + opp. gov.

in which the election occurred. In addition, neither party has an advantage in ultraclose races versus very close, close, or not-so-close races. It does not appear that there is even a small number of cases of election-night corruption in Japan, a finding that is consistent with other tests presented earlier for Japan.

Similar tests run for Canada and the United States, however, do show evidence of election-night corruption in both countries, consistent with the findings of the tests for these countries presented earlier. For example, the Democratic Party in the United States has a statistically significant advantage in only the first category (ultraclose races) of the twenty regressions run. There are greater numbers (statistically significant) of Republican winners in nearly half of the categories analyzed, but these results are only in the categories of not-so-close races (victory margins from 3.5 percent to 10 percent). These results, in contrast to those in the Japanese example, are consistent with explanations of election-night corruption. The Republican advantage disappears in close races and is replaced by an anomalous, statistically significant Democratic advantage that exists only in ultraclose races. It is extremely difficult to manufacture enough bogus votes on election night to steal an election that your opponent is winning by 5 or 10 percent of the vote, but a 2 or 3 percent margin of victory for an opponent can be converted into a slim majority for a candidate. Thus, it is possible that there are fewer Republican victories in close races because some of those races that would have been a close Republican victory have been changed by election-night corruption into extremely narrow Democratic victories. This trend culminates in the results for ultraclose races in which the Democrats have an anomalous, statistically significant advantage over the Republicans, the only such advantage for the Democrats in all twenty separate regressions.

We ran additional tests on the U.S. data, but we were unable to substantiate a link between control of the governorship and a greater number of ultraclose victories by candidates of the governor's party in that state. We also tried controlling for the tendency of a state toward corruption, using Mayhew's categories of the types of party organizations in each state, and the results did not show such a link (Mayhew 1986:196).[7] Thus, it appears that election-night corruption occurs in the United States and it is associated with Democratic candidates, but there is no link between control of the governorship and ultraclose victories.

The same set of regressions run for Canada shows that the Liberal Party has disproportionately fewer victors of close races. These numbers are statistically significant for close races but not for ultraclose races (again, those won by less than 0.5 percent). Liberal Party candidates win more ultraclose races than very close races, a finding consistent with patterns of election-night corruption. Similarly, there are greater numbers of Liberal Party winners in ultraclose races if the province has a Liberal Party premier than in provinces controlled by other parties. In provinces with Liberal premiers, there are fewer Liberal winners in close races but more Liberal winners in ultraclose races, and the results for that category of winner are the only statistically significant results (at a 90 percent level of confidence). These results suggest that control of the provincial government is a crucial factor in explaining only ultraclose races, a finding consistent with our theoretical descriptions of election-night corruption, but surprising given the conventional wisdom that Canadian politics and the Canadian bureaucracy are less corrupt than their American counterparts.

Further research into the election bureaucracies of Japan, Canada, and the United States helps explain our findings. Any electoral bureaucracy has a local component, even if the procedures are centralized at the national level, because ballots must be cast and collected at decentralized locations. Crucial questions for ensuring the integrity of the electoral process are (1) how many supervisors of the election process are in place, (2) how those supervisors are selected, and (3) whether ballot counting is disaggregated sufficiently to create opportunities to steal elections.

On all of these measures, the Japanese electoral bureaucracy scores high, making it very difficult to steal an election on election night. Japanese election procedures are mandated by national legislation.[8] Though the actual administration of elections is done by local committees selected at the municipal level, the members of these committees are chosen in a public vote by municipal assemblies. In addition, the actual counting of ballots has several safeguards that make election-night stealing nearly impossible in Japan. First, each candidate is allowed to name witnesses who observe the counting of ballots. Second, ballots are typically gathered at the municipal level before being counted. Third, by law, no ballots may be counted until all the ballots have been delivered to the municipal office for counting. Fourth, ballots are mixed from all the polling places in a municipality before any ballots are counted. It still might be possible in Japan for one municipality to delay its counting of ballots until the results from the other municipalities in the district are known, but even so, the counting of ballots in that municipality would have to occur under the eyes of witnesses from all political parties.

In contrast, until recent reforms in Canada were enacted, election administration, including the counting of ballots, was under the control of the party that won the previous election in that district. Canadian practice allowed major parties to nominate election workers, but the district election official, selected by the party that won that district in the previous election, was not required to accept those nominations. It was possible for the district election official to appoint only his or her allies as the poll workers serving throughout the election district.[9] In addition, ballots in Canada are counted at the polling place and reported to the district election official, making it possible for only one or two corrupt officials to steal the election by waiting until the number of ballots needed to win is known and then adjusting their ballot totals. Recent Canadian reforms have changed this situation, creating a more independent electoral administration similar to the Japanese electoral bureaucracy, but this new administration has only been used in Canada's most recent elections.

These Canadian procedures fail to explain the link between control of the provincial government and disproportionate numbers of Liberal Party victories in the ultraclose category, but it would not be surprising if there were a correlation between the party that won the district in the previous election and the party that controlled the provincial government. Obviously, additional research is needed to probe whether there is a strong correlation between ultraclose victories by candidates from the party that won that district in the previous election (and thereby controlled the local election machinery on the night of the election).

In the United States, the lack of a clear connection between the occurrence of election-night corruption and control of the state government likely occurs because U.S. electoral administration is extremely fragmented. Most electoral rules are not specified at the national level as they are in Japan and as they are in Canada for federal elections. Even state electoral rules give considerable leeway to local jurisdictions regarding many electoral procedures. Furthermore, the decentralized administration and counting of ballots opens the door for a corrupt electoral official at the local level to steal the election. Indeed, all the notorious stories of election-night stealing in Texas or Nevada, recounted earlier, involved local election officials rather than state officials.

To further explore this link in the United States, we also conducted some case studies of election-night corruption in Utah and Nevada, two states with disproportionately high numbers of ultraclose races. Our results provided provocative evidence of a link between incumbents and election-night corruption. We analyzed nine Utah races and ten Nevada races. Six of the nine Utah races and seven of the ten Nevada races had fact patterns consistent with election-night corruption. In each of these thirteen races, the lead changed between contenders before one candidate took the lead toward the end of the vote count. Even more interesting was our finding that of the fifteen races contested by an incumbent, eleven of them were won by the incumbent. In addition, of the four incumbents who lost ultraclose races, two of them were not true incumbents, having been appointed or elected to office less than six months before the ultraclose election. Though we might expect incumbents to be a disproportionate share of winners in races with a 10 percent margin for the victor, it is odd that in races so evenly matched (in which the victor wins by less than 0.5 percent), incumbents would disproportionately win so many of the races. Perhaps, in the United States, incumbents are more likely to successfully use the techniques of election-night corruption. Incumbents are likely to have better ties to local electoral officials—ties that are needed if a candidate is going to steal the election on election night.

Conclusion and Implications

This chapter has raised more questions than it has answered, but the questions raised are intriguing and potentially fruitful. The purpose of this chapter was to test the simple idea that if there is significant election-night corruption, it should show up by anomalies in the number and characteristics of ultraclose elections. We put forward the hypothesis that such corruption should be rarer in Japan and Canada than in the United States. The Japanese data confirm that even in a country with widespread corruption, national rules for election administration that guarantee the integrity of the balloting and ballot-counting process make it nearly impossible to steal an election on election night. This absence of election-night corruption in Japan was evident in multiple tests of the Japanese data.

In contrast, the United States has disproportionately high numbers of ultraclose races when these races were disaggregated by political party, and additionally, in Canada, a similar finding was correlated with Liberal Party control of provincial governments. Though election-night corruption in the United States is not correlated with which party controls the state house, an examination of ultraclose races in two states suggests that incumbency is a possible conduit of the occurrence of election-night corruption in the United States.

It is also significant that general perceptions of corruption are not the best predictors of corruption in the Japanese and Canadian cases. Rather, institutions served as better predictors of this specific form of corruption. Canada has one of the best reputations for the absence of corruption, and Japan is notorious among the advanced industrialized democracies for its high levels of corruption. Yet the results for election-night corruption correlate better with the independence and centralization of the electoral bureaucracy than they do with general levels of corruption or perceptions of corruption. These results suggest a note of caution when using general perceptions of corruption to analyze a cause or effect of a specific form of corruption. The correlation between general perceptions of corruption and a specific form of corruption may not be reliable, especially among countries that are grouped toward a similar end of the corruption spectrum. The use of general perceptions of corruption, for example, may be of limited usefulness in analyzing differences among relatively similar countries with regard to a specific form of corruption.

Notes

[1] All of these announced tallies were unofficial. The official tally was not released until several days after the election.

[2] We use a percentage measure rather than an absolute measure because we believe that the number of votes that can be created or manipulated using election-night corruption increases with the size of the electorate.

[3] The Canadian data are for House of Commons races from 1945 to 2000. The data are from the official parliament Web site (Parliament of Canada 2005). The Japanese data cover House of Representatives elections from 1947 to 2003 and are based on a data set originally created by Steven

R. Reed and supplemented with data from recent elections. The U.S. data set are an ICPSR data set (1991) that include all presidential, congressional, gubernatorial, and some state office races, and in some analyses we have included southern primaries from the ICPSR (1994) data sets.

[4] We take a running average of the second through the fourth categories (victory margins of 0.5 to 1 percent, 1 to 1.5 percent, and 1.5 to 2 percent). We also calculate an average for the third through fifth and fourth through sixth categories (1 to 2.5 percent and 1.5 to 3 percent). We calculate the increase or decrease between each of these averages and then add that increase or decrease to the first average calculated. We also add the trend number twice to the average of the second through fourth categories because we are predicting the first category, and this first average is centered on the third category and is therefore two units away from the ultraclose category that we are trying to predict. We also use two other variants of the calculation (adding the trend only once to the first average and adding the trend to the second category) and obtain similar results to those reported.

[5] We ran twenty binary logistic regressions. It would have been perhaps simpler to run one multinomial logistic regression, but running twenty separate regressions is a more conservative estimator, so we chose this less efficient method. We also ran the twenty additional regressions using an absolute measure of the margin of victory (250 vote increments in each category) and obtained similar results.

[6] This finding is shown by calculating predicted values for LDP and opposition candidates in prefectures with opposition governors. In these twenty regressions, not reported in the main text of this chapter, opposition candidates had a slight advantage over LDP candidates in ten of the twenty categories. In the five categories for the closest races, there were more opposition winners in two of the five categories and more LDP winners in the other three categories. There is no pattern of opposition candidates winning a disproportionate number of ultraclose races in prefectures in which their party controls the local bureaucracy.

[7] There are many other possible measures of the potential corruption of a state electoral bureaucracy. Elazar (1972) presents cultural explanations that Meier and Holbrook (1992) reject. Meier and Holbrook, among others, use numbers of prosecutions of public officials. Of these and other measures, Mayhew's measure had two distinct advantages. First, his measure seemed most relevant to election-night corruption rather than to general patterns of corruption and dishonesty. Second, his measure was created specifically to cover state politics in the 1960s and even earlier periods, an important fact for our data set, which extends back to the 1870s.

[8] The procedures are listed in the Public Offices Election Law (POEL; Koshoku Senkyo Ho), sections 6, voting (*tohyo*), and 7, counting ballots (*kaihyo*). A useful summary of these provisions, translated into English, is given in Ministry of Home Affairs, 1996.

[9] The rules recently enacted are provided at http://www.elections.ca, the Web site of Elections Canada, the organization that administers federal elections

in Canada. The description of the previous rules was provided in an interview with an Elections Canada official.

References

Alesina, Alberto, and Beatrice Weder. 2002. Do corrupt governments receive less foreign aid? *The American Economic Review* 92 (September): 1126–37.

Anderson, Christopher J., and Yuliya V. Tverdova. 2003. Corruption, political allegiances, and attitudes toward government in contemporary democracies. *American Journal of Political Science* 47 (January): 91–109.

Becker, David, Daniel Kessler, and Mark McClellan. 2005. Detecting Medicare abuse. *Journal of Health Economics* 24 (January): 189–210.

Caro, Robert A. 1991. *The years of Lyndon Johnson: Means of ascent.* New York: Vintage Books.

Dallek, Robert. 1991. *Lone star rising.* New York: Oxford Univ. Press.

Davis, Charles L., Roderic Ai Camp, and Kenneth M. Coleman. 2004. The influence of party systems on citizens' perceptions of corruption and electoral response in Latin America. *Comparative Political Studies* 37 (August): 677–703.

Duggan, Mark, and Steven D. Levitt. 2002. Winning isn't everything: Corruption in Sumo wrestling. *American Economic Review* 92 (December): 1594–605.

Elazar, Daniel J. 1972. *American federalism: A view from the States.* New York: Thomas Y. Crowell.

Fund, John. 2004. *Stealing elections: How voter fraud threatens our democracy.* San Francisco: Encounter Books.

Garicano, Luis, Ignacio Palacios-Huerta, and Canice J. Prendergast. 2005. Favoritism under social pressure. *Review of Economics and Statistics* 87 (May): 208–16.

Gerring, John, and Strom C. Thacker. 2004. Political institutions and corruption: The role of unitarism and parliamentarism. *British Journal of Political Science* 34 (April): 295–330.

———. 2005. Do neoliberal policies deter political corruption? *International Organization* 59 (Winter): 233–54.

Golden, Miriam A., and Eric C. C. Chang. 2001. Factional conflict and political malfeasance in postwar Italian Christian democracy. *World Politics* 53 (July): 588–622.

Imai, Kosuke, and Gary King. 2004. Did illegal overseas absentee ballots decide the 2000 U.S. presidential election? *Perspectives on Politics* 2 (September): 535–50.

Inter-university consortium for political and social research (ICPSR). 1991. Southern primary candidate name and constituency totals, 1920–1972. Electronic text file. Ann Arbor, MI: ICPSR. http://www.icpsr.umich.edu.

———. 1994. Candidate and constituency statistics of elections in the United States, 1788–1990, 5th ed. Electronic text file. Ann Arbor, MI: ICPSR. http://www.icpsr.umich.edu.

Jacob, Brian A., and Steven D. Levitt. 2003. Rotten apples: An investigation of the prevalence and predictors of teacher cheating. *Quarterly Journal of Economics* 118 (August): 843–77.

Kallina, Edmund F., Jr. 1988. *Courthouse over White House: Chicago and the presidential election of 1960.* Orlando, FL: Univ. of Central Florida Press.

Mayhew, David R. 1986. *Placing parties in American politics, organization, electoral settings, and government activity in the twentieth century.* Princeton, NJ: Princeton Univ. Press.

Mebane, Jr., Walter R. 2006. Detecting attempted election theft: Vote counts, voting machines, and Benford's law. Paper presented at the Midwest American Political Science Association annual convention, Chicago, IL., April 20–23.

Meier, Kenneth J., and Thomas M. Holbrook. 1992. I seen my opportunities and I took 'em: Political corruption in the American states. *Journal of Politics* 54 (February): 135–55.

Ministry of Home Affairs. 1996. *Election system in Japan.* Tokyo: Jichi Sogo Center.

Parliament of Canada. 2005. Library of parliament, history of the federal electoral ridings since 1867. http://www.parl.gc.ca/information/about/process/house/infer/infer.asp?Language=E.

Simpser, Alberto. 2005. Strategic incentives for electoral corruption. Paper presented at the American Political Science Association annual convention, Washington D.C., September 1–4.

Treisman, Daniel. 2000. The causes of corruption: A cross-national study. *Journal of Public Economics* 76 (June): 399–457.

Xin, Xiaohui, and Thomas K. Rudel. 2004. The context for political corruption: A cross-national analysis. *Social Science Quarterly* 85 (June): 294–309.

WOMEN IN POLITICS

THE PUZZLE OF THE JAPANESE GENDER GAP IN LIBERAL DEMOCRATIC PARTY SUPPORT

Barry C. Burden[1]

After three decades of remarkable economic growth, the last twenty years have brought tremendous uncertainty to Japan. These social, political, and economic changes presumably have tremendous ramifications for the role of women in national politics. The critical "lost decade" of the 1990s saw the collapse of the Japanese economic "miracle" and, not coincidentally, the Liberal Democratic Party's (LDP's) first electoral loss after forty years of uninterrupted rule. The conservative LDP's surprising defeat was attributed in part to discontent among women voters who were disproportionately affected by the nation's poor macroeconomic performance. Junichiro Koizumi's success in the 2005 elections was also attributed to female voters; the prime minister strategically recruited women to run for office on the LDP ticket. These events occurred in the wake of more general challenges to social norms, particularly the traditional division of household duties between husband and wife. Although Japan has been much slower to change than other industrial powers, today women are waiting longer to get married, are having fewer children, and are more likely to work outside the home.

These are notable changes in a nation where women were unable to vote until 1945, and only then under a constitution imposed by the military victors of World War II. Yet Japanese women have not taken up the same role as their peers in Western democracies. Women hold a smaller share of seats in the Diet than in the legislatures of other industrialized democracies.[2] The United Nations Development Programme (UNDP) puts Japan near the top of its list of nations on the measure of human development, but ranks it a mediocre forty-third on gender empowerment. This poor ranking is due to Japan's sparse representation of women in professional ranks and the low wages of Japanese women compared with men. These sorts of indicators make it easy for observers to conclude that Japan is "arguably the most gender-inegalitarian industrialized country" (Raymo 2003:84).

The economic and political instability of modern Japan appears to have a strong gender component. Prominent political science theories would suggest clear relationships between social and economic change on the one hand and gender differences in political preferences on the other hand. Based on theories from the field of political economy, one might expect Japanese men and women to have starkly differing political views. As in other nations, these differences would be encapsulated in a "gender gap" in partisan preferences that would evolve as society does. If experiences in the United States, Britain, and other Western democracies also hold in Japan, one would expect that as women's roles in family life and business evolve, this gap would widen. Surprisingly, this turns out not to be the case.

In this chapter, I describe an investigation of the historical politics of the Japanese gender gap. By assembling a data series of public opinion data on the LDP and merging this with economic and social indicators, I am able to identify causal relationships between macroeconomic performance and gender differences in support for the ruling party. Replicating an analysis of the U.S. gender gap by Box-Steffensmeier, De Boef, and Lin (BDL 2004), I found a the economy, or practically any other explanatory variable to be negligible aside from support for the prime minister's cabinet. The near-constancy of the gender gap over the last forty-five years in Japan remains puzzling because it runs against conventional explanations in every way. It appears that the economic factors that are crucial to understanding gender gaps in Western democracies have simply not been influential in Japan.

Theoretical Guidance

Despite the fact that there has been little empirical investigation of gender differences in Japanese public opinion, the political science literature provides concrete guidance on how to conceptualize the gender gap and the factors that might affect it. Because these theories are based largely on experiences in Western democracies, how well they apply in Japan remains an open question. We will begin by reviewing the conventional arguments about economics and the gender gap, and consider their relevance to Japan.

Gender differences in political opinions have been linked to stages of national development. Economic development is thought to shape cultural values, which often prescribe clear societal norms for men and women. Specifically, theory suggests gender gaps ought to emerge most strongly in postindustrial societies such as Japan rather than in developing societies. In *Rising Tide*, Inglehart and Norris (2003) argue that the shift from agrarian to industrial and then postindustrial society will expand gender differences. These developments exacerbate the gender gap because they generally bring about greater participation of women in the workforce, depress fertility rates, and produce more gender equality in society. These processes produce a cross-national relationship between economic development and attitudes toward gender equality such that the most advanced nations also see larger political differences between men and women in the electorate. Using a variety of data from many nations, Inglehart and Norris demonstrate that women have shifted toward parties on the left in recent decades and that this movement is greatest in the most developed societies. Given its rapid economic development after World War II, Japan would seem to provide an ideal environment for observing this relationship. As women became more independent of men economically, their preferences should have shifted left and away from the LDP.

Inglehart and Norris find a strong relationship between economic development and gender equality. In their 1998 analysis of several dozen nations, citizens with a per capita gross domestic product (GDP) above $20,000 almost universally agreed that women ought to have equal rights to a job, political leadership, and university education, and that it is acceptable for women to be childless or unmarried but with a child. These nations include Western democracies such as the United States, Canada, Norway, Sweden, Spain, and other democracies such as Australia. In contrast, in countries where per capita GDP is below $10,000, support for gender-equality statements ranged mostly between 50 and 80 percent. Japan is an outlier since it does not belong to either group. Japanese benefit from some of the highest per capita GDP in the world yet fall in the middle of the gender-equality scale with nations such as Belarus, Turkey, and Tanzania. While these results raise some questions about how well Japan conforms to experiences in other nations, the "rising tide" theory clearly hypothesizes that a gender gap should have emerged and grown in Japan over the postwar period.

Not only do Inglehart and Norris make this prediction but women's participation in the labor force has also been shown to affect the gender gap across a range of nations. Women who work outside the home show increasing support for parties of the left (Iversen and Rosenbluth 2006). Single working women in particular tend to be more supportive of progressive government policies because they make lower salaries, and so the gender gap is expected to be inversely related to the marriage rate as single women gravitate toward parties on the left (BDL 2004; Edlund and Pande 2002). Delayed marriage and increased divorce rates, both of which are found in Japan, ought to push women away from the conservative LDP. High marriage rates also encourage gender-specific household duties and thus smaller differences in the political preferences of men and women. Unmarried women in a country with high divorce rates are especially likely to support parties on the left, whereas married women in low-divorce-rate countries are least likely to do so (Iversen and Rosenbluth 2006).

When women work outside the home, gender differences in wages ought to contribute to divergent political views as well (Patterson and Nishikawa 2002). In Japan it seems that economic downturns harm men less than women because female workers serve as a "buffer" for male workers (Houseman and Abraham 1993). As Leonard J. Schoppa's *Race for the Exits* (2006) argues, women in Japan have long played the role of "shock absorbers," taking lesser-paying jobs when unemployment was low and facing termination or resignation when the economy deteriorated. Government policies actually reinforce these differential employment practices. In fact, some would argue that this division of labor was a necessary part of the massive growth in the Japanese economy from the 1960s to the 1980s. As a result of these inequalities, part-time workers in Japan are disproportionately female and suffer lower wages and fewer benefits (Broadbent 2003). As temporary, "pink collar," and otherwise dispensable employees, women are more likely to be laid off by their employers in times of economic difficulty. Hence they serve as buffers to protect men from unpleasant side effects of economic downturns. This asymmetry is well established in the literature and could be the key to understanding how fluctuations in the economy would change the size of the gender gap.

While the "buffer" theory predicts that women will be more responsive to economic fluctuations than men, other facts challenge this view. Women express less interest in politics, yet vote at higher rates than men (Steel 2004). This suggests that voting is more a social than instrumental act for Japanese women, who are not particularly well represented by the fiscally conservative and somewhat hawkish LDP (Patterson and Nishikawa 2002). Unlike women in the United States (Norrander 1997), Japanese women are more likely to report that they do not support any party. Consequently, we would expect women's opinions to be less responsive to economic conditions even though their wages and economic well-being might paradoxically be more affected by the macroeconomy. This fundamental irony could go a long way in explaining why women are underrepresented in the party system despite being more sensitive to national economic performance.

There is some support for differential attention to the economy in the case of the United States. Research shows that men's ratings of the president reflect evaluations of the economy more than do women's, yet women are also more pessimistic about the economy than are men (Clarke et al. 2004). At the same time, American women are more likely to rely on assessments of the national economy in judging political leaders, whereas men are more likely to base opinions on their personal financial situations (Clarke et al. 2004; Welch and Hibbing 1992). Drawing upon multiple economic measures, I will assess whether Japanese men and women react differently to economic indicators as appears to happen in other developed democracies.

In addition to these clear predictions based on a political economic understanding, it is possible that old-fashioned politics might also matter. Since the dependent variable of interest here is support for the LDP, it is plausible that factors that contribute to LDP support in general could also influence the relative support of men and women for the party. There is unfortunately much less theoretical work to motivate this sort of argument. Yet in my study of strategies used by the LDP to maintain popular support, I find no evidence that economic variables have direct influence on party support (Burden 2006). Economic variables shape attitudes toward LDP leaders but do not spill over to affect the party itself. It is a curious but important fact that party support is affected by prime ministerial support but not the other way around. Using some of the same data that are analyzed here, I have found that support for the LDP is heavily driven by support for its leaders, namely the prime minister and his cabinet. The prime minister is a key figure in Japan because he is the head of the party and the one person in politics most clearly responsible for the government's actions. If this relationship is different in any way for men and women, then we would expect changes in prime minister support to affect the gender gap in LDP support.

Data

To understand the relationships among economics, leadership politics, and gender, I use survey data on the partisan preferences of Japanese men and women toward the LDP over a long period of time. Fortunately, the Jiji Press Service provides an ideal source: nationwide polls with representative samples of Japanese citizens conducted monthly since the formation of the modern political system in the 1950s. Early each month a representative voter sample is interviewed in person and asked which party they currently support and whether they support the current prime minister's cabinet. Remarkably, the methodology and wording of the questions have remained unchanged through this entire period. Included in the surveys are batteries of questions about economic performance, ideology, support for the prime minister, and preferred political party. I analyze the period from June 1960 to December 2004. Given the tremendous growth of the Japanese economy in the postwar era and the great dominance of the LDP through at least the 1980s, this forty-four-year period is ideal for testing Inglehart and Norris's thesis about economic development.

Because the LDP has formed the government or has been the major partner in every coalition government in this era (aside from a short spell in 1993–1994), the party provides a convenient baseline for assessing public opinion over a long time period.[3] Although party positions are not completely fixed, the LDP has long been considered to be center-right on the ideological spectrum and is almost always described as conservative (Hrebenar 2000). Kato and Laver (2003) show that the LDP is especially conservative on social policy and on issues of national identity, although perhaps less so on spending policy. We will consider in the conclusion how this mix of policy positions figures into the LDP's support.

Figure 11.1 shows support for the LDP by gender over this time span. Because the data are collected monthly, the raw time series show significant bobbling across periods. To make the trends more apparent and to smooth out the variability due to sampling error, I have fit flexible splines through both time series.

One fact that emerges from the figure is that men are consistently more supportive of the LDP than are women.[4] Men average about 34 percent support and women about 26 percent support, with men being somewhat more variable.[5] This translates to an eight-point gender gap, on average.

A second fact that emerges is that the gender gap is relatively stable over time. The two lines tend to move up and down in tandem, indicating that men and women's views of the LDP often shift for the same reasons and at the same times. When the LDP suffered from inflation and scandals in the 1970s and was defeated in the 1989 Upper House and 1993 Lower House elections, both sexes became less supportive of the party. The gap appears to have grown somewhat during good times for the LDP in the 1960s and 1980s. But, overall, it is striking just how consistent the difference in LDP support is, despite great social, political, and economic change.

Figure 11.1 LDP Support by Gender

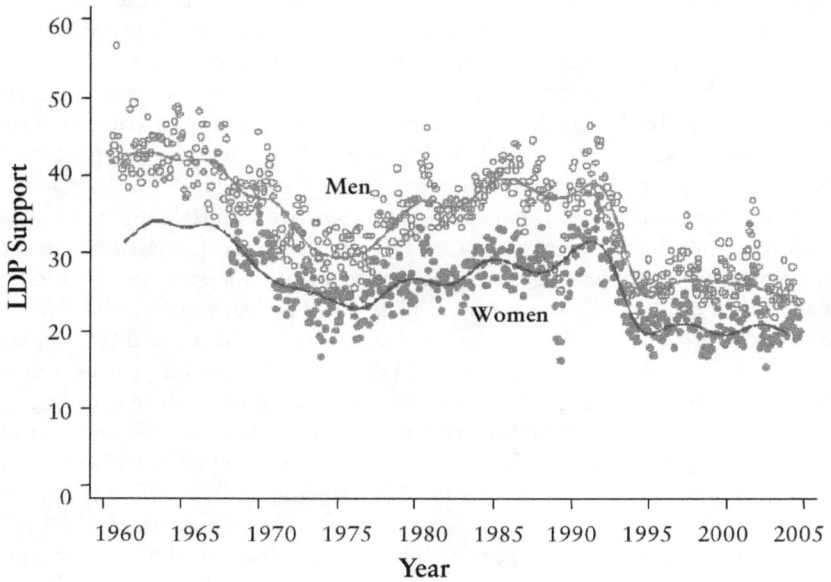

Before moving to the statistical analysis, I convert these two time series into a single gender gap indicator. My measure is simple: the difference in support for the LDP between men and women (Matsuda 2005). Figure 11.2 displays the monthly gender gap in LDP support. The mean gap during this time period is 7.7 percentage points. It ranges from essentially 0 to almost 18 points, with a standard deviation of 3.2 points. When we examine the smoothing spline, however, it seems that, practically speaking, the gap seldom exceeds 10 or 12 points and seldom falls below 5 points for more than a month or two. The gap begins at a relatively high level in the 1960s, and then declines into the early 1970s before returning to its peak in the mid-1980s. Gender differences in LDP support fall through the early 1990s but rise in the second half of the decade, only to fall again after 2000. This pattern suggests a possible relationship between the gender gap in LDP support and the support ratings of the LDP prime minister. The gap was rising just as support for Keizo Obuchi and Yoshiro Mori was falling; the gap fell when Koizumi was earning record support ratings starting in 2001.

Figure 11.2 Gender Gap in LDP Support

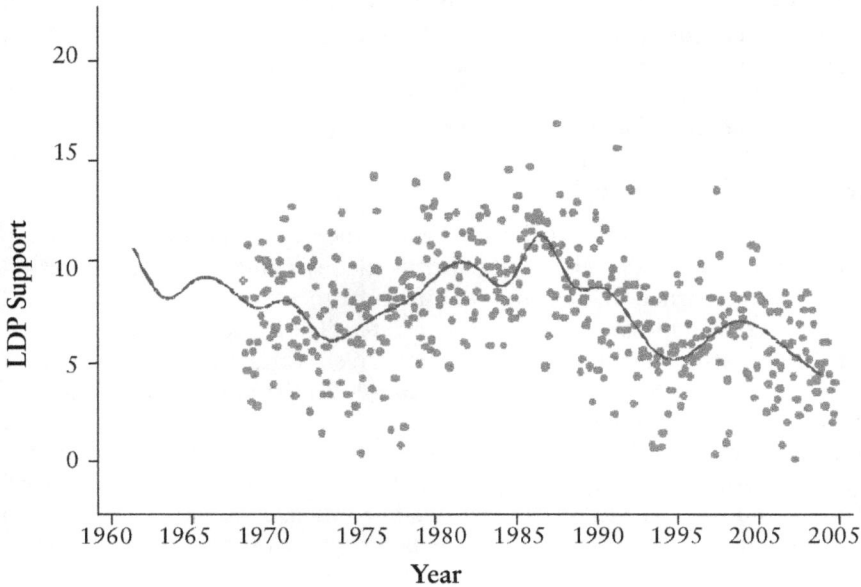

Note: Vertical axis is the difference between male and female support for the LDP.

Considering the clear expectations raised by other scholars, figure 11.2 is puzzling on several counts. First, the trend is not that predicted by Inglehart and Norris (2003). Unlike in the United States and Western Europe, where the gender gap emerged and then grew, in Japan it appears to cycle up and down without trending upward. If anything, the overall trend is downward; the correlation of the gap and time is -0.29 ($p < 0.001$). The gender gap in Japan simply does not display the secular increases in gender differences that are observed in other postindustrial democracies. Despite massive changes in industrialization, urbanization, gender roles, and the party system over the past forty-five years, the gender gap has hovered consistently between 5 and 10 points. It thus seems implausible that standard structural variables will account for much of the fluctuation, since the radical changes in the national economy and even the more modest secular changes in social structure are not reflected in the figure. Short-term political effects are more likely explanations.

Second, the gap does not appear to correspond to commonly understood changes in gender consciousness in Japan. One might have expected women to assert their independence from the LDP in the late 1980s and early 1990s. The "Madonna boom" and the identification of the Socialists (and their female leader, Takako Doi) with women's causes could have drawn female support and widened the gender gap. Despite claims that women responded more strongly to LDP scandals (Pharr 1998), it is difficult to see evidence that the gap grew after Recruit, Lockheed, or other major scandals (Aldrich and Kage 2003). The challenges faced by the LDP in assembling governing majorities over the last decade have also not exacerbated the gap. In fact, the gap appears smaller just at the points where the LDP is most vulnerable—for example, in the early 1990s and mid-2000s. This suggests a negative relationship between support for LDP leaders (presumably the prime minister and his cabinet) and the gap.

Variables and a Statistical Model

I use multivariate time-series analysis to explain the rise and fall of the gender gap between 1960 and 2004. The explanatory variables come from the theoretical literature cited earlier. To capture the effects of the overall macroeconomy, I use national unemployment and inflation rates. These are standard variables in the comparative study of economic effects on electoral outcomes and appear in other studies of the gender gap (BDL 2004). To the degree that the gender gap is a product of economic performance, it should increase in magnitude as unemployment and inflation rise. Two other variables gauge the unique economic positions of women. It is likely that women respond less to general economic indexes than to those that pertain to their own well-being (Iversen and Rosenbluth 2006). I account for the percentage of women who are single (Matsuda 2005) and the percentage who are unemployed to assess the "buffer" hypothesis. Again, the gender gap ought to grow as these measures increase. All four of these variables are straightforward structural indicators suggested by theories of gender and economics.

To these economic measures I add one purely political variable: support for the prime minister's cabinet. Other research has already shown that cabinet support affects support for the LDP (Burden 2006). By extension, cabinet support might also influence the gender gap. All that is required is that men and women respond differently as their views of the prime minister change. If the Koizumi era is typical, figure 11.2 would suggest that an increase in cabinet support will decrease the gender gap. This appears to happen because women adjust their views of the LDP more acutely when support for the cabinet fluctuates.

I adopt the time-series framework proposed by BDL (2004). They posit that both male and female partisanship are linear functions of a common set of explanatory variables. In my framework,

$$\text{Female LDP support} = \mathbf{X}\beta + u$$
$$\text{and}$$
$$\text{Male LDP support} = \mathbf{X}\gamma + v$$

where $\mathbf{X}$ is a matrix of covariates such as economic conditions, β and γ are vectors of coefficients, and u and v are random disturbances. If men and women react identically to the variables in $\mathbf{X}$ (and have identically distributed error terms), then the two equations would need not be separated, since $\beta = \gamma$. This would also result in a constant gender gap over time, even if overall levels of LDP support rise and fall.

Since we hypothesize that variables influence men and women differently, our interest is in how β and γ compare. Following BDL, I subtract one model from the other so that

LDP gender gap = male LDP support - female LDP support = $X(\beta - \gamma) + (u - v)$.

This specification allows for direct tests of whether explanatory variables affect men and women's support for the LDP differently, or the null hypothesis that $\beta - \gamma = 0$. The variables in X include the five just described, as well as several others used as controls in the BDL analysis. These controls are macroideology (the proportion of self-identified progressives among both progressives and conservatives) and lagged values of female and male support for the LDP.

Using this specification, I estimate a linear regression model after "prewhitening" the series to avoid spurious relationships. I use the autoregressive fractionally integrated moving average (ARFIMA) approach of BDL and others (see Box-Steffensmeier and Smith 1998; Lebo, Walker, and Clarke 2000). This requires estimating the standard autoregressive (AR) and moving average (MA) terms, as well as the degree of fractional integration in the parameter d. Unlike traditional ARIMA formulations, in which the degree of integration must be an integer, ARFIMA permits fractional estimates that put a series somewhere between the standard categories of integrated and stationary. I use the semiparametric estimator developed by Geweke and Porter-Hudak (1983).[6] Although not reported here, the most notable of these is the 0.38 estimate of d for the gender gap variable. This is strikingly close to BDLs' estimate of 0.47 for the U.S. gender gap and supports the view from figure 11.2 that the gender gap is relatively resistant to political and economic shocks.

After stripping these variables down by filtering out the ARFIMA elements, I estimate simple ordinary least squares (OLS) regression models of the gender gap. Recall that each coefficient is an estimate of the effects of $\beta - \gamma$, or whether men's and women's support for the LDP responds differently to explanatory variables. I specify several versions, beginning with the most basic economic and control variables in X and then sequentially adding others. One reason for doing this is to evaluate hypotheses sequentially once a baseline model has been fit; the other reason is that two of the variables (macroideology and unemployed women) do not exist for the full time period. Table 11.1 presents the results of these models.

Table 11.1 Models of the Gender Gap in LDP Support

	Model I	Model II	Model III	Model IV	Model V
Unemployment $_t$	-1.23	-2.15	-1.28	-0.34	-0.05
	(0.93)	(1.19)	(0.93)	(0.99)	(1.02)
Inflation $_t$	0.02	0.07	0.01	-0.06	0.06
	(0.15)	(0.17)	(0.15)	(0.16)	(0.18)
PM cabinet support $_{t-1}$			-0.02*	-0.02*	-0.02*
			(0.01)	(0.01)	(0.01)
Macroideology $_{t-1}$		-0.03			
		(0.03)			
Macroideology $_{t-2}$		-0.05*			
		(0.03)			
Single women $_t$					-0.81
					(0.75)
Unemployed women $_t$				-2.22	
				(1.26)	
Female LDP support $_{t-1}$	0.37**	0.33**	0.38**	0.37**	0.41**
	(0.04)	(0.05)	(0.04)	(0.05)	(0.05)
Female LDP support $_{t-2}$	0.10**	0.07	0.11**	0.13**	0.24**
	(0.04)	(0.05)	(0.04)	(0.05)	(0.05)
Male LDP support $_{t-1}$	-0.24**	-0.20**	-0.23**	-0.21**	-0.23**
	(0.04)	(0.05)	(0.04)	(0.04)	(0.05)
Male LDP support $_{t-2}$	-0.17**	-0.20**	-0.17**	-0.15**	-0.15**
	(0.04)	(0.05)	(0.04)	(0.04)	(0.05)
Constant	0.53	1.39*	1.09*	1.05	-0.06
	(0.54)	(0.79)	(0.61)	(0.64)	(0.70)
Adjusted R^2	0.16	0.12	0.16	0.15	0.18
Number of cases	530	370	530	462	379
Durbin-Watson	2.02	2.09	2.01	2.00	1.98
Mean square error	2.82	2.94	2.82	2.68	2.62

Note:*$p < 0.05$, one-tailed tests
**$p < 0.01$, one-tailed tests

Model I begins with the basics: unemployment and inflation, plus controls for the previous LDP support level among men and women. The economic variables are far from statistically significant. Lagged female support has positive effects while lagged male support has negative effects, suggesting positive feedback for women and negative feedback for men. More analysis is required before we can understand these effects. For now, it is important to note that general macroeconomic indicators play no role in governing the gender gap. Model II reinforces this result by adding lagged values of macroideology to the model. Again, neither unemployment nor inflation is statistically significant, challenging the standard political economic explanation for gender differences in partisan preferences.

Model III introduces politics in the form of lagged support for the prime minister's cabinet. Economic variables remain insignificant, but cabinet support is negative and statistically significant, indicating that the gender gap in LDP support decreases when support for the prime minister's cabinet increases. That is, an unpopular prime minister harms the party's image primarily by lowering evaluations of the party more among women than among men, thus widening the gap. When the cabinet's favorability rises, women are more likely than men to rally behind the LDP, and so the gender gap shrinks.

Finally, models IV and V introduce the two measures of female economic independence. These models are not strictly comparable to the others, because the additional variables lower the sample size. The cabinet approval variable is retained in these models, since it demonstrated importance in model III. Although cabinet support remains just as important in these last two models, neither the percentage of single women nor the proportion of women who are unemployed seems to affect the gender gap.

These results paint a portrait of gender and politics in Japan that is surprisingly void of economics or other influences due to changing structures of the family and workplace. Despite the clear theoretical expectations of the political economy literature and findings in other nations, indicators of macroeconomic performance or the gendered nature of labor appear to play little role in driving the gender gap in attitudes toward Japan's dominant political party. A casual inspection of the gender gap time series implied as much, since it exhibited no clear secular increase despite massive changes in Japanese society and its economy. This would seem to make Japan unlike other industrialized democracies. Instead, the gender gap seems to be a product of its own feedback and of attitudes toward the performance of the LDP's leaders, namely the prime minister and his cabinet. The gender gap has fluctuated between 0 and 15 points, depending mostly on how the prime minister was doing in the eyes of the public. Opinion toward the prime minister's cabinet alters support for the LDP, although differentially for men and women.

Conclusion

In the wake of these results, much remains to be done both theoretically and methodologically to understand gender differences in Japanese political attitudes. Although the explanatory power of the models presented here is equivalent to that in BDL, my results seem less satisfying because they fail to parallel the predictions of the scholars. The standard political economic accounts for gender differences in partisan preferences do not find any support in the multivariate models. If economic development did not lead to gender equality and the independent political views that normally ensue, then it suggests that the more appropriate research question may be why industrialization and growth did not transform gender roles in Japan as they did in other Western nations (Gelb 2003).

Beyond feedback effects of male and female support for the LDP, the only explanatory variable that affects the gender gap is support for the prime minister's cabinet. This follows quite naturally from my other work showing that support for the prime minister affects support for the LDP (Burden 2006; Patterson and Maeda 2007). It suggests that gender differences wax and wane in response to politics rather than for structural or economic reasons. This would set Japan apart from Western democracies. It is most striking that the gender gap shrank rather than grew over time, contrary to what prominent developmental theories such as Inglehart and Norris's "rising tide" would predict.

Perhaps Japan fails to follow the patterns of other nations because of its unusual party system, namely the dominance of a single political party over a long time period, and the fragmentation of the opposition (Hrebenar 2000). Many of the political economic explanations for gender differences in political views identify variables that push women away from conservative parties and toward leftist parties. In Japan the center-right of the ideological spectrum is dominated by the LDP, but the left has typically been segmented into the Communists, Socialists, and—recently—the Democratic Party of Japan (DPJ). We should entertain the possibility that the lack of desirable options on the center-left has inhibited the emergence of a partisan gender gap in Japan.

For much of the postwar period the most durable opposition on the left came from the Japanese Socialist Party (JSP), which was associated not only with labor unions and workers, but also, late in its development, with women. So while economic variables might not explain a gender gap in LDP support, perhaps they are more potent in explaining a gender gap in JSP support. To test this proposition I reestimated the models in table 11.1, replacing the dependent variable with a measure of the JSP gender gap. This test failed on two fronts.

First, as shown in figure 11.3, the gender gap runs the wrong way. Men, not women, are more likely to support the JSP. From July 1960 to June 1991 the average gap is 3.6 points. This is partly due to the fact that women are more likely to say that they support no party at all (Patterson and Nishikawa 2002). Second, none of the regression models showed any effects for unemployment, inflation, the percentage of single women, or the percentage of unemployed women. Moreover, prime minister cabinet support is statistically insignificant, as my theory about LDP-specific effects would suggest (Burden 2006). Similar results hold for the gap in "no party" support, where women do outnumber men. In summary, although the hypothesis that fragmentation on the left is responsible for the failure of the gender gap to blossom or even to respond to economic variables, this preliminary exploration of JSP support provides little encouragement for this line of thinking.

Figure 11.3 JSP Support by Gender

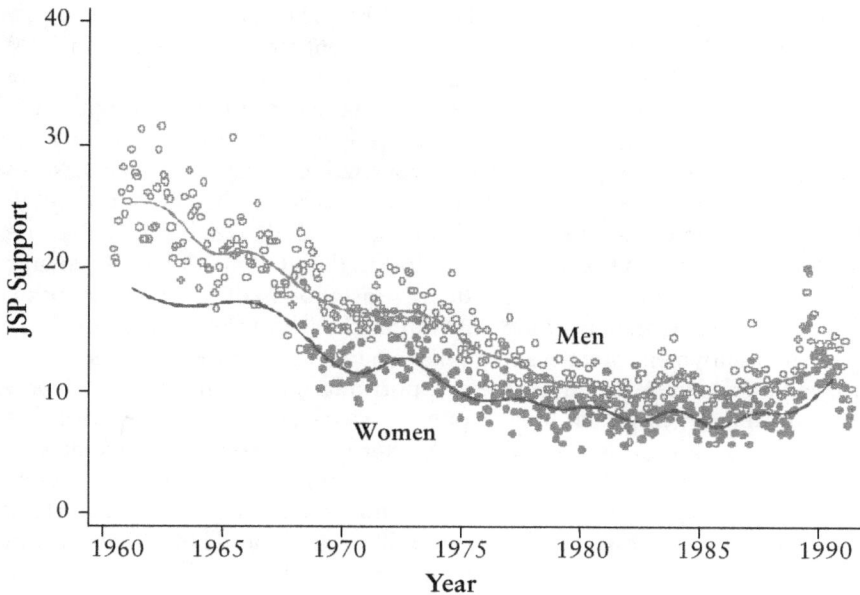

Peculiarities of the LDP itself require further exploration. The LDP's inconsistency in positions across policy dimensions might also limit the effects of economic factors on the gender gap. The expert surveys of Kato and Laver (2003), mentioned earlier, indicate that the LDP is in fact as liberal as other parties on issues of taxing and spending. To the degree that these are the positions that economically vulnerable women care about most, abandoning the LDP in times of economic turmoil might not be the rational reaction. Some have suggested that LDP governments have in fact produced rather "family friendly" workplace policies (Gelb 2003). So perhaps the LDP's evolving positions on such issues have been just progressive enough to prevent large-scale abandonment of the party by women. Koizumi's strategy of placing women prominently in the party's electoral operations would be another way to ward off female dissatisfaction with a party that might not otherwise represent them well.

One might have expected a significant widening in the gender gap in the mid-1980s and 1990s as economic slowdowns took a harder toll on female workers than on their male counterparts. Yet it was precisely at that time that the LDP agreed to make policy changes to alleviate these inequalities. A series of legal victories in the courts was followed by the passage of the Equal Employment Opportunity Law (EEOL) by the Yasuhiro Nakasone government in 1985. The EEOL encouraged employers to give women equal treatment but at the same time allowed firms to ask female employees to work overtime and night shifts, did not alter other discriminatory practices that discourage full-time work, and offered little in the way of enforcement of real equal-opportunity workplace provisions (Gelb 2003; Schoppa 2006). The Child Care Leave Law was created in 1991 by the Toshiki Kaifu government after it announced in 1990 that the fertility rate had fallen to a record low. Like the EEOL, the child-care law was more a set of recommendations than mandates, and it came with little enforcement power. The late 1990s saw more legislation aimed at easing the child- and family-care responsibilities of women, including symbolic measures such as the Basic Law for a Gender Equal Society, a strengthening of the EEOL in 1997, and a domestic-violence-prevention law in 2001 (Gelb 2003). Because of its flexible policy positions (Hrebenar 2000), the LDP might have been able to thwart the rise of a gender gap. It offered legislation to diffuse the perception that women were treated as economic "buffers" in the 1980s and 1990s.

Other employment practices might have had effects as well. A large public sector can increase female employment opportunities when the private sector is more favorable toward men. Japan's public sector—small compared with that of other industrialized democracies in Western Europe—thus contributes to fewer women being employed in traditionally female-dominated occupations (Estévez-Abe 2006). Japan's meager state is unusual among peer nations, which in turn contributes to more gendered divisions of household labor (Iversen and Rosenbluth 2006). Strong employment protection also disadvantages female employees, since employers are more likely to invest in male human capital. Thus, the slow unraveling of "lifetime employment" in Japan might very well shake up the relatively constant gender differences in political attitudes.

The LDP might be able to subvert attention from economic effects in other ways as well. In another work (Burden 2006) I suggest that the LDP manages to limit the impact of macroeconomic troubles on the LDP by shifting blame to outgoing personnel in the party. To the degree that this calibration strategy is successful, changes in economic indicators will produce gendered attitudes toward the prime minister and his cabinet but not toward the party—and might just be the key to LDP longevity. Whether by adapting its policy positions or distracting from its performance failures by focusing blame on individuals within the party, the LDP has managed to prevent a disproportionate withdrawal of party support by women in the Japanese electorate.

Evaluations of the prime minister turn out to be critical elements in the larger political dynamics in Japan. A widely popular prime minister like Koizumi can pull his party upward and thus win the goodwill of his LDP colleagues, despite their possible concerns about his policy priorities or governing style. But the prime minister's popular support also affects gender dynamics because Japanese men and women rally around leaders to different degrees. In particular, the data suggest that women's support for the LDP waivers somewhat more in response to evaluations of the party's leadership. Because men are less responsive, the gender gap tends to widen under disliked prime ministers but shrink under popular ones. As a result, a well-regarded LDP president such as Koizumi helps his party in yet another way by disproportionately drawing women into the fold. This would help to insulate the party from opposition parties—such as the Socialists in the late 1980s or the DPJ in the early 2000s—who want to make a bid for the "women's vote."

Notes

[1] A more extensive version of this chapter was presented at the Stanford Conference on Electoral and Legislative Politics in Japan, June 11–12, 2007, and at the 2007 annual meeting of the Midwest Political Science Association. I thank Kentaro Fukumoto, Natsu Matsuda, and Tiffany Nagano for assistance in data collection. The editors and Mike Thies provided extremely useful comments. The Reischauer Institute of Japanese Studies at Harvard University provided financial support.

[2] The Inter-Parliamentary Union ranks Japan 100th in terms of female representation in the lower chamber of the national legislature (90.6 percent male), http://www.ipu.org/wmn-e/classif.htm.

[3] The LDP was not part of the governing coalition for the eleven months from August 1993 through June 1994. For these observations the cabinet-support measure is reversed, so that it represents nonsupport. The results are unchanged if these observations are removed from the analysis.

[4] Using the formula in BDL (2004, footnote 4), the observed gap in LDP support is significantly different from 0 in 475 out of 533 months or about 90 percent of the time using a 95 percent confidence interval.

[5] The standard deviation is 6.8 for men versus 5.4 for women.

[6] Although a full-maximum likelihood estimator might be preferable when the sample size is small (BDL 2004), I have over five hundred observations, which is an adequate length to justify the semiparametric approach. Lebo, Walker, and Clarke (2000) use much shorter time series and find no substantive differences between the two kinds of estimators. I estimated d using the $gphudak$ command in Stata 9.0.

References

Aldrich, Daniel, and Rieko Kage. 2003. Mars and Venus at twilight: A critical investigation of moralism, age effects, and sex differences. *Political Psychology* 24:23–40.

Box-Steffensmeier, Janet M., Suzanna De Boef, and Tse-Min Lin (BDL). 2004. The dynamics of the partisan gender gap. *American Political Science Review* 98:515–28.

Box-Steffensmeier, Janet M., and Renee M. Smith. 1998. Investigating political dynamics using fractional integration methods. *American Journal of Political Science* 42:661–89.

Broadbent, Kaye. 2003. *Women's employment in Japan: The experience of part-time workers*. New York: Routledge.

Burden, Barry C. 2006. Economic accountability and strategic calibration in Japan's Liberal Democratic Party. Unpublished manuscript.

Clarke, Harold D., Marianne C. Stewart, Mike Ault, and Euel Elliott. 2004. Men, women, and the dynamics of presidential approval. *British Journal of Political Science* 35:31–51.

Edlund, Lena, and Rohini Pande. 2002. Why have women become left-wing? The political gender gap and the decline in marriage. *Quarterly Journal of Economics* 117:917–61.

Estévez-Abe, Margarita. 2006. Gendering the varieties of capitalism: A study of occupational segregation by sex in advanced industrial democracies. *World Politics* 59:142–75.

Gelb, Joyce. 2003. *Gender politics in Japan and the United States: Comparing women's movements, rights, and politics.* New York: Palgrave Macmillan.

Geweke, J., and S. Porter-Hudak. 1983. The estimation and application of long memory time series models. *Journal of Time Series Analysis* 4:221–38.

Houseman, Susan N., and Katharine G. Abraham. 1993. Female workers as a buffer in the Japanese economy. *American Economic Review* 83:45–51.

Hrebenar, Ronald J. 2000. *Japan's new party system.* Boulder, CO: Westview Press.

Inglehart, Ronald, and Pippa Norris. 2003. *Rising tide: Gender equality and cultural change.* New York: Cambridge Univ. Press.

Iversen, Torben, and Frances Rosenbluth. 2006. The political economy of gender: Explaining cross-national variation in the gender division of labor and the gender voting gap. *American Journal of Political Science* 50:1–19.

Kato, Junko, and Michael Laver. 2003. Policy and party competition in Japan after the election of 2000. *Japanese Journal of Political Science* 4:121–33.

Lebo, Matthew J., Robert W. Walker, and Harold D. Clarke. 2000. You must remember this: Dealing with long memory in political analyses. *Electoral Studies* 19:31–48.

Matsuda, Natsu. 2005. The Japanese partisan gender gap: Why are women less likely to support the ruling party than men? Paper presented at the annual meeting of the Midwest Political Science Association, Chicago, April 7–10.

Norrander, Barbara. 1997. The independence gap and the gender gap. *Public Opinion Quarterly* 61:464–76.

Patterson, Dennis, and Ko Maeda. 2007. Prime ministerial popularity and the changing electoral fortunes of Japan's Liberal Democratic Party. *Asian Survey* 47:415–33.

Patterson, Dennis, and Misa Nishikawa. 2002. Political interest or interest in politics? Gender and party support in postwar Japan. *Women and Politics* 24:1–34.

Pharr, Susan J. 1998. Moralism and the gender gap: Judgments of political ethics in Japan. *Political Psychology* 19:211–36.

Raymo, James M. 2003. Educational attainment and the transition to first marriage among Japanese women. *Demography* 40:83–103.

Schoppa, Leonard J. 2006. *Race for the exits: The unraveling of Japan's system of social protection.* Ithaca, NY: Cornell Univ. Press.

Steel, Gill. 2004. Gender and political behaviour in Japan. *Social Science Japan Journal* 7:223–44.

Welch, Susan, and John Hibbing. 1992. Financial conditions, gender, and voting in American national elections. *Journal of Politics* 54:197–213.

WOMEN RUNNING FOR NATIONAL OFFICE IN JAPAN: ARE KOIZUMI'S FEMALE "CHILDREN" A SHORT-TERM ANOMALY OR A LASTING PHENOMENON?

Alisa Gaunder[1]

Women are underrepresented in Japanese politics. At the national level, however, women have experienced major increases in strength in two very distinct political parties. The first increase came when the Japan Socialist Party (JSP) successfully supported ten women for office under the leadership of Takako Doi. This "Madonna boom" increased the percentage of women in the Upper House to 17.5 percent. Similarly, a record number of women from the Liberal Democratic Party (LDP) were elected in the 2005 Lower House elections, when Prime Minister Junichiro Koizumi decided to run several women against postal reform "rebels" in high-profile districts. With the victory of twenty-six conservative women, the percentage of women in the Lower House increased to 9.4 percent. Both of these increases in female representation were the result of top-down party leadership, not bottom-up institutionalization. But the Madonna boom faded and the majority of these women members of the Diet disappeared. Can we expect a similar fate for Koizumi's female "children"?

Including the significant increases of the 1989 Upper House elections and the 2005 Lower House elections, female representation in both houses of the Diet has risen—slowly but steadily—since World War II. Figure 12.1 illustrates the overall pattern of female representation in the Lower House and Upper House during the postwar period. While it remains to be seen if the 2005 Lower House elections are an aberration, the 1989 Upper House elections stand out as a spike in a more gradual increase in female representation. The results of the 2007 Upper House elections might suggest that Koizumi opened the door for female representation to increase at a relatively fast pace. In those elections, a record twenty-six women were voted into office, bringing the percentage of women in this chamber to 21.5 percent. A closer examination of these results, along with a comparison of the 1989 and 2005 cases, reveal that significant barriers remain for female candidates at the national level. Without institutional reform at the party level, the number of women in the Diet will continue its gradual upward trend.

Figure 12.1 Percentage of Women Elected to the Diet

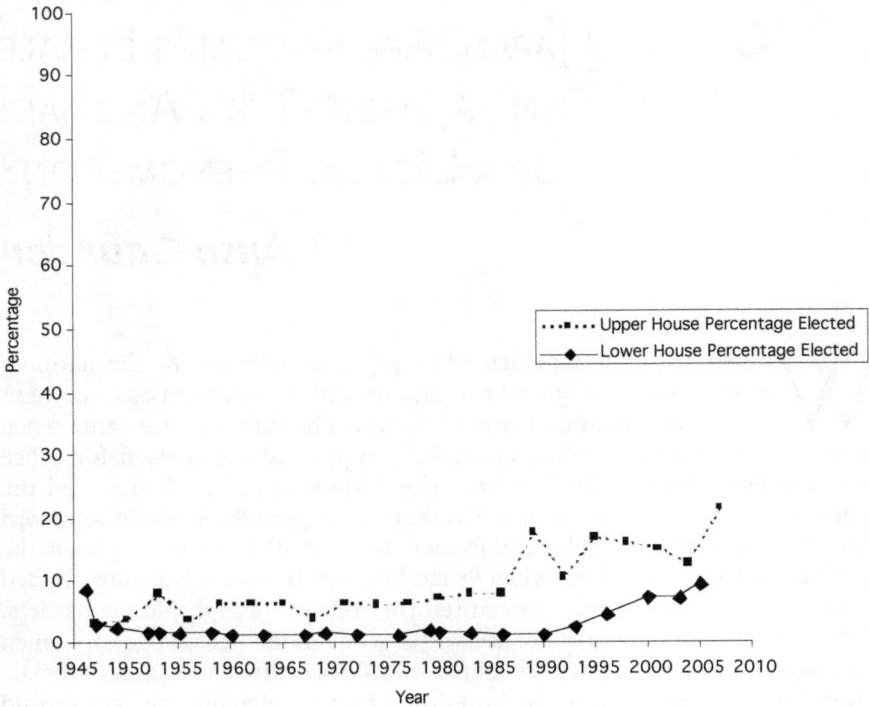

Source: 2005 Cabinet Whitepaper for Planning Gender Cooperation, http://www.gender.go.jp/whitepaper/h17/danjyo_hp/danjyo/pdf/DKH17H01.pdf.

Electoral Obstacles in Japan

In Japan all candidates face three major obstacles when running for national office: building a constituency (*jiban*), publicity/endorsements (*kanban*), and money (*kaban*). In addition to the traditional electoral constraints, women also face constraints embedded in cultural and social norms. Women in Japan tend to think of politics as distant from their lives (Iwao 1993; LeBlanc 1999). Even if women become more interested in politics through their involvement in local activism, certain gender expectations remain. Specifically, a tendency still exists to see a woman's role as that of a "good wife, wise mother." Indeed, a woman candidate's family remains a large obstacle to running for office (Katsuko Nishimoto, personal interview, March 28, 2005; Mitsuko Yamaguchi, personal interview, March 24, 2005).[2] If a woman runs for office, people ask, "Who is going to take care of the family?" This question never emerges for men running for office.[3]

Because of more limited access to party resources and the constraints posed by cultural and social norms, women have had to seek additional means for challenging these electoral obstacles. In particular, activities of "backup schools," sponsored by organizations such as the Ichikawa Fusae Memorial Association and campaign-funding organizations such as WINWIN, have provided women with additional resources. In general, however, women have performed the most strongly when party leaders have made the election of women a priority.

Traditional Resources for Challenging Electoral Obstacles

Traditionally, candidates have challenged the obstacles of *jiban, kanban*, and *kaban* using a certain set of institutional resources. Specifically, personal support organizations (*koenkai*) allow candidates to cultivate the personal vote. Party and factional support provide publicity and endorsements, while party and factional financial aid alleviate some of the fund-raising pressures. These resources are less available to women running for office than to men.

Koenkai

Koenkai play a critical role in building a constituency (*jiban*). LDP politicians (as well as JSP politicians) created *koenkai* to respond to the incentives and constraints created by the electoral system. For the LDP especially, the system of multimember districts (MMDs) under a single nontransferable vote (SNTV)—in place in the Lower House from 1947 to 1993—created incentives for candidates to compete based on personal vote, not on policy. Under this system, 2 to 6 representatives were elected in 129 districts. In order to gain a majority in the Lower House, which had 511 seats, a party needed to win 2 seats in each district on average. The LDP was the only party with enough resources to field multiple candidates in every district.[4] Unable to distinguish themselves on policy—since the LDP votes down party lines in the Diet—these candidates were forced to compete by providing personal favors and pork to their constituents. *Koenkai* became the institutional means for cultivating this personal vote. Incumbents with established *koenkai* proved very difficult to unseat (Darcy and Nixon 1996:14). Very few women had entered politics before the momentum of incumbency had taken hold under this system.[5]

Koenkai are difficult for all aspiring LDP politicians to build, but women face even greater obstacles because they often are excluded from the old boys' networks crucial to the creation of these organizations. These connections come from education, work, and family. Women who graduate from elite universities and work as bureaucrats, local politicians, or political assistants to Diet members do have some relevant connections, but only a small number of women have this background. Women without this pedigree do not. If women candidates are married, they are likely to have moved to a region based on their husband's career. This common practice denies them family connections in the district where they live and would run for office (Bochel et al. 2003:27). Because of the

241

personal allegiances that *koenkai* foster, these organizations often are passed from a retiring politician to a family member or a former political assistant. Daughters and wives have occasionally inherited *koenkai*, but the norm has been to pass these personal support groups on to a male representative of the family or to a male political assistant.

Many people predicted that *koenkai* would become obsolete with the 1994 revisions to the Public Office Election Law (POEL). Among other things, these revisions created a new electoral system for the Lower House. This system combines single-member districts (SMDs) with a proportional representation (PR) tier and comprises 300 SMD seats and 180 PR seats. The hope was that under the combined SMD-PR system, candidates would compete based on policy, not on personal favors and connections. The logic of competition in SMDs continues to reward candidates with *koenkai* (Krauss and Pekkanen 2004). The critical role of *koenkai* in both the old and new electoral systems favors candidates with money or connections to money. Thus, while women were expected to perform better under the new system, women continue to struggle to cultivate the personal connections to local politicians and businesses necessary to support *koenkai*. The PR component of the electoral system does provide opportunities for women to gain seats without building a *koenkai*, but as we will see, success on the PR list is contingent on receiving a party's nomination.

Party and Factional Endorsements

Party and factional endorsements are a key element in gaining the publicity (*kanban*) necessary to win elections. Gaining party support has been difficult for women in Japan. In particular, the LDP's party structure, rules, and norms have not favored women candidates. Specifically, the historically closed nature of the nomination and recruitment process, along with the characteristics and priorities of party gatekeepers, have kept the number of officially endorsed female candidates low. Under the old MMD system, the LDP established an Electoral Strategy Committee to oversee nominations. This committee is composed of twelve members with factional representation proportional to faction size. The LDP president and vice president also serve on the committee (Cox and Rosenbluth 1996:261; Shiratori 1988:171). The consideration of official candidates is a bottom-up process, with the Electoral Strategy Committee considering recommendations from the local branch offices. The committee passes its recommendation to the executive council. If the executive council is unable to resolve who should receive official party endorsement in any of the districts, the decision is left to the five major party officials—the LDP president, vice president, secretary-general, the Policy Affairs Research Council (PARC) chairperson, and the executive council chairperson (Shiratori 1988:172–73). Under the old electoral system, factional balancing was a major determinant of official endorsements. After incumbents, second-generation politicians or candidates who could demonstrate strong support in a given district were given priority (Woodall 1996:108). It was also common for LDP members who did not receive official party endorsement to run as independents, provided they had a sufficient personal support network. The LDP would issue these independents a certificate of party membership and retroactively give these candidates the party nomination if they won (Shiratori 1988:172). This practice increased the number of conservative candidates running in any district and favored candidates with resources and connections who could establish their own local political machines (Shiratori 1988:175).

Under both the old and new electoral systems, local party branch offices and factions have played a key role in the recruitment and nomination process in the LDP. Women face barriers to entry in both areas; local branch offices as well as factions are patriarchal. Iwamoto notes that one of the largest obstacles that potential women candidates face is "the aged male gatekeepers who select candidates in almost all the districts" (2001:226). Very few women have the type of experience rewarded by local party gatekeepers and/or factions. The favored career paths of LDP politicians are in the civil service or politics: bureaucrats, local and prefectural assembly members, or political assistants (Ogai 2001:208). Far fewer women are bureaucrats or local politicians because of similar gender barriers in these professions as in national politics.

The obstacles posed by factions have not lifted under the new electoral system. Factions fight to receive party endorsement when open seats become available in the SMDs, because such openings provide an opportunity for a faction to increase its overall strength in the LDP (Park 2001:438). The factions of the LDP president and secretary-general often are able to recruit more potential candidates because they have greater weight in deciding party endorsements (Park 2001:438–39). Candidates who receive LDP endorsement, however, have an incentive to keep their factional affiliation a secret during the election so as to secure more votes (Köllner 2004:94). Since no faction has made it a priority to increase its number of women members, many of the same constraints to recruitment and nomination as found under the old electoral system remain.

Even if these structural barriers did not exist, the conservative ideology of the LDP acts as a deterrent to the recruitment of female candidates. The LDP has not advocated progressive gender policies. LDP-sponsored legislation tends to support women in their traditional gender roles (Ogai 2001:209). As a result, the LDP does not have much to offer potential women candidates. Not surprisingly, the Socialist and Communist parties historically have attracted more women (Aiuchi 2001:221; Ogai 2001:209).

In contrast to the LDP, the Democratic Party of Japan (DPJ)—the largest opposition party in Japan—has a party structure, rules, and norms that have been slightly more favorable to women candidates. Unlike the now-defunct Japan New Party (JNP), the DPJ did not incorporate quotas for women as part of its party platform upon its formation in 1996. It did, however, establish certain institutions and rules to attract more women candidates. Specifically, it has a recruitment program for women and provides some open political training classes to potential women candidates. If women decide to run as DPJ candidates, the party provides funding to help them get their campaigns off the ground.[6] Also, its highest-profile members are committed to campaigning on behalf of women candidates (Aiuchi 2001:221).

The DPJ's Committee for Gender Equality oversees the recruitment of women for party nomination. DPJ candidates are recommended by local party officials or representatives of supporting organizations such as unions. Candidates also can express their interest in receiving the DPJ's endorsement through the party's open recruitment program (Aiuchi 2001:221–22).[7] This program offers the greatest opportunity for the entry of women. Still, only 10 percent of program applicants were women in the 2000 Lower House election cycle, illustrating the reluctance of women to self-select themselves as potential candidates (Aiuchi 2001:222).

Party and Factional Financial Assistance

Financial assistance from parties and/or factions has been the primary resource for money (*kaban*), the third major electoral obstacle. LDP factions in particular played a major role in supporting candidates for office under the old electoral system. During the first two decades of LDP dominance, factions provided direct monetary support. With the revisions to the Political Funds Control Law in 1976, however, factions began to play a more indirect fund-raising role, providing such services as introductions to donors (Curtis 1988:179). Factions provided this support in return for allegiance to their candidates in the party presidential election, which determined the prime minister during the period of LDP dominance (1955–1993). Party and/or factional endorsements were a prerequisite for this assistance, and as we have seen, women rarely were tapped as official candidates.

The influence of factions in elections has decreased even further since the passage of the 1994 political reforms (Krauss and Pekkanen 2004). Significantly, these reforms created government-supported party subsidies that were supposed to lessen the burden on the individual. One would expect that this would make it easier for women to run, since women generally have less access to private funding. But, once again, in order to benefit from these subsidies, a candidate needs to receive party endorsement, a feat more difficult for women.

Especially in the LDP, the burden of raising funds falls on the individual candidate. A survey of LDP Lower House members revealed that the money received from the LDP prefectural branch offices through the party-subsidy provision covers only 14 percent of the average politician's annual expenses (Taniguchi 2006). Candidates in the SMD constituencies continue to rely on *koenkai* to cultivate the personal vote (Krauss and Pekkanen 2004). Building and maintaining *koenkai* is expensive. Seiko Noda, a prominent female member of the LDP, reflected on the barriers that financing campaigns poses for women who want to run with LDP endorsement:

> In the conservative party, it [campaigning] is all self-financed. The amount that the party gives us is really not much, and so in Japan, members receive election and daily operation support not from individuals but from companies. The corporate culture is a male one, so companies do not bother giving money to women. Thus, it is difficult collecting donations. The reason why men can run again and again even if they lose is because they are able to receive so many donations. In contrast, if women use up donations [from companies], they do not receive additional donations. As a result, they cannot run in the next [race]. (Personal interview, June 10, 2005)

According to Noda, women are held to a higher standard when they run for office: they often get only one chance. Moreover, women often do not have connections to the most likely funding sources.

As mentioned earlier, the DPJ does provide some direct financial assistance to its women candidates (Aiuchi 2001:221). Overall, however, the DPJ has a smaller monetary resource base to draw from, presenting additional obstacles to all of its officially endorsed candidates.

The Effects of Constraints on Election Outcomes

The electoral fortunes of women candidates during the postwar period reflect the fact that women often do not have access to the traditional resources used to challenge the obstacles of *jiban*, *kanban*, and *kaban*. For example, until Koizumi's recruitment of women candidates in 2005, the LDP had the second-fewest women candidates in both SMD and PR constituencies in most Lower House elections. In most instances the Komeito (Komei and the New Peace Party had joined hands and formed the New Komeito in 1998) was the only party with fewer women candidates than the LDP.[8]

In comparison to the LDP, though, the DPJ has attracted and supported more women candidates in both SMD and PR contests in most elections. In fact, the LDP supported more PR candidates only in the 2005 election (with 25 Koizumi-supported women candidates versus the DPJ's 24). In all other elections the DPJ endorsed 2 to 3 times more women candidates than the LDP.

Table 12.1 compares the election success rates of female and male candidates since 1993. In most instances, the success rates for both male and female LDP candidates are higher than for DPJ candidates, especially in SMDs. In the LDP, women were less successful than men in constituency contests in 1996 and 2005. With the exception of 1996, though, women have had a higher success rate than their male counterparts in PR contests. Thus, while the LDP historically has nominated only a few women candidates, it has prioritized their election in the PR tier and placed them in SMDs where they were competitive.

Table 12.1 Election Success Rates of Male and Female Candidates, by Party

Year	LDP		DPJ		JSP		Komeito	
	Male (%)	Female (%)	Male (%)	Female (%)	Male (%)	Female (%)	Male (%)	Female (%)
1993	78.4 (283)	50 (2)	–	–	50.8 (132)	30 (10)	94.2 (52)	100 (2)
1996 (SMD)	59 (283)	40 (5)	13.5 (126)	0 (17)	8.1 (37)	16.7 (6)	–	–
1996 (PR)	21.5 (317)	20 (10)	23.4 (317)	13.6 (22)	22.5 (40)	25 (8)	–	–
2000 (SMD)	65 (266)	80 (5)	35.5 (217)	12 (25)	2 (51)	15 (20)	41.2 (17)	0 (1)
2000 (PR)	16.5 (316)	40 (10)	18.9 (233)	11.5 (26)	14.8 (54)	31.8 (22)	44.7 (47)	18.8 (16)
2003 (SMD)	60.6 (269)	62.5 (8)	40.2 (241)	30.8 (26)	2.2 (45)	0 (17)	90 (10)	0 (0)
2003 (PR)	21.4 (304)	40 (10)	26.5 (245)	24.1 (29)	4.2 (48)	17.6 (17)	53.8 (39)	66.7 (6)
2005 (SMD)	76.5 (268)	63.6 (22)	18.4 (266)	13 (23)	3.6 (28)	0 (10)	88.9 (9)	0 (0)
2005 (PR)	21.2 (311)	48 (25)	21 (271)	16.7 (24)	13.3 (30)	15.4 (13)	51.4 (37)	66.7 (6)

Sources: Success rates for candidates were calculated using raw election data from the following sources: Somusho Jijigyoseikyoku Seijibu, *Senkyo Nenkan, Heisei 8–Heisei 11*; Jijisho Senkyobu, *Heisei 12 Shugiingiin Sosenkyo Saikosaibansho Saibankan Kokuminshinsa Kekkashirabe*; Somusho, *Heisei 15 Shugiingiin Sosenkyo Saikosaibansho Saibankan Kokuminshinsa Kekkashirabe*; Shugiingiin Jimukyoku, *Shugiingiin Sosenkyo Ichiran Dai 39 kai*; Shugiingiin Jimukyoku, *Shugiingiin Sosenkyo Ichiran Dai 40 kai*; http://www.soumu.go.jp/ senkyo/ h17sousenkyo.

Note: The number of candidates fielded is listed in parentheses. Several candidates ran in both SMD and PR contests. These candidates are counted twice.

The difference in the success rates of male and female DPJ candidates shows even less variation; it consistently narrowed from 13 percentage points in 1996 to 5 percentage points in 2005 in SMD contests. This trend implies that voters are not necessarily more inclined to vote for men than for women.

Finally, with the exception of a few contests in the LDP, the success rates for LDP and DPJ politicians move in the same direction for men and women, suggesting that party popularity is more significant than gender in determining election outcomes. Thus, the low number of female representatives across parties seems to be the result of low self-selection combined with low party support, not low voter support and election rates.

Alternative Resources: The Role of Women's Organizations

A vibrant women's movement provides women with additional resources to overcome electoral obstacles, thereby increasing the chances of candidate self-selection. Women's organizations provide the chance to gain administrative and political experience as well as the opportunity to build a support base. A reputable organization can provide legitimacy to a woman's candidacy and even help an aspiring candidate gain party affiliation. It can also provide resources such as a volunteer base or financial backing that can aid a woman candidate's campaign (Matland 2005:95).

While politics traditionally has not been the realm of women in Japan, many have become active in community activities and organizations, such as local parent-teacher associations, consumer movements, and citizen/protest movements (Iwao 1993:242). Predominantly middle-class, educated women initially join these groups in accordance with their roles as wives and mothers, expressing concern over issues that directly affect the household, including education, the environment, and food safety (Iwao 1993:244). Participation in these groups has provided Japanese women with an opportunity to challenge society's dominant image of women and their role, and thereby has increased their participation in the political realm (Pharr 1981). Indeed, many of these women realize that they can affect real change only by becoming part of the political decision-making process, at least at the local level (Iwao 1993:244). Several scholars have found a connection between local-level organizations, social movements, and involvement in politics (Eto 2001; Gelb and Estévez-Abe 1998; Ogai 1999, 2004).

In this section, I consider the role of four distinct organizations in training, recruiting, and supporting women for political office in Japan. Two of these organizations—the Seikatsu Networks[9] and the Ichikawa Fusae Memorial Association—focus on supporting candidates at the local level. A third organization—the Politics School for Women—run by Yoriko Madoka, a DPJ Lower House representative, focuses on training women to run for office at all levels. Finally, WINWIN is a nonpartisan organization that provides financial backing to first-time women candidates running for office, mainly at the national level.

These four organizations are significant because, to varying degrees, each provides women with certain alternative resources to build a constituency, gain publicity, and raise funds. These alternative resources allow women to compete against other candidates who might have greater access to traditional party tools. Table 12.2 compares the traditional resources discussed in the previous section and the alternative resources provided by each organization discussed in this section. As we will see, the Seikatsu Networks officially endorses its candidates, funds their campaigns, and mobilizes others to support its candidates at the local level. WINWIN provides direct financial assistance to first-time candidates. The key focus of the Seikatsu Networks, the Ichikawa Fusae Memorial Association, and the Politics School for Women, however, is increasing the political awareness of women and educating them on how to run a campaign. These services are an important first step but fall short of directly confronting some of the obstacles to gaining party endorsement at the national level.

Table 12.2 A Comparison of Traditional Party Tools and Alternative Resources for Challenging Electoral Obstacles

Obstacle	Traditional party tools	Alternative resources
Organized support (*jiban*)	*Koenkai*	Seikatsu Networks volunteers
Publicity (*kanban*)	Party, factional endorsement	Seikatsu Networks, party leader support (Doi, Koizumi)
Money (*kaban*)	Party, factional subsidies	WINWIN, Seikatsu Networks
Policy/election expertise	Factional support	Seikatsu Networks, Ichikawa Fusae Memorial Association, the Politics School for Women

The Seikatsu Networks helps women overcome the obstacles of building a constituency, gaining publicity, and financing a campaign at the local level. The Seikatsu Networks is the political arm of the Seikatsu Club, a consumer group that was formed as a cooperative to purchase environmentally sound household products. The Seikatsu Club's concern with safe household products has attracted housewives to its membership, although men hold significant leadership positions (Gelb and Estévez-Abe 1998:268). Over time, the group's activities have become more political as members have begun to realize that securing safe products is greatly facilitated by government regulations that protect the environment. To directly influence politics at the local level, the consumer group established a separate branch of the organization—the Seikatsu Networks—which directly focuses on getting members elected to local office. Candidates supported by the Seikatsu Networks benefit from the aid of volunteers belonging to the Seikatsu Club. Seikatsu Club members provide an initial support base from which candidates can build an even greater backing. These candidates can also draw on the Seikatsu Club's other resources to help them overcome the obstacle of financial backing. The Seikatsu Networks represents the success of a social movement translating its organizational power into political representation for women in local areas where it is organizationally strong (Gelb and Estévez-Abe 1998; LeBlanc 1999; Ogai 1999, 2004).

The fact that the Seikatsu Networks focuses on electing proxies[10] at the local level reflects the relationship between women and politics in Japan. As described earlier, women see politics as distant from their lives in Japan. Women do show interest in education and the environment, however. But, interestingly enough, they do not define these areas as political. Instead, they see these as public issues (Steel 2004:227). The Seikatsu Club provides housewives with a way to address these public issues, and the Seikatsu Networks offers a path to connect the experience gained in the cooperative to local politics. With such involvement, politics becomes less distant (Pharr 1981). But very few proxies serving in local assemblies aspire to politics at the national level. Instead they see local politics as the most appropriate arena for influencing the policies they care about (Gelb and Estévez-Abe 1998:271).

Unlike the Seikatsu Networks, the Ichikawa Fusae Memorial Association supports the Center to Promote Women's Involvement in Politics by training candidates for local office and educating current local politicians—but without an explicit policy agenda. This association is named after Ichikawa Fusae, a leader of the prewar women's suffrage movement and an independent member of the Upper House of the Diet from 1958 to 1981. The Ichikawa Fusae Memorial Association's main goal is to promote "cleaner" politics and elections and—to this end—foster greater female involvement in the political arena (Bochel and Bochel 2004). Mitsuko Yamaguchi, executive director of the association explains, "In national elections, parties are responsible for advancing women. In local elections, organizations [such as the Ichikawa Fusae Memorial Association] need to support many qualified women through education" (personal interview, March 24, 2006). The association strives to increase the number of women serving as local assembly members across Japan.

The education provided by the Ichikawa Fusae Memorial Association's so-called "backup school" indirectly helps women challenge electoral obstacles. That is, this education provides them with information on how to confront *jiban*, *kanban*, and *kaban*; it does not directly provide its participants with supporters, publicity, or money. And it does help build participants' self-confidence, allowing them to reach beyond traditional gender expectations. The backup school's courses for new candidates focus on practical skills for running for office, including how to run a legal campaign, build a support organization, give speeches, and develop policy expertise. For example, since it is often difficult to collect individual financial contributions, the association encourages women to ask for volunteer support instead. According to Yamaguchi, a band of volunteers working in your living room instead of in a costly campaign office near the train station can reduce many of the costs of running for office. This kind of support has clearly been successful; approximately 80 percent of the women who take classes at the Ichikawa Fusae Memorial Association and run for office win a seat in local assemblies (Yamaguchi, personal interview, March 24, 2006).

The Ichikawa Fusae Memorial Association's backup school is not alone. Several variations of this kind of educational resource exist, such as the Politics School for Women, which was created in response to a perceived lack of interest in politics among women. According to Madoka, the broad goal of the school is "to create a network for women and get them excited about making policy." She resists the notion that women's interests should stem only from their role as housewives, and says that women need to have a more macro view of policy, including foreign policy and defense, as opposed to a microview that centers on issues such as the environment and education (personal interview, March 27, 2006). The school does not focus exclusively on candidate training and recruitment. Instead, it seeks to educate and excite more women about politics.

To date, 103 participants in the Politics School for Women have been elected to office at the national, prefectural, ward, city, town, and village levels (Madoka, personal interview, March 27, 2006).[11] Only two of the participants have been elected to national office, though, suggesting that education alone is not enough to confront the obstacles women face when running for the Diet.

In contrast to the other organizations, WINWIN is a nonpartisan organization focused on raising funds to support first-time women candidates running for office, mainly at the national level. WINWIN models itself on EMILY's List in the United States, which has had great success in nationalizing races for Congress by mobilizing financial support for pro-choice female Democrats. The key innovation of EMILY's List has been to exploit the willingness of pro-choice women across the country to financially support candidates running in districts other than their own (Sarah Brewer, personal interview, June 19, 2006).[12]

WINWIN has not been as successful as EMILY's List at challenging the financial obstacles faced by female candidates, precisely because it lacks a unifying policy issue that would mobilize support. WINWIN is already fighting an uphill battle, since there is no custom of individual contributions in Japan. Without a unifying issue, the steering committee's decisions about whom to financially back simply appear ad hoc. In some cases the organization has supported candidates who did not need financial backing. The lack of transparency in the decision-making process has disillusioned many of the contributors who initially offered financial support (Ogai Tokuko, personal interview, March 24, 2006).[13] As a result, this organization is struggling.

While all these organizations attempt to challenge the obstacles faced by women running for office, most of them have achieved only partial success, largely limited to the local level. Women tend to have the greatest success at the national level when party leaders prioritize their election. Since party-leader support nearly always results in official party endorsement, it allows women access to the traditional party resources necessary to build a constituency, gain publicity, and raise money.

The Role of Leadership

Party leaders have played a large role in elections when there have been significant increases in the number of women running for office and winning. Specifically, Doi's commitment to seeing JSP women candidates elected in the 1989 Upper House elections and Koizumi's support of LDP women candidates in the 2005 Lower House elections directly led to dramatic increases in female representation in the Diet.

The success of women in both the 1989 Upper House and 2005 Lower House elections was closely associated with the popularity of the party leaders who selected the candidates and the political climate of the time. It was not the result of changes made to the institutional rules and norms for recruiting and nominating candidates in either party.

Doi, the head of the JSP in 1989, was extremely popular and attracted a large amount of media attention as the first female party leader. Doi used her popularity to campaign for the women her party endorsed in the 1989 Upper House elections. In all, ten of the twelve women endorsed by the JSP won seats. The party did not expect their phenomenal success and did not have a strategy to exploit the new perspective these women brought to office. The party did not have quotas for women or any other institutions to ensure the high level of nomination of women in the future (Iwai 1993).

The environment was favorable for Doi's "Women Changing Politics" campaign in 1989; Upper House elections that year followed one of the largest political scandals in Japanese history, the Recruit Cosmos stocks-for-favors scandal. The public was disillusioned with LDP money politics and was open to alternatives. Doi's manipulation of public opinion and media coverage allowed her to exploit the scandalous image of the LDP and to promote an image of female JSP politicians as "clean" (Ogai 2001:209). While women were already conceived culturally as "clean," Doi's speeches emphasized that fact. She used a window of opportunity created by the Recruit scandal to contrast the Socialist candidates with the scandal-ridden images of the LDP members (Gaunder and Terrel 2006).

Media coverage and public opinion became vital resources for Doi's campaign to exploit this window of opportunity and to elect women candidates to the Diet. Doi's selection as JSP chairperson drew significant media attention and raised the public's awareness of the possibility of female involvement in politics (Iwamoto 2001:225). During her tenure as party head, Doi commanded a tremendous amount of coverage in the media, evident in numerous pictures and articles (Stockwin 1994:21). Doi's positive media exposure resulted in an increase in public support, which then allowed her to challenge the cultural stigma associated with women's involvement in politics. Her refreshing campaign style mobilized public opinion in her favor as well as earning her a large support base among women (Iwao 1993).

Media coverage and popular public opinion also increased her power within the JSP, a party plagued by factionalism with splits among left, right, and center groupings. During the height of her popularity she became indispensable in party electioneering. Doi was able to maintain her position of leadership as long as she could demonstrate that her popularity translated into more votes for the JSP. The media attention, public support, and electoral successes gave her outside legitimacy that she was able to use to rise above internal disputes within the JSP, at least in the short term (Stockwin 1994:25).

Doi's "Women Changing Politics in Japan" can be considered a success in 1989 because of the immediate gains in the number of women politicians. The press dubbed this influx of women politicians on the national scene as the "Madonna boom." But, according to Iwamoto, Doi resigned as the chair of the JSP after "perceiving her own failure in realizing the dream of 'Women Changing Politics in Japan'" (Iwamoto 2001:226). Doi's evaluation of her failure seems to be based on the fact that the newly acquired women in the JSP did not lead to overall JSP success. In a personal interview (May 26, 2005), Doi classified the Madonna boom as a failure, because the JSP did not capture the majority in the Lower House in the 1990 elections.

This failure does not discount the record-breaking number of women candidates she recruited and helped get elected. Doi's Madonna boom helped increase the acceptance of women in the political realm, a trend that continues today. Mizuho Fukushima, the current head of the Social Democratic Party (formerly referred to as the JSP), explained the significance of the Doi-led Madonna boom in this way:

> Until that time politics was considered a man's world. After [the Madonna boom] there was a feeling that politics was near and that one can change politics. When Doi became the leader of the JSP, I shook her hand. Maybe that was the reason why I became a politician. (Personal interview, May 24, 2005)

Doi's campaign for women confronted idea that a woman's place was in the home. The Madonna boom can be seen as a significant step in getting women involved in politics at the national level, even if the perception of these women as "clean" was informed by traditional values.[14]

Like Doi, Koizumi played a crucial role in the election of women in the 2005 Lower House elections by creating an environment that was favorable for the election of women candidates. While passing comprehensive postal reform was his top priority, a significant number of LDP members opposed this legislation. His postal-reform bill barely passed the Lower House in July 2005, with 37 LDP members voting against it. Koizumi threatened to use one of his most powerful formal powers as prime minister and dissolve the Lower House if the Upper House rejected the bill. Despite this threat, the bill failed in the Upper House because of the LDP rebels who voted against it. Many predicted Koizumi would not follow through with his threat, but he proved them wrong. He dissolved the Diet, kicking the rebels who had voted against his postal-reform package out of the party. This election turned into a referendum on change in general and postal reform in particular. Women candidates fitted nicely into this theme of change.

As the gatekeeper for party endorsements in this election, Koizumi gave LDP support to a record number of women. Twenty-six women won as LDP candidates, almost tripling the number of LDP women elected to the Lower House in 2003 (where there were nine). Eleven of the twenty-six women were selected as "assassins" to replace rebels who had voted against Koizumi's postal-reform package in SMD contests. The LDP under Prime Minister Koizumi's leadership also placed women in the first slot in the PR ranking in seven of the eleven regional PR lists. As Christensen points out, the selection of women supported Koizumi's reformist image and symbolically suggested that he was changing the LDP by selecting nontraditional candidates to run for office (2006:509). But only five of the female candidates who ran in SMDs that were not part of the postal-reform controversy were not incumbents, former incumbents, or "assassins." This suggests that the increased number of women candidates was not indicative of a structural change in party recruitment procedures, but rather a reflection of Koizumi's personal quest to punish LDP rebels (Christensen 2006:509).

Koizumi's reformist (anti-LDP) stance helped him recruit these candidates to the traditionally conservative party, allowing him to partially challenge the ideological obstacle that had prevented the LDP from attracting women candidates in the past. It is important to note that many of the women he recruited were conservative careerists. Others, however, were enticed by Koizumi's promise to change the LDP. For example, Representative Naomi Tokashiki, one of Koizumi's recruits, explained, "I had gotten offers from the LDP in the past, but I thought the party was old-fashioned. After hearing Koizumi, I thought the LDP was changing, and I thought that I might be able to contribute." Tokashiki said that her character matched Koizumi's, and that when Koizumi campaigned for her, the constituents in her district witnessed this compatibility and supported her (personal interview, March 28, 2006).

Koizumi's decision to support women in a high-profile manner directly influenced their success. For example, Representative Nishimoto Katsuko recognizes that her success was related to the fact that Koizumi put women at a higher rank on the PR list. Knowing how important this ranking was to her success, she acknowledges that her reelection partially depended on the approach of the prime minister in office during the next Lower House elections. It is not

POLITICAL CHANGE IN JAPAN

clear that future LDP leaders will support women in the same way (personal interview, March 28, 2006). Clearly, Koizumi's support of the women nominated by the LDP was critical.

Koizumi's leadership skills provided women candidates with additional resources to challenge obstacles to their election. Specifically, Koizumi's popularity, positive media coverage, and effective speaking skills brought more publicity to these female candidates, and publicity is one of the three critical elements to getting elected in Japan. Koizumi's position within the LDP was weak. He did not have the backing of a powerful faction, and his policies challenged most of the senior power wielders in the party. As a result, throughout his tenure as prime minister, Koizumi used his popularity to pressure LDP members to conform to his policy priorities. The LDP kept him at the helm because he delivered electoral victories. When his second postal-reform package failed in 2005, his public-support ratings were at a personal low, hovering around 50 percent. His decision to dissolve the Diet and his crusade to punish the LDP rebels reinvigorated his public appeal and caused his support ratings to soar.

Significantly, Koizumi did not support women candidates based on a policy agenda supporting gender issues. Instead, as mentioned earlier, he seemed to be drawn to women candidates because they symbolically increased his reformist credentials (Christensen 2006:509). Koizumi exploited the nontraditional nature of these female candidates; he also chose strong personalities. Whereas Doi's Madonnas ran more as a bloc, Koizumi's female assassins boldly distinguished themselves as individuals. They refrained from invoking traditional conceptions of women to woo voters. These differences mark a significant shift in female representation in the Diet.

Conclusion

Two of the most significant increases in the number of women in the Diet occurred when a party leader made the election of women a priority, thereby easing the normal constraints that women face in receiving party endorsement. The fact that Doi and Koizumi represent separate parties underscores the importance of leadership in bringing women to office. While it is impossible to determine the effects of the recent election of Koizumi's assassins, it is significant to note that the number of women elected to the Upper House following the 1989 Madonna boom dropped from 17.5 percent to 10.3 percent in the 1992 Upper House elections, suggesting that the election of Socialist women was not the result of structural party change in the JSP. The women elected in 1989 were not up for reelection until 1995, but the JSP was not able to maintain the momentum in electing women to office in the election following the Madonna boom.

Can we expect a similar fate for the women elected under Koizumi's leadership? Indeed, the LDP is unlikely to elect as many women in the next Lower House elections. Several women LDP incumbents actually switched districts in 2005. Similarly, many of the LDP female newcomers ran in districts where they did not have any family or residential ties. All newcomers benefited from the support of independent swing voters, and such support is often fleeting. All these factors will work against their reelection, especially without Koizumi's long coattails. The LDP, however, will most likely elect more women than it had in the party prior to 2005. Female representation in the LDP jumped from nine women (five SMD, four PR) in 2003 to twenty-six women (fourteen SMD, twelve PR) in 2005. To the extent that these candidates have been able to cultivate personal support organizations in their constituencies, incumbency should guarantee the reelection of at least some of the women elected in SMDs. Party policy, however, will determine the fate of the women who were elected on a PR list. Koizumi did open up more space for new candidates by imposing an age limit on the LDP's members, throwing rebels out and electing new members in 2005. He also established greater control over the candidate-nomination process for the party president. The legacy of Koizumi's changes to both the office of the prime minister and the LDP presidency is widely contested (Christensen 2006; Estévez-Abe 2006). The key issue for the long-term participation of women is whether they can continue to gain representation. The record number of women elected to the Upper House in July 2007 suggests a continued positive upward trend.

Increasing the number of women in any given party, however, hinges on active recruitment. While Doi and Koizumi clearly influenced the number of women in their respective parties by prioritizing the candidacy of women, party leaders are not the only force that can increase recruitment. Recruitment is a component of party policy. This kind of policy shift is more likely to happen when women constitute a critical mass in the party.[15] For example, parties implemented quotas in many European countries after women increased their voice in the parties.

Indeed, looking at the experience of other countries, implementing quotas for women seems to be the best way to increase their presence in national legislative bodies (Kittilson 2006). Quotas, however, have not been seriously considered by most political parties in Japan. The now-defunct JNP did have a quota for women, but, significantly, it was unable to find enough women candidates to meet it in the elections it contested. PR electoral systems also favor women candidates. The move from an MMD system to a combined SMD-PR electoral system in 1994 marked a step in this direction. Increasing the number of women in the Diet was not one of the motivations behind this proposal, though. Instead, the PR element was promoted to protect the smaller parties that the MMD system had fostered.

The current electoral system does provide an avenue to promote women candidates. Leaders or parties can guarantee candidates a high rank on the PR list in return for their willingness to fight in highly competitive SMD races (Reed 1995). Koizumi exploited this avenue by giving preferential treatment on the PR list to high-profile women candidates who were acting as assassins in the SMDs. To the extent that parties and/or party leaders use this avenue to promote women in the future, we will continue to a see an increase in their numbers. Recruitment, however, is key. The trend toward open recruitment in the DPJ in 2000 and in the LDP in 2002 is a step in the right direction. New party policy that favors the institutionalized recruitment of women is critical for sustained increases in numbers. Unfortunately, Koizumi's support of women candidates fell far short of such institutionalization. Thus, while the gradual trend of increasing numbers of female representatives is likely to persist, it will continue to be marked by its slow pace.

Notes

[1] I would like to thank Steven R. Reed, Kenneth Mori McElwain, Kay Shimizu, Steven Vogel, Mari Miura, and Sarah Wiliarty for their comments, and Tomoko Kadota, Hikari Nishimoto, and Lissa Terrel for their research assistance.

[2] Katsuko Nishimoto is a first-term member of the Lower House who ran in the proportional representation (PR) constituency race as one of Koizumi's "children" in 2005. Mitsuko Yamaguchi is the executive director of the Ichikawa Fusae Memorial Association.

[3] Survey data from the United States reveal that qualified women are less likely to run for office than qualified men, because women are more likely to take into account the effects of candidacy on their family lives. This decision process prevails even though female and male candidates have roughly equal election rates in the United States (Lawless and Fox 2005). A similar decision process might be affecting women's self-selection in Japan.

[4] In fact, the JCP was the only other party to field one candidate in every district. Other parties ran multiple candidates only in regions where their support base was strong.

[5] One of the largest totals of women elected to the Diet, however, actually occurred in the 1946 Lower House elections (Ogai 1996). Once Japan adopted the SNTV system in the following elections, the number of women elected declined dramatically, due to the differences in the electoral rules (Darcy and Nixon 1996).

[6] In 2000 the DPJ provided approximately $10,000 to its women candidates (Aiuchi 2001:221).

[7] The LDP instituted an open recruitment program in 2002.

[8] In the 1996 Lower House elections the Socialists also ran fewer candidates than the LDP in PR constituencies.

[9] Depending on translation, the political wing of the Seikatsu Club has been referenced in a variety of ways in the scholarly literature. References include "the Seikatsu Networks" (Gelb and Estevez-Abe 1998), "the Netto" (LeBlanc 1999), and "the Seikatsusha Net" (Ogai 1999, 2004).

[10] Elected representatives from the Seikatsu Networks are referred to as proxies (*dairinin*) because they must consult the organization on policy matters, as well as turn over a large portion of their salary (Gelb and Estévez-Abe 1998:267).

[11] This figure includes politicians with prior experience who participated in the school. Not all school participants are first-time politicians.

[12] Sarah Brewer is the associate director of the Women and Politics Institute at American University.

[13] Ogai Tokuko is an expert on women and politics in Japan and the author of *Jenda to seiji sanka: The Impact of Women in Politics* (Seori Shobo 2005).

[14] The discussion of Doi's leadership in this section draws on an unpublished conference paper coauthored with Lissa Terrel. See Gaunder and Terrel 2006.

[15] Karen Beckwith and Kimberly Cowell-Meyers (2007) provide a nice overview of the critical-mass literature.

References

Aiuchi, Masako. 2001. How women won or lost in the Japanese Lower House election: Case studies of women candidates who ran as challengers. *PS: Political Science and Politics* 34 (2): 221–24.

Beckwith, Karen, and Kimberly Cowell-Meyers. 2007. Sheer numbers: Critical representation thresholds and women's representation. *Perspectives on Politics* 5 (3): 553–65.

Bochel, Catherine, and Hugh Bochel. 2004. Challenging the dominant culture: Women in Japanese local politics. Paper presented at the Political Studies Association International Conference, Minneapolis, MN, September 5–11.

Bochel, Catherine, Hugh Bochel, Masashi Kasuga, and Hideko Takeyasu. 2003. Against the system? Women in elected local government in Japan. *Local Government Studies* 29 (2): 19–31.

Christensen, Ray. 2006. An analysis of the 2005 Japanese general election: Will Koizumi's political reforms endure? *Asian Survey* 46 (4): 497–516.

Cox, Gary W., and Frances Rosenbluth. 1996. Factional competition for the party endorsement: The case of Japan's Liberal Democratic Party. *British Journal of Political Science* 26 (2): 259–69.

Curtis, Gerald L. 1988. *The Japanese way of politics.* New York: Columbia Univ. Press.

Darcy, R., and David L. Nixon. 1996. Women in the 1946 and 1993 Japanese House of Representative elections: The role of the election system. *Journal of Northeast Asian Studies* 15 (Spring): 3–19.

Estévez-Abe, Margarita. 2006. Japan's shift toward a Westminster system: A structural analysis of the 2005 Lower House election and its aftermath. *Asian Survey* 46 (4): 632–51.

Eto, Mikiko. 2001. Women's leverage on social policymaking in Japan. *PS: Political Science and Politics* 34 (June): 241–46.

Gaunder, Alisa, and Lissa Terrel. 2006. How female politicians overcome party constraints: The cases of Doi Takako, Fukushima Mizuho, and Moriyama Mayumi. Paper presented at the Association of Asian Studies meeting, San Francisco, CA, April 6–9.

Gelb, Joyce, and Margarita Estévez-Abe. 1998. Political women in Japan: A case study of the Seikatsusha Network Movement. *Social Science Japan Journal* 1 (2): 263–79.

Iwai, Tomoaki. 1993. The Madonna boom: Women in the Japanese diet. *Journal of Japanese Studies* 19 (Winter): 103–20.

Iwamoto, Misako. 2001. The Madonna boom: The progress of Japanese women into politics in the 1980s. *PS: Political Science and Politics* 34 (2): 225–26.

Iwao, Sumiko. 1993. *The Japanese woman.* New York: Free Press.

Kittilson, Miki Caul. 2006. *Challenging parties, changing parliaments: Women in elected office in contemporary Western Europe.* Columbus: Ohio State Univ. Press.

Köllner, Patrick. 2004. Factionalism in Japanese political parties revisited, or how do factions in the LDP and the DPJ differ? *Japan Forum* 16 (1): 87–109.

Krauss, Ellis S., and Robert Pekkanen. 2004. Explaining party adaptation to electoral reform: The discreet charm of the LDP? *Journal of Japanese Studies* 30 (Winter): 1–34.

Lawless, Jennifer L., and Richard L. Fox. 2005. *It takes a candidate: Why women don't run for office.* Cambridge: Cambridge Univ. Press.

LeBlanc, Robin M. 1999. *Bicycle citizens: The political world of the Japanese housewife.* Berkeley: Univ. of California Press.

Matland, Richard E. 2005. Enhancing women's political participation: Legislative recruitment and electoral systems. In *Women in parliament: Beyond numbers,* ed. Julie Ballington and Azza Karam, 93–111. Stockholm: International IDEA.

Ogai, Tokuko. 1996. The stars of democracy: The first thirty-nine female Diet members. *U.S.-Japan Women's Journal* 11:81–117.

———. 1999. The political activities of Japanese housewives: From invisible to visible political participation. *The Journal of Pacific Asia* 5:59–97.

———. 2001. Japanese women and political institutions: Why are women politically underrepresented? *PS: Political Science and Politics* 34 (2): 207–10.

———. 2004. From the personal to the political: Women activists in Japan. In *Promises of empowerment: Women in Asia and Latin America,* ed. Peter H. Smith, Jennifer L. Troutner, and Christine Hunefeldt, 88–102. New York: Rowman and Littlefield.

Park, Cheol Hee. 2001. Factional dynamics in Japan's LDP since political reform: Continuity and change. *Asian Survey* 41 (3): 428–61.

Pharr, Susan J. 1981. *Political women in Japan: The search for a place in political life.* Berkeley: Univ. of California Press.

Reed, Steven R. 1995. The nomination process for Japan's next general election: Waiting for the Heiritsu-sei. *Asian Survey* 35 (12): 1075–86.

Shiratori, Rei. 1988. Japan: Localism, factionalism, personalism. *Candidate selection in comparative perspective: The secret garden of politics*, ed. Michael Gallagher and Michael Marsh, 169–89. London: Sage Publications.

Steel, Gill. 2004. Gender and political behaviour in Japan. *Social Science Japan Journal* 7 (2): 223–44.

Stockwin, J. A. A. 1994. On trying to move mountains: The political career of Doi Takako. *Japan Forum* 6 (April): 21–34.

Taniguchi, Masaki. 2006. Recent changes in Japanese politics, the trends and outlook. Speech presented at Young Professionals Project, Univ. of Sydney.

Woodall, Brian. 1996. *Japan under construction: Corruption, politics, and public works*. Berkeley: Univ. of California Press.

Surrogate Representation: Building Sustainable Linkage Structures in Contemporary Japanese Politics

Sherry L. Martin

E lecting Lower House politicians who represent the growing diversity of views within the Japanese electorate was among the multiple goals of the 1994 electoral-reform bill.[1] In the months preceding the passage of the bill, voters who were polled expressed hopes that electoral reform would produce results—in the distribution of seats and substantive policy positions—that reflected public opinion.[2] In July 2007, over a decade after electoral reform, Japanese voters delivered a majority of Upper House seats to the opposition Democratic Party of Japan (DPJ), penalizing the Liberal Democratic Party (LDP) administration, headed by Prime Minister Shinzo Abe, for failing to respond to the "public mood" (Ito 2007). An overwhelming majority of Japanese voters maintains that politicians do not think about everyday people after elections are over and that elections do not represent public views well. Yet, an equally sizable majority agrees that legislative politics helps people to be heard and is satisfied with the overall performance of representative democracy in Japan.

This chapter uses national election data to examine attitudes about the relationship between voter choice and legislative representation. I suggest that constraints on voter choice offer an explanation for voter dissatisfaction with the electoral process, but that dissatisfaction is ameliorated when voters find "surrogate" parties and politicians who articulate their views—even if found outside their own district. The existence of a surrogate who reflects one's views is vital to mass approval of democratic performance when elections fall short of expectations and are not the primary vehicle by which the majority of citizens articulate their interests.

Electoral Reform and Mending Broken Linkage Structures

The 1994 electoral reforms raised voters' hopes that the connection between voting and quality leadership and representation would be strengthened. Most notably, voters expected alteration in power between two moderate, programmatic parties in national politics (Reed and Thies 2001). Instead, there has been more continuity than change in Japanese politics as the LDP managed to regain its dominant position in Japanese politics upon passage of the reform package. Japanese politics in the aftermath of electoral reform has experienced incremental change—not a sea change. How unmet expectations might fuel widespread political cynicism has been a source of concern for politicians and political scientists alike. Voter disappointment, dissatisfaction, and distrust erode institutional legitimacy over the long term as more citizens begin to question whether elections produce just outcomes.[3]

Ten years after the passage of electoral reform, over three-quarters of voters surveyed immediately prior to the 2004 Upper House elections did not think that electoral outcomes expressed their views. Only 23.9 percent of Japanese respondents agreed that elections facilitated the representation of public views "very well" or "quite well." This makes Japan an outlier among advanced industrialized nations, and earns it a rank alongside newly emerging democracies, where citizens' expectations often outpace the performance of brand-new institutions. Figure 13.1 places twenty established democracies, including Japan, on a continuum from those least satisfied to those most satisfied with electoral outcomes. Japanese voters, on the far-left side, are the least likely to agree that elections represent their views well. Portuguese and Canadian voters are also unlikely to agree that elections represent their views well, but more than 15 percentage points separate them from the Japanese. In marked contrast, Danes (79.3 percent), followed by Americans (71.6 percent), have the highest percentage of respondents indicating that elections represent views well. Over one-half of voters in nearly three-quarters of these established democracies are pleased with electoral outcomes. The Japanese are an exception.

Still, the Japanese are no more or less satisfied with democracy than voters in any other advanced industrialized democracy (see figure 13.2). Seventy percent of Japanese respondents were satisfied with democracies even though one of its fundamental linkage structures is clearly not working as well as many would like.

Unsurprisingly, trends over time reveal that a large and increasing percentage of Japanese voters believe that politicians stop listening to voters immediately after elections are over (see figure 13.3). This finding is consistent with the dominant opinion that elections do not reflect voters' views. It is inconsistent, however, with the equally large percentage of voters who think that the Diet represents views quite well. The legislative process produces outcomes that voters agree are substantively representative despite the fact that elections do not immediately produce a legislative decision-making body that, on its surface, impresses voters as a direct translation of ballots into seats. These findings suggest that the existence of a range of ideological perspectives in the legislature, coupled with the right institutional norms, serves as a corrective to electoral outcomes; the deliberative process produces outcomes that the public accepts as good democratic governance.[4] How? In this chapter, I argue that surrogate representation plays an important role in Japanese politics. When voters are not directly represented by a party and/or politician with positions close to their own, their agreement that political processes work well are contingent upon their views finding expression elsewhere in the system.

Figure 13.1 Elections Ensure the Representation of Voters' Views (Very well / Quite well)

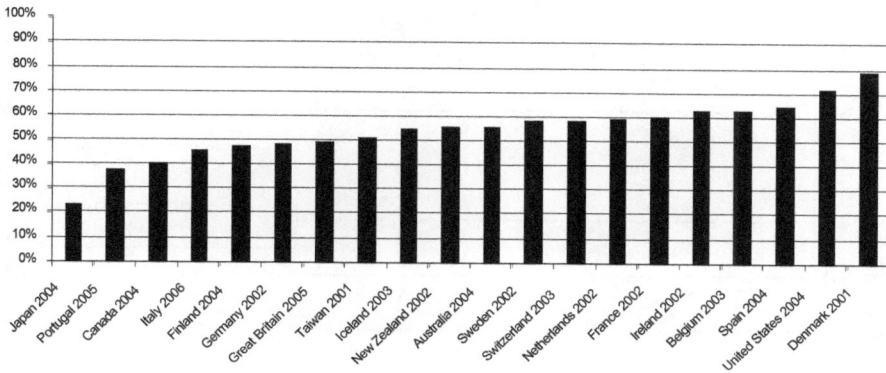

Source: *The Comparative Study of Electoral Systems*, Module 2, CSES Module 2 Full Release (data set), June 27, 2007, http://www.cses.org.

Note: The text of the original question reads as follows: *Thinking about how elections in [country] work in practice, how well do elections ensure that the views of voters are represented by MPs: very well, quite well, not very well, or not well at all?* Bars represent the combined response pattern for voters who responded that elections ensured representation well or quite well.

Figure 13.2 Satisfaction with Democracy (Very satisfied / Fairly satisfied)

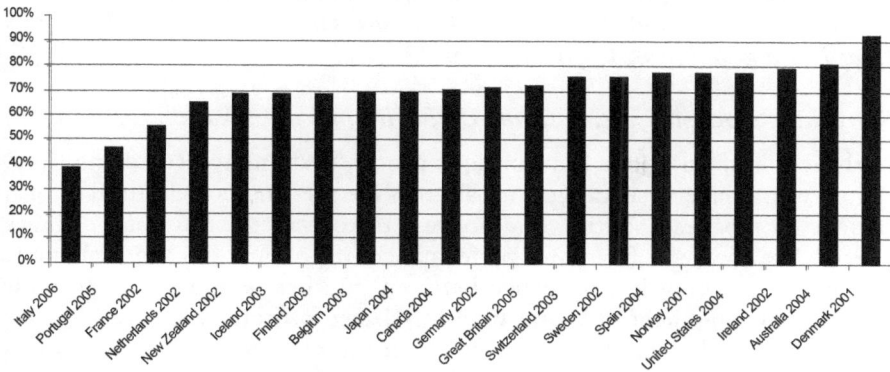

Source: *The Comparative Study of Electoral Systems*, Module 2.

Note: The text of the original question reads as follows: *On the whole, are you very satisfied, fairly satisfied, not very satisfied, or not at all satisfied with the way democracy works in [country]?* Bars represented the combined response pattern for voters who indicated that they were very or fairly satisfied.

263

Figure 13.3 The Representation Gap

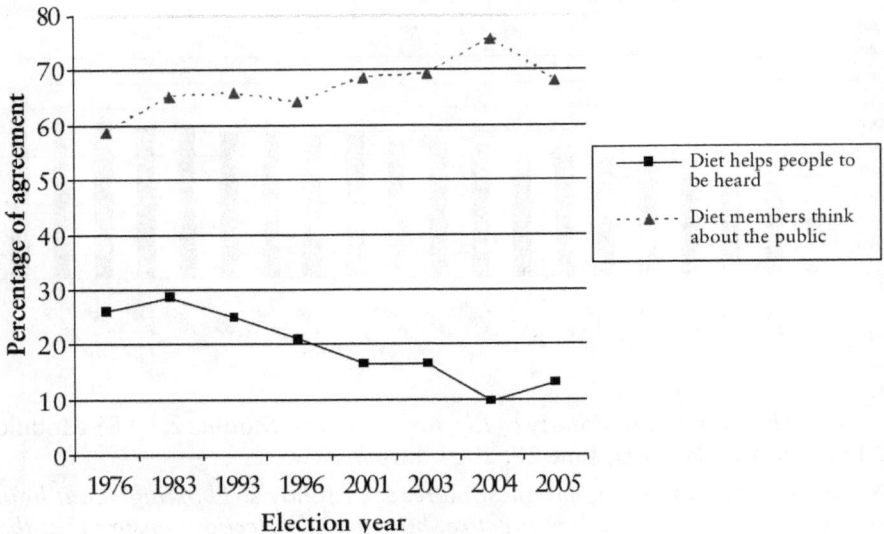

Source: Watanuki et al. 1976, 1983; Kabashima et al.1993–96; Ikeda et al. 2001–2005.

Note: The selected questions read as follows: *What do you think of the people we elect to the National Diet? Speaking generally, do you think they stop thinking about the people's interests immediately after taking office? Or do you think this is not the case? And, The National Diet makes it possible for people's voices to be heard in politics. Do you agree or disagree?*

Surrogate Representatives: Patching Up Fault Lines in Linkage Structures

In this section, I use Jane Mansbridge's article "Rethinking Representation" (2003) to frame representative norms across the pre- and postelectoral reform periods in Japanese politics, and address the specific institutional changes intended to alter the form and performance of political linkage structures. There is a growing incongruence between politicians and voters in their expectations about the role and work of elected officials. Electoral reforms reflect already changing expectations about the relationship between voters and elected officials, including that institutional changes will make a qualitative difference. In the aftermath of electoral reform, unmet expectations—boosted by anticipation of the difference reforms will make—are reflected in a notable decline in public confidence that elections ensure that elected representatives will give voice to voters' views.

Electoral reformers pursue "better" representation by altering direct and indirect linkages between the voting public and elected officials. In Japan, reformers introduced a system of single-member districts (SMDs) to stimulate inter- and intraparty competition and to give voters choices between opposing parties offering alternative positions on substantive policy issues. A parallel proportional representation (PR) round was meant to ensure that minority perspectives would not be entirely squeezed out of the system. SMDs typically strengthen ties between representatives and constituents, allowing the former to act independently when the party advocates national policy positions that representatives deem detrimental to their own narrower constituencies and their potential for reelection. PR districts provide incentives for candidates and parties to appeal to a broader constituency to increase the appeal of the party's list overall. The institutional framework of this new electoral system gives incentives for the emergence of different, but complementary, representational styles that do not altogether conform to the demands of promissory representation that reformers reinforced as a normative ideal. Unfortunately, promissory representation may be an unattainable ideal, and its place in the public imagination holds dire consequences for how voters evaluate the performance of representatives in the short term and systemic legitimacy in the long term.

Much of the debate around representation in Japan takes place within the normative framework of promissory representation, which assumes one of two alternative styles: mandate or trustee (Wakata 1977; Feldman 2000). Given a mandate, representatives promise to follow constituents' instructions; as trustees, representatives promise to further the constituency's interests and those of the nation at large, even if that means deviating from constituents' expressed wishes in the short term on the basis of long-term calculations. Both versions assume that candidates make promises during an initial authorizing election, and reelection is contingent upon how satisfied voters are with representatives' fulfillment of their promises. Interestingly, while politicians who keep promises help to build public trust, the promissory model requires little trust because officials who do not keep promises can be easily kicked out; those who do keep promises build up a "reservoir" of trust.

Promissory representation was arguably hard to enforce under the 1955 system in Japan. First, decision-making took place behind bureaucratic doors and in the upper echelons of the LDP party apparatus. Consequently, transparency was compromised and voters had a difficult time attributing accountability to backbenchers in their own districts. Second, the system of old multimember districts (MMDs) with a single nontransferable vote (SNTV) pitted politicians running under the same party label against one another in an attempt to win as many party seats as possible in the medium-sized districts. The ability of voters to kick the rascals out was further compromised because the MMD system made it difficult for voters to coordinate to kick out one specific party representative, much less all party representatives in the same district. Replacing one LDP politician in an MMD had little impact on LDP dominance in the aggregate and over the long term. Greater transparency in decision-making and elected officials' increased accountability to voters were also among the expressed goals of electoral reformers. SMDs and issue-based competition would help voters to more easily assign blame to and penalize unresponsive representatives.

Mansbridge notes that promissory representation coexists with three other forms of representation prominent in democratic systems: anticipatory, gyroscopic, and surrogate. Each form is best suited to a separate socioeconomic context, and requires distinct types of electoral connections between representatives and voters that breed various expectations about representative democracy with different consequences for how voters evaluate politics. All forms of representation operate simultaneously in any given system, and their effects are "cumulative" and "complementary, not oppositional" (Mansbridge 2003:525–26).[5] Further, representatives change their styles over time and across various electoral and policy spaces. While I will briefly summarize anticipatory and gyroscopic representation, I will focus on surrogate representation as an important counterbalance to the promissory ideal, because it is the only form that "plays the normatively critical role of providing representation to voters who lose in their own district" (Mansbridge 2003:523).

Anticipatory representatives make decisions over the course of their term in office in anticipation of voters' evaluations in future elections. Successful anticipatory representation requires close and ongoing communication between representatives and constituents between election cycles as each tries to educate, persuade, and influence the other. This is a relationship of "reciprocal power" and "continuing mutual influence" that requires little trust and is well suited to periods of rapid change (Mansbridge 2003:516–20). In the gyroscopic model of representation, voters use candidates' observable attributes and behaviors as insight into their fundamental worldviews in an effort to select representatives who can be trusted to make choices that voters would make under similar conditions. Voters make their selections based on deliberative processes during elections but, having chosen candidates who presumably share similar internal motivations, allow gyroscopic representatives tremendous freedom between elections (Mansbridge 2003:520–22).

A politician is a surrogate representative when she represents groups residing outside her own district (Mansbridge 2003; Tremblay 2006). In representing interests beyond the geographic confines of district boundaries, her constituency is broadened and may be regional, national, or supranational in scope. I focus on surrogate representation because Japanese politics has always had its share of perpetual political outsiders,[6] and this group expanded within the electorate in the years preceding electoral reform and has not shown signs of decrease. Under the 1955 system, the traditional opposition parties played the part of surrogate for voters unaffiliated with the dominant LDP. The steady erosion of the opposition presence[7] in national-level politics was matched by a steady increase in the proportion of unaffiliated and dissatisfied voters in the system (Tanaka 2003). Even though traditional opposition parties held a minority of seats in the national Diet, they were able to effectively influence debate and enforce norms of accountability through strategies of protest and legislative delay. By the 1990s, the opposition was unraveling. Patterns of sociodemographic change and economic upheavals frayed traditional social networks that linked voters and elites (Otake 1999). The proportion of unaffiliated voters began to approach one-half of the electorate, and cynicism about politics reached new depths among voters already predisposed to cynicism (Tanaka 2003).

We can envision communication between voters and representatives in Japan as a series of concentric circles with the representative in the middle and voters of varying degrees of closeness or distance representing each circle. "Organized voters" (business interests, union members, neighborhood association members, and those firmly integrated into clientelist networks) and members of candidates' support organizations (*koenkai*) fill the innermost circles (which have been contracting in recent decades) and floating voters fill the outermost circles (which have been expanding). Communication with representatives increases between and during elections with advancement from the outermost to the innermost circle. Increasingly, there is no contact between representatives and voters between elections, and communication during elections, is conducted indirectly through media outlets. Effective surrogate representation, according to Mansbridge, rises in relative importance under these circumstances because voters retain some level of confidence in the democratic electoral process as long as their interests find voice somewhere.

Always being on the losing team impacts voters' attitudes about politics and political actors. If there are few access points available to underrepresented interests in the system, losing can generate mass attitudinal orientations and behavioral outcomes that threaten regime legitimacy (Anderson et al. 2005). The introduction of SMDs further increases the likelihood that more voters will witness the loss of their preferred candidate or party. Seeing their favored candidates and parties win in PR districts becomes more salient. In giving voice to underrepresented interests, surrogate representation can improve upon the proportionality of interests by presenting alternative perspectives relevant to decision-making processes (Mansbridge 2003). This is important to maintain systemic-level confidence among individuals who feel that their ability to directly influence government actors is limited.

Surrogate representation may be both conscious and unconscious. Politicians may consciously seek to appeal to voters beyond their own constituencies to further their political careers. For example, Prime Minister Koizumi was elected to the premiership over the usual suspects because he gained the support of local party leaders. He was later able to act independently of his own party because of his popularity among voters across Japan. Politicians are also surrogates when they actively advocate for a geographically dispersed set of minority interests. Kanako Otsuji, who made a failed bid in 2007 for an Upper House seat as a DPJ candidate, is a surrogate for sexual minorities across Japan and would have been the first openly gay national politician. Otsuji brought discrimination against sexual minorities in Japan to the fore and planned to advocate for same-sex partnership (see *International Herald Tribune/Asia-Pacific* 2007). Politicians are unconscious surrogates when they represent a set of principles held by voters inside and outside their constituencies. Even though politicians from the Japan Communist Party (JCP) have been most successful in urban Japan (Kyoto is a stronghold), JCP supporters are in evidence throughout Japan in districts that are LDP strongholds and that have never elected a JCP politician to office.

Many reasons for voters' dissatisfaction with electoral outcomes precede the actual election. Voters' choices are already limited by the time they arrive at the polls. As indicated by Robert Weiner in chapter 5 of this volume, there are many uncompetitive districts across Japan. Many incumbents run unopposed at the subnational level. In national and subnational elections, large margins of victory suggest that the runners-up were not viable contenders and, as such, voters were not offered a true choice. Further, opposition parties other than the JCP have not amassed the resources to run candidates in every district. Opposition-party supporters might not have the option of directly voting for their own party's candidate in elections at every administrative level. Under these conditions, the tasks that representatives of other districts accomplish while in office attain even more importance among minor-party supporters.

The fact that there are opposition-party politicians elected from districts other than one's own is important to voters who hear some of their interests articulated during legislative deliberation, see evidence of policies that grant them some of their priorities, and observe opposition politicians actively obstructing governing-party policies that are not in their best interests.

Data and Findings

To test whether there is some degree of surrogate representation at work in the Japanese system, I used data from the 2004 House of Councillors elections. A national random sample of respondents was asked, "Is there a political party in Japan that reflects your views well?"[8] This question is qualitatively different from questions about party identification and vote choice. Respondents may indicate that they support the LPD and voted for the party and its candidates in the election without feeling that this party—or any other—represents their views. Expressed party identification and vote choice may reflect a strategic choice among equally poor alternatives. This question taps into voters' sincere evaluations of whether there is a party in the system that reflects their views without asking them to differentiate between winning and losing teams, and without regard to whether they had the option of directly voting for that party or candidate in the election. This question also taps into a response pattern that is often absent from existing survey research, because it begins from the assumption that there may be no party that represents a respondent's views, rather than from the assumption that she is closest to the party that she voted for.

If surrogate representation is at work, I hypothesize that voters who identify a party in the system that represents their views are more likely to be satisfied with how democracy is carried out in Japan and are more likely to agree that elections ensure that the views of voters are represented by Diet members. If having a party that reflects one's views operates independently of party support and vote choice, this variable should be more important in determining satisfaction with democracy and views of electoral outcomes. I limit my presentation of findings in this section to reporting significant response patterns, bivariate relationships, and predicted outcomes that deepen our understanding of how the (non)existence of a party that represents one's views shapes the propensity for voters to be satisfied with democratic outcomes and linkage structures.[9]

Parties Reflect the Views of Less than One-Half of Voters: Consequences for Evaluations of Electoral Outcomes and Democratic Performance

When asked if there was a party in the system that represented their views, fewer than one-half (46.5 percent) of respondents indicated that such a party existed. Approximately one-third (34.7 percent) indicated that there was no such party, and nearly one-fifth (17.9 percent) indicated that they did not know if there was a party that represented their views. Over one-half of voters surveyed did not feel that there was a party that represented their views or were unsure that such a party existed. Undoubtedly, this uncertainty helps to explain the large proportion of floating voters (that is, nonpartisans) and weak partisans in the Japanese electorate, and why voters are dissatisfied with elections as linkage institutions.

The likelihood of a Japanese voter being satisfied with the performance of democracy, and agreeing that elections ensure that Diet members represent voters' views, is higher when she actively supports the party that reflects her views than when she expresses support for a party while nonetheless feeling that there is no party that reflects her views.[10] Figure 13.4 suggests that the congruence of these factors—the existence of a party that reflects one's views and support for that party—do not coincide in contemporary Japanese politics. Having a party that reflects one's views is an important indicator of how one will evaluate the performance of democracy and elections as a linkage structure. Whereas having a party that reflects one's views improves voters' evaluations of democracy (top two lines) to the extent that the most satisfied Japanese voters are as satisfied as American voters and others in countries listed on the right side of figure 13.2, the existence of such a party improves the gap in evaluations of elections without eliminating it altogether (bottom two lines). The most positive Japanese respondents remain significantly less likely than voters in other democracies to think that elections work well as a linkage structure (see figure 13.1).

Having a party that reflects one's views does not boost evaluations of elections as linkage institutions, because voting has not typically been an effective tool for holding Japanese politicians accountable, and electoral reforms have not yet led to the transformation of the ballot into this type of tool. The limited influence of having a party that reflects one's views or the likelihood of seeing elections as a means of ensuring representation reflects the programmatic weakness of Japanese parties. Elections under the MMD system revolved around the patron-client relationship and the delivery of pork to constituents. Competition between multiple candidates from the same party in any given district was not conducive to issue-based competition as a means of making ideological distinctions between candidates. Parties in the postelectoral reform era continue to struggle with the task of using issue positions to craft their electoral identities in a manner that sets the political agenda and frames the terms of public debate.

Figure 13.4 Surrogate Representation and Changing Evaluations of Democracy and Elections

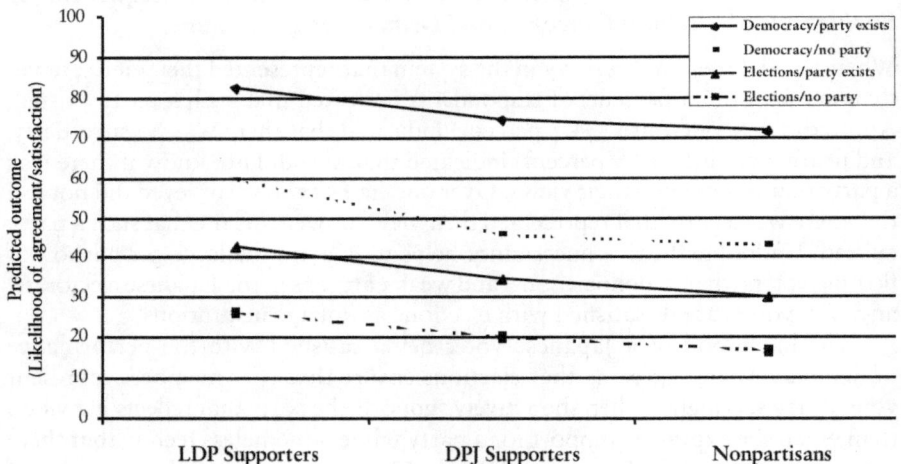

Source: Ikeda et al. 2001–2005.

Note: Lines represent the percentage of respondents satisfied with democracy and the percentage who agree that elections help voters' voices to be heard.

Figure 13.4 provides tentative support for my hypothesis that surrogate representation plays the important role of providing voters with a sense that democracy is working and that their interests find expression in the system even when the ballot box is viewed as an ineffective means of directly influencing politics. How one feels about democratic performance and elections as a linkage institution measures external and internal efficacy, respectively. Having a party that represents one's views influences both dimensions of efficacy, but is likely to have a larger impact on external efficacy than on internal efficacy when electoral choices are limited at the district level. External efficacy sustains feelings that political outcomes in the aggregate are fair even when voters lose the sense that they exert direct influence. External efficacy refers to "system-regarding" attitudes, and internal efficacy refers to a "personal dimension of belief" (Pollack 1983:400). Evaluations of democratic performance tap into attitudes about external efficacy; Japanese voters have confidence that democratic institutions are responsive. Similarly, voters feel that the institutional context of the Diet promotes democratic outcomes in the aggregate even if they feel relatively powerless in directly electing and communicating with their preferred parties and politicians.

The extent that individual voters feel that politicians listen, or that elections ensure that politicians represent their interests, taps into attitudes about internal efficacy. Internal efficacy captures whether individuals feel that they can personally exert a direct influence on political outcomes. Elections can never ensure that your views are represented if you cannot directly vote for the party that represents your views; voters are unable to vote for a party that does not run candidates in their districts. But legislative processes can produce better outcomes if an individual thinks that having elected politicians from a party that represents her views present at the bargaining table matters, even if they were not directly elected from her district. Japanese voters feel that legislators are responsive, but not as a direct consequence of what happened at the polls.

Surrogate Representation: An Alternative Source of Efficacy When Partisanship is Weak

Respondents who are most likely to agree that elections ensure that voters' views are heard are not LDP supporters, but Clean Government Party (CGP) supporters, with a predicted outcome of 49.2 percent (figure 13.5).[11] Entering into coalition with the LDP gave the CGP and supporters of this small party a voice in government that exceeded both its size and expectations as a traditional opposition party. Even though the CGP does not run candidates in every district, and in fact mobilizes supporters to vote for LDP candidates in districts where there is no CGP candidate, CGP supporters rank only behind LDP supporters in their satisfaction with democracy and are the most likely to agree that elections ensure that members of parliament represent the views of its supporters. What is a reality for the CGP's experience, however, is unusual for other parties in the system: it enjoys a strong partisan support base. The party's image and communication between party elites and supporters are more robust than is the case with other parties in the system. CGP supporters are the most likely to report that the party they support is also the party that represents their views. When these two factors coincide, Japanese voters' sense of internal efficacy, as measured by their evaluations of elections, approximates that of the cross-national "average" in figure 13.1; CGP supporters are at least as efficacious as voters in Germany and Great Britain.

Figure 13.5 Surrogate Representation and Evaluations of Elections and Democratic Performance

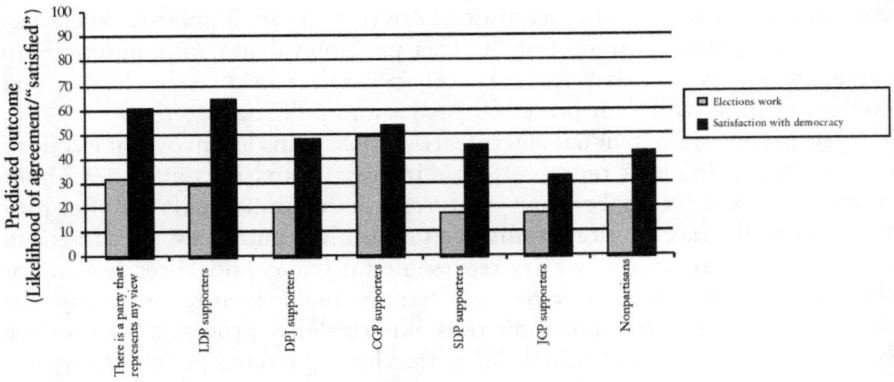

Source: Ikeda et al. 2001–2005.

Note: Bars represent the percentage of respondents satisfied with democracy and the percentage who agree that elections help voters' voices to be heard.

Figure 13.5 separates predicted probabilities for the impact of "surrogate representation" (that is, having a party that represents one's views even if one is unable or unwilling to vote for its candidates) relative to party support on voters' evaluations of elections and democratic performance, in an effort to disentangle the relative influence exhibited by each. While the CGP suggests that these two factors are bound up, the relative strength of surrogate representation relative to weak partisan ties to other parties in the system suggests that surrogate representation plays an independent role in boosting both internal efficacy and external efficacy. However, surrogate representation plays a much larger role in boosting external efficacy among voters who are weak partisans and do not support either the LDP or coalition partner CGP. The existence of a party that represents one's views somewhere in the system, even if one is unable to vote directly for its candidates, operates independently of party support in shaping political orientations, and helps to narrow the representation gap (see figure 13.3).

Gender and Surrogate Representation

Surrogate representation has a specific valence in the broader debate about the descriptive and substantive representation of underrepresented groups such as women and ethnic minorities. At the heart of this debate is whether the election of representatives bearing the same social (descriptive) attributes as an underrepresented group translates into substantive policy outcomes that benefit group members. Do we need more women elected to office to see the enactment of more policies that benefit women as a group? Or can men represent women's interests? These questions remain contentious, and the empirical evidence does not clearly favor one perspective over the other.[12] This is all the more reason to test whether having a party that best represents one's interests plays an even more significant role in boosting feelings of internal and external efficacy for Japanese women who as a group achieve significantly fewer nationally elected parliamentary seats than women in other, similarly advanced, industrialized democracies.[13]

The same models were run for separate samples of men and women to assess the impact of having a party that reflects one's views, regardless of whether one votes for that same party, on (1) one's level of satisfaction with democratic performance and (2) one's likelihood to agree that elections are fundamental to helping voters to be heard in the political arena. We can assume that women are more likely than men to express less satisfaction with democratic performance and less agreement that elections reflect views, because existing research has already established that women are overrepresented among the large proportion of nonpartisan voters in the Japanese electorate (Patterson and Nishikawa 2002; Martin 2004). In this sample, one-third of women and just over one-quarter of men are self-identified nonpartisans. This means that having a party that represents one's views should play an even greater role in creating and sustaining feelings of efficacy among women voters in the absence of partisanship. Though it is impossible to determine whether or how women voters assess the performance of individual politicians, male or female, that represent districts other than their own, having a party that reflects one's views could indicate the importance to women voters of opposition parties such as the Social Democratic Party of Japan (SDPJ, formerly the Japan Socialist Party, JSP) or the Japan Communist Party (JCP), both of which have had a reputation for fielding more women as candidates for national office. Similarly, these parties might be important because they prioritize policies (such as social welfare) that resonate more strongly with women voters than with men.[14]

Though controlling for gender does not change the response patterns evident in figures 13.4 and 13.5, women are nearly 10 percentage points less likely than men to say that there is a party in the system that represents their views (42.1 percent compared with 51.9 percent). This difference is salient because having a party that represents one's views is more important than expressed partisanship in fostering positive outlooks about the representativeness of elections among both men and women. Gender is insignificant among voters who respond that there *is* a party in the system that represents their views. Support for the CGP is the only party-support variable that exerts a significant impact for women, but not for men, on agreement that elections represent voters' views. This can likely be attributed to the fact that the CGP has typically supported social welfare initiatives that tend to matter more for women voters than for men. In this regard, elected CGP representatives might serve a surrogate function for Japanese women voters beyond their own districts and in districts where the party does not run candidates.

Women across all categories of partisanship are significantly less likely than men to express satisfaction with democratic performance in Japan. Again, having a party that represents one's views substantially increases satisfaction with democratic performance among men and women, but it is more important for women because they are less likely to say that such a party exists in the first place. Men's greater satisfaction with government performance indicates that men have a higher sense of external efficacy than women. Given that men as a group dominate electoral politics in Japan—they constitute the majority of candidates, win the majority of seats, make the majority of political contributions, and are generally the gatekeepers to elite politics—it is to be expected that men as a group are more likely to feel that democratic institutions and political actors are responsive.

It is notable that having a party that reflects one's views eliminates significant gender differences in internal efficacy, as measured by agreement with the statement that elections reflect voters' views. Traditionally, women have been more likely to say that they are unable to personally influence politics. The narrowing of this gap suggests that men and women are feeling equally constrained by limited electoral options, and underscores the importance of small and opposition parties in advocating for a wider range of perspectives than are currently represented in the Japanese system. Krauss and Pekkanen (2008) argue that leftist voters' views are marginalized under the new, but still evolving, electoral order, due to the disappearance of the old opposition and its replacement by the DPJ, a right-of-center party that has yet to distinguish itself from the LDP–New Komeito coalition.

Conclusion

The disproportionate focus on promissory representation means that we have an insufficient understanding of the connections among institutions, sociopolitical contexts, and the full range of modal forms of representation available to voters. Our understanding of the range of styles that capture representative-constituent relationships in postwar Japanese politics is incomplete, making the task of examining continuity and change against the backdrop of socioeconomic and institutional change a difficult one. How do we reconcile voters' satisfaction with the performance of representative democracy with their dissatisfaction with parties and elections as linkage institutions? How do we capture what happens between election cycles to ameliorate the gap between external and internal efficacy? This chapter considers the role of surrogate representation in Japanese politics in an attempt to begin to fill this void. I find evidence that surrogate representation sustains high levels of external efficacy as measured by voters' positive evaluations of democratic performance and other items that are correlated with democratic performance (that is, the Diet helps to ensure that voters' voices are heard). Surrogate representation sustains external efficacy even when internal efficacy weakens with the loosening of partisan ties across Japan.

The quality of the representative-constituent relationship in Japan has been measured against the normative criteria associated with promissory representation and has been found lacking. One-party dominance violates basic assumptions about the control that voters exercise over candidates and parties through the ballot box. The threat of "kicking the rascals out" loses credibility if the competition is not perceived as viable. At the same time, it is difficult to say that voters are definitely getting what they want if, again, there are no viable alternatives that can be rejected. While not arguing that the promissory model is inadequate, I suggest that it is worthwhile to think about other types of representative-constituent relationships that operate alongside the promissory model. Doing so might help us to assess change in the quality of representation over time, even in the absence of an alteration in power.

Notes

[1] See Reed and Thies (2001) for a detailed discussion of electoral reform as a solution to multiple problems that emerged out of a more concentrated effort to curtail money-power politics in Japan, but quickly opened an opportunity for a wide array of political actors to advance other directly and loosely related goals. Reform proponents also sought to reduce LDP dominance and promote competition and alteration in power between two moderate parties, foster issue-based competition, and reduce malapportionment.

[2] Source: NHK Broadcasting Culture Research Institute, December 4–5, 1993, Japan Public Opinion Library. A national random sample was asked, "What do you think is most important about an electoral-system reform?" Respondents could choose one response from a list. The largest group of respondents (21 percent) chose "make it reflect public opinion." Twenty percent responded "reduce campaign costs," 17 percent "emphasize the character and views of each candidates," and 11 percent "make the value of votes equal." Less that 10 percent chose each of the following goals: "make change in power possible," "stabilize the political parties," and "change elections so that they are party based with an emphasis on their policies."

[3] Kabashima et al. have made this point, as each election cycle after reform has failed to dislodge the LDP.

[4] See Tyler (2000), who finds that when decision-making procedures are seen as fair, citizens are more satisfied with their outcomes.

[5] Though these four models are presented separately as "ideal types" for analytical clarity, they are not mutually exclusive.

[6] By "political outsiders," I refer to traditional opposition parties (JSP, JCP, Komeito, Democratic Socialist League, and others), as well as to demographic groups that are also underrepresented in politics (women, urban voters, consumers, ethnic minorities, and others).

[7] See Scheiner (2006) for a discussion of the extent of opposition failure in postwar Japanese politics, the conditions that facilitated it, and the challenges that remain for parties seeking to gain a foothold as a viable opposition force in postelectoral reform politics in Japan.

[8] I also examine responses to a follow-up question in which respondents were asked whether there was a particular party leader that best represented their interests. I did not use this question for analysis, because most respondents replied "no" or were unable to identify a party leader. See Massey (1975) for a discussion of the institutional constraints on strong leadership in Japan. Constraints are beginning to loosen (see Krauss and Nyblade 2005) in the postreform era, as evidenced by Koizumi.

[9] I ran separate multinomial logistic regression models for (1) democratic satisfaction and (2) for the extent that elections ensure representation, as dependent variables. In addition to my variables of interest, I also introduced socioeconomic (gender, income, education, city size, and so on) and other attitudinal variables (such as government performance and satisfaction with seats won by each party) as controls. I do not report the full model because, aside from income and government performance, all other socioeconomic and attitudinal variables, with the exception of those that figure prominently into my hypothesis, dropped out of the equation. Here, I prefer to concentrate on the most salient and significant predictors—existence of a party that reflects a respondent's (R's) views and R's party support—for clarity.

[10] Over 80 percent of LDP (81.2 percent) and DPJ (84.2 percent) supporters named their respective parties as those that reflected their views. Similarly high percentages (83.4 percent for LDP; 75.1 percent for DPJ) also voted for the party that they said most represented their views. I concentrate on party support because it takes into consideration attitudinal orientations that this chapter is most concerned with.

[11] A multinomial logistic regression was used to generate the predicted probability of a voter agreeing that elections ensured that members of parliament represented her views, while controlling for self-expressed party support and whether or not she indicated that there is a party in the system that represents her views.

[12] For a comprehensive review of the evolution of the "critical mass" debate and arguments in favor of increasing the substantive and/or descriptive representation of women, see Dolan and Tripp (2006).

[13] Japan currently ranks 96th worldwide, alongside Gambia and Georgia, with women holding 9.6 percent of seats in the Lower House of the Diet. The United States is ranked 65th, with women holding 16.3 percent of seats in the House of Representatives. Women hold between one-third and just under one-half of seats in the top-ranked countries—Rwanda, Sweden, Finland, Costa Rica, Denmark, Norway, Netherlands, Cuba/Spain (shared rank), Mozambique, and Belgium. See the Inter-Parliamentary Union's "Women in National Parliaments" at http://www.ipu.org.

[14] Patterson and Nishikawa (2002) argue that higher rates of support for smaller parties among Japanese women voters (for example, CGP, the New Liberal Club, and the JCP) are due to the fact that these political parties represent issues of specific concern to more women than men (for example, social welfare, education, and the environment).

References

Anderson, Christopher J., Andre Blais, Shaun Bowler, Todd Donovan, and Ola Listhaug. 2005. *Losers' consent: Elections and democratic legitimacy*. New York: Oxford Univ, Press.

Dolan, Kathleen and Aili Mari Trip. 2006. Critical perspective on women and gender. *Politics and Gender* 2 (4):491–530.

Feldman, Ofer. 2000. *The Japanese political personality: Analyzing the motivations and culture of freshman diet members*. New York: St. Martin's Press.

Flanagan, Scott C., Shinsaku Kohei, Ichiro Miyake, Bradley M. Richardson, and Joji Watanuki. *JABISS: The Japanese Election Study, 1976* (electronic file). ICPSR04682-v1. Irvine, CA: Univ. of California, Irvine, Center for the Study of Democracy (producers), 2007. Ann Arbor, MI: Inter-university Consortium for Political and Social Research (distributor), February 27, 2008. doi:10.3886/ICPSR04682.

Ikeda, Ken'ichi, Yoshiaki Kobayashi, and Hiroshi Hirano. *Nationwide time-series survey on voting behavior in the beginning of the 21st century, 2001–2005*, Japan Election Study III (JES III, SSJDA version).

International Herald Tribune/Asia-Pacific. 2007. Gay candidate in Japan fails to win a seat. July 30. http://www.iht.com. (This and other newspaper articles cited in this chapter are available upon request from the author.)

Ito, Joichi. 2007. In Japan, stagnation wins again. *New York Times*, September 18. http://www.nytimes.com.

Kabashima, Ikuo, Joji Watanuki, Ichiro Miyake, Yoshiaki Kobayashi, and Ken'ichi Ikeda. *Japan Election Study II 1993–96* (JESII).

Krauss, Ellis S., and Benjamin Nyblade. 2005. Presidentialization in Japan? The prime minister, media and elections in Japan. *British Journal of Political Science* 35:357–68.

Krauss, Ellis S., and Robert Pekkanen. 2008. Reforming the Liberal Democratic Party. In *Democratic reform in Japan: Assessing the impact*, ed. Sherry L. Martin and Gill Steel. Boulder, CO: Lynne Rienner Publishers.

Mansbridge, Jane. 2003. Rethinking representation. *American Political Science Review* 97 (4): 515–28.

Martin, Sherry. 2004. Alienated, independent, and female: Lessons from the Japanese electorate. *Social Science Japan Journal* 7:1–19.

Massey, Joseph A. 1975. The missing leader: Japanese youths' view of political authority. *American Political Science Review* 69:31–48.

Otake, Hideo. 1999. Political realignment and policy conflict. In *Power shuffles and policy processes: Coalition government in Japan in the 1990s*, ed. Hideo Otake, 129–30. Tokyo: Japan Center for International Exchange.

Patterson, Dennis, and Misa Nishikawa. 2002. Political interest or interest in politics? Gender and party support in postwar Japan. *Women and Politics* 24:1–34.

Pollack, Philip H., III. 1983. The participatory consequences of internal and external political efficiency: A research note. *Western Political Quarterly* 36 (3): 400–09.

Reed, Steven R., and Michael F. Thies. 2001. The causes of electoral reform in Japan. In *Mixed-member electoral systems: The best of both worlds?* ed. Matthew Soberg Shugart and Martin P. Wattenberg, 152–72. Oxford and New York: Oxford Univ. Press.

Scheiner, Ethan. 2006. *Democracy without competition in Japan: Opposition failure in a one-party dominant state.* Cambridge: Cambridge Univ. Press.

Tanaka, Aiji. 2003. Decline of trust in Japanese party system, 1976–2001: Why has the LDP stayed in power? And what is the consequence? *Waseda Political Studies* 35:35–59.

Tremblay, Manon. 2006. The substantive representation of women and PR: Some reflections on the role of surrogate representation and critical mass. *Politics and gender* 2 (4): 502–10.

Tyler, Tom R. 2000. Social justice: Outcome and procedure. *International Journal of Psychology* 35 (2): 117–25.

Wakata, Kyoji. 1977. *Japanese diet members, social background, general values, and role perception.* PhD dissertation, Houston, TX: Rice Univ.

Watanuki Joji, Ichiro Miyake, Takashi Inoguchi, and Ikuo Kabashima. *Japan Election Study 1983* (JESI).

CONCLUSION

Japanese Politics in the Koizumi Era: Temporary Anomaly or a Paradigm Shift?

Kenneth Mori McElwain and Steven R. Reed

When the Liberal Democratic Party (LDP) lost its majority in the 1993 Lower House elections, many observers declared (or hoped for) an end to business as usual under the "1955 system." The new eight-party coalition invoked political change through electoral reform. While legislators and analysts had long pointed out the relationship between money politics and the old system of multimember districts (MMDs) and a single nontransferable vote (SNTV), the Recruit (1989) and Sagawa Kyubin (1992) scandals revealed the breadth and magnitude of corruption in the LDP's electoral machine. At the same time, the nation's policy paralysis during the first Gulf War confirmed the inability of a consensus-oriented deliberation process to end in decisive action. By adopting a mixed-member majoritarian (MMM) system with a single-member district (SMD) tier, most observers predicted the gradual emergence of a two-party system, à la Duverger's Law. Under alternating two-party competition, elections would begin to prioritize ideological differences over clientelist appeals, voters would have clear alternatives in the government party and its opposition, and national politicians would seize authority from the powerful bureaucracy to achieve their policy goals.

Most observers have been disappointed with how political events have unfolded since the early 1990s. True, one should not expect that parliamentarians, bureaucrats, interest groups, and voters will adjust to a new political environment overnight. Many researchers have hedged their predictions with a wait-and-see attitude. This is analytically appropriate, but at a certain point, it becomes incumbent on experts to distinguish slow change from no change.

As this book goes to press, it has been over fifteen years since the LDP's historic collapse. While some changes unfold more gradually than others, we believe there is sufficient data—about both the past and the present—to draw some conclusions about the state of Japanese politics today. Each chapter in this volume has explored a different facet of electoral and legislative politics, comparing the country's historical trajectory and recent events with the broader comparative literature. In concluding this volume, we eschew individual reviews of the contributors' chapters, and instead address common theoretical and empirical findings that will help us gauge the evolution of Japanese politics. We believe there are three broader themes that are of particular note: the importance of leadership, the prospects of government turnover, and pluralism in policymaking.

Does Leadership Matter?

Junichiro Koizumi's tenure as LDP president and Japanese prime minister demonstrated the political value of policy leadership and electoral popularity. As Chao-Chi Lin shows, however, Koizumi's ascension was far from assured. He had competed in previous leadership contests to no avail, and his tendency to espouse policies that went against party orthodoxy led to his widespread characterization as a *henjin* (charitably translated as "eccentric," less charitably as "weirdo"). Koizumi had always painted himself as a reformer, however, and this political brand was exactly what the party needed in the wake of Yoshiro Mori's memorably unpopular stint as prime minister. Koizumi rode to victory in 2001 by virtue of an internal rule change in the LDP, which granted prefectural party branches a larger voice in the party presidential election. In the past, local party bosses mostly supported candidates who were backed by their districts' parliamentarians, and conventional models predicted that the establishment candidate, Ryutaro Hashimoto, would corral factional support and win handily. This time around, however, most prefectural branches decided to choose their delegates through primaries open to all party members. This allowed the more widely popular Koizumi to corner 90 percent of the local votes and ride the reformist wave to victory. For the first time in LDP history, the party leader was chosen on the basis of his popularity with the public instead of his power within the party.

Accounts of Koizumi's victory accord with the burgeoning literature on the "presidentialization of prime ministers," which suggests that the media and electorate are increasingly attentive to the individual identity and power of prime ministers (Poguntke and Webb 2005; Krauss and Nyblade 2005). This attention, in turn, gives leaders some ammunition in intra- and interparty legislative bargaining. At the most basic level, a popular leader has electoral value to his or her party's candidates. Kenneth Mori McElwain finds that in the 2005 Lower House elections, LDP candidates performed better in districts where support for Koizumi was high. Indeed, the LDP successfully leveraged Koizumi's coattails: the value of Koizumi actually visiting a particular district was a 2 to 3 percent increase in LDP vote share. In addition, Barry C. Burden demonstrates that a prime minister's popularity has a disproportionate influence on how female voters perceive the LDP. The role of leadership in female political participation extends into the composition of parliament. Alisa Gaunder argues that the gender imbalance in the Diet improves only when party leaders make it a priority to recruit female candidates. While previous leaders from both opposition and governing parties have also tried to rectify the Diet's paucity of women, Koizumi is the most recent champion of nominating female candidates in competitive districts.

Electoral popularity is valuable not only for its own sake. Entrepreneurial leaders with strong policy preferences can leverage their popularity to enact controversial reforms. The traditional LDP model of politics involved consensus-building and factional balancing. The LDP shied away from contentious ideological issues, focusing instead on redistributive politics that benefited all members. However, a crucial pillar of Koizumi's reform plans was the privatization of the postal system and the separation of its delivery services from its banking and insurance functions. Although this was opposed by the postmasters' union and its patrons in the LDP, Koizumi used his bully pulpit to put the issue on the policy agenda, oust factional dissidents, and fight the 2005 election on an issue with minimal public salience in the past. Many LDP members were hesitant to follow Koizumi's gamble, and there was widespread dissatisfaction with his top-down leadership style. *Because* he was popular with the electorate, however, Koizumi held a valuable bargaining chip: his coattails were long enough to offset potential losses in factional or interest-group backing. As Patricia L. Maclachlan discusses in depth, Koizumi leveraged this chip to dominate the policymaking process, establishing cabinet-led committees and imbuing them with sufficient authority to override opposition from both LDP and bureaucratic dissidents.

On the one hand, our analysis suggests that Japanese leaders can utilize their popularity to enact their preferred reforms while simultaneously benefiting the party overall. On the other hand, this does not ensure that Koizumi's political style will persist in the future. Neither the selection of Yasuo Fukuda nor Taro Aso as party leaders indicates an attempt by the party to build upon the Koizumi legacy or emulate his style. After all, there have been other popular prime ministers in the past, and not all were successful in realizing their agenda. Kakuei Tanaka, the original populist prime minister, sought to transform Japan by extending infrastructure projects to all corners of the country. Although he succeeded in crafting a political machine that distributed vast amounts of public works, its accompanying tolls—bribery scandals and government debt—eventually delegitimized his agenda. Yasuhiro Nakasone, who was prime minister in the 1980s, focused more heavily on making Japan a relevant player in foreign policy and international security. His attempts to change the Article 9 Peace Clause and increase the military budget failed, however, due to his inability to override parliamentary opposition and convince voters of his cause's merits. More recently, Hashimoto worked on the structural liberalization of Japan, emphasizing reductions in trade barriers, weakening the power of the bureaucracy, and reducing the budget deficit. However, he was pressured to resign following the LDP's dismal performance in the 1998 House of Councillors elections, caused by rising unemployment and slow economic growth in the wake of the Asian financial crisis.

This leads us to a broader question: is Koizumi an anomaly, or a symptom of deeper political transformation? Koizumi's rise was due in part to being in the right place at the right time; Hashimoto, not Koizumi, may have become

LDP president in 2001 if there hadn't been changes to the party's selection procedures. As Lin argues, Koizumi won precisely because of the primary system: local prefectural branches voted overwhelmingly in his favor, making it costly for Diet members to risk their supporters' wrath by casting their votes for Hashimoto. To the extent that institutional rules structure the incentives of political actors, future LDP presidential candidates may also prioritize broad policy alternatives over purely factional alliances in order to win the support of grassroots members. However, there is no reason to think that this format for selecting leaders will necessarily become the norm. The LDP has seldom used the same rules to select two consecutive leaders. When it becomes necessary to select a new leader, the first question has always been, "What procedures shall we use?" Although the LDP's internal constitution requires periodic presidential elections, the party can choose leaders by a vote among Diet members when they resign midterm. At the same time, faction bosses can obviate the need for an election if they coordinate around a consensus candidate to run unchallenged.

The LDP currently appears to be committed to running presidential primaries, at least in part because presidential elections provide an effective venue for the party to campaign unofficially in front of the public and dominate the news cycle. When Abe resigned abruptly in 2007, the party could have chosen its next leader through a parliamentary vote, but the LDP nevertheless held a primary, which was won by Fukuda. One reason for Fukuda's victory was the bandwagon effect created by the support of almost all the faction leaders. While this was not a return to disciplined factions determining the vote, neither was it a primary dominated by the candidates' popularity with the public.

There are reasons to believe the LDP will continue to use primary processes, thereby increasing the salience of mass popularity over factional power-sharing when choosing party leaders. First, the LDP cannot afford to look more insular and undemocratic than the Democratic Party of Japan (DPJ). This concern was muted in the past when the opposition was fragmented, but the rise of the DPJ—which mostly uses open selection processes—increases the costs to the LDP of adhering to traditional mechanisms. Second, party leaders are more visible in the media, raising the value of leaders who look good and speak eloquently on the evening news. As McElwain shows, popular leaders are an electoral asset; catching Koizumi's lightning in a bottle may not be easy, but an open selection process has the best odds of finding a popular leader.

Will Parties Alternate in Power?

Has Japan evolved into or toward a two-party system? Will there be alternation in power? The answer depends on what data one decides to analyze, because the concept of a two-party system is ill-defined and thus gives analysts no guide to what data are the most relevant. Steven R. Reed and Kay Shimizu analyze the failure to produce an alternation in power and wind up betting on Duverger's

Law. Robert J. Weiner analyzes the gap between the SMD winner and the runner-up and winds up betting against Duverger's Law. Only time will tell.

We do, however, see the emergence of two camps—the LDP-Komei on the center-right, and the DPJ and Social Democratic Party (SDP) on the center-left—and we do have good evidence of the increasing relevance of both policy and leadership in electoral competition. A crucial aspect of the LDP's past dominance was the electorate's ability to divorce feelings about local district candidates from feelings about those candidates' parties. The LDP's popularity has frequently sagged below 30 to 40 percent in national polls, and yet many voters are satisfied with the ability of their candidates to "bring home the bacon" (Richardson 1988). Ko Maeda finds, however, that this disconnect between candidate and party preferences is dissipating. The correlation between LDP vote swings in the SMD versus proportional representation (PR) tiers of the ballot is strengthening, indicating that the party label is becoming more relevant in elections. In turn, this strengthens the value of having a popular party leader.

Fluctuations in the value of the party label may end up deciding the evolutionary direction of the Japanese party system. Weiner cautions that a bipartisan trend at the national level does not equate to competitive elections at the district level. Many district races in the SMD tier are uncompetitive, and this result is replicated in local government elections, as well as in SMD competition in other countries. Of course, this does not preclude alternations in power altogether, but when the modal margin of victory is large and few districts are in play, only large changes in partisan vote trends will be sufficient to unseat the LDP. This matters particularly from a policy perspective, since accountability to voters is weaker when politicians feel invulnerable.

The key issue, then, is the likelihood that large groups of voters will change their ballots from one election to the next. Reed and Shimizu argue that the increasing salience of party leadership and structural reform issues makes ideology more important in elections. In effect, public opinion is sufficiently volatile to generate large vote swings. Weiner warns that this does not guarantee close individual district races: a large vote swing to the DPJ will make LDP strongholds more competitive but DPJ bailiwicks even less so. However, Maeda's finding that vote choices are increasingly based on party labels, combined with the Reed and Shimizu thesis that vote choices are more volatile, indicate that uncompetitive districts today may become competitive districts tomorrow. In effect, while well-known incumbents who embrace their party label will be rewarded when the party is popular (hence uncompetitive districts in the short term), they will be penalized for their devotion when voters change their minds (hence competitive districts in the long term). Because more votes are in play today than in the past, party leaders have stronger incentives to design policy platforms that attract a broad range of voters and to campaign in districts where they are not presently strong. In fact, while many individual districts are uncompetitive, the number of *uncontested* districts is extremely low.

The key to the magnitude of vote swings may be independent voters. As Sherry L. Martin shows, the anchors of traditional partisanship are weakening, with more and more voters identifying themselves as independents in national surveys. Floating voters are more likely to switch their ballot preferences than true partisans, increasing the number of competitive districts. To the extent that these floating voters are dissatisfied with the traditional LDP model of clientelist politics, there is significant opportunity for aggressive parties to offer an alternative vision. The effects of weaker partisanship and a declining organizational vote on the emergence of new policy dimensions and parties have already been observed in a range of European cases (Dalton and Wattenberg 2000; Wren and McElwain 2007). At the same time, floating voters with weaker allegiances may be more willing to punish poorly performing governments, regardless of their ideology, resulting in greater policy accountability. Indeed, as Reed and Shimizu indicate, the DPJ's stunning victory in the 2007 Upper House elections was driven by popular dissatisfaction with the LDP's policy performance.

Of course, partisanship is not a trait specific to voters. Even before the 1990s, the LDP manufactured parliamentary majorities by being willing and able to entice independent politicians to join the party *after* the election. If the LDP continues to do this better than the opposition, then changes in voter behavior will have a smaller impact on the distribution of parliamentary seats. However, recent trends suggest the stabilization of politicians' party affiliations. Jun Saito examines the causes and timing of party switching among legislators over the past two decades. A large proportion of party switching was by Diet members who left the LDP in the early 1990s, contributing to the party's ouster in 1993. While previous studies have found that ideological commitment to political reform, broadly defined, was a strong predictor of switching (Reed and Scheiner 2003), Saito argues that ideology matters particularly for Diet members who do not rely heavily on pork-barreling. Each successive infrastructure project generates declining marginal returns to constituents; politicians who have satisfied their voters' particularistic needs must rely on alternative tactics to generate electoral support. While some interest groups—particularly the construction and transportation industries—have an insatiable demand for government projects, the eventual saturation of pork-barreling may serve to strengthen partisanship over time.

One sign of stabilizing bipartisanship is that no members of the LDP have voluntarily defected to another party since 1996. The only defectors have been those denied the LDP nomination. The postal rebels of 2005 did not defect; they were kicked out. Some of the rebels decided to join the DPJ or form new parties, but most sought paths back into the LDP. Other candidates have been denied the LDP nomination because they lost the election and another candidate was better placed to win it for the LDP. Some of these candidates have decided to run for the DPJ or for a minor party, but such decisions can hardly be characterized as defections. Similarly, only two DPJ incumbents have switched to the LDP since the party was founded in 1996. Three candidates defected from the LDP to the New Conservative Party, which turned out to be a half-way house to the LDP and was probably intended to be so. With these several exceptions, neither of the major parties has suffered any serious defections. Candidates without nominations are up for grabs. The LDP welcomes rebels back into the party, and the DPJ welcomes LDP rejects and rebels who want to change sides. Both the LDP and the DPJ have been magnets, absorbing both candidates and minor parties.

Is Policymaking More Pluralistic?

As the value of leadership increases and parties become more cohesive, it is natural to ask, "How have public policies changed?" A generation of scholars since Chalmers Johnson's (1982) volume on the Japanese developmental state has debated the relative influence of bureaucrats versus politicians in policy decision-making (Calder 1988; Okimoto 1989; Ramseyer and Rosenbluth 1993; Curtis 1999). Most acknowledge that bureaucrats are relatively insulated from legislative politics, having had to serve only one master—the LDP—for most of the postwar period. At the same time, the policy *input* process itself has been narrow. The LDP has always catered to a broad coalition of interest groups, but its strongest clients have been domestically oriented industries such as construction and agriculture, which provide hefty donations in exchange for favorable protectionist policies.

With the end of LDP rule, many expected policymaking to become more pluralistic. When electoral reform was debated in the early 1990s, one of the motivations was to increase the government's policy performance and accountability. Under a two-party system, each camp would need to win close to 50 percent of the electorate to secure a majority, forcing it to appeal to a broader cross-section of voters. This would lead to new or underrepresented social groups, such as consumer associations, environmental activists, and new industries, to gain a seat at the policy table. Moreover, because voters dissatisfied with the incumbent government would have a clear alternative to vote for, both major parties would carefully monitor each other's performance. This, in turn, would strengthen political involvement in policymaking and monitoring the bureaucracy.

By the 1990s, the Iron Triangle of the LDP, bureaucrats, and big businesses had already begun to unravel. On the heels of successive corruption scandals, Keidanren—the Japan Business Federation—halted campaign contributions to the LDP in 1993. Ethan Scheiner and Michio Muramatsu argue that the willingness of the bureaucracy to cooperate with the 1993–1994 eight-party coalition created a schism between LDP politicians and bureaucrats. The competitive as opposed to cooperative relationship between the two has decreased the effectiveness of government responses to policy crises, as seen in the bungled and slow-moving reaction to the nonperforming loans.

Although interest groups focused their lobbying activities on the bureaucracy during the rapid party realignment of the mid- to late 1990s, political parties have begun to regain the upper hand (Scheiner and Muramatsu). This was made abundantly clear when Keidanren resumed contributions to the LDP in 2004. Moreover, structural reforms during the Hashimoto and Obuchi cabinets weakened the policy autonomy of the bureaucracy. Various government ministries with broad mandates have been split: the Ministry of Finance, for example, lost banking supervision powers to the Financial Services Agency and monetary authority to the Bank of Japan. Numerous bribery scandals within the government ministries diminished public trust in the once-vaunted bureaucratic elite.

Political—as opposed to bureaucratic—leadership in policy reform was clearest during Koizumi's postal-privatization saga. Koizumi succeeded in pushing through a bill that weakened both LDP clientelism and bureaucratic autonomy by bypassing the traditional policymaking process (Mahlachlan). He established study groups and commissions within the Cabinet Agency, appointing like-minded reformers such as Heizo Takenaka to key leadership posts without regard for factional balancing. While Koizumi's strong commitment to postal reform reflected his personal policy preferences more than national economic need, he was successful in quelling intra-LDP opposition because of his electoral leverage.

Of course, it is still premature to conclude that Japanese policymaking has turned a corner. Some of Koizumi's policies failed to materialize fully, such as his attempts to privatize and depoliticize the Japan Highway Public Corporation. The DPJ picked up the issue by opposing road-designated tax revenues (*doro tokutei zaigen*), such as gasoline and tonnage taxes, which are earmarked specifically to fund Japan's ubiquitous road construction projects. The public, of course, favors lower gasoline prices, but the LDP managed to win the media debate by framing the issue as one of local finance and accusing the DPJ of depriving local governments of millions of yen in revenues. The DPJ tried but failed to frame it as an issue of bureaucratic control over large sums of money without parliamentary oversight. Without much fanfare, and timed to limit damage to the LDP, Koizumi came out in favor of the DPJ position over that of his own party. As of this writing, the debate is moving toward a compromise position, particularly since the DPJ has greater authority to block legislation using its plurality position in the Upper House.

The most important long-run effect of postal reform is unlikely to be any of the issues debated at the time, but rather the removal of the huge sums of money in postal savings from bureaucratic control. The same can be said of current debates over road-designated tax revenues. The LDP may want to avoid controversial issues such as reforming the bureaucracy, but events and DPJ pressure will make it much harder to avoid in the future. Reed and Shimizu demonstrate that public interest in bureaucratic and fiscal reform is stronger than ever, as evinced by Koizumi's 2005 electoral victory based on postal reform. The

LDP cannot afford to be on the wrong side of public opinion for very long.

There are signs that pluralism in both the electoral and policy processes is strengthening. Gaunder describes the emergence of grassroots organizations and policy schools to help women get elected to the Diet. At the same time, voters seem pleased with the legislative process, even as they are disappointed with their choice of political parties. This is due partially to the consensus-oriented norms of Diet proceedings, which give opposition parties legislative voice despite LDP dominance (Martin). With the DPJ capturing a plurality in the Upper House, policy accountability and electoral competition can only increase in the future.

Conclusion

Political reform has changed Japanese politics in many ways, some intended and some unintended. The clearest example of reform living up to its promise is the increase in policy-based elections, symbolized most notably by the use of party manifestos since 2003 and by an increased emphasis on leadership. The clearest case of failure is the fact that the LDP remains in power and there has yet to be an alternation in power. Evidence for the evolution of a two-party system is more complex and ambiguous.

Though we have not addressed the issue of political corruption directly, there is also evidence that political reform has reduced corruption. Ray Christensen and Kyle Colvin address election-night corruption, which may turn out to be the exception to this trend. They show that there was not much corruption under the old electoral system, and we may well see more election-night cheating in the SMDs. However, SMDs have reduced the capacity of entrenched incumbents to survive corruption scandals. Though we do not yet have systematic statistical comparisons, it seems clear that scandal-tainted incumbents are less likely to receive a nomination, less likely to run, and more likely to be defeated if they do run. The exceptions tend to be rural areas in which the DPJ cannot find a candidate to run against the established incumbent, but the number of such exceptions is declining rapidly. Perhaps even more important is the fact that the DPJ will not allow the LDP to cover up bureaucratic corruption and incompetence.

These transformations (or lack thereof) in electoral and legislative politics will continue to impact the salience and outcomes of policymaking. Recent upswings in economic performance have temporarily diminished public concerns about the "lost decade," although the country is still not out of the woods. Instead, public opinion is increasingly focused on issues that have an ideological bent. One example is foreign policy, where LDP leaders are competing openly about how to engage the country's Asian neighbors. Until the 1980s, open discussions about Japanese remilitarization were verboten, due to concerns—both domestic and international—about Japan's militaristic history. However, Koizumi defied regional outrage by repeatedly visiting Yasukuni Shrine, and Abe made his name by taking North Korea to task over its abduction of Japanese citizens. Fukuda has backtracked from his predecessors by being more accommodating to international sentiment, although Aso—the prime minister at the time of this writing—is known for his hawkish views. Since Koizumi, however, debate over foreign policy has been brought before the public for the first time in over four decades. Another example is structural economic reform, especially with respect to labor market fluidity, unequal wealth distribution, and government involvement in the economy overall. The postal reform and road construction debates described previously speak to Koizumi's success in raising public awareness about inefficiencies in government performance.

In the American political lexicon, there is the saying, "Only Nixon could go to China." When Richard Nixon visited Mao Zedong in 1972, he was able to deflect accusations of being soft on Communism precisely because he (and his Republican Party) had a history of staunch anti-Communism. A Democrat doing the same would have been raked over the coals for being a Communist sympathizer, and thus would be less likely to take on prevailing orthodoxy. In many ways, Koizumi's criticisms of Japanese politics, and particularly of the LDP electoral machine, resonated with the public because of this Nixonian logic. As an LDP lifer—and a third-generation politician to boot—Koizumi's positions were credible precisely because he was taking on issues that had benefited his party in the past. Opposition parties in their various incarnations—the Socialists, the New Frontier Party, and now the Democrats—have similarly accused the LDP for its close relationship to the bureaucracy and interest groups. Although their arguments are as valid—theoretically—as Koizumi's, they are less credible to the public when coming from outside the LDP, because they could be perceived as self-serving electioneering.

In other words, the most important legacy of the 1990s and of Koizumi's tenure may be the opening of long-delayed debates. There are no more "sacred cows" in Japanese politics, and this is important to a country facing short- and long-term problems related to tax and pension reform, a growing demand for female and immigrant participation in the labor force, and a tenuous economic future. In addition to the outcome of policies, politicians and voters care about *how* decisions are made, and it is no longer seen as sour grapes for the opposition to take the LDP to task. Even though the LDP continues to hold on to the powerful Lower House of parliament, the prospects of political change—both electoral and legislative—are much greater now than in the past.

References

Calder, Kent E. 1988. *Crisis and compensation: Public policy and political stability in Japan, 1949–1986.* Princeton, NJ: Princeton Univ. Press.
Curtis, Gerald L. 1999. *The logic of Japanese politics: Leaders, institutions, and the limits of change.* New York: Columbia Univ. Press.

Dalton, Russell J., and Martin P. Wattenberg. 2000. *Parties without partisans: Political change in advanced industrial democracies*. Oxford: Oxford Univ. Press.

Johnson, Chalmers. 1982. *MITI and the Japanese miracle: The growth of industrial policy, 1925–1975*. Stanford, CA: Stanford Univ. Press.

Krauss, Ellis S., and Benjamin Nyblade. 2005. Presidentialization in Japan? The prime minister, media, and elections in Japan. *British Journal of Political Science* 35:357–68.

Okimoto, Daniel I. 1989. *Between MITI and the market: Japanese industrial policy for high technology*. Stanford, CA: Stanford Univ. Press.

Poguntke, Thomas, and Paul Webb. 2005. *The presidentialization of politics: A comparative study of modern democracies*. Oxford: Oxford Univ. Press.

Ramseyer, J. Mark, and Frances McCall Rosenbluth. 1993. *Japan's political marketplace*. Cambridge, MA: Harvard Univ. Press.

Reed, Steven R., and Ethan Scheiner. 2003. Electoral incentives and policy preferences: Mixed motives behind party defections in Japan. *British Journal of Political Science* 33:469–90.

Richardson, Bradley M. 1988. Constituency candidates versus parties in Japanese voting behavior. *American Political Science Review* 82 (3): 695–718.

Wren, Anne, and Kenneth Mori McElwain. 2007. Voters and parties. In *The Oxford handbook of comparative politics*, ed. C. Boix and S. Stokes. Oxford: Oxford Univ. Press.

INDEX

A

Abe, Shinzo
  cabinet, 43
  government of, 17t
  performance, 19
  relations with North Korea, 289–90
  relationship with postal rebels,
    40, 173
  resignation, ix, 126–27, 284
abortion debate, 8
Administrative Reform Council
  (Gyosei Kaikaku Kaigi), 159
Akita Prefecture, election results,
  76–78, 123
Alice, Texas, 200, 202
alternation in power
  factors that prevent, 34, 44, 62
  failure of, under MMD system, 32, 33
  moves toward, 14, 36, 87, 284–85,
    289
  in two-party systems, viii, 19, 29
amakudari bureaucrats
  debates about, 22
  postal positions, reforms of, 161
Amyx, Jennifer
  on reasons for slow response to
    banking crisis, 184, 191
  on politician-bureaucrat relations,
    192
anticipatory representation, 266
antipollution citizen's movement, 8
Article 9, Japanese Constitution (Peace
  Clause), 150, 283
Asian financial crisis, 283
Aso, Taro
  candidacy for LDP president, 43, 115
  electoral support, 120t
  leadership approach, 283
  opposition to postal privatization,
    163, 165
assassins. *See* postal assassins
association of retired postmasters
  (Taiju no Kai), 158

B

banks. *See also* financial crisis, 1990s
  bailouts for, opposition to, 184–85,
    191, 196n3
  impact of capital market
    liberalization, 191
  insulation of, as form of protection,
    191
  ties to the Ministry of Finance
    (MOF), 183, 190–11, 193
Basic Law for a Gender Equal Society,
  2001, 234
bipartisanship
  gerrymandering, 205
  growing evidence of, 286
  at national *vs.* district levels, 68, 285
  possibilities and limits of, ix–x
Blair, Tony, 18, 34, 41, 149
bullet-train (*shinkansen*) construction.
  See also infrastructure
    Ashikaga Prefecture, 72–75, 74t
    Hachinohe, Aomori Prefecture,
      74t, 75–77
    Hirosaki, Aomori Prefecture,
      74t, 75–77
    Nagano Prefecture, 78–79
    Oyama Prefecture, 72–75, 74t
    Yamagata Prefecture, 74t
bureaucracy, bureaucrats. *See also*
  corruption; politician-bureaucrat
  relations
  corruption and incompetence,
    21–22, 181
  civil service elites, viii, 243
  diminishing power of, 187–88, 287
  incorporation into postal-reform
    process, 164
  insulation from legislative politics,
    vii, 287
  policymaking role, 171–72, 185–
    86, 188–90
  amakudari, 22, 161, 171
  relationships with banks, 181–85, 195

relationships with court system,
196n4
sources of information, 187
sources of power, 6, 189

C

campaigns, campaign expenditures.
See elections
Canada
election rules, 215n8
election-night corruption in, 203–5
party control over candidate
selection, 51
satisfaction with election outcomes
in, 262
victory margins in
impact of party affiliation, 206–7
ultraclose elections, 207–8, 214
candidates. *See also* elections;
incumbents; Liberal Democratic
Party (LDP) *and specific elections*
candidate-centered elections
district-level elections as, 87–88
nomination rules and, 51
party loyalty, 67, 98–99
personal *vs.* party focus, 32, 41,
47, 48–49
and power of elected officials, 87
predictable outcomes from, 99
programmatic policies *vs.* pork-
barrel tactics, 71
in SMD tier, x
and type of electoral system, 50
under the "1955 system," 47, 55
dual candidacy (*chofuku rikkoho*)
and "best loser" provisions, 32–
36, 48, 151n2
endorsement requirement, 127n4
fees paid by, 135–36
fund-raising, 244
independents, 33, 52
koenkai (support groups)
communication with
representatives, 267
as political machines, 32, 51–52
role in winning elections, 115,

117, 139–40, 169, 241
for women, challenges of
creating, 241–42
nomination process and policies
MMD-SNTV *vs.* SMD-PR
system, 31
party endorsements, 242–43
U.S. *vs.* U.K., 51
obstacles faced by, 240–41
ranking system for, 48
competition for, 117
Koizumi's ranking of women
candidates, 253
for SMD *vs.* PR seats, 48
success rates, male *vs.* female
candidates, 245–47, 246t
visits from party leaders, 134,
139–40
voter satisfaction with
representation by, 271–72
women, 241–44
capital market liberalization, 183, 191
CEFP. *See* Council on Economic and
Fiscal Policy
CGP. *See* Clean Government Party
(CGP)
Chiba Prefecture
competition among candidates, 36
LDP losses in, 122
LDP support from, 112
Child Care Leave Law, 1991, 234
Christian Democratic Party (Italy)
clientelist system, 8, 9
disintegration of, 29
LDP *vs.*, vii
civil service elites. *See* bureaucracy,
bureaucrats
Clean Government Party (CGP,
Komei, Komeito)
base of support, 69
coalition with LDP, 285
complexity of, 37–40
electoral strategy, 99–100
emergence from the NFP, 16
formation of, 11–12
mechanisms of, 30
nomination coordination, 135

vote bartering, 151n3
in government coalitions, 17t
support for LDP candidates, 69–70
satisfaction with, 271–73
clientelist systems, 8–10
closeness ratios, district-level elections, 90–91, 91f
Committee for Gender Equality, DPJ, 244
consensus-based policymaking system, 283
Conservative Party
campaign financing, 245
in England, 62
formation of, 16, 70
in government coalitions, 17t
merger with LDP, 100
constituencies, organized (*jiban*), 248t
constitutional revision
Abe's efforts, 19, 23n1
debates about, 6–7, 11, 150
historical efforts, 30
corruption. *See also* election-night corruption; scandals
bureaucratic, 10, 21–22
elections, 212
impact of election reform, x–xii, 289
perceived, 199
personal politics and, 48–49, 281
during Tanaka era, viii, 8–10, 21–22
"Costa Rica arrangements" (tag teams), 34–35, 57
Council on Economic and Fiscal Policy (CEFP), 162–63, 172
court system, 196n4
Curtis, Gerald, 11–12, 32

D

Damore, David F., 135
De Boef, Suzanna, 222
democracy. *See also* opposition parties; two-party system
alternation in power
factors that prevent, 34, 44, 62
failure of, under MMD system, 32, 33

moves toward, 14, 36, 87, 284–85, 289
in two-party systems, viii, 19, 29, 52
anticipatory representation, 266
promissory representation, 265–66
public satisfaction with
gender differences, 274
Japan *vs.* other countries, 262–63, 263f
party identification and, 269
role of surrogate representation, 270–71, 270f
Democratic Party of Japan (DPJ, Minshuto)
alliance with SDP, 285
candidates switching from, 75
candidates switching to, 36
competing parties to, 97–98
criticisms of *amakudari*, 22
electoral success, success rates, 19, 42t, 61–63
formation of, 14
incorporation of Liberal Party, 70
incorporation of NFP affiliated candidates, 70
media coverage of, 284
1998 House of Representatives elections, 121
no-confidence vote against Mori, 121
nomination process, 33
policies, 52, 67
opposition to postal privatization, 42–43, 166, 168–69
opposition to road-designated taxes, 288
role in development of two-party system, 29, 52
success of "new LDP" over, 41
support for women candidates, 244, 256n6
supporters
growing numbers of, 16, 44, 60–62, 112
satisfaction with election outcomes, 272f

women, 243–44
2005 election campaign
  candidate visits, 141–49, 143t,
    147t
  strategy, 134
  withdrawal of weaker
    candidates, 102
2007 House of Councillors elections
  implications, 67, 261, 286
  success in rural areas, 43
Democratic Party, U.S.
  election-night corruption, 199–
    200, 202
  victory margins, 207–8, 212
Democratic Socialist Party (DSP), 11,
  17t
"dentists" (Nihon Shika Ishi
  Renmei), in LDP, 118t
Diet. See also House of Councillors
  (Upper House); House of
  Representatives (Lower House);
  Liberal Democratic Party (LDP)
  bank regulation
    passage of, 195
    rejection of proposals for, 183
  district-level elections
    candidate-based focus, 87–88
    closeness ratios, 90–91
    competition among candidates,
      93–95
    RU (runner-up) ratios, 88–90
  evidence of increasing pluralism
    in, 29, 289
  gender gap in, 239, 240t, 282
  impact of LDP election rule
    changes, 115
  inability to obtain policy
    information or develop bank
    legislation, 183
  Koizumi's dissolution of, 42, 165
  LDP majority status, vii–viii
  postwar purging of, 6
  role in electing LDP party leaders,
    110, 128n13
  support staffs, 189
"doctors" (Nihon Ishi Renmei), in
  LDP, 118t

Doi, Takako
  impact on gender consciousness,
    227
  leadership of JSP, 20, 239
  promotion of women candidates,
    251–52
Douro Chosakai (LDP Road
  Investigation Panel), 72
DPJ. See Democratic Party of Japan
  (DPJ, Minshuto)
dual candidacy rule (chofuku
  rikkoho), 33, 48, 51, 99, 151n2
Duverger's Law
  avoidance of, LDP policy
    approaches, 34–43
  and disappearance of smaller
    parties, 37
  in Japan
    evidence for and against, 43,
      135, 284–85
    impacts, 100
  Japan vs. other countries, 29–30, 44

E
economy. See also infrastructure;
  postal privatization
  economic development
    as political platform, 6
    and pollution control issues, 30
    rapidity of, until the 1990s, 181
    role of bureaucracy in, vii
    role of transportation
      infrastructure, 71–72
    and voting patterns, Japan vs.
      U.S., 223–24
  economic growth
    initial investment in
      infrastructure and, 71–72
    as key to Tanaka's reform plans, 8
  and gender gap in politics, 222–23,
    233–34
  impact of postal privatization,
    157–58, 167–68
  recession, and Koizumi's election
    success, 122
Eda, Saburo, 11
EEOL (Equal Employment

Opportunity Law), 233–34
election-night corruption
  analytic approach, 208–9, 215
  characteristics and examples,
    199–201
  factors mitigating, 201–2, 289
  identifying and measuring in
    United States, Canada and Japan
    hypotheses, 203–4
    study design, 204–5
  other forms of election corruption
    vs., 202–3
  role of bureaucracy in, 212–14
  role of party control, 209–12, 211t
  in ultraclose vs. very close
    elections, 208–9, 209t
elections. See also candidates;
  election-night corruption; electoral-
  law reform; House of Councillors
  elections; House of Representatives
  elections
  administration, 212
  campaign costs, 32
    administrative activities, 136
    expenditure limits, 151n4
    spending limits, 136, 151n4
  candidate-centered vs. party-
    centered, 47
  coattail effects, x, 79, 133–134,
    149–150, 255, 282–83. (See also
    under Koizumi)
  competition in
    following electoral reform, 91, 281
    impact of nomination rule
      changes, 51
    impact of party manifestos, 52
    impact of party realignments,
      96–100
    impact of strategic entry and
      withdrawal of candidates,
      100–2, 104n15, 104n16
    impact of voter swings and
      shifts, 95–96
    Japan vs. other countries, 87,
      92–93
    measuring, approaches to,
      103n3, 103n4, 103n6
    moves toward two-party system,

  ix, 12–13, 16, 19–20, 29, 69,
    209–10
  national-level vs. district-level,
    87–88
  and SMD-PR electoral system,
    87, 94–95
  in SMTV districts vs. prefectural
    SMDs, 93
elected officials
  voter expectations for, 264
  voter satisfaction with, 261–63,
    263t, 269–70
electoral success, factors that affect
  party affiliation, 149
  pork-barrel projects, 71–72
  strategic party behavior, 135
funding sources
  factions, 244
  fees paid by candidates, 135–36
  for LDP candidates, 244
  as obstacle for women
    candidates, 244–45
  resource allocation decisions, 135
  WINWIN, 250
hoshu bunretsu (running against
  own party), 59
as referenda on LDP performance,
  32
victory margins
  gubernatorial elections, Japan,
    210, 211t
  in Japan vs. Canada and the
    U.S., 206, 206t
  male vs. female candidates,
    245–47, 246t
  party affiliation and, 206–7, 207f
  party control and, 207–13, 211t
  ultraclose elections, 207–8
Electoral Strategy Committee, LDP, 242
electoral-law reform, 1994. See also
  elections; SMD-PR electoral system
  "Chusenkyokusei haishi sengen"
    (resolution to ban middle-sized
    districts), 70–71
  factors leading to, x–xii, 12–14,
    49, 275n1
  goals of, 47
  Hata's support for, 78

impact on LDP leadership, 67, 69
Kato's opposition to, 78
and marginalization of leftist
  voters, 274
and move toward two-party
  system, electoral competition,
  ix, 12–13, 16, 19–20, 29, 69,
  209–10
nomination coordination, 135
political change following, 14, 29,
  48–49, 51, 70, 185, 261–62, 270
possibilities and limits of, ix–x
role of factions following, 243, 244
role of *koenkai* following, 242
employment, women's, 223
endorsement, party
  automatic, for incumbents, 51
  impact on women candidates,
    242–44
  in Japan *vs.* other countries, 51
  Koizumi's use of, 166, 170
  resources for developing, 248t
  role in faction-centered
    competition, 127n4, 242–43
  rules regarding, 113, 151n5, 152n9
  as source of legitimacy, 38
  as source of publicity, 241
Equal Employment Opportunity Law
  (EEOL), 1985, 233–34
ethnic minorities, surrogate
  representation for, 272–73
Eto, Seiichi
  candidacy, 40
  readmission to LDP, 40
Eto-Kamei faction, LDP
  role in 1998 presidential election,
    115, 128n16
  role in 2001 presidential election,
    120

F

factions, LDP
  affiliations, determinants of, 115
  balancing during nomination
    process, 242–43
  campaign funding provided by, 244
  competition among, 127n4

declining power of, 120
industrial association
  representatives, 118t
mainstream *vs.* nonmainstream,
  128n14
as obstacle to women candidates,
  243
role in postal privatization, 168
role in presidential elections, 5,
  115, 119, 119t, 120, 128n16
under the SNTV system, 110
structure of, 114–15
during the Tanaka era, 9
FILP. *See* Fiscal Investment and Loan
  Program (FILP)
financial crisis, 1990s
  bank bailouts, opposition to, 184–
    85, 191, 196n3
  causes, 181–84
  "fire alarms" for, 182, 187, 190,
    193, 195
  government response to, 181–85
  interest group responses to, 194
  and politician-bureaucrat relations,
    182–83, 195
  role of Ministry of Finance during,
    190–94
Financial Reconstruction Agency, 195
Fiscal Investment and Loan Program
  (FILP)
  competition with MPT, 160
  establishment of, 157–58
  impact of postal privatization on,
    167–68
foreign policy debates, viii, 6, 281,
  283, 289–90
Fukuda, Takeo
  economic policies, 8
  Koizumi's support for, 160
  leadership approach, 283
  primary wins, 284
Fukuda, Yasuo
  coalition formed by, 17t, 19
  management skills, ix
  replacement of, 126–27
Fukuoka Prefecture
  LDP-Komei interactions in, 39
  party-leader visits to, 140

Fukushima, Mizuho, 137, 252
Funada, Naka, 21

G

gatekeepers, party
 impact on nomination process, 242
 impact on women candidates, 243,
  253, 274
gender consciousness. *See also*
 women; women candidates
 and rise of the JSP, 232
 timing of, in Japan, 227
gender gap in politics
 analytic approach, statistical
  analysis, 225, 235n4, 235n5,
  235n6
 importance of the candidate for
  prime minister, 232
 in Japan *vs.* other countries, 222–23
 manifestations, 221–22
 national development and, 223–24
 role of limited party options, 232
Germany, electoral system, 32, 50
Gerring, John, 203–4
globalization, impact on financial
 system, 183
Grimes, William W., 190–93
gubernatorial elections, Japan, 209–
 12, 211t
Gulf War, first, policy paralysis
 during, 281
Gyosei Kaikaku Kaigi (Administrative
 Reform Council), 159
gyroscopic representation, 266

H

Hashimoto, Ryutaro
 coattail effects, 150
 electoral defeat, 2001, x, 109, 117,
  119–24, 282
 in government coalitions, 17t
 party support for, 123
 postal reform initiatives, 159–60
 public dissatisfaction with, 120–21,
  123
 resignation as prime minister, 116
 role as party leader, 115, 129n29

 tax and economic policies, 121, 283
Hashimoto faction
 candidate for LDP president, 115
 formation of, 114
 support for Koizumi, 129n31
 support from postmasters, 117
Hata, Tsutomu
 coalition formed by, 17t, 69
 political career, 13, 77–79
 supporters, 81–83
Headquarters for Political Reform,
 114–15
heiritsu-sei (SMD-PR) electoral
 system, 135
Hiroshima Prefecture, 2005 election
 campaign, 42–43
Hirschman-Herfindahl index, 103n4
HIV-tainted blood scandal, 22, 181
home mortgage lending (*jusen*)
 problem, 184
Horie, Takefumi, 42–43
Horiuchi faction, LDP
 alliance with Hashimoto, 114
 Horiuchi, Yusaku, opposition to
  bank bailouts, 196n3
 role in 2001 presidential election,
  120
 withdrawal of support for
  Hashimoto, 119
Hosokawa, Morihiro
 coalitions formed by, 13, 17t, 68–69
 coattail effects, 79
 founding of JNP, 13
 politician-bureaucrat relations, 190
 scandals and resignation, 69
House of Councillors (Upper House).
 See also SMD-PR electoral system
 factional affiliations, 118t
 rejection of postal privatization
  bills, 2005, 165
 support for Koizumi in, 129n31
House of Councillors elections
 closed-list PR system, 117
 DPJ electoral successes, 289
 electoral competition
  pre- and postreform, 100
  voting patterns, 94
 1974, 8–9

1989, "Women Changing Politics" campaign, 239, 251
1992, JNP success during, 68
1995, NFP success during, 69
1998, and Hashimoto's resignation, 283
role of postmaster associations, 158
2001, LDP strategy, 112
2004, LDP losses during, 41
2007
    DPJ electoral success, 19, 36, 67, 261, 286
    evidence of two-party system in, 29
    LDP losses during, 43
    LDP-Komei cooperation during, 40
    and questioning of Ministry of Finance, 191
    role of postmaster associations in, 173
House of Representatives (Lower House). See also SMD-PR electoral system
    DPJ seats in, 52
    LDP losses in, 44, 68
    no-confidence votes in, 12, 68, 79, 83t, 121
    and 1998 bank reform, 185
    postal-privatization bill, 165
    SMD districts and PR tiers, 48
    support for Koizumi in, 129n31
House of Representatives elections
    campaign costs, 135–36
    closeness ratios, 90–91, 91f
    electoral competition, 87, 93, 100
    disincentives for, 88
    1946, success of women candidates, 20, 256n5
    1986, impact of pork-barrel spending, 76
    1990, JSP losses during, 252
    1993
        LDP losses during, x, 12–13, 68
        results by party, 15t
    1996
        closeness ratios, district-level elections, 91f
        results by party, 14, 15t

success of LDP-led coalition, 69
1998, LDP loss of urban support during, 121
role of koenkai in, 241
RU (runner-up) ratios
    postreform (1996–2005), 89–90, 89f
    pre-reform (1958–1990), 88–89, 89f
time limits on campaigns, 136–37
2000
    closeness ratios, district-level elections, 91f
    declining support for LDP, 112
    female candidates, 244
    LDP victories during, 16
    LDP-Komei negotiations during, 38
    results by party, 15t
2003
    closeness ratios, district-level elections, 91f
    Koizumi's loss during, 41
    LDP losses during, 41
    "major-party-slate-change districts," 97
    results by party, 15t
    role of DPJ, 70
    voter swings during, 95–96
    women candidates, 253
2005
    campaigning by pro- and anti-postal-reform groups, 133, 166
    closeness ratios, district-level elections, 91f
    importance of, 18
    JCP vote share, 151n8
    LDP victories during, 150
    "major-party-slate-change districts," 97
    Okada's vs. Koizumi's visits to SMDs during, 134, 141–49, 143t, 147t
    precipitating factors, 166
    results by party, 15t
    success of party-affiliation over the personal during, 50

voter swings during, 95–96
women candidates, 239

I

Ichikawa Fusae Memorial Association
goals and activities, 249–50
promotion of women candidates,
241, 247–48, 248t
Ikeda, Hayato, 6, 18
Ikuta, Masaharu
heading of Postal Services Agency,
161
opposition to postal privatization,
163
proposals for postal reform, 161,
173–74
resignation from Japan Post, 174
incumbents
party affiliation and loyalty
defections from the LDP, viii,
12–13, 68–71, 78, 101, 286
generational factors, 67
infrastructure hypothesis of
party alignment, 71–83, 82t
party switching among, 72–73
role in electoral success, 285
shifting voter support for, 32, 95–96
support for, during 2005 election,
134
support organizations, 51–52, 241
in uncompetitive districts, 268
independent voters
impact on elections, 36, 122, 286
LDP support for, 243
as political outsiders, 266, 275n6
satisfaction with representation
and democracy, 269, 272f
under SMD-PR system, 33
industrial associations
electoral dilemmas faced by, 129n27
inability to mobilize support for
Hashimoto, 123
role in LDP, 118t
infrastructure development,
transportation (bullet-trains)
economic growth from, 71–72
impact on electoral politics, 73, 74t

importance of FILP revenues to, 158
infrastructure needs index (INI),
80–83
party alignments and, 72–80, 80f
Inglehart, Ronald, 222–23
insurance system, postal
privatization of, 159, 164
state revenues from, 157–58
interest groups
party affiliation, 190–91, 194
role in policymaking process,
187–88, 190
use of under clientelist system, 8–9
Internet use during campaigns, limits
on, 137, 151n5
Italy
corruption in, 10
Duverger's Law in, 29
SMD system, small parties under, 37
Iwamoto, Misako, 243, 252
Iwate Prefecture, 123

J

Japan Communist Party (JCP)
candidates from, 99
competition, 97–98
impact of strategic voting on, 100–1
platform and appeal, 11–12
supporter satisfaction with, 272f
surrogate representation by, 268
vote share during 2005 elections,
151n8
Japan Highway Public Corporation,
effort to privatize, 288
Japan New Party (JNP, Nihon Shinto)
efforts to attract women to, 243
formation of, 68
in government coalitions, 13, 17t
Japan Post Bank, 167, 171
Japan Post Co. (Nihon Yusei Kosha),
161, 176n19. See also Nihon Yusei
(Japan Post)
Japan Renewal Party (Shinseito). See
Renewal Party.
Japan Socialist Party (JSP)
gender differences in support for,
232, 233f

in government coalitions, 14, 17t,
30, 69
policy positions, 6, 11, 67
splintering of, 11–12
women activists and candidates,
20, 239, 251–52
jiban (organized constituency),
challenges of building, 241, 248t
Johnson, Chalmers, 188, 287
Johnson, Lyndon, 199–200, 202
jusen (home mortgage lending)
problem, 184, 196n2

K

Kaifu, Toshiki
Child Care Leave Law, 234
political reform proposals, 78, 127n7
popularity, 127n5
report to on electoral reform, 49–50
Kakuei, Tanaka, 5
Kamei, Shizuka
candidacy for LDP president, 115
government service, 128n11
opposition to postal privatization,
133
2001 presidential election, 119
2005 election campaign, 42–43
Kan, Naoto, 22
Kanagawa Prefecture, 160
kanban (endorsements, publicity). *See*
endorsement, party (*kanban*)
Kanemaru, Shin, 192
Kato, Junko
analysis of 1993 LDP split, 70
on conservatism of LDP, 225
on policymaking process, 186
on politician-bureaucrat relations,
182, 189
Kato, Koichi
opposition to electoral reform, 78
political alliances, 17, 78, 114,
128n15
political career, 77–79
supporters of, INI scores, 83
Kishi, Nobusuke, 5, 6
Kitschelt, Herbert, 8
koenkai (candidate support groups)

communication with
representatives, 267
role in winning elections, 32, 115,
117, 139–40, 169, 241
for women, challenges of creating,
241–42
Koga, Makoto
changes in presidential election
rules, 115
response to demands of local
chapters, 124, 128n13
Koike, Yuriko, 22
Koizumi, Junichiro
call for dissolution of factions, 115
coattail effects
media popularity, 136
policy impacts, 282–83
and recruitment of women
candidates, 254–55
sources of, 150
2005 election, 134
electoral losses, 41
emergence and success,
examinations of, x
in government coalitions, 17t
infrastructure spending by, 84
leadership positions, 109, 115
leadership skills, 168, 169
long-term impact, debates about,
x, 283–84
political alliances with Kato and
Yamazaki, 128n15
political successes and failures,
17–18, 288
popularity of, 123
among women voters, 221,
234–35
approval ratings, 133–34
broadness of appeal, 30
impact of local visits, 147–49,
148f
influence on SMD-PR linkages,
55–57
postal-privatization policy, 117
conflicts with Aso over, 165
contentious nature of, 283
efforts to overcome stalemate
over, 163–64

financial goals, 157–58
initial failure, 133
insistence on, 159–60
rejection of alternative
proposals, 164–65
steps toward, 161
reform image, viii, 122–23, 253–54, 288
support for Tanaka, 7, 160
support for women candidates, 239, 252–54, 282
support from Hashimoto faction, 129n31
2001 election campaign
excitement about, 41
prefectural primaries, 119
reasons for success, 120–27
votes for, 119–20, 120t
2005 election campaign, 42–43
precipitating factors, 133, 165
resource allocation strategy, 143t
visits to new candidates, 134
visits to SMDs during, 137–39, 138t, 141–49, 147t, 151n7, 152n9
use of media, 129n25
use of surrogate representation, 267
visits to Yasukuni Shrine, 289–90
women in government of, 20, 233
in YKK coalition, 78
Kokumin Shinto. See People's New Party.
Komei (Komeito). See Clean Government Party (CGP).
Kono, Yohei
LDP presidency, 127n2
rejection as party leader, 129n29
kouenkai (candidate support groups). See koenkai.
Krauss, Ellis S., 274

L
Labor Party (Israel), vii
land improvement associations (tochi kairyo jigyo), 9
land reform, and LDP's clientelist system, 8

Laver, Michael, 225
Laxalt, Paul, 200, 202
LDP. See Liberal Democratic Party (LDP)
leftist voters, marginalization of following electoral reform, 274
Liberal Democratic Party (LDP). See also factions; financial crisis, 1990s; politician-bureaucrat relations; prime ministers, scandals
alternatives to, 11–12, 32, 43, 97–98
conservative ideology, 243
contributions from Nippon Keidanren to, 287–88
economic focus, 6, 11, 30
election rules
candidate nominations, 51–52
changes in, 111–17, 284
role in Koizumi's election success, 282
election successes and losses
House of Councillors elections, 94
loss of parliamentary majority, viii
1993 election, 13, 68–69, 87
1994 return to power, 14, 69, 192
1996 election, 69
2000 elections, 61–63
2003 and 2004 elections, 41
2005 campaign, 29–30, 42–43, 102, 166
factions
coalition formation under the SNTV system, 110
impact of rules changes on, 113–14
mavericks, 110
power of, 111
role in election rule changes, 114–15
during the Tanaka era, 9
Financial Affairs Research Council, 193
founding, 5
funding support for candidates, 244–45
gender gap among supporters, 222, 224–31, 230t

in government coalitions, 13–14,
17t, 69, 127n2
impacts of financial crisis on, 195–96
interest groups in, 118t, 194, 287
Koizumi's revitalization of, 17–18
land-improvement associations
(*tochi kairyo jigyo*), 9
leadership
importance of personal
popularity, 282
importance to electoral success,
285
role in promoting women
candidates. 252–54
maintenance of power by, 7, 30
membership
growth following election rule
changes, 111
nominal membership, 116–17
occupation members, 117
open recruitment program, 256n7
popular support and, 128n18
readmission of postal rebels, 173
regional *vs.* occupation
members, 117
rejoining of by defectors, 69
nomination coordination
Electoral Strategy Committee, 242
factional balancing during,
242–43
impact on electoral success, 135
nomination rules governing,
51–52
postreform, 33
party affiliation and loyalty
defections from, viii, 12–13,
68–71, 78, 101, 286
impact of infrastructure
investment, 75, 77
incumbents, 79–80, 80f, 82t, 83t
Koizumi's coattail effects, 136
party discipline, 7, 9
switches to DPJ, 36
party leadership
failure to respond to local
chapters, 123–24
1998 presidential election, 115–16,
116t

policies, policy debates
adoption of opposition policy
positions, 32
consensus-based approach, 283
manifestos, 52
over road-designated taxes, 288
policy inconsistencies, 233–34
policymaking process, 186
postal reform, 163–68
Policy Affairs Research Council, 72
political alliances
with JSP, 30
with Komei, 16, 37–40, 69–70,
151n3, 285
with Liberal Party, 69
nomination coordination, 135
political dominance
and bureaucratic dominance
over policymaking, 189
and capacity to reinvent itself,
7, 30
clientelist networks, 8–9
diminishing power, evidence of,
vii–ix, 44, 60–62, 112, 122, 286
and electoral advantage, 36
loss of voter support and, 7,
23n3, 32, 84n1, 113f
role of pork in, 285
in rural areas, 53t
tag teams, 34–36
pre- and postreform incarnations,
x, 70, 83, 261–62
presidential elections
changes in election rules, 126–27
1978 primary, 160
1999 election, 128n14
outcomes and factional
affiliation, 1995 and 1999, 119
reasons for Koizumi's election
success, 120–27
rule changes, 109, 110
sensitivity to public opinion,
129n30
2001 election, 18, 41, 119–27, 120t
primary elections, 111, 116–17, 119
relationship with the court system,
196n4
relationship with postmaster

association, 169–71, 173
slow response to financial crisis,
192–93
split over privatizing postal service,
133
support from New Komeito party,
59
supporter satisfaction with
elections and democracy, 272, 272f
women candidates
gender gap in, 239
during Koizumi's tenure, 253
party-related constraints on,
242–43
Liberal Party, Japan
candidates from in 1949 elections, 6
defections from, 70
founding of the Liberal
Democratic Party, 5
in government coalitions, 17t, 69,
70
Ozawa's leadership of, 16
local chapters of political parties
demands for equal voting rights,
128n12
failure of leaders to respond to, 124
importance of, following election
reforms, 168
role in LDP recruitment and
nomination process, 243
local politics, women's involvement
in, 247–50
Lockheed scandal, 9–10, 12, 111, 228
Lower House. See House of
Representatives (Lower House)

M
Madoka, Yoriko, 247–48, 250
"Madonna boom," 227, 239, 252, 254
mail delivery services, 162, 164
"major-party-slate-change districts,"
96–97
Manabu, Masayo, 77
"mass clientelism party," 9
Mihara, Asahiko, 39–40
Ministry of Finance (MOF)
policymaking role, 183–85

reduced role, following 1998
reforms, 195
reluctance to bail out banks, 184,
191
role in preventing scrutiny of
banking sector, 183, 191–94
ties to banking sector, 190–91, 193
Ministry of Health and Welfare,
HIV-tainted blood scandal, 22, 181
Ministry of Internal Affairs and
Communications (MIC)
impact of postal privatization on,
171, 174
postal-reform proposals, 164–65
Ministry of Posts and
Telecommunications (MPT)
competition with FILP, 160
opposition to Hashimoto's postal
reform proposals, 159
mixed-member majoritarian (MMM)
electoral systems
competition under, 32
continuing role of koenkai in, 242
double candidacy and "best loser"
provisions, 32–33, 99, 151n2
elections under, 40, 69, 135–36,
269–70
electoral competition and, 87
emphasis on SMDs in, 32
establishment of, 32
House of Representatives elections, 48
MMD-SNTV vote system vs., 31
tendency to draw centrist
candidates, 67
House of Councillors elections, 100
in Japan, 14
parallel vs. proportional systems,
50–51
RU (runner-up) ratios, 89–90, 89f
Miyazawa, Kiichi
bank bailout proposal, 185, 191
efforts to prevent banking crisis,
184
faction of, Kato's inheritance of, 78
factional support, 127n7
in government coalitions, 17t
Koizumi's role in cabinet of, 160
local support, 119

no-confidence vote against, 68
MMD-SNTV electoral system
  (multimember districts [MMDs])
  "1955 system"
    candidate-centered elections, 47,
      48, 55
    demise of, 12–13
    indicators, 52, 157
    predictions about, viii
    surrogate representation in,
      266–67
    in Japan, 1947–1993, 31
    nomination procedures, 35, 242–43
    patron-client relationships and
      pork, 269–70
    problems associated with, 32
    redrawing of, under SMD system, 32
    representatives, fulfillment of
      promises by, 265
    role of koenkai in, 241
    small parties under, 37
    SMD-PR electoral system vs., 31
    victory margins in, 206, 210
MMM system. See mixed-member
  majoritarian (MMM) electoral
  systems
mobilization effects, party-leader
  visits, 139–40
Moe, Terry
  "extreme case" scenario, 189
  structural politics, 182, 186
Mori, Yoshiro
  declining support for, 112
  leadership roles, 112, 115, 122,
    128n11
  postal-reform efforts, 162
  resignation, 112
  role in changing presidential
    election rules, 115
  unpopularity of cabinet of, 79,
    113f, 121, 282
Muramatsu, Michio
  on policymaking process, 186
  on politician-bureaucrat relations,
    171, 182
Murayama, Tomiichi
  in government coalitions, 17t
  leadership position, 69, 127n2

N
Nagano Prefecture
  competition for the Olympics, 85n8
  impact of infrastructure
    investment, 74t
  LDP losses in, 122
Nakasone, Yasuhiro
  Equal Employment Opportunity
    Law (EEOL), 233–34
  foreign policy initiatives, 283
  Kato's service in cabinet of, 78
  popularity of, and coattail effects,
    150
  support of by largest LDP faction,
    111
National Association of
  Commissioned Postmasters
  (Zentoku Tokutei
  Yubinkyokuchokai), 123
  compromise proposals for postal
    reform, 173–74
  departure from LDP during 2005
    campaign, 166
  meetings with Noda, 176n16
  opposition to postal reform, 158–59
  role in LDP elections, 160, 170
National Public Service Law (Kokka
  Komuin Ho), 1948, 169
Nevada, 1944 senate election, 200, 202
New Conservative Party, 287
New Frontier Party (NFP, Shinshinto)
  dissolution of, 14, 69
  formation of, 69
  incorporation into the DPJ, 70
  Komei component, 37–38
New Komeito, 59, 64n11
New Labour campaign, England, 41
"new LDP," 41–43
New Liberal Club (NLC)
  electoral strategy, 100
  formation of, viii, 12
New Party Harbinger (Shinto Sakigake)
  formation of, 13–14, 68
  in government coalitions, 69, 127n2
  role in formation of DPJ, 14
New Zealand
  electoral competition, 94

mixed-member electoral system in, 50
RU (runner-up) ratios, 92–93, 93f
SMD-PR electoral system in, 32
Nihon Ishi Renmei (doctors), in LDP, 118t
Nihon Izokukai (war-bereaved), in LDP, 118t
Nihon Kango Renmei (nurses), in LDP, 118t
Nihon Shika Ishi Renmei (dentists), in LDP, 118t
Nihon Shinto. See Japan New Party (JNP)
Nihon Yakuzaishi Renmei (pharmacists), in LDP, 118t
Nihon Yusei (Japan Post)
  assumption of Japan Post responsibilities, 171
  compromise with Zentoku on postal reform, 173–74
  establishment of, 176n23
  naming of, 176n19
Nippon Credit Bank (NCB), accounting irregularities, 191
Nippon Keidanren (Japan Business Federation), 191, 287–88
Nippon Telegraph Telecommunications (NTT), privatization of, 171
Nishikawa, Yoshifumi, 174, 176n24
Nishimoto, Katsuko, 253, 256n2
Noda, Seiko
  meetings with Zentoku, 176n16
  on obstacles faced by women candidates, 245
  readmission into the LDP, 173
  reelection, 166
nominations
  kateba jiminto system (MMD system), 35
Nonaka, Hiromu
  changes in presidential election rules, 115
  corporatization of postal system, 160
  government service, 128n11
  opposition to postal reform, 159

response to demands of local chapters, 124
non-LDP government coalition, 13–14
nonperforming loan (NPL) problem. See banks; financial crisis, 1990s
Norris, Pippa, 222–23
North Korea, 289–90
noukyou (farm cooperatives), in LDP clientelist system, 8
nurses (Nihon Kango Renmei), in LDP, 118t

O
Obuchi, Keizo
  in government coalitions, 17t
  leadership position, 78, 115–16
  role of factions in election of, 127n9, 128n10, 128n14
  sudden illness, political impact, 112
occupation members, LDP
  industrial association, 118t
  strength of, vs. regional members, 117
  support for Hashimoto's presidency, 117
Ohira, Masayoshi
  leadership position, 111
  postmaster association support for, 160
  role of factions in election of, 111
Oita Prefecture, 2005 elections, 40
Okada, Katsuya
  compromise on postal reform, 169
  2005 election strategy
    resource allocation, 143t
    visits to incumbents, 134
    visits to SMDs, 141–49, 147t, 151n7, 152n9
opposition parties
  Komei, success of coalition with LDP, 37–40. See also Democratic Party of Japan (DPJ, Minshuto); Komei (Komeito) party
  ongoing failure of, 276n7
  role in surrogate representation, 266–67, 268
  small, disappearance of, 37
  weakness of, under MMD, 31–32

organizational voting, decline of, 10, 286
Otsuji, Kanako, 267–68
Ozawa, Ichiro
    campaign strategy, 43
    INI score, 71–79
    leadership of DPJ, 70
    leadership of Liberal Party, 16
    leadership of NFP, 69
    leadership position during change
        of government, 13–14
    resignation from LDP-led
        coalition, viii, 70

P

parliamentary systems
    and election-night corruption, 204
    "presidentialization" of elections,
        136, 149, 282
partisan realignment. See party
    switching
party affiliation, party switching. See
    also specific parties
    among incumbents, generational
        factors, 67
    defectors from the LDP, 35, 78
    at the district level, 94–95
    and emphasis on candidates over
        parties, 31
    importance of, in SMD elections,
        285
    increase in independents,
        "floaters," 67
    limited number of, 286–87
    MMD-SNTV vs. SMD-PR system,
        31
    role of pork in decisions about,
        71–83, 286
    and victory margins, Japan vs. U.S.
        and U.K., 207–8
    women
        in Japan vs. U.S., 224
        recruitment quotas, 255
party-centered elections. See also
    electoral competition; electoral reform
    following electoral reform,
        empirical findings, 53–55
    as goal of electoral reform, 47, 49–50

    impact of SMDs on development
        of, 51
    move toward in Japan, 60
    slate changes, impact on electoral
        competition, 98–99
    2005 election campaign, 50
party-leader visits. See yuuzei (visits by
    party leaders)
peace, as political focus, 6–7, 11
Pekkanen, Robert, 274
pension contributions, loss of, 22
People's New Party (Kokumin Shinto)
    postmaster support for, 166, 173, 84n2
pharmacists (Nihon Yakuzaishi
    Renmei), in LDP, 118t
pluralism. See alternation of power;
    democracy; two-party system
Policy Affairs Research Council, LDP, 72
policy councils (shingikai), 188
policymaking. See also politician-
    bureaucrat relations; postal
    privatization; postal reform
    dependence on interest groups, 187
    impacts of electoral reform on,
        287–88
    policy councils (shingikai), 188
    policy reform, 287–88
    political vs. bureaucratic leadership
        in, 288
    postwar, 6
    prime ministerial approaches to, 283
Political Funds Control Law, 1976,
    244
political reform
    "Chusenkyokusei haishi sengen"
        (resolution to ban middle-sized
        districts), 70–71
    Ozawa support for, viii
    role of women, xi
politician-bureaucrat relations. See
    also Ministry of Finance (MOF)
    competitive, 182, 187–88, 190–91,
        194–95
    cooperative, 182, 186–87, 287–88
    delegation of authority, 185–86
    impact of single-party dominance,
        186, 189, 192
    interdependency of, 189

and new bank regulation rules, 195
politician dependence on
  bureaucrats for information, 185–86
relations with non-LDP politicians,
  190
role of interest groups in
  policymaking, 187, 190
role of party affiliation in response
  to financial crisis, 193–94
traditional explanations for, 188
Politics School for Women, 247, 248t,
  250
"Pollution Diet," 1970, 30
pork-barrel legislation
  as basis for personal appeals,
    48–49, 50
  and candidate popularity, 285
  new *vs.* established infrastructure
    projects, 71–72
  and party switching, 286
  role in incumbent party loyalty,
    70, 71
post offices
  commissioned, social service
    responsibilities, 175n2
  guarantees regarding, 164
postal assassins (*shikaku*)
  female, Koizumi's choice of, 253–55
  Koizumi's use of in 2005 election,
    18, 20, 30, 42, 133, 141
  tag teams with postal rebels, 35–36,
    145
postal family (*yusei famirii*)
  demand for single postal
    corporation, 161
  opposition to postal reform, 159
  reemergence following privatization,
    172–75
  Zentei (postal workers union)
    LDP protection of postmasters
      from, 170
    as members of the postal family,
      175n1
    opposition to postal
      privatization, 169
postal privatization. *See also* Koizumi,
  Junichiro; postal reform
  concessions, 164

efforts to delay implementation,
  170–71
failure of legislation for, 2005, 165
financial goals, 157–58
impact on financial system, 167–68
impact on postmaster association,
  169–71
impact on postmasters, 175
impact on the LDP, 167–68
implementation, 166, 168–69, 171–75
incorporation of bureaucracy into
  reform process, 164
Koizumi's advocacy for, 109, 160–61
legislation for, 161–62
opposition to, 163
passage of, 163
passage of legislation for, 163–64, 166
political goals, 158
post-2003 policymaking process,
  162–65
underlying principles, 163
Postal Privatization Basic Plan (Yusei
  Min'eika Kihon Hoshin), 2004, 163
Postal Privatization Preparation Office
  (PPPO, Yusei Min'eika Junbi Shitsu)
  establishment of, 163
  MIC pressure on, 171
  successor organization, 171–72
Postal Privatization Promotion Office
  (Yusei Min'eika Suishin Shitsu)
  implementation responsibilities,
    171–72
  membership, 176n17
postal rebels (*zohansha*)
  Koizumi's association of the DPJ
    with, 42
  Koizumi's public campaign against,
    166
  readmission to LDP under Abe, 40,
    43
  tag teams with assassins, 35–36, 145
postal reform. *See also* Koizumi,
  Junichiro; postal privatization
  corporatization of postal system,
    159–60
  debate about, 17, 19, 133, 283
  Hashimoto's initiatives regarding, 159
  Ikuta's initiatives regarding, 161

Japan Post (Nihon Yusei), 161
long-term impacts, 288–89
MIC alternatives to Koizumi's
proposal, 164–65
postmaster associations, 158
as source of conflict between LDP
and Komei, 40
split within LDP over, 84n2, 133
use of tag teams to address, 35
Postal Service Agency, 161
postal savings system
competition for control over, 160–61
privatization of, 164, 167
state revenues from, 157–58
postmasters, postmaster associations
efforts to preserve influence, 173
LDP courting of, 173
loss of status as public servants, 175
opposition to postal privatization,
160, 169–71
prefectural chapters and delegates,
LDP
allocation of votes to, 115,
128n16, 128n20
allocation of votes within, 116
party loyalty among, 115
reduction in numbers of, 127n3
role in 2001 presidential primaries,
119
role in electing LDP party leaders,
110
role in Koizumi's election success,
121–22, 282
timing of primary elections,
123–24
presidential elections, LDP.
changes in election rules, 126–27
1999 election, 128n14
outcomes and factional affiliation,
1995 and 1999, 119
primary elections
allocation of votes during,
129n21
changing rules for, 128n20
expectations for, among party
leaders, 116–17
introduction of, 111
LDP commitment to, 284

1978 primary, 160
policy debates during, 160
role in Koizumi's election
success, 121–22, 282
role of local chapters in, 168
timing and sequence of, 123–24
United States primaries vs., 51,
129n26
reasons for Koizumi's election
success, 120–27
rule changes, 109, 110
sensitivity to public opinion,
129n30
2001 election, 18, 41, 119–27, 120t
2007 elections, 126–27
presidentialization of prime ministers,
136, 149, 282
prime ministers. See also specific
individuals
coattail effects, collective vs.
selective benefits, 136
1991–2007, coalition governments,
17t
popularity of, and gender gap in
voting preferences, 234–35
role of factions in election of, 5,
127n7, 127n9
promissory representation
defined, 265
mandate vs. trustee frameworks
for, 265
vs. surrogate representation,
274–75
proportional representation (PR)
closed-list system for ranking
candidates, 48, 117, 253, 255–56
Duverger's Law and, 44
impact on Japanese politics, ix
LDP lead over DPJ in, 42t
LDP support for Komei candidates
in, 38–40, 39t
in reformed electoral system, 14, 32
relationship to single-member
districts (SMDs), 48, 50–51
voter representation in, 265
voting patterns
party affiliation and, 55–59,
56f, 58t

urban *vs.* rural areas, 53, 53t
  variability in, 53–55, 54f
women candidates, 242
Public Office Election Law (POEL).
  See also electoral reform
  limits on media coverage, 152n10
  limits of duration of campaigns,
    136–37
  limits on online communications,
    137, 151n5

R

Ramseyer, J. Mark, 188
real estate speculation, 183–84
rearmament, policy debates, 6, 11,
  289–90
Recruit scandal, 1989, 12, 68, 228,
  251, 281
Reed, Steven R., xii
  on alternation of power, ix–x, 284–85
  on LDP split, 1993, 70–71
Renewal Party (RP, Shinseito), 68, 69
  formation of, 68, 77–78, 81
  in government coalitions, 69
  party switching from, 81
representation, forms of
  gyroscopic, 266
representation, political
  anticipatory representation, 266
  communication between voters
    and representatives, 267
  incongruence with voter
    expectations, 264
  gyroscopic representation, 266
  promissory representation, 265–66
  and public satisfaction with, role
    of surrogate representation,
    270–72, 270f
  in SMD-PR electoral system, 265
  surrogate representation, 266–67
  and voter choice, 261
Republican Party, U.S., 207–08, 212
resource allocation strategies. *See*
  yuuzei (party-leader visits)
  nomination coordination and
    party-based efforts, 135–37
  yuuzei (party-leader visits) as

resource allocation metric
  Okada's *vs.* Koizumi's strategy, 134
  statistical analysis, 141–19, 143t,
    147t, 152n14, 153n15, 153n16
  visits to SMD candidate
    districts, 2005 election, 137–
    39, 138t
"rising tide" theory of gender
  equality, 222–23
Rosenbluth, Frances
  analysis of 1993 LDP split, 70
  on slow response to banking crisis,
    185, 188
RU (runner-up) ratios
  Cox's "SF ratio" *vs.*, 103n3
  in "major-party-slate-change
    districts," 96–97
  methods for calculating, 88, 104n8
  pre-reform *vs.* postreform, 88–90
  in U.K. elections, 92
running against own party (*hoshu
  bunretsu*), 59
rural and underdeveloped areas. *See
  also* intrastructure development
  candidate relationships with party
    leaders, 52
  impact of infrastructure
    investment in, 71–72
  inclusion in regular-city category,
    104n13

S

Sagawa Kyubin scandal, 1992, 281
Sakigake. *See* New Party Harbinger
  (Shinto Sakigake)
same-sex partnership, 267–68
Sato, Eisaku, 18
  consensus-based policymaking
    system, 7
  leadership of largest LDP faction, 111
scandals
  HIV-tainted blood scandal, 22, 181
  Hosokawa's money scandals, 69
  impact on electoral-law reform,
    1994, 12
  impact on LDP election rules, 111
  involving LDP candidates, impact

on party support, 68
Lockheed scandal, viii, 9–10, 12, 21–22, 111, 228
Recruit scandal, 12, 68–69, 228, 251, 281
Sagawa Kyubin scandal, 281
sex scandals, 20–21
Shin Kanemaru scandal, 192
Social Insurance Agency scandal, 181, 196
Schaap, Ross, 185
Schoppa, Leonard J., 223
seiji kaikaku (political reform), 49
Seikatsu Networks, Seikatsu Clubs
goals and activities, 248–49
impact on women in politics, 247–48, 248t
political wing, 256n9
proxies (dairinin), 249, 256n10
sekihai-ritsu (proportion of votes relative to winner), 48, 151n2
sex scandals, 20–21
shingikai (policy councils), 188
shinkansen (bullet-train) stations, 73, 74t. See also infrastructure
Shinseito party. See Renewal Party
Shinshinto party (New Frontier Party, NFP), 14
Shinto Nippon, postmaster support for, 166
Shinto Sakigake (New Party Harbinger)
formation, 13
in government coalitions, 1991–2007, 17t
role in formation of DPJ, 14
Shinzo, Abe, 172
single-member districts (SMDs)
competition in
and development of a two-party system, 29
disincentives for, 88
districts with major party realignments, 96–97
districts with minor party realignments, 97–98
Japan vs. U.S. and U.K., 93
party- vs. candidate-centered

elections, 51
district-related differences in party strength, 94–95
double candidacy, 48
relationship to proportional representation districts (PRs), 14, 30, 50–51
victory margins
Japan vs. Canadian and U.S., 206
2000 election, 61–63
ultraclose elections, 210
voter representation
and efforts to promote intra-party competition, 265
strengthening of ties between representatives and constituents, 265
voting patterns
consistency in votes cast, 55–57
impact of local versus party-related factors, 57–59, 58t
urban vs. rural areas, 53, 53t, 59–60, 61f
variability in, 53–55, 54f
single-party dominance. See also Liberal Democratic Party (LDP)
and bureaucrat role in policymaking, 186, 189
and candidate-centered elections, 47–48
small and medium enterprises (SMEs), importance of FILP revenues to, 158
SNTV (single nontransferable vote) system
abolition of, 47
candidate-centered elections, 48–49
coalition building under, 110
electoral competition under, 99–100
RU (runner-up) ratios, 88–89, 89f
Social Democratic League (Shaminren, SDL), 11
Social Democratic Party of Japan (SDPJ)
in coalition governments, 127n2, 285

Doi-led Madonna boom, 227, 239, 252, 254
supporter satisfaction with elections and democracy, 272f
weakness of, 87
Social Insurance Agency, scandal involving, 181, 196
Soka Gakkai Buddhist sect, Komei Party, 16, 37, 69
Stevenson, Coke, 199–200, 202
strategic entry of candidates, 104n15, 104n16
strategic voting, electoral competition and, 97–100
strategic withdrawal of candidates, 100–2
structural politics, 182, 186–87
surrogate representation
    characteristics, 266
    effectiveness of, for women and minorities, 272–73
    in "1955 system," 266–67
    promissory representation vs., 274–75
    public satisfaction with democracy, 270–71, 270f
    role in Japanese politics, 262
    and voter-representative communication, 267
    voters' perception of, statistical analysis, 268–69, 276
Suzuki, Zenko, 76

T

tag teams ("Costa Rica arrangements"), 34–35
Taiju no Kai (association of retired postmasters)
    departure from LDP, 166
    LDP courting of, 173
    party membership and representatives, 118t
    role in LDP elections, 158, 170
    support for Hashimoto's presidency, 117
Takemura, Masayoshi, 13, 71–79
Takenaka, Heizo
    conficts with Aso over postal

privatization, 165
    role in postal-reform process, 162–65, 164
Takeshita, Noboru
    faction leadership, 127n7
    party leadership, 111
    policy positions, 49
    popularity, 127n5
    resignation as prime minister, 68
Tanaka, Kakuei
    background and reform proposals, 7–8
    clientelist system, 8
    connections to the postal lobby, 159
    corruption scandals, viii, 9–10, 21–22, 111
    faction leadership, 9, 111
    policymaking approach, 8
    transportation infrastructure, 76
Tanaka, Makiko
    2001 candidacy of, 41
    incompetence shown by, 41
tatoka (multipartization), 11
telephone/telegraph service, privatization of, 160, 171
Tetsudou Chousakai (LDP Railroad Investigation Panel), 72
Thacker, Strom C., 204
Thatcher, Margaret, 149
tochi kairyo jigyo (land-improvement associations), 9
Tochigi Prefecture
    electoral politics, role of infrastructure investment, 72–75, 74t
    LDP losses in, 122
tokiwakai (former Japan Railway employees), 118t
Tokusuiren (MIC-administered postal organization), 170, 173–74
Tokyo
    LDP support for Komei candidates in, 38
    special ward (tokubetsu ku) assembly elections, JCP candidates, 101
transportation infrastructure. See infrastructure
trustee framework for promissory

representation, 265
21-Seiki Wo Tsukuru Kai (Society for the 21st Century), 118t
two-party system
and alternation of power, 29, 284–85
and candidate-centered elections, 47–48
creating, challenges of, ix, 19–20, 135, 157, 284–85
and decline in smaller parties, 52
in district elections, failure of, 88
and electoral competition, 91, 97–102
expectations for, 29, 87, 281
fundamental components, 41
impact of SMDs on development of, 29, 51
running against own party, 41
surrogate representation, 268

U

ultraclose elections
factors in, 208–12, 209t
very close elections vs., 208
uncertainty, political
impact on gender gap, 221
and increasing number of independent voters, 269
and politician-bureaucrat relations, 183, 185–86
role of primary elections, 116
United Kingdom
party influence over candidate selection, 51
two-party system and electoral competition, RU ratios, 92–94, 93f
United Nations Development Programme (UNDP), 221
United States
campaign expenditures, 135
candidate selection, 51
candidate withdrawal strategies, 102
election-night corruption in, 203–5
two-party system and electoral competition, 87, 92

victory margins in
role of party affiliation, 206f, 207–8
ultraclose elections, 214–16
voter satisfaction with election outcomes, 262
voting patterns, 224
Upper House. See House of Councillors (Upper House)
urban and developed areas
appeal of Koizumi's reform image in, 122–23
emergence of two-party system in, 53t
impact of infrastructure investment, 72
party switching among incumbents, 72–73
primary elections in, 121–22
rural and underdeveloped areas vs. declining importance of schism between, 67
move toward party-centered elections in, 60
party affiliation and loyalty, 71–83
voting patterns, 61f
U.S.-Japan Security Treaty (Ampo), efforts to amend, 6

V

Vogel, Steven
on privatization of telephone system, 171
on slow response to banking crisis, 184
voters
party identification, 269
relationship with representatives satisfaction with, 261, 269–72
types of, 265–67
voting patterns
"contamination" effects, 64n8
gender differences, 223–24
impact of local versus party-related factors, 57–59, 58t
LPD voting margin over DPJ in SMDs, 2000 election, 61–63

SMD tier *vs.* PR tier, 53–57,
54f, 56f
swings and shifts in, 95–96, 286
urban *vs.* rural areas, 53, 53t

W

war-bereaved association (Nihon
Izokukai), in LDP, 118t
WINWIN, 241, 248t
goals and activities, 250
role in increasing women's
involvement in politics, 247–48
women
attraction to DPJ, 243–44
changing role in electoral politics,
20–21
family pressures on, 240
political opinions
"buffer" theory, 224
impact of economic conditions
on, 222–24
role in electoral process and
government, xi, 22, 221–22,
235n2
satisfaction with representation
and democracy, 274
support for Koizumi, 221, 282
support for smaller parties,
277n14
surrogate representation for,
272–73
wage differentials, 223–24
women candidates
barriers to recruitment and
nomination, 243
DPJ support for, 243–44
electoral success rates, 245–47,
246t, 276n12, 276n13
expectations for, 245
and gender gap in the Diet, 282
Koizumi's support for, 253
1946 House of Representatives
election, 256n5
obstacles faced by, 240–45
recruiting of, 251–55
sources of funding, 241
support from women's

organizations, 247–51
training opportunities, 250
2000 House of Representatives
election, 244
2003 House of Representatives
election, 253
"Women Changing Politics"
campaign, 1989, 251
women's organizations
Seikatsu Networks, Seikatsu
Clubs, 248–49
support for women candidates,
247–51

Y

Yamazaki, Taku
political alliances, 17, 78, 114, 128n15
sex scandal involving, 21
Yasukuni Shrine, Koizumi visit to, 289
YKK (Yamasaki, Kato and Koizumi)
coalition, 17, 128n15
Yomiuri Shimbun (newspaper)
coverage of party-leader visits, 137
reports on irregularities at Nippon
Credit Bank, 191
Yoshida, Shigeru, 6
Yucho/Kampo Seimei Hoken Kanri
Kiko fund, 171
Yusei Min'eika Junbi Shitsu (Postal
Privatization Preparation Office,
PPPO). *See* Postal Privatization
Preparation Office
Yusei Min'eika Suishin Shitsu (Postal
Privatization Promotion Office).
See Postal Privatization Promotion
Office
yuuzei (party-leader visits), 2005
election
allocation of visits to SMDs, 136–39,
138t
electoral impacts, 136, 139–40
Okada's *vs.* Koizumi's during 2005
election
statistical analysis, 141–43,
145–49, 152–53
strategies, 134, 137–39, 138t

Z

Zentoku Tokutei Yubinkyokuchokai.
  See National Association of
  Commissioned Postmasters.
"zombie legislators," 48

About the Contributors

Barry C. Burden is a professor of political science at the University of Wisconsin. His research and teaching focus on electoral politics and representation. He has written about partisanship, third-party campaigns, public attitudes toward political leaders, legislative politics, candidate strategies, and voter turnout. He is coauthor of *Why Americans Split Their Tickets: Campaigns, Competition, and Divided Government* (2002), editor of *Uncertainty in American Politics* (2003), and author of *Personal Roots of Representation* (2007). Burden has also published articles in the *American Political Science Review, American Journal of Political Science, British Journal of Political Science, Legislative Studies Quarterly, Political Science Quarterly,* and *Electoral Studies.*

Ray Christensen is an associate professor of political science at Brigham Young University. A specialist in Japanese elections—especially on issues of gender representation, malapportionment, electoral reform, and election rules—he is the author of *Ending the LDP Hegemony: Party Cooperation in Japan* (2000).

Kyle Colvin is a recent graduate of Brigham Young University's political science department. He is currently attending law school at Brigham Young University.

Alisa Gaunder is an associate professor of political science at Southwestern University in Georgetown, Texas. Gaunder received her Ph.D. in political science from the University of California, Berkeley. Her research interests include comparative political leadership, campaign finance reform in Japan and the United States, and women and politics in Japan. She is the author of *Political Reform in Japan: Leadership Looming Large* (2007) and the editor of *The Routledge Handbook of Japanese Politics* (forthcoming).

Chao-Chi Lin is an assistant professor of political science at National Chengchi University in Taiwan. Her research interests include comparative political institutions, contemporary Japanese politics, and East Asian political economy.

Patricia L. Maclachlan received her Ph.D. in comparative politics from Columbia University in 1996 and is now associate professor of government and Asian studies at the University of Texas, Austin. She is the author of *Consumer Politics in Postwar Japan: The Institutional Boundaries of Citizen Activism* (2002), and a contributor and coeditor (with Sheldon Garon) of *The Ambivalent Consumer: Questioning Consumption in East Asia and the West* (2006). Maclachlan is currently completing a book manuscript on the history and politics of the Japanese postal system.

Ko Maeda is an assistant professor of political science at the University of North Texas, specializing in political institutions, political parties, and elections. He received his B.A. (1998) from the University of Tsukuba and M.A. (2001) and Ph.D. (2005) from Michigan State University. His work has appeared or is forthcoming in the *British Journal of Political Science, Electoral Studies,* the *Journal of Theoretical Politics, Asian Survey,* and *Comparative Political Studies.*

Sherry L. Martin earned her A.B. in politics from Princeton University and her Ph.D. in political science from the University of Michigan. She is an assistant professor jointly appointed in the government department and the Program in Feminist, Gender, and Sexuality Studies at Cornell University. A comparativist interested in gender and politics, political participation, electoral institutions, and political socialization, Martin's research has examined the connections between gender, a decline in partisanship, and widespread feelings of political alienation in contemporary Japanese politics. Her work has appeared in *the Social Science Japan Journal* and the *Journal of Women, Politics & Policy.* She is the coeditor, with Gill Steel, of *Democratic Reform in Japan: Assessing the Impact* (2008).

Michio Muramatsu is a professor in the department of political science at the Law Faculty, Gakushuin University, Tokyo, where he researches Japanese politics and the relationship between bureaucrats and politicians in comparative perspective. He is the author of *Local Power in the Japanese State* (1997) and has published a number of articles on Japanese and comparative politics in journals including *American Political Science Review, British Journal of Political Science, Asian Survey,* and *Journal of Japanese Studies.*

Kenneth Mori McElwain is an assistant professor in the department of political science at the University of Michigan, where he studies the comparative politics of institutional design. His current book manuscript examines how partisan incentives influence the initial selection and subsequent manipulation of electoral systems, and how these choices can help unpopular governments to stay in power. Other research topics include the organizational principles of political parties and the procedural complexity of constitutional amendments. He was born and raised in Tokyo, Japan, and he received his A.B. from the Woodrow Wilson School at Princeton University, and his Ph.D. from Stanford University.

Jun Saito is an assistant professor in the department of political science at Yale University. His research focuses on distributive politics and electoral foundations of international relations. Between 2002 and 2003, he served in the Japanese House of Representatives.

Ethan Scheiner is an associate professor in the department of political science at the University of California, Davis. His research focuses on Japanese politics and general issues surrounding democratic representation. He is the author of *Democracy Without Competition in Japan: Opposition Failure in a One-Party Dominant State* (2005) and a number of articles on Japanese and comparative politics in the *British Journal of Political Science*, *Comparative Political Studies*, *Electoral Studies*, *Japanese Journal of Political Science*, and *Legislative Studies Quarterly*.

Kay Shimizu is an assistant professor in the department of political science at Columbia University. Her research concerns the political economy of development in Japan and China with a focus on financial reform, corporate governance, elections and grassroots politics. Shimizu received her B.A., M.A., and Ph.D. from Stanford University.

Steven R. Reed is a professor of modern government at Chuo University in Japan, where all of his classes are taught in Japanese. His major areas of research are parties, elections, electoral systems, and Japanese politics. He edited *Japanese Electoral Politics: Creating a New Party System* (2003) and has collected two data sets on Japanese elections, one under the 1947–1993 electoral system and one under the new electoral system in effect since 1994. He has published in the *British Journal of Political Science*, the *Journal of Japanese Studies*, *Comparative Politics*, *Comparative Political Studies*, *Party Politics*, *Electoral Studies*, and several Japanese journals.

Robert J. Weiner is an assistant professor of political science at the Naval Postgraduate School (NPS) in Monterey, California. His research focuses on Japanese and East Asian politics, political parties and elections, and democratic institutions. He earned his Ph.D. in political science from the University of California, Berkeley.

RECENT AND FORTHCOMING PUBLICATIONS OF THE WALTER H. SHORENSTEIN ASIA-PACIFIC RESEARCH CENTER

Books (distributed by the Brookings Institution Press)

Rafiq Dossani, Daniel C. Sneider, and Vikram Sood. *Does South Asia Exist? Prospects for Regional Integration.* Stanford, CA: Walter H. Shorenstein Asia-Pacific Research Center, forthcoming 2009.

Jean C. Oi, Scott Rozelle, and Xueguang Zhou. *Growing Pains: Tensions and Opportunities in China's Transformation.* Stanford, CA: Walter H. Shorenstein Asia-Pacific Research Center, forthcoming 2009.

Karen Eggleston, ed. *Prescribing Cultures and Pharmaceutical Policy in the Asia-Pacific.* Stanford, CA: Walter H. Shorenstein Asia-Pacific Research Center, 2009.

Donald Macintyre, Daniel C. Sneider, and Gi-Wook Shin, eds. *First Drafts of Korea: The U.S. Media and Perceptions of the Last Cold War Frontier.* Stanford, CA: Walter H. Shorenstein Asia-Pacific Research Center, 2009.

Donald K. Emmerson. *Hard Choices: Security, Democracy, and Regionalism in Southeast Asia.* Stanford, CA: Walter H. Shorenstein Asia-Pacific Research Center, 2008.

Henry S. Rowen, Marguerite Gong Hancock, and William F. Miller, eds. *Greater China's Quest for Innovation.* Stanford, CA: Walter H. Shorenstein Asia-Pacific Research Center, 2008.

Gi-Wook Shin and Daniel C. Sneider, eds. *Cross Currents: Regionalism and Nationalism in Northeast Asia.* Stanford, CA: Walter H. Shorenstein Asia-Pacific Research Center, 2007.

Stella R. Quah, ed. *Crisis Preparedness: Asia and the Global Governance of Epidemics.* Stanford, CA: Walter H. Shorenstein Asia-Pacific Research Center, 2007.

Philip W. Yun and Gi-Wook Shin, eds. *North Korea: 2005 and Beyond.* Stanford, CA: Walter H. Shorenstein Asia-Pacific Research Center, 2006.

Jongryn Mo and Daniel I. Okimoto, eds. *From Crisis to Opportunity: Financial Globalization and East Asian Capitalism*. Stanford, CA: Walter H. Shorenstein Asia-Pacific Research Center, 2006.

Michael H. Armacost and Daniel I. Okimoto, eds. *The Future of America's Alliances in Northeast Asia*. Stanford, CA: Walter H. Shorenstein Asia-Pacific Research Center, 2004.

Henry S. Rowen and Sangmok Suh, eds. *To the Brink of Peace: New Challenges in Inter-Korean Economic Cooperation and Integration*. Stanford, CA: Walter H. Shorenstein Asia-Pacific Research Center, 2001.

Studies of the Walter H. Shorenstein Asia-Pacific Research Center
(published with Stanford University Press)

Jean Oi and Nara Dillon, eds. *At the Crossroads of Empires: Middlemen, Social Networks, and State-building in Republican Shanghai*. Stanford, CA: Stanford University Press, 2007.

Henry S. Rowen, Marguerite Gong Hancock, and William F. Miller, eds. *Making IT: The Rise of Asia in High Tech*. Stanford, CA: Stanford University Press, 2006.

Gi-Wook Shin. *Ethnic Nationalism in Korea: Genealogy, Politics, and Legacy*. Stanford, CA:Stanford University Press, 2006.

Andrew Walder, Joseph Esherick, and Paul Pickowicz, eds. *The Chinese Cultural Revolution as History*. Stanford, CA: Stanford University Press, 2006.

Rafiq Dossani and Henry S. Rowen, eds. *Prospects for Peace in South Asia*. Stanford, CA: Stanford University Press, 2005.

The authorized representative in the EU for product safety and compliance is:
Mare Nostrum Group
B.V Doelen 72
4831 GR Breda
The Netherlands

www.ingramcontent.com/pod-product-compliance
Lightning Source LLC
Chambersburg PA
CBHW020335270326
41926CB00007B/197

9 781931 368148